Europe Divided 1559–1598

Blackwell Classic Histories of Europe

This series comprises new editions of seminal histories of Europe. Written by the leading scholars of their generation, the books represent both major works of historical analysis and interpretation and clear, authoritative overviews of the major periods of European history. All the volumes have been revised for inclusion in the series and include updated material to aid further study. *Blackwell Classic Histories of Europe* provides a forum in which these key works can continue to be enjoyed by scholars, students and general readers alike.

Published

Europe: Hierarchy and Revolt 1320–1480
Second Edition
George Holmes

Renaissance Europe 1480–1520
Second Edition
John Hale

Reformation Europe 1517–1559
Second Edition
G. R. Elton

Europe Divided: 1559–1598
Second Edition
J. H. Elliott

Europe Transformed: 1878–1919
Second Edition
Norman Stone

Forthcoming

Europe in Crisis: 1598–1648
Second Edition
Geoffrey Parker

Europe Unfolding: 1648–1688
Second Edition
John Stoye

Europe: Privilege and Protest 1730–1798
Second Edition
Olwen Hufton

Revolutionary Europe 1783–1815
Second Edition
George Rudé

EUROPE DIVIDED
1559–1598
Second Edition

J. H. Elliott

Copyright © J. H. Elliott 1968, 2000

The right of J. H. Elliott to be identified as author of this work has been asserted in accordance with the Copyright, Designs and Patents Act 1988.

First published 1968
Second edition published by Blackwell Publishers Ltd 2000

2 4 6 8 10 9 7 5 3 1

Blackwell Publishers Ltd
108 Cowley Road
Oxford OX4 1JF
UK

Blackwell Publishers Inc.
350 Main Street
Malden, Massachusetts 02148
USA

British Library Cataloguing in Publication Data

A CIP catalogue record for this book is available from the British Library.

Library of Congress Cataloging-in-Publication Data is available for this book.

ISBN 0–631–21779–7

    0–631–21780–0 (pbk)

Typeset in 10.5 on 12 pt Sabon
by Kolam Information Services Pvt Ltd. Pondicherry, India
Printed in Great Britain by TJ International, Padstow, Cornwall

This book is printed on acid-free paper

Contents

Preface to the Second Edition   viii
Preface to the First Edition   xiii

Maps   xv

1   Later Sixteenth-Century Europe   xvi
2   The Mediterranean   xviii
3   The Atlantic   xix
4   The Netherlands   xx
5   The Netherlands Divided   xxi
6   France   xxii

Genealogical Tables   xxiii

1   Spanish and Austrian Habsburgs   xxiii
2   Houses of Valois and Bourbon   xxiv
3   House of Guise   xxv
4   Montmorency and Coligny   xxvi

PART I: THE EUROPE OF CATEAU-CAMBRÉSIS   1

1   **The International Scene**   3

    1   Dynastic Peace   3
    2   Confessional Strife   15

2   **The European Economy**   24

    1   The Baltic and the East   24
    2   The Atlantic and the Mediterranean   29
    3   Silver and Prices   35

3   **The Problem of the State**   42

1   Monarchy   42
2   Estates   51
3   National Unity and Religious Diversity   57

PART II: 1559–1572   67

4   **Protestantism and Revolt**   69

1   Wars of Religion?   69
2   The Huguenots at War   75
3   The Revolt of the Netherlands   81

5   **Catholicism and Repression**   94

1   The Council of Trent and the Catholic Reformation   94
2   The Counter-Reformation and the Secular Power   104

6   **The War with Islam**   115

1   Prelude to Conflict   115
2   The Confrontation of Empires   120
3   The Aftermath of Lepanto   128

PART III: 1572–1585   133

7   **Crisis in the North: 1572**   135

1   The Capture of Brill   135
2   The Massacre of St Bartholomew   144

8   **A Middle Way?**   154

1   Poland and the West   154
2   Sweden and Germany   163
3   France and the Netherlands   168

9   **The Growth of Spanish Power**   178

1   The Problems of Philip II   178
2   Portugal and the Azores   185
3   Recovery in the Netherlands   190

PART IV: 1585–1598   201

10 **The International Conflict**   203

1   The Problems of Intervention   203
2   The Brink of War   211
3   The Armada and the League   216

11   The Discomfiture of Spain   229

   1   France and Spain   229
   2   The Rallying to the King   237
   3   Nantes and Vervins   241

12   The Divided Continent   248

   1   The Mediterranean World   248
   2   Rome and the North   255
   3   Division and Unity   262

Notes   269

Further Reading   276

Index   292

Preface to the Second Edition

The first edition of this book was written to a specific brief and with a particular purpose in mind. It was designed to provide a clear and accessible narrative account of a complex but critical forty-year period of European history, during which the lines of religious division hardened, and the Spain of Philip II, the self-appointed champion of the Roman cause, found itself confronted, and finally checked, by the increasingly dynamic Protestant societies of northern Europe.

The story-line was therefore essentially political, and this helped to give the book the unity and coherence demanded by the nature of the series for which it was written. But at the same time no self-respecting historical work written during the 1960s and covering a broad canvas of European history could confine itself purely to political and diplomatic narrative. This was the great age of the so-called *Annales* School in Paris, dominated by the grandest of *grands maîtres*, Fernand Braudel, whose *The Mediterranean and the Mediterranean World in the Age of Philip II*, first published in 1949, transformed our approach not only to the history of the period which he made his own, but also to the historical enterprise itself. Turning his back on traditional political and diplomatic narrative, Braudel insisted on the priority of geography and the environment, and of economic and social forces, over mere 'events'. History, it seemed, could never be the same again.

Braudel's message, conveyed in page after page of brilliant insights and coruscating prose, was highly seductive. It was now clearly impossible to produce an account of European history in the second half of the sixteenth century which ignored economic and social developments. This book, therefore, was written under the shadow of Braudel's *Mediterranean*. Yet at the same time I, for one, was unable to go the whole way with Braudel. In the first place, his interpretation seemed to me to place an unacceptably strong emphasis on environmental, social and economic forces at the expense of what is now known as *mentalités* – religion, culture, ideas – which were relegated to a very secondary position. This seemed particularly inappropriate in the discussion of an age of violent religious passions. Secondly, his interpretation seemed to me excessively determinist. Was Philip II, for instance, quite such a prisoner of circumstances as Braudel suggested? At that very moment my own research students, to some of whom I refer in the preface to the first edition, were turning up fascinating evidence in the archives about the decision-making process in the Spain of Philip II and about the part played by personality and human agency in the development of events. Finally, the events themselves seemed to merit something more than the dismissive treatment they received from Braudel. Relegating them to the third and final place in the structure of his book, he failed, as I saw it, to interpret them convincingly in the light of the social and economic developments he had analysed with such brilliance, and as a result was unable to integrate them successfully into his overall framework. The 'total history' to which he aspired was, and remains, a noble ideal. But total history can scarcely be described as total if it fails to take into account not only the impact of ideas and individuals, but also of chance, along with sheer muddle and confusion, on the unfolding sequence of events.

My account of the history of Europe in the second half of the sixteenth century, therefore, was written both under the influence of Braudel, and in reaction to him. I wanted to restore 'events' to the position they seemed to me to deserve, while not ignoring the impact of the Braudelian revolution on our understanding of the age of Philip II. The enterprise, inevitably, was a difficult one, especially given the tight limitations on space imposed by the series. Much – too much – had to be sacrificed for the sake of coherence and readability.

Some thirty years after its original publication the gaps seem all the greater. During those thirty years, a vast historical literature has appeared on many aspects of the period. But, when reviewing this literature as I prepared the book for a new edition, I became persuaded that it still met a need. Although the bibliography is now so much more massive than it was even in the 1960s, and works of great quality have been produced in the intervening years, the dominant trends in historical writing have favoured some aspects of sixteenth-century history over others, with consequent losses as well as gains.

The kind of social and economic analysis favoured by Braudel and the *Annalistes* has lost ground, partly as a result of what came to be a rather mechanical repetition of *Annaliste* methods and formulas, but also because of the growing rejection of Marxist and *marxisant* thinking in large parts of the western world. In particular, the swing to the history of *mentalités*, which affected historians working within the *Annales* tradition as well as those outside it, represented an attempt to restore to the study of the past a concern with the influence of ideas, attitudes and values which had been missing in the dominant historiography of the post-war period. The result was a new insistence on the importance of 'cultural' history – a cultural history strongly coloured by anthropology, which seemed to offer to a new generation of historians the key to the locked doors of the past. As the key was turned, so particular kinds of cultural studies – for example inquires into the history of witchcraft – proliferated.

There has also been a significant shift away from the study of those great impersonal forces so beloved of Braudel to the personal and the individual, and a consequential shift from the macro-historical to the micro-historical. A miller of Friuli with a bizarre personal cosmology, or a one-legged French soldier belatedly returned from the wars, have received the kind of close historical attention once accorded to entire social groups or communities. While this has notably enriched our appreciation of certain aspects of sixteenth-century life, it has also raised difficult questions about the degree to which individual case-histories, capable of being reconstructed through the chance survival and discovery of a dossier, can legitimately be regarded as truly representative of the cultural and social world from which they were singled out by a combination of accident and ingenious historical sleuthing.

Even as the new preoccupation with cultural history, regarded primarily as the history of what came to be known as 'popular culture', was extending the range of historical knowledge to embrace unstudied or understudied areas of social experience, so the proliferation of research into individual or local case-histories was tending to splinter the past into a multitude of fragments. This fragmentation of the past meant the blurring or loss of that larger picture which the Marxist or *marxisant* historians had sought to capture through their concentration on large issues of economic and social development.

In due course a reaction set in against what came to be seen as an excessively populist interpretation of 'society' and 'culture', and also against the neglect, by the new cultural and anthropological historians as much as by the *Annales* historians of the previous generation, of the historical dimension of power. Politics, understood primarily as 'high politics', forced their way back onto the historical agenda, giving a new impetus both to political narrative and to political biography, a genre which, while it never ceased to be practised, had for long been under something of a cloud. But, for many historians, the new concern with high politics was an arid pursuit if it turned its back on recent historical gains. These included a heightened sensitivity to social and cultural issues, and a belief – bordering at times on the obsessive – that the analysis of language, imagery and representation offered an indispensable key both to the intentions of historical actors and to the understanding of the society in which they operated.

As far as European history of the later sixteenth century is concerned, these shifts of historical focus have been especially reflected over the past two decades in the increased attention paid to the ways in which government operated through a social hierarchy vertically articulated by ties of kinship, patronage and clientage, so that the exercise of power from the centre became a process of continuous negotiation between the various parties involved. The breakdown of power, as in the course of the French Wars of Religion, thus reflects the failure of the crown, for whatever reason, to control and manipulate successfully the existing networks of clientage for its own political advantage. But, as I have sought to indicate in this book, if there were failures, as in the France of the later Valois, there were also successes. The Spain of Philip II, or the England of Elizabeth, showed how political skill and the deployment of the resources inherent in sixteenth-century kingship, could help maintain effective government even in a period of acute religious tensions and international conflict.

The resources inherent in kingship included not only the more obvious sources of patronage, but also the symbolic aspects of power. The marriage of history and anthropology, combined with our contemporary preoccupation with the symbolic manifestations of power, has led to a new and sophisticated interest in the nature of the court and court society, and in the ways in which monarchs sought to strengthen, project and celebrate their majesty through elaborate court spectacles, and through their patronage of artists and men of letters. This concern with the representation of power has benefited from, and to some extent assisted, the most important of all the recent trends in contemporary scholarship in the field of the humanities: the dismantling of traditional disciplinary barriers, as historians of politics and society cooperate with literary specialists, art historians and historians of ideas in a joint venture designed to recover and reconstruct the language of the past.

The widening of traditional history reflected in these and other developments – the resurgence, for instance, of military history, especially in its social context – has had many beneficial consequences, but it has also greatly complicated the task of producing a convincing historical synthesis. Both 'war' and 'religion' carry more historiographical freight than they carried forty years ago. If writing today a survey of later sixteenth-century European history, I would have had to take this historiographical freight on board, even if subsequently rejecting some of it as superfluous or excessively inflated baggage. But the wholesale incorporation of new freight, while still preserving the best of the old, would have hopelessly unbalanced the cargo, and led to the capsizing of the ship. In the circumstances, therefore, I have contented myself with making adjustments to the text where I felt that it looked misleading or outdated in the light of more recent research, and in replacing the original bibliography with an extended bibliographical essay which will alert readers to those areas which are not covered, or are inadequately covered, in the text they have before them. I am grateful to Mr Timothy Watson of Magdalen College, Oxford, for his suggestions both for revision of the text and for additional reading.

In presenting the book with these amendments to a new generation of readers, I do so in the belief that it goes some way towards meeting a need which has still to be fully met by a new generation of writers. It seeks to provide a broad picture which identifies and analyses some of the principal forces working for both continuity and change in a period of political and religious upheaval. It seeks, too, to show the interaction of developments across the continent – something that has tended to get lost in recent years in the proliferation of national and local studies. Above all, it seeks to tell a coherent and comprehensible story of a continent in turmoil, at a time when the importance of mere 'events', and the virtues of narrative history after a long period of disparagement, have once again come to be recognized.

Oxford
September 1999

Preface to the First Edition

In approaching the considerable body of literature on the history of later sixteenth-century Europe I felt that the outstanding need at this moment was for a primarily political narrative, which would take into account the recent advances in our knowledge of the economic and social history of the period, and would attempt to relate to each other some of the simultaneous and complementary events occurring in the various European States. We have become so accustomed to separate accounts of the French religious wars and the revolt of the Netherlands that we are in danger of losing the sense of that interaction of events in different parts of the continent, of which contemporaries themselves were so sharply aware. The limited amount of space at my disposal has inevitably led to foreshortenings and omissions; but I hope to have conveyed some idea of the complex interplay of events across the continent, and of the feeling of contemporaries that they were involved in a great European drama. In selecting 1572 and 1585 as the moments of chronological division in the narrative I was influenced only by what appeared to me to be the great significance of those particular years. The consequent division of the thirty-nine years 1559–1598 into thirteen-year periods is not intended to suggest any mystical faith in a cyclical movement of history.

I should like to express my gratitude to Mr Alastair Duke and Mr Brian Pearce for drawing my attention to certain publications on the Netherlands and France respectively. Four of my research students working on different aspects of the history of this period – Mr R. J. W. Evans, Mr R. L. Kagan, Mr A. W. Lovett and Mr N. G. Parker – have done their best to keep me up to the mark, and I have benefited greatly from conversations with them. When their theses eventually see the light of day, this book will require revision and amendment in several places. I am grateful also to Professor J. H. Plumb and Professor G. R. Elton, both of whom read the typescript and made valuable comments on it. Professor R. B. Wernham, Professor Orest Ranum and Dr N. M. Sutherland all gave generously of their time in reading the proofs, and in pointing out errors which I have done my best to correct. Mr Richard Ollard has been both vigilant and encouraging at every stage of the book's career. The index was compiled by my wife, to whom this book is gratefully dedicated.

King's College, London
9 July 1968

Maps

Map 1 Later Sixteenth-Century Europe

Map 2   The Mediterranean

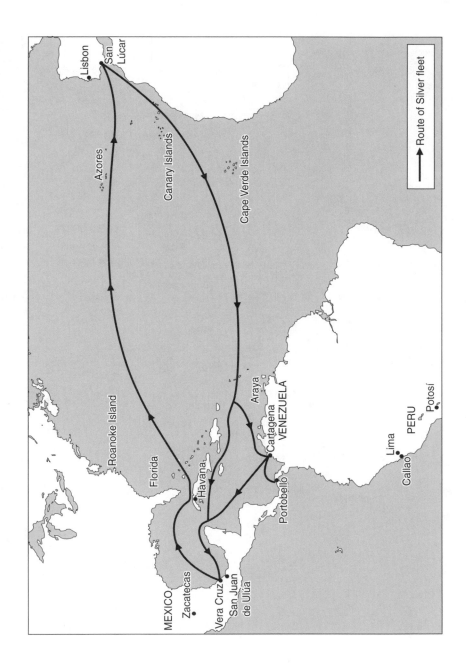

Map 3   The Atlantic

Map 4 The Netherlands

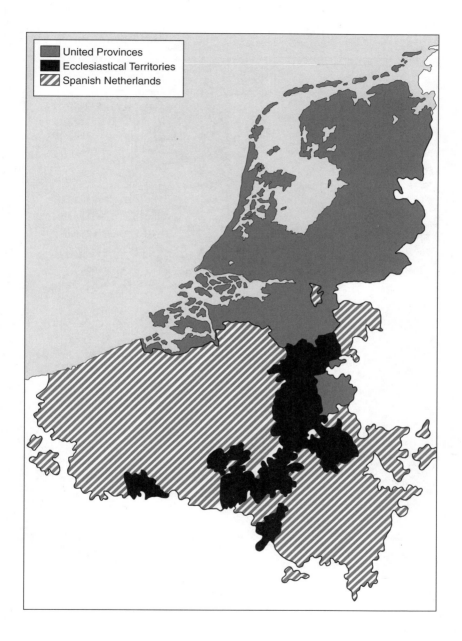

Map 5   The Netherlands Divided

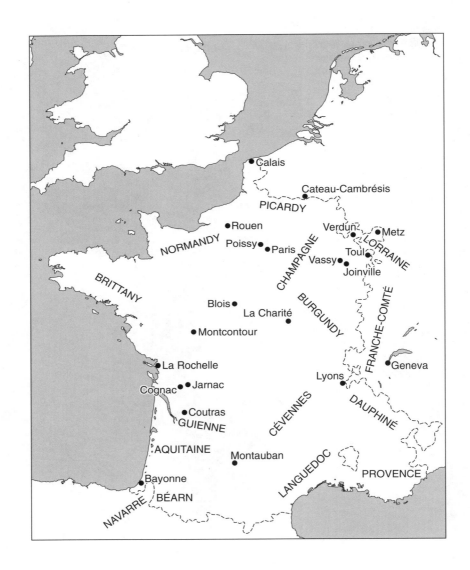

Map 6 France

Genealogical Tables

1 Spanish and Austrian Habsburgs

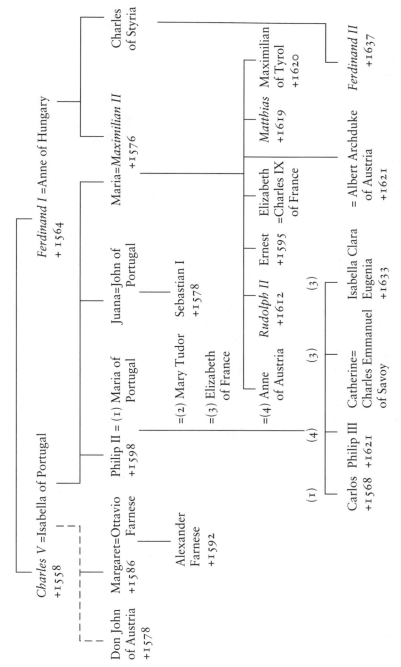

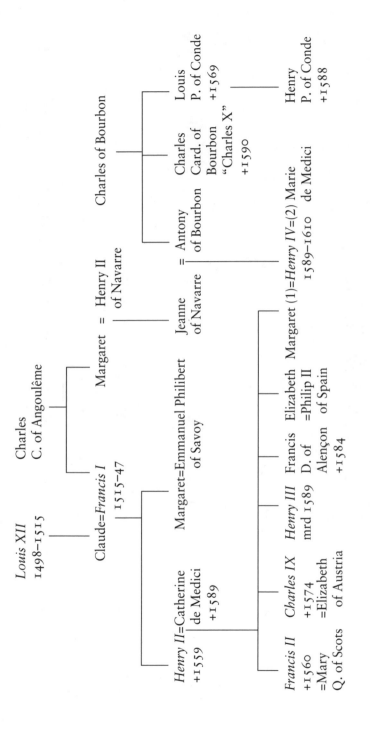

2 Houses of Valois and Bourbon

3 House of Guise

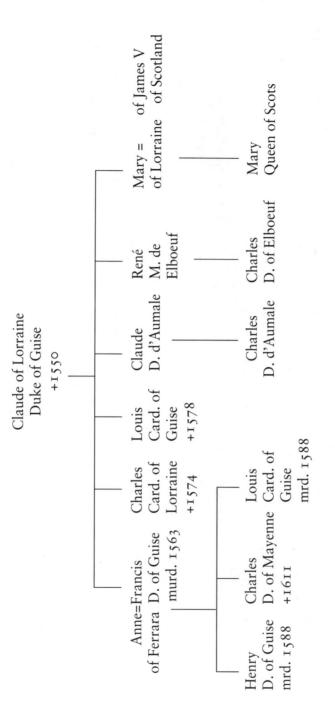

Claude of Lorraine
Duke of Guise
+1550

Anne=Francis D. of Guise
of Ferrara murd. 1563

Charles
Card. of
Lorraine
+1574

Louis
Card. of
Guise
+1578

Claude
D. d'Aumale

René
M. de
Elboeuf

Mary =   of James V
of Lorraine   of Scotland

Henry
D. of Guise
mrd. 1588

Charles
D. of Mayenne
+1611

Louis
Card. of
Guise
mrd. 1588

Charles
D. d'Aumale

Charles
D. of Elboeuf

Mary
Queen of Scots

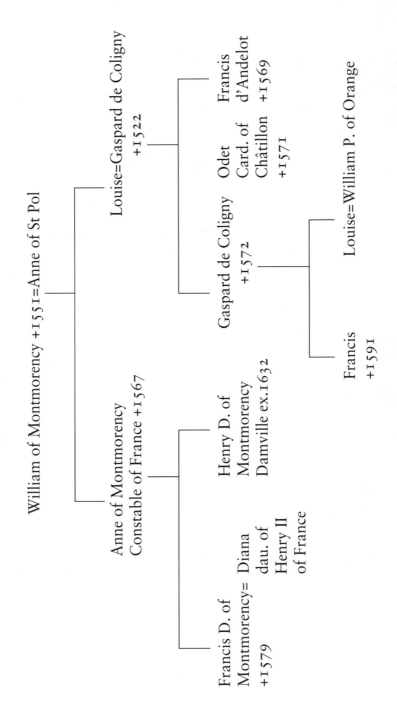

4 Montmorency and Coligny

William of Montmorency +1551=Anne of St Pol

Anne of Montmorency
Constable of France +1567

Louise=Gaspard de Coligny
+1522

Francis D. of
Montmorency=
+1579

Diana
dau. of
Henry II
of France

Henry D. of
Montmorency
Damville ex.1632

Gaspard de Coligny
+1572

Odet
Card. of
Châtillon
+1571

Francis
d'Andelot +1569

Francis
+1591

Louise=William P. of Orange

PART I

The Europe of Cateau-Cambrésis

I

The International Scene

1 Dynastic Peace

The Europe of Cateau-Cambrésis was born beneath the double sign of bankruptcy and heresy, and never escaped from the potent influences which attended its birth. The mounting cost of war had forced the Spanish Crown to default on its obligations to its bankers in 1557, and the French Crown promptly followed suit. After this, peace between Habsburg and Valois was only a question of time. There was, after all, a limit to the goodwill and the resources of even the most compliant bankers, just as there was also a limit to the capacity of States to meet the steeply rising rates of interest on their accumulating debts. Sixteenth-century kings were no strangers to insolvency, although they would ignore its threatening presence for as long as they could. But there were moments when the reckoning could no longer be deferred. One such moment came in 1557, and there would be similar painful episodes in the decades ahead.

Bankruptcy, however, was not alone in driving Philip II of Spain and Henry II of France towards a settlement of their differences. Heresy, and the fear of it, were having the same effect. The authority of princes and the stability of States seemed everywhere to be jeopardized, in these middle years of the century, by the alarming spread of religious dissidence. Spain itself, although protected by its powerful Inquisition, felt dangerously exposed; and France was faced with imminent disaster. This, at least, was the warning which the bishop of Arras, Antoine Perrenot, conveyed to Charles of Guise, cardinal of Lorraine, when the two men met in May 1558 to discuss the possibility of a peace settlement. As an adviser to Philip II and a member of the Netherlands council of state, Perrenot spoke with some authority. Heresy, he warned the cardinal, was to be found in the very highest quarters. It was true that no trace of suspicion attached to Henry II's favourite, the Constable Montmorency, who had been held a prisoner by the Spaniards since the French defeat at the battle of St Quentin. But the same could not be said of two other French prisoners, the Constable's nephews, Gaspard de Coligny and his brother François d'Andelot. The Spanish authorities had irrefutable evidence that Coligny had been in communication with Calvinist Geneva. In the circumstances, the king of France would be well advised to abandon a war from which only the heretics now stood to gain, and to devote all his energies to the spiritual salvation of his troubled kingdom.

Although the warning was not lost on Henry II, peace was not easily achieved. Formal discussions opened in October 1558, but any immediate prospect of a settlement was destroyed by an event of the greatest concern to the monarchies of Western Europe – the death on 17 November of Mary Tudor, queen of England and wife of Philip II of Spain. The Anglo-Spanish union had been a cornerstone of Charles V's policy in the final years of his reign, and its future must now be regarded as highly uncertain, with Mary dead and no child of the marriage to succeed her. Nobody knew what policies the new queen, Elizabeth, would adopt in questions of doctrine and foreign affairs, although Philip's envoy in London expressed the prophetic fear that 'in religion she will not go right'. The best means of disproving the prophecy and averting the calamity was to provide her with a devoutly Catholic, and Spanish, husband. Her former brother-in-law Philip, at this time in Brussels, was ready enough to oblige. For this prematurely care-worn king, twice a widower by the age of thirty-two, the political advantages of a second English marriage needed no rehearsal. French influence was dangerously strong in Scotland, whose young queen Mary had recently become the daughter-in-law of Henry II of France, and whose queen regent, Mary of Lorraine, was a sister of the duke of Guise. On Mary Tudor's death, Henry II had proclaimed his daughter-in-law the rightful queen of England. If Spain were to retain any influence in Northern Europe, and if the Netherlands were to be saved from subjection to France, Henry's attempt to gain control of the British Isles must at all costs be foiled.

The jockeying between Philip and Henry for domination over England was bound to interrupt Habsburg-Valois negotiations, especially as Elizabeth, who must be a party to any settlement, was unwilling to contemplate peace with France as long as Calais remained in French hands. But while Philip was anxious to humour Elizabeth, he soon appreciated that his marriage prospects in that particular quarter were distinctly discouraging, and that England needed peace as urgently as Spain. When Elizabeth, for her part, realized that Philip was not prepared to postpone negotiations indefinitely for the sake of her claims to Calais, she could only acquiesce. By the beginning of February 1559, therefore, all three powers were ready to resume their discussions.

The site suggested for the negotiations was the neutral territory of Cateau-Cambrésis, where the bishop of Cambrai possessed a derelict *château*. Windows of paper set in wooden frames were hastily installed, and a little furniture was hurried to the empty building. The Spanish delegates arrived on 5 February, and the French on the 6th, soon to be followed by the English. All three delegations contained men whose names would be famous throughout Europe before the century was done. The strong Spanish representation consisted of that great commander, the duke of Alba; Ruy Gómez de Silva, the Portuguese favourite of Philip II, and Alba's future rival in the struggle for influence at the court of Spain; Antoine Perrenot, bishop of Arras, soon to be raised to the purple as cardinal Granvelle; Ulrich Viglius of the Netherlands council of state, and William, prince of Orange, the greatest of the Netherlands nobles and a loyal servant of Philip II. The French delegation, by contrast, was weak; and it suffered from having operated at a disadvantage during the earlier round of discussions in 1558 because two of its members, the Constable Montmorency and the Maréchal de Saint-André, were both prisoners-of-war at the time, and had been released on parole in order to take part. Since then, Montmorency had ransomed himself for a large sum, and had used his influence with Henry II to work for peace with Spain. But he had lost much of his credit in France through his defeat at St Quentin, and he would lose more when the terms of the settlement were announced. A more effective figure in the French delegation was the cardinal of Lorraine, the brother of the duke of Guise and the most intelligent member of that great house of Guise-Lorraine whose star was rising as that of their rival Montmorency began to wane. The English delegation of three was a relatively modest affair: the bishop of Ely, Nicholas Wootton (formerly ambassador at Paris) and Lord Howard of Effingham, whose son would lead the English fleet to victory in 1588.

When general discussions opened on 11 February, the ambassadors were at least agreed on the acute discomfort of their lodgings. But the talks themselves went slowly. The three delegations occupied different corners of the room, and spokesmen would periodically be despatched from their respective corners to argue the case for their principals. There were language problems, too, since the discussions were conducted in Latin – a tongue in which the military men among the ambassadors, Alba, Montmorency and Saint-André, found some difficulty in expressing themselves. The bishop of Arras and the cardinal of Lorraine were therefore in constant demand as interpreters. But the difficulties, both diplomatic and linguistic, were in due course overcome. Many of the major decisions had already been taken in the October negotiations, and the obligatory English rearguard action over Calais proved to be the principal cause of delay. By the end of March matters were nearly settled, and the discussions were formally concluded by the signing of two separate peace treaties on 2 and 3 April respectively.

The first treaty, between England and France, provided Elizabeth with a face-saving formula by which the French should keep Calais for eight years and then either restore it, or – since this was highly improbable – pay compensation for its retention. For years to come, bitter memories of Calais haunted Anglo-French relations, but for practical purposes the issue was dead, and England had lost her last permanent outpost on the continent of Europe.

The second, and more important, treaty, signed on 3 April, was between France and Spain. Apart from an exchange of towns along her north-eastern frontier, where France also kept the Imperial cities of Metz, Toul and Verdun, the treaty was primarily concerned with a settlement in Italy, the battleground of France and Spain for over half a century. Here, the peace confirmed what had already been determined by a succession of wars: the almost total exclusion of France from the Italian peninsula, to the benefit of Spain and her allies. It was with bitterness and disillusionment that the French occupying army received its orders to abandon Piedmont, which it had originally invaded in 1536. By the treaty, Piedmont and Savoy were restored to their rightful owner, the duke Emmanuel Philibert, who had served Philip II faithfully as his governor in the Netherlands and as his victorious general at St Quentin. The French retained a few strongholds on the Italian side of the Alps, but their days as an Italian power were effectively over. Some compensation was perhaps to be found in the stipulation that Emmanuel Philibert should marry Henry II's sister, Margaret of Valois. But Margaret's loyalty to her husband proved stronger than her family allegiance, and the ducal pair set about restoring the fortunes of their duchy and of the House of Savoy without regard for France.

The reappearance of a strong Alpine State ruled by a shrewd and determined duke tended to overshadow the other decisions affecting Italy taken at Cateau-Cambrésis. One other Italian ruler besides Emmanuel Philibert, however, had good reason to be pleased with the settlement. In 1555 a combined force of Spaniards and Florentines had captured the independent city of Siena. Two years later, Philip II handed over the captured town to the duke of Florence, Cosimo de Medici, and his action was ratified at Cateau-Cambrésis. The acquisition of Siena fulfilled one of the great ambitions of Cosimo's ambitious life. It also increased the power and the reputation of a ruler who was already beginning to acquire a position of pre-eminence among his Italian colleagues.

The transfers of territory to the dukes of Savoy and Florence were accomplished with relative smoothness. Another of Spain's allies, however, had considerable difficulty in harvesting the fruits of victory.

At Cateau-Cambrésis the island of Corsica, which had been under French occupation since 1553, was restored to the republic of Genoa. The Corsicans, under the leadership of one of the most flamboyant Mediterranean adventurers of the sixteenth century, Sampiero Corso, had long been struggling to free themselves from Genoese domination. It was Sampiero who had originally called in the French, and it was Sampiero who now resumed the struggle when the French were forced to depart. While the Genoese attempted to gain control over a hostile island, Sampiero scoured the Mediterranean for allies. He received promises of help from France, along with a number of banners bearing the heroic device *pugna pro patria*; and thus armed, he landed in 1564 with a handful of friends at Ajaccio. It took four years, and the assassination of Sampiero, to crush the ensuing insurrection. The Corsicans were the first, but not the only, people who would fight for their *patria* in the years after Cateau-Cambrésis.

Whatever the practical difficulties involved in fulfilling the terms of the treaties, Western Europe was formally at peace from the spring of 1559. The official policy in France was to welcome warmly the reconciliation of the two great Catholic powers – a reconciliation that was to be solemnly ratified by the marriage of Philip II to Henry II's thirteen-year old daughter, Elizabeth of Valois. But some Frenchmen felt deep resentment at the alleged humiliation of France in the peace treaty. The country had abandoned its allies and its conquests in Italy, and it seemed as if the lives and the treasure of France had all been expended for nothing. 'By a stroke of the pen,' wrote one critic, 'all our conquests of thirty years have been handed back'. The man generally held responsible for the humiliation of Cateau-Cambrésis was the Constable Montmorency; and the Guises, as might be expected, did nothing to dispel the impression that the Constable was the architect of disaster. But Montmorency still retained the favour of the king, and the Guises still found themselves unable to capture the commanding heights of power.

Within three months of Cateau-Cambrésis, however, everything had changed. Henry II ordered that the marriages of the king of Spain and the duke of Savoy to the two French princesses should be celebrated with the most spectacular festivities. On 28 June, the day of the betrothal of Emmanuel Philibert and Margaret, the tournaments began. On the 30th, Henry himself entered the lists, and was mortally wounded by the count of Montgomery's lance. He died on 10 July, leaving a widow, Catherine de Medici, and a brood of sickly sons, of whom the eldest now became king, as Francis II, at the age of fifteen.

The accession of Francis brought with it the downfall of the Constable Montmorency, and his replacement by the duke of Guise and the cardinal of Lorraine, the uncles of Mary Queen of Scots, the new queen of France. With their House now dominant in the courts of

Paris and Edinburgh, tempting new possibilities suggested themselves to the ambitious leaders of an ambitious family. By a swift military stroke they might succeed in wiping out the humiliation of the recent peace settlement, and so confirm the duke of Guise's reputation, first gained at Calais, as the national saviour of France. Once again, as at the time of Mary Tudor's death, the fortunes of Western Europe turned on those of the British Isles. A French military intervention might establish Mary Queen of Scots on the English throne in place of Elizabeth. Even if this failed, it would still help to restore and consolidate French influence in Scotland, where at this moment the regency government of Mary of Lorraine was finding itself in difficulties.

John Knox, returning from his Geneva exile in May 1559, had already sounded his trumpet, with no uncertain note, against the rule of the foreign and popish queen regent. Knox's trumpet-call was answered by a popular outbreak of image-smashing, and by an insurrection of Protestant nobles, the 'Lords of the Congregation'. While Mary of Lorraine appealed to France for help in restoring her authority, the rebels turned to Elizabeth, although at first without great hopes of success. By the terms of Cateau-Cambrésis Elizabeth was pledged to non-intervention in Scotland, and she was anyhow reluctant to support a rebellion against a lawful queen. Yet so much was at stake in Scotland that she simply could not afford to let her northern neighbour fall into French hands by default. Coaxed along by her secretary William Cecil, she overcame her scruples about offering help to rebels in general and to John Knox in particular, to the extent of sending a fleet to the Firth of Forth in January 1560. Then, calculating to a nicety the probable international repercussions, she ordered an army across the border at the end of March, to lay siege to the French forces at Leith.

The English invasion of Scotland aroused acute concern in the courts of Western Europe. If Elizabeth were defeated by the French, as Philip of Spain had feared that she might be, then both Scotland and England would fall into French hands, and the Netherlands would be in danger. But could the Catholic king of Spain come to the help of a queen who had now made clear her Protestant inclinations, and who was herself assisting a rebellion instigated by heretics against a lawful sovereign? Philip's problem was an early example of the dilemma which would afflict every European ruler in the age of Cateau-Cambrésis – whether national or religious interests should take precedence on those unfortunate occasions when they failed to coincide. But by the time an envoy from Philip had arrived in England to urge on the queen a cessation of hostilities and Spanish mediation, the matter was already as good as settled. Although the English army made a miserable showing, the military inadequacies of the English proved of less importance than the political and religious dissensions of the French. Shaken by the discovery in February of the Huguenot conspiracy of Amboise, the Guise régime lost its first enthusiasm for foreign adventure, and French commissioners were sent to Scotland to treat for peace. By the treaty of Edinburgh of 6 July 1560 it was agreed that all French troops should leave Scotland, and that Mary Stuart should renounce her claims to the English throne. Francis II and Mary subsequently refused to ratify the treaty, but Francis died on 5 December, and the interests of the new regent of France, the Florentine Catherine de Medici, did not extend to the remote and incomprehensible regions of the north. Mary Stuart was therefore left to fend for herself, and when she returned to Scotland in August 1561, it was without the French military backing that alone could give substance to her pretensions to sovereignty over England.

The success of Elizabeth and Cecil in Scotland in 1559–1560 was of major European significance, for nothing would more quickly have disturbed the balance of forces registered in the treaty of Cateau-Cambrésis than the consolidation of French power on England's northern border. In establishing herself as the effective protector of the new, Protestant, Scotland, Elizabeth had immeasurably strengthened her own position, and had ensured her independence of the leading continental powers. At the same time, she had also helped to give some degree of permanence to the West European settlement of 1559. The continuity of this settlement was now based on the recognition of two major facts of international life. The first was the recognition by France that the Italian peninsula was for the time being beyond the sphere of its effective interest. The second was the mutual recognition by France and Spain that the domination of the British Isles was not at present practical politics for either. Given the acceptance of these two fundamental premises, there was a reasonable expectation that the peace of Cateau-Cambrésis would last rather longer than previous attempts at a Habsburg-Valois settlement.

The reasons for this were to be found partly in the mutual exhaustion of the rival powers, partly in their common concern at the spread of heresy, but most of all in the crippling decline of the French Crown's authority following the death of Henry II in the summer of 1559. The abortive Scottish adventure had brought home the difficulties of conducting an ambitious foreign policy during a period of acute domestic uncertainty, and the lesson was not lost on Catherine de Medici. As long as the queen-mother had the upper hand in France, she would do her best to avoid a confrontation with Spain. As a result, the old Habsburg-Valois struggle – the principal cause of West European instability during the previous half-century – went into abeyance after 1559. The mutual rivalry inevitably persisted;

but for the next thirty years there was a vacuum at the heart of European life – a vacuum created by the inability of a weakened French monarchy to sustain consistently its interests beyond the borders of France.

The eclipse of French power, had it come a generation earlier, might have saved the Emperor Charles V; but by 1559 Charles and his empire both belonged to the past. His brother Ferdinand I (1556–1564) had succeeded to the title, but hardly to the realities of Imperial power. Instead it was Charles's son, Philip II of Spain, who – although disappointed of the Imperial title – stood to gain most by the peace of Cateau-Cambrésis and the death of Henry II. While Ferdinand had to content himself with a nominal authority over a Germany whose political and religious disunity had been formally confirmed by the peace of Augsburg of 1555, his nephew Philip of Spain was the master of an impeccably orthodox Castile; and while Ferdinand's financial and military resources were slender, and were heavily committed to the defence of Europe's eastern frontier against the Turk, Castile's resources, while momentarily depleted, hinted at reserves of strength far beyond the dreams of an Austrian Habsburg. Philip, therefore, if he could once exploit those reserves, was in a far stronger position than his uncle to capitalize on the weakness of France.

Philip's dominions consisted of Spain and its possessions in Italy and the New World, together with the Netherlands and that ancient Burgundian relic, the Franche-Comté, lying between France and the Swiss Confederation. For four years he had ruled these territories from Brussels, a convenient centre from which to follow the campaigns against the French, and to watch over his interests in the Netherlands and England. But by some strange twist of irony this chilling man, who somehow conveyed the impression that he had never felt the warm touch of the Mediterranean sun, never really felt at home in the north, and looked forward to the day when he could return to Castile. By the summer of 1559 this day was in sight. The death of Mary Tudor and the conclusion of peace with France made his presence in the north less necessary than before. At the same time, his ministers in Spain were clamouring for his return to the peninsula, where urgent administrative problems demanded his personal attention. But above all it was the need for money which drew him back to Spain. In recent years the Netherlands had proved increasingly disappointing as a source of royal income, and Philip had become overwhelmingly dependent on remittances from Castile. 'I will gain nothing by staying here,' he wrote to Antoine Perrenot in June 1559, 'except lose myself and these states ... The best thing that can be done is for all of us to seek the remedy ... and if the remedy is not here then I will go to seek it in Spain.'[1] Whether he would find it there was another matter, but the search was worth the journey, and in

August 1559 he left the north for the Iberian peninsula, never to return.

Philip's homecoming to Spain in the early autumn of 1559 marks as well as any event the division of the century. On one side was the age of Charles V, on the other that of Philip II; and although the son borrowed much from his father, and would have borrowed more if he could, there were, none the less, profound differences between the empires of father and son, which became still more pronounced as the century progressed. For Charles's empire had been the Holy Roman Empire, universal in its aspirations and commitments, and based, in so far as it had a geographical base, on the German lands. The empire of Philip II, on the other hand, was technically not an empire at all. Contemporaries knew it as the *monarquía española* – the Spanish Monarchy – and the title, while scarcely suggesting the extent and the diversity of the territories of which it was composed, at least acknowledged the central fact about Philip II's power: its firm Spanish basis. If Philip inherited, along with his Spanish lands, many of the universal obligations that had once belonged to his father, this was less because of commitments implicit in his style and titles, than because of the economic, geographical and religious realities of the world in which he had been called upon to assume his inheritance. For, by 1559, the kingship of Spain was a uniquely powerful position, carrying with it responsibilities and opportunities which in an earlier age would automatically have accompanied the title of Holy Roman Emperor.

There is no one single explanation of the unique pre-eminence enjoyed by Spain in the affairs of Europe in the two or three generations after 1559. Part of it naturally derived from the accident of France's temporary eclipse. This was especially apparent in Italy, where Spain benefited decisively from her possession of Italian territory and from the absence of serious competition. After 1559 it was no longer possible for Venice and the Italian princes to pursue with any real hope of success their traditional policy of playing off the French against the Spaniards. Most of them, with varying degrees of resignation, accepted the inevitable and chose to hitch their fortunes to the rising star of Spain. The Venetian Republic, it is true, sought to preserve some freedom of action by drawing closer to the Papacy, and to the Florentine duchy of Cosimo de Medici, who greatly enhanced his standing in 1569 by securing from Pope Pius V the right to style himself Grand Duke of Tuscany. Emmanuel Philibert of Savoy, with a spirit of independence befitting the victorious general of St Quentin, managed to ensure from Philip II a degree of cautious respect as he methodically set about building up the resources of his shattered Alpine duchy. But in general the power of Spain was too overwhelming in the years immediately following Cateau-Cambrésis for the rulers of Italy to court the risk of any serious argument with Madrid. Philip II, after all, was the master of Lombardy and Milan, of Naples, Sardinia and Sicily. Spanish garrisons were strung across the peninsula, and Milan was an impregnable *plaza de armas*, from which the Spaniards could dominate the entire north Italian plain. Moreover, the Turks were too uncomfortably close for any petty Italian prince to indulge in excessive defiance of the only power capable of offering him some protection in the event of an Ottoman attack.

As the behaviour of the Italian States suggested, much of Spain's European pre-eminence under Philip II rested on its military power, which itself was a strange composite of reputation and reality. The famous Spanish *tercios* – those formations of massed pikemen and musketeers which had dominated the battlefields of Europe during the first half of the century – had understandably acquired a reputation for invincibility. The Spanish infantryman, toughened by service in North Africa or Italy, or sometimes in the Indies, was a remarkable soldier who, if well led, had no equal in Europe. But native Spaniards represented only a small proportion of the 40,000–60,000 men who might at any one time be serving in the king of Spain's armies. The bulk of the troops consisted of foreign mercenaries – Walloons, Germans, Italians – whose effectiveness as a fighting force was closely related to their hopes of remuneration. Money, as contemporaries insisted, provided the sinews of war, or, as Rabelais chose to express it, '*les nerfs des batailles sont les pécunes*'. If foreign soldiers of fortune elected to enter the service of the king of Spain, they did so because they expected him to be able to offer them ample opportunities for profitable employment, and reasonably regular pay.

The expectation, while frequently disappointed, was at least understandable. The power of Philip II rested ultimately on his wealth, and this far exceeded the wealth of contemporary rulers in Christian Europe. Essentially it was derived from two sources: the taxes, lay and clerical, levied in his dominions, and especially in Castile; and the annual remittance of silver from his possessions in America. But in 1559, when Philip returned home to Spain, neither of these sources was as productive as it might have been, or as it needed to be if he were to maintain and increase his power. The full-scale exploitation of the silver mines of the New World had as yet barely begun, and the position was aggravated by the fact that Spain's trade with the Indies was at this moment in recession.[2] In Spain itself, the royal bankruptcy of 1557 had revealed the hollowness of the Crown's finances under the pressures of war; and the existing taxes, while making heavy demands on certain sections of the population of Castile, were inadequate to meet even Philip's most pressing needs.

The new international opportunities awaiting Spain in the years immediately after 1559 were therefore to some extent counterbalanced by the urgent character of its domestic difficulties. Time was needed to sort out the financial and administrative inheritance of the reign of Charles V, and to discover and mobilize fresh sources of revenue. But, even given time, Spain could not expect to go unchallenged; for although France was no longer an effective competitor, there remained another, and more formidable, rival in the Ottoman Empire of Sulaiman the Magnificent.

For over a hundred years now, Europe had been living uncomfortably close to the Turks. On the coasts of Italy and the Hungarian plain, ravaged homesteads and depopulated villages bore stark witness to the terrors of Ottoman power. Charles V had done what he could, but Charles was dead, and the Emperor Ferdinand lacked the resources to continue the fight. In 1562 a series of frustrating diplomatic negotiations on which he had embarked culminated in a humiliating truce, whereby the Emperor agreed to pay punctually his annual tribute to the Sultan, and was compelled to recognize the independence of Transylvania under its prince John Sigismund Zapolyai.

During 1558 Philip II had himself taken a discreet and indirect part in these negotiations in the hope of securing a truce on the Mediterranean front. Some temporary settlement might in the end have been achieved, but in 1559, just after the signing of the treaty of Cateau-Cambrésis, Philip changed his mind. The diplomatic approaches to the agents of the Sultan were suspended, and in June Philip approved the plans prepared by his viceroy in Sicily and the Grand Master of the Knights of St John of Malta for an expedition to recover Tripoli, from which the Turks and their allies had expelled the Knights in 1551.

This crucial change in Philip's Turkish policy in the spring of 1559, while partly inspired by reports of internal dissensions in the Ottoman Empire, was made possible by the ending of the war with France. Cateau-Cambrésis had freed Spain from its preoccupations in Northern Europe, and at the same time had deprived the Turks of the help of their traditional Christian ally. Philip, afraid that a peace settlement would endanger his reputation, and still unaware of the state of Spain after the long years of war, seems to have assumed that this was a favourable moment for seizing the initiative in the Mediterranean, but it soon became clear that he had badly miscalculated. The Turks were at this moment much stronger, and Spain much weaker, than Philip had believed.[3] As a result, Spain found itself committed to a protracted Mediterranean conflict, in the course of which Philip naturally came to assume the mantle of his father as the champion of Christendom against the forces of Islam.

The peace which had come to North-West Europe in 1559 was not, therefore, accompanied by a corresponding peace in the south. The Mediterranean basin, however, was not the only region to be troubled by conflict in the years after 1559, nor was the Ottoman Empire the only power on the fringes of Europe to be a disturber of the peace. Away to the north-east, along the shores of the Baltic, the precarious balance of rival States – Poland, Sweden, Denmark – was at this moment being upset by the sudden intrusion of Muscovy, a power which had until now played little active part in European international life. During the first years of his personal government, its ruler Ivan IV, who had assumed the title of Tsar in 1547, had devoted his attention to extending the eastern boundaries of his State. His annexation in 1552 of the Tartar Khanate of Kazan gave him command of the Middle Volga, and access through the Urals to western Siberia. Four years later, the capture of Astrakhan brought the Russians to the shores of the Caspian, and during the following decades they pressed steadily eastwards. But Ivan's interests were not exclusively confined to the East. He was also concerned to break Muscovy's dependence on Hanseatic middlemen by securing direct access to Western Europe by way of the Baltic. It was in the 1550s, over the question of Livonia, that the chance occurred for an opening to the West.

Livonia, along with Estonia and Courland, belonged to the Knights of the Teutonic Order, whose Grand Master, Albert of Brandenburg, had startled Europe by his conversion to Lutheranism in 1525. Since then, the Order had been riddled with dissension, and the Baltic powers had been hungrily eyeing its lands. Ivan was quick to appreciate the advantages to be derived from the weakness and demoralization of the Order, and in 1558, after various attempts at intimidation, his forces seized the Estonian port of Narva. The Russian occupation of Narva, the principal port of entry for West European goods into Eastern Europe, produced predictable repercussions throughout the North. The Imperial Diet deliberated; the Swedes and Poles, fearful for the future of Livonia, but anxious to avoid a confrontation with the Tsar, moved hesitantly to the support of the Teutonic Knights, whose lands they coveted. As the Russians inflicted a new and crushing defeat on the Teutonic Order, the seismic shocks set off by their invasion of Livonia brought about a new alignment of forces around the Baltic shores. In 1561 the Grand Master of the Order, recognizing his inability to stand alone, agreed to the reunion of Livonia with the Grand Duchy of Lithuania, which itself, in 1569, was formally united to Poland by the Union of Lublin. In 1561, too, Eric XIV of Sweden occupied Estonia, hoping to establish himself on the eastern side of a Danish-dominated Baltic, and to gain control over Russia's trade with the West. The Swedish intervention precipitated a savage conflict with Denmark, a Northern Seven Years War lasting from 1563 to 1570.

It was a measure of the European importance of the Baltic trade that the peace congress which assembled at Stettin in 1570 included representatives of England and Scotland, and even of Spain. Only the Russians were excluded from the congress, which proclaimed freedom of navigation in the Baltic, and attempted a general settlement among the northern powers. Sweden, although keeping Estonia, fared badly at the congress. It was true that Frederick II of Denmark had failed in his attempt to reconquer Sweden, and that Danish plans for a restoration of the Scandinavian union were as good as dead. But Eric XIV's grand design for a Baltic expansion which would bring the Russian trade under Swedish control had come to nothing, and its author was languishing in prison, after being deposed by his nobles in 1568. Those parts of Livonia which had not fallen to the Poles were placed under Danish protection, in order to keep them out of Russian hands. The Tsar would do his best in the following years to upset the settlement, but, in the end, his own domestic problems defeated him, and Muscovy would have to wait a long time yet for its access to the West. The peace of Stettin of 1570 was therefore in some respects a North European equivalent of the peace of Cateau-Cambrésis of eleven years before. While it left many unsolved problems behind it, it created a relatively long-lived settlement, to the benefit, in the first instance, of the Danes and the Poles. Like Cateau-Cambrésis the settlement proved reasonably durable because Muscovy, like France after Cateau-Cambrésis, soon showed itself in no condition to dispute the verdict effectively. Late sixteenth-century Europe would fight out its conflicts without reference to Muscovy, an empire too remote, too alien and unstable, to be regarded with more than passing fear or curiosity by the nations of the West.

2 Confessional Strife

The dynastic peace that came to Western Europe in 1559 held out hopes of a long period of international tranquillity, in which the wounds of Christendom might be bound up and healed, and its religious unity restored. These hopes were to be cruelly disappointed. Although traditional dynastic rivalries lost much of their former importance in the two or three decades that followed Cateau-Cambrésis, there was to be no slackening of the international tension. Instead, within a few years animosities not only flared up with a new vigour, but burned with an intensity unparalleled in an earlier age. For national rivalries had been overlaid with a new layer of hatred and suspicion, the product of the principal legacy of the sixteenth century to European life – confessional dispute. It was religious differences which came to the forefront after 1559, cutting across national frontiers, exacerbating old hatreds and fomenting new, and disrupting national communities, and then the international community, to such devastating effect that within thirty years of Cateau-Cambrésis the political character of Europe was profoundly, and permanently, changed.

Already in the age of Charles V, religious controversy had helped to shatter the nominal unity of a Christendom confronted by the advances of Islam. But by the 1550s Martin Luther was dead, and his religion, deprived of its founder's intensely personal leadership, was becoming intellectually torpid and politically quiescent. In Germany, the principal scene of confessional strife during the first half of the century, the peace of Augsburg had established an equilibrium, however uneasy, between the Lutheran and the Roman Catholic princes, and in so doing had deprived the Lutherans of any real incentive to further militancy. The Calvinists, however, were excluded from the terms of the Augsburg settlement; and as torpor overcame the second generation of Lutherans, it was the Calvinists who became the most dynamic representatives of the Protestant faith.

At a time when the Roman Church was at last beginning to respond with some measure of success to the challenge of heresy, Calvinism enjoyed certain obvious advantages over Lutheranism as a militant creed. Its doctrines were more clear-cut and more sharply formulated; its adherents were better disciplined; its cellular system of church organization made possible its propagation and independent growth even where the secular authorities were opposed to its establishment; and it had in Geneva a central headquarters from where Calvin himself, until his death in 1564, could command the field of battle. After years of struggle the ageing Calvin had become, from the mid-1550s, the undisputed master of Geneva. The opposition in the city council had been silenced; his enemies had fled. Now that he was entrenched in Geneva beyond any possibility of overthrow, Calvin could turn the city into the effective capital of his new religion, a Protestant Rome. The Calvinists of Europe had long been accustomed to turn to Geneva for advice and instruction, and they had fled to it as a refuge in times of persecution. But it still lacked an institute of higher education for the training of pastors, the men who would act as missionaries of the faith. The Lausanne Academy, although to some extent meeting the need, was subject to the government of Bern, which did not take kindly to the more rigid forms of Calvinist orthodoxy. After protracted wrangling, most of the Lausanne professors, including Theodore Beza, the professor of Greek, were expelled by the Bernese government in 1558. With their assistance, Calvin founded an academy at Geneva in 1559, and Beza became its rector. The new institution was an immediate success. Within three years, one hundred and sixty-two students had enrolled in it, and the number had risen to over three hundred by the time of Calvin's death.

The opening of the Geneva Academy in June 1559 coincided with the reopening of Europe's national frontiers after the peace of Cateau-Cambrésis. Already, at a funeral oration for Mary Tudor, the bishop of Winchester had given a bleak warning of the horrors ahead: 'The wolves be coming out of Geneva and other places of Germany, and have sent their books before, full of pestilent doctrines, blasphemy and heresy to infect the people.'[4] With the reopening of the frontiers in 1559–1560 the packs began to prowl. The Marian exiles flocked back to England on Elizabeth's accession, and pushed the queen in 1559 into the acceptance of a more Protestant settlement than she had either envisaged or desired. Elizabeth successfully resisted the imposition of a Calvinist form of organization on her church, but two European States began to remodel their churches on Calvinist lines in the early 1560s – Scotland, under the revolutionary leadership of the returned exile John Knox, and the Palatinate, in uniquely respectable circumstances, as a result of the conversion of its new ruler, the Elector Frederick III. In the Low Countries, where heresy had been savagely repressed, the return of peace allowed the Calvinist exiles to infiltrate across the frontiers and establish themselves in Tournai, Valenciennes and the cities of Flanders. Under the leadership of the most prominent of the returned exiles, Guy de Brès, Calvinism during the early 1560s made considerable headway in the southern Netherlands – more so than in the north, where such Calvinist influence as existed came from the church at Emden, across the German frontier. But it was in France that Geneva scored some of its most notable successes. Every year a fresh group of Geneva-trained pastors was despatched into France. Most of them native Frenchmen, drawn from middle-class or aristocratic homes, they made influential converts and founded new churches, which looked to Geneva for guidance and advice.

The wolves, as the bishop of Winchester had said, had 'sent their books before.' Bibles, Psalters, pamphlets, and copies of Calvin's *Institutes* poured from the Geneva presses, which at their peak may have been producing as many as 300,000 volumes a year. These books, whether in Latin or the vernacular, recognized no frontiers. A leading Geneva printer like Henri Estienne, the son of the royal printer to Francis I of France, would meet bulk orders from the book merchants for editions of his annotated Bible and of other works in popular demand, or would dispose of them at the great Frankfurt book fair. Pedlars and itinerant vendors would carry them along the trade-routes of central and western Europe; bales of books mysteriously found their way into the holds of ships; and grubby copies passed surreptitiously from hand to hand. Even Spain, where the authorities were especially alert to the threat of subversive literature, was by no means immune. 'One has to consider,' wrote Luis de Ortiz, an official at Burgos in 1558, 'what bad printed works enter these kingdoms from outside. Apart from those full of abominable errors which Luther and his followers have sown . . . even the good ones have scandalous introductions and marginal notes.'[5]

In order to check the flood of subversive religious propaganda, the princes of mid-sixteenth century Europe were compelled to resort to increasingly stringent measures of censorship and prohibition. Since Pope Leo X's prohibition of 1520 on the dissemination and reading of Lutheran-tainted literature, individual universities like Louvain and the Sorbonne had issued their own lists of forbidden books. The Spanish Inquisition issued its first Index in 1546, and the famous Placards or edicts published in the Netherlands in 1550 by Charles V prohibited the reading, copying or dissemination of heretical literature on pain of death. Now, in the late 1550s, still tighter restrictions were introduced. A few months after Luis de Ortiz had written his treatise, the Regent of Spain issued a pragmatic forbidding the import of foreign books, and ordering that all books printed in Spain should in future be licensed by the Council of Castile. The first papal Index, that of Paul IV, appeared in 1559, and the Spanish Inquisition published in the same year, for home consumption, a new and more severe Index of its own.

In spite of the new measures and the increasingly heavy penalties, the smuggling of books continued on an enormous scale. Calvinism, it was clear, was making its impact on the educated and the literate classes of Europe. For the illiterate peasantry, on the other hand, the appeal of a religion so dependent on the written word was relatively slight. It was possible, but difficult, for Calvinism to cross the barrier of literacy – a barrier which tended to separate the countryside from the town. Criteria for gauging literacy are hard to establish, but a rough clue is provided by a man's ability to sign his name, or at least his initials, as distinct from making a mark. On this basis, it has been estimated that 90% of the agricultural population of the Narbonne region in France were strangers to the written word in the later sixteenth century, as against only some 33% of the artisans.[6] This pattern is reflected in the social distribution of Calvinists in the province of Languedoc. In 1560 there were 817 registered attenders at Calvinist meetings in the city of Montpellier, of whom 561 indicated their occupational status.

Profession	Number	Percentage
Artisans	387	69%
Professional classes (lawyers, doctors, notaries, etc.)	87	15.4%
Merchants	24	4.3%
Bourgeois	23	4.2%
Nobles	13	2.3%
Farmers and rural labourers	27	4.8%

The obvious absentees were the rural labourers, who constituted no less than one fifth of Montpellier's total population, but who barely figured on the Huguenot list.

The Montpellier figures suggest that Calvinism suffered even in the cities from the distinction between town and countryside, between literate or semi-literate artisan and the illiterate agricultural labourer. It was the artisans of Montpellier, especially the textile and leather-workers, who came out in sympathy with Calvinism in the early 1560s. The peasants and farm-labourers, on the other hand, proved recalcitrant or actively hostile to the reformed religion. As early as 1561 they were protesting angrily against Huguenot attempts to abolish the mass and to deprive them of saints' days and festivals and dancing. It was only slowly, and with supreme difficulty, that this ancient Catholic world of the countryside was conquered and colonized by the combined forces of Calvinism and literacy. The peasant society of the rough mountain land of the Cévennes became fervently Calvinist – largely, it seems, through the influence of the artisan-élite of leather-workers which lived among it. But the conversion of the Cévennes astonished even Beza, for it was usually considered impossible to sow the Word with success on such unpromising ground. Calvinism, at least in its early years, proved itself essentially a religion for the urban and the literate.

It is easy enough to single out the broad classes of society to which Calvin's doctrines appealed – skilled artisans, merchants, lawyers, gentry, and the professional classes in the towns. But the popularity of Calvinism cannot be explained, still less explained away, merely by reference to economic categories. Its own innate qualities – its clear appeal to the gospel, its insistence on high ethical standards, the sense of unswerving confidence in the purposes of an omnipotent Deity – were of a type which crossed the frontiers of wealth and class. It postulated a desire for self-improvement and self-discipline which might be found at every level of society, although its social range was no doubt restricted by the prerequisites of a degree both of literacy and of leisure for study of the Scriptures. Perhaps the ability to meet those prerequisites helps to explain its considerable success among women of the middle and upper-classes – it was not infrequently through their wives or their mothers that French nobles and gentry made their first acquaintance with the teachings of Calvin. In some places, such as Spain, Italy, or eastern France, in all of which repression was unusually severe, Calvinism failed to establish itself. Elsewhere, it benefited from the educational improvements of the sixteenth century, and from the inability of a Roman Church only slowly waking from its lethargy, to understand and to satisfy the spiritual needs of its flock.

How could the challenge of Calvinism be most effectively met? A crude, but undoubtedly rewarding, method would be to track down the wolves to their lair, that home of heresy, the city of Geneva. The city's geographical position made it highly vulnerable, particularly to the ambitions of its uncomfortably close neighbour, the duke of Savoy. The restoration of his lands in 1559 had made the duke a powerful European figure once more, and the moment seemed opportune for a renewal of traditional Savoyard designs on Geneva, all the more so because the duke's Vaudois subjects had recently turned away from their former heterodoxy to embrace the more dangerous doctrines of Genevan Calvinism. Emmanuel Philibert's plans to dispose simultaneously of the Vaudois and Geneva may have aroused the sympathetic interest of the Papacy and Spain, but the French Crown, at this moment walking a delicate tightrope between Catholic and Protestant, declined to cooperate. As a result, the moment for action passed. A revolt of the Vaudois against the duke ended in 1561 with a compromise settlement, under which Emmanuel Philibert, with a display of political wisdom regrettably rare among his contemporaries, conceded liberty of conscience within strict geographical limits. And Geneva itself was for the time being left untouched, warily surveying the world from behind its well-defended walls.

Failing the extermination of Geneva, the only adequate response to the Calvinist advance lay in the continuing reform of the Roman Catholic Church. Already, the new or reformed religious orders, especially the Jesuits, had achieved some success in countering Calvinism, particularly in central and eastern Europe. But the Church as a whole remained obstinately unreformed, and the Council of Trent, which had been summoned to advance the work of reform, had been in a state of suspension almost without interruption since 1548. As long as the great powers remained at war, there was no prospect of resumption, and it was only with Cateau-Cambrésis that the reconvening of the Council became once more a practical possibility.

A number of serious obstacles, however, blocked the path to a new session at Trent. One major obstacle, Paul IV, was mercifully removed by death in August 1559, but it was not until the end of December that a new Pope of very different character, Pius IV, emerged from the conclave. A comfortable pontiff, more remarkable for being the uncle of St Charles Borromeo than for any very exceptional virtues of his own, Pius hardly appeared a very appropriate standard-bearer for the Roman Church at this moment of crisis. But he was shrewd enough to appreciate that the case for a resumption of the Council was overwhelming, and that this could only be achieved if he could free the Church from the political entanglements in which it had been involved by his rash and irascible predecessor. 'We desire this council,' he announced, 'we wish it earnestly, and we would have it to be universal . . . Let what requires reformation be reformed, even though it be our own person and our own affairs.'

These were brave words, but the secular princes did not greet them with the enthusiasm that might have been expected. Philip II considered that a further meeting of the Council was quite unnecessary in so far as Spain was concerned, and that it might even cause complications in respect to the delicate religious situation in the Netherlands; but if the Pope did reconvene the Council, it must be regarded as a continuation of the old Council, and not as a new one. A continuation of the old Council, however, was held to be out of the question by both the Emperor and the French. The Emperor was afraid that a mere continuation of Trent would upset the delicate Augsburg settlement of 1555. He therefore supported the French demand for a new General Council that might lay the foundations for the reunion of Christendom – the fervent, if illusory, ambition of a French monarchy which saw little other way of escape from the religious feuds that now beset it. Failing such a new General Council, the cardinal of Lorraine threatened to summon a French national Council, which would bring French Catholics and Calvinists together in an attempt at mutual compromise on an exclusively national basis.

Confronted with such irreconcilable points of view, Pius IV could do little more than wait on events, while doing his best to edge the princes into acceptance of the idea of a new session at Trent. The very diversity of views, however, finally played into his hands. The prospect of a French national Council so alarmed Philip of Spain that in the summer of 1561 he at last waived his objections to the Pope's design. Now that one of the leading powers had formally agreed to let its bishops attend, Pius felt strong enough to press ahead with his schemes. The Council officially reopened at Trent on 18 January 1562. The work of ecclesiastical reform was at last to be resumed.

The success of Pius IV in organizing a new session of the Council of Trent did much to shape the character of events in the half-century following the peace of Cateau-Cambrésis. The Roman Church would not, after all, go leaderless and disorganized into battle against international Calvinism; and if Rome was still weak, and would for long remain heavily dependent on the secular power for aid, its belated willingness to set its own house in order offered the best, and perhaps the only, hope that one day it might make good its heavy losses. The guide-lines, in fact, were now drawn for the great religious struggle of the later sixteenth century – a struggle in which two rival faiths, with their international headquarters at Rome and Geneva respectively, would compete with every weapon at their command for the allegiance of men and the salvation of souls.

This bitter confessional conflict came in time to overshadow every aspect of European life. Individuals and nations found themselves confronted with problems of loyalty which created painful dilemmas and tortured the sensitive conscience. Did an individual's first duty lie with his king or his God? Should a State's foreign policy be guided by considerations of national interest or religious allegiance when, as so often happened, the two failed to coincide? Could Spain, for instance, legitimately temporize in its relations with Protestant England, when the overthrow of Elizabeth would redound to the benefit of France? Should Catherine de Medici support the French Protestants in their anti-Spanish policy, or make common cause with France's traditional rival, Spain, against the enemies of the Holy Catholic Church?

The very insolubility of these problems created new tensions of its own, and served to raise still further the temperature of international debate. All Europe found itself involved – even outlying regions like Scandinavia and Eastern Europe which had hitherto conducted their affairs in relative isolation from the States of the West. But it was one of the ironies of the new situation that the incorporation of the East and the North into the European state-system to create for the first time something approaching a single European diplomatic community should have coincided with the breakdown of international life itself. For the principal victim of the confessional struggles was the international community – that common corps of Christendom to which lip-service continued to be paid long after it had ceased to have any foundation in fact.

The breakdown could be detected in widely different fields. Merchants, always the first to be affected by any worsening of international relations, found themselves subjected to a new hazard when foreign authorities began to show as great an interest in their creeds as their cargoes. Students, accustomed to travel the continent to pursue their studies in the university of their choice, now began to discover that this was not as easy for them as it had been for their fathers. The young Swiss, Felix Platter, was safe enough at Montpellier in 1552 as long as he did not flaunt his Protestant beliefs,[7] but the universities of Europe were already beginning to divide along confessional lines. Calvinist nobles in the Netherlands or Hungary would send their sons to the Geneva Academy, while the Catholics sent theirs to Padua or Louvain. In 1559 Philip II forbade Spaniards to study abroad, except in specified colleges at Bologna, Rome, Naples, and Coimbra. In 1570 royal letters patent, addressed to the *Parlement* at Dôle, prohibited the inhabitants of the Franche-Comté from 'studying, teaching, learning or residing in any universities or public or private schools other than in this country or other countries, states and realms in our obedience, excepting always the town and university of Rome.' Governmental prohibitions were often evaded and ignored, but the fact remained that the eighty or so universities of mid-sixteenth-century Europe were being transformed from international into national institutions, and that the European community of scholars was itself being fragmented by the new confessional strife.

The diplomatic institutions and procedures of European States, painfully evolved over the course of the centuries, were also subjected to almost intolerable strains. As the continent divided into two warring camps, it became increasingly difficult to maintain the traditional international courtesies, or to continue the dialogue between sovereign States. In a world in which the Papacy frowned on diplomatic relations between Catholics and heretics it was inevitable that the normal change of diplomatic intercourse should shrink, and that embassies, where they survived, should become centres for religious propaganda and political subversion at the heart of alien territory. Operating in a climate of intense distrust and suspicion, diplomats were transmuted into plotters and spies, while their embassies sheltered secret agents and informers, and a host of dubious characters who flitted through the shady underworld of international life. The host government responded in similar fashion. Mail-bags were mysteriously rifled, codes of increasing complexity were deciphered, couriers were bribed and sometimes found dead.

As the traditional links between States were snapped one by one, and as allegiances polarized around Geneva and Rome, it was natural that nostalgia for the old, united Christendom should grow. Sixteenth-century aspirations for religious reconciliation and reunion seem so hopelessly ill-founded in the light of what actually occurred, that it is easy to dismiss them as the dreams of cranks and visionaries, devoid of any significance for the contemporary scene. But in practice they were widely, and even desperately, cherished by influential figures in many States, who could not bring themselves to accept a permanent division of the society in which they lived; and because they were cherished, and entered into the calculations even of hard-headed statesmen, they still played their part in shaping the pattern of events. Cateau-Cambrésis, after all, had been designed to bring a lasting peace to a Europe weary of war. If the sudden intrusion of confessional strife shattered this design, it did not mean that the design itself was ill-conceived, or that the evil itself was at once beyond repair. In the event, it was left to later generations to perceive that the men who framed the treaty of Cateau-Cambrésis had themselves already passed the point of no return; that Christendom as a unity was lost beyond recall, and that the Europe which replaced it would be sharply and permanently divided in the years that lay ahead.

The European Economy

1 The Baltic and the East

The wars of the 1550s placed an intolerable burden on the economies of the States of Western Europe. Trade routes were disrupted, frontier regions devastated, and heavy State expenditure for military purposes strained to its limits the delicate mechanism of international finance. Nemesis came in 1557–1559, when the great banking houses of Europe were rocked to their foundations by the decision, first of the Spanish Crown and then of the French, to repudiate their debts. Some banking houses, built on the sand, collapsed. Others, more firmly established, weathered the storm. But, after the wreckage had been cleared, it was seen that the contours of the landscape had been permanently changed. When Anton Fugger died in September 1560, leaving the family business in the hands of a new generation about whose competence he felt a justifiable concern, his death was more than the death of a prince among merchant-bankers – a man who for thirty years had handled the affairs of the greatest house in Europe with an exemplary skill. It symbolized in effect the passing of an age. New bankers, especially Genoese, would rise to international prominence, but the later sixteenth century could not compete with that earlier age of a uniquely intimate relationship between kings and great merchants, which has proudly passed into history as the 'Age of the Fugger'.

Yet although the great merchant-princes were gone, and there were no longer any towering figures in the world of international finance, this does not necessarily imply that the second half of the sixteenth century was a period of 'crisis' for the growth of capitalism. The 1550s were undeniably difficult years, but European economic activity revived rapidly as soon as peace was signed. In the ten years following Cateau-Cambrésis, commercial exchanges between France and Spain are thought to have reached their highest level of the century, and conditions throughout north-western and Atlantic Europe were generally favourable to international trade. The situation deteriorated in the later 1560s as a result of the troubles in the Netherlands; but even so sensitive a region for the European economy as the Low Countries did not at this moment dictate the whole pattern of economic life. In practice, the major restraints on Europe's economic growth remained the same as in the first half of the century – the weakness of its financial institutions, the inadequacy and high cost of the prevailing methods of transport, and the primitive nature of most of its agrarian and industrial techniques. But, within the limits imposed by these deficiences, some regions showed an increased economic vitality even as others declined; and in the broad perspective of European development, the years between Cateau-Cambrésis and the end of the century seem less remarkable for their economic hesitations and uncertainties than for the successful assimilation of two vast areas into the orbit of Western Europe's economic system – the New World across the Atlantic, and the almost equally New World to the east of the Elbe.

While it was in the second half of the sixteenth century that the East European economy began to be effectively integrated with that of the West, this was only the culmination of a process which had begun long before. Its origins can be traced back to the period of Western Europe's slow recovery from the Black Death and its aftermath. As population figures began climbing again in the late fifteenth century, the pressure on the land – which in some regions had been extensively turned over to pasture for sheep – inevitably mounted. The great landowners east of the Elbe, and especially those living close to the Baltic or to the rivers flowing towards it, saw an opportunity in the rising demand for grain to recoup their own fortunes and to acquire the luxury articles and manufactured goods which only the West could provide. Consequently, as more food was needed in the West, more land was brought under the plough in the East. But the exploitation of land demanded the exploitation of labour, which had been made scarce by the mass defection of peasants to the towns. As a result, nobles and towns throughout Eastern Europe in the late fifteenth and early sixteenth centuries clashed over the fate of the runaway peasants, and in the end it was the towns which went down in defeat. At the very time, then, when serfdom was disappearing in Western Europe, it embarked on a new career in the East. A series of increasingly harsh measures tied the peasants of Eastern Europe to the soil, imposed heavy labour obligations on them, and gave to their landlords the virtual disposal of their lives.

The character of East European life therefore began to diverge markedly in the sixteenth century from that of the West. In much of Western Europe, economic and social organization were tending to become more varied and complex. Expanding overseas trade led to growing imports of such products as sugar, which needed processing and marketing; traditional industries, notably textiles, expanded to fresh areas and developed special branches to meet minority needs; new, and high-quality, industries attempted to cater for the increasingly sophisticated tastes of the European rich. The century saw not only a marked increase in the size of towns, particularly those of the middle rank, but also the emergence of a new phenomenon – the really big city of over a hundred thousand inhabitants. At the start of the century, probably only four cities entered this category: Paris, Naples, Venice and Milan. By the end of it, eight or nine other cities had joined them, including London, Lisbon, Rome, Palermo and Seville.

This striking development of industrial and urban civilization does not mean that Western Europe had become, by the end of the sixteenth century, a 'bourgeois' society. On the contrary, in some respects it was more aristocratic in 1600 than it had been a hundred and fifty years before. But the contrast was none the less marked with the lands beyond the Elbe, where the majority of towns had tended to stagnate or decay since the early years of the century. Nor were the Eastern and Western aristocracies in strictly comparable positions, although they shared many of the same interests and tastes. The nobles of the West, while still immensely powerful, had seen their seigneurial jurisdiction eroded by the advance of royal justice; and although they had managed to infuse urban society with many of their own values, they none the less found themselves competing with their social inferiors, whether gentry or townsmen, for the effective control of power in a monarchical State. The magnates of the East, on the other hand, had little competition to fear. With kings and towns alike too weak to contest their authority, they dominated an overwhelmingly agrarian society, in which their economic predominance as great landowners was backed up by exclusive judicial rights over the serfs on their estates.

The position, admittedly, was not uniform throughout Eastern Europe; nor, even in areas of similar social development, were its causes uniformly the same. The character of individual princes, proximity to the Turks, remoteness from the major waterways, or the continued vitality of towns (as in Transylvania) – all these caused major variations between one region and the next. Muscovy, in particular, remained a law unto itself. Here, unlike other parts of Eastern Europe, there was no question of large-scale exports to the West. Trading contacts, whether through Archangel or the Baltic, were severely limited, and Russia's exports included very little grain. But, in spite of this, several of the features of life in the march-lands of Europe repeated themselves on Russian soil. Muscovy's territorial expansion in the sixteenth century, together with its natural population increase, had created a large internal market for grain. This was essentially an urban market, for Muscovite towns, unlike their East European equivalents, were growing in number and importance during the course of the century. Many landowners responded to their new economic opportunities in the same way as those of Germany or Poland – by bringing more land under cultivation, and demanding heavier labour services of their peasants. At the same time, the power of the State was increasing in Muscovy, as it was not in much of Eastern Europe. In 1556 Ivan IV ordered all landowners to perform service to the State; and the new service nobility, owning small estates allotted by the Tsar, was dependent for its survival on the control of peasant labour. This resulted in a series of increasingly stringent decrees, which permanently clamped serfdom on Russia by the end of the century.

The serf society of Muscovy, however, remained a world on its own, threatening to its neighbours because of its growing military power, but still economically unrelated to the European world. On the other hand, Poland, Silesia, Brandenburg and Prussia were being inexorably drawn into the orbit of West European life; and ironically it was this very process of closer association with the West which was doing more than anything else to divide Europe into two distinctive halves. To the west of the Elbe lay an increasingly varied and complex society; to the east, a society consisting essentially of landlords and serfs. And the closer they came together, the farther they moved apart. Eastern Europe was in effect drifting into a type of colonial relationship with the West, with most of the consequences which such a relationship implies. The Prussian Junkers and the Polish nobles naturally responded to their new market opportunities by the intensive exploitation of their estates to provide the West with food and raw materials. In exchange, they acquired western manufactures and luxury articles. The import of these goods at advantageous rates was bound to prejudice domestic production and to help stultify the industrial development of East European towns. The eastern lands, in consequence, were subjected to a long period of economic backwardness and social stagnation at a time when some parts of Western Europe were displaying the first signs of a capacity to change.

But the East's loss was the West's gain. From the East, Western Europe could obtain not only essential raw materials – wood, fibres, metals – but also the grain which in some areas represented the margin of safety between survival and starvation for a rapidly swelling urban population. Between 1562 and 1569 no less than 23% of the grain consumed in the Netherlands was imported from the Baltic. Although the demands of the Netherlands were exceptional, it was of supreme importance to Western Europe as a whole that it could turn in times of emergency to its granary east of the Elbe. But the increasing economic interdependence of Eastern and Western Europe was also beneficial to the West in other ways. It stimulated industrial growth by providing a valuable outlet for western manufactures, and it gave a powerful impetus to shipping and trade. Polish and east German timber and grain, shipped from Danzig and the other Baltic ports, would be carried through the Danish Sound to Antwerp, or, from the 1550s, increasingly to Amsterdam. From here it was often re-exported to other parts of the continent, especially southern Europe. The major carriers were the shippers of the Netherlands, which had acquired, by the treaty Speyer of 1544, a privileged status in the payment of dues and tolls in the Danish Sound. The merchants of the Low Countries made the most of their advantage: of the 3,000 ships which passed through the Sound between 1560 and 1569, 75% were Dutch.

The growing importance of the Baltic trade and of the north-south maritime routes helped shift Europe's centres of economic gravity as the century progressed. Charles V's world had been dominated by the financial and commercial axis of Antwerp and south Germany, but by the 1550s the importance of this axis had already begun to diminish. The central European silver-mines had been fatally hit by competition from American silver, and the prosperity of southern Germany was further reduced by the Emperor's financial irresponsibility, which brought disaster not only to the Antwerp money-market but also to the Augsburg bankers. The decline of the south German continental economy, however, was accompanied by the advance of a north German maritime economy, as the northern ports – Hamburg, Bremen, Emden, Riga and Reval – benefited from the growing vitality of the Baltic trade.

It might have seemed that the maritime prosperity of the north would enable Antwerp to retain its proud position as the commercial capital of Europe. The competition, however, eventually proved too strong. In the early 1560s a series of trading disputes between England and the Netherlands led to the shift of the English cloth trade from Antwerp to Emden and then to Hamburg and other ports of north Germany. It became clear at the same time that Bremen and Hamburg were better placed than Antwerp for trade with the German hinterland and for trans-continental trade with the Italian peninsula, while Amsterdam became an increasingly successful rival for control of the east-west transit trade in grain. But Antwerp's decline was gradual, rather than dramatic. If it failed to hold its position as the main European entrepot for Baltic grain, it was still able to participate in the thriving Baltic trade as the principal export centre for South European commodities and for local manufactures to the lands of North-East Europe. On the strength of its industrial exports, such as Flemish linen, it seemed for a moment around 1559 that the city might weather the storm. Its population rose to 90,000 in the course of the

1560s, and the building industry boomed. But the revival was decept-
ive, and the upsurge of the early 1560s could not be sustained. At a
time when its commercial pre-eminence was threatened by an increasingly ominous combination of economic and political misfortune, it
discovered that it had also lost its unique financial position. For
Antwerp proved to be an early and spectacular casualty of the most
important of all the economic developments of the later sixteenth
century – the incorporation of the New World of America into
European life.

2 The Atlantic and the Mediterranean

Although Mexico fell to the Spaniards in the 1520s and Peru in the
1530s, it was not until after 1550 that the effective exploitation of the
New World's resources can be said to have begun. Some delay was
unavoidable, for discovery and conquest, however heroic, were not in
themselves enough. The newly found territories had to be subjugated,
settled, and at least nominally Christianized, before the Spaniards and
Portuguese could hope to create on the other side of the Atlantic
viable societies in the image of their own. Until this was done, America would remain no more than a marchland of Europe, an advancing
frontier pushed forward by rival warring gangs. But by the 1550s the
process of settlement and consolidation was well under way. In the
wake of the soldiers had come the clergy and the administrators to
organize, to convert, and to govern; and by the middle years of the
century New Spain and Peru were equipped with the full-scale
apparatus of Spanish government, in the form of viceroys, *audiencias*
or judicial tribunals, and that horde of officials who had become
indispensable adjuncts of the sixteenth-century State. The age of the
conquistador was over, and the less spectacular age of the bureaucrat
had begun.

The officials who governed the 'Indies', as the Spaniards persisted
in calling their American possessions, entertained no doubts about
either the reasons or the justification for Spain's presence on the far
side of the Atlantic. The New World had been entrusted by God to the
special care of the Kings of Spain, in order that its heathen inhabitants
might be brought to an understanding of the true Faith; and, with the
obligation, went also the reward, in the form of the gold and silver
which these God-given lands were producing in such gratifying quantities. Since the designs of Providence were so unequivocally clear,
there could be no question of Spain's sharing either the duties, or the
riches, with any other nation. The New World therefore remained, at
least in Castilian eyes, the exclusive preserve of the Crown of Castile,
however much other European states might contest the validity of the

papal bulls of donation of 1493. But, in the event, there was a considerable, and growing, discrepancy between theory and practice. Since the 1520s, both foreign traders and foreign raiders had been infiltrating into the Caribbean with increasing success, and French privateers rounded off the Franco-Spanish war to their own satisfaction by seizing and burning Cartagena in 1559. The Treaty of Cateau-Cambrésis itself was significantly silent on the subject of America, for the clause in the truce of Vaucelles of 1556 by which France explicitly renounced its claims to trade with the Indies was dropped from the final peace settlement – partly, no doubt, because it had proved to be unenforceable, and partly because Philip's advisers seem to have felt that any specific reference to the Indies in an international agreement might of itself help to call Spain's absolute rights into question. Instead of an agreed clause, therefore, the powers agreed only to disagree over the Indies in 1559. While Spain insisted on her absolute rights, based on prior discovery and papal donation, her rivals insisted no less firmly on the principle of the freedom of the seas (a principle for which some of them showed less enthusiasm at home). A compromise solution was found in the tacit acceptance of the idea of the 'Lines of Demarcation', which had been fixed to the west on the Canary Islands, and to the south on the Tropic of Cancer, by the treaty of Tordesillas between Spain and Portugal in 1494. To the south and west of the Lines the European powers would not necessarily be bound by the same standards of conduct as those that regulated their relations in Europe. If the French still chose to enter American waters, then equally Spain could choose to deal with these encroachments in such ways as it saw fit. The results of the compromise were predictable. The treaty of Cateau-Cambrésis may have brought peace to western Europe, but there was to be 'no peace beyond the Line' in the years that lay ahead.

Although foreign intrusions into the Caribbean were a source of constant, and growing, concern to the Spanish Crown, they were too weak and too sporadic in the middle years of the century to prevent the development of that great Spanish-American trading system on which the power of Philip II ultimately rested. This system derived logically from the mutual needs of Spain and its colonies. The growing colonial population of Mexico and Peru – perhaps some 150,000 by 1570 – was heavily dependent on the mother country for the foodstuffs, the clothes, and the luxuries which would enable it to lead a life resembling as closely as possible the life led by the well-born and the rich in the world it had left behind. Spain, on the other hand, needed the produce of the New World – the pearls, the dye-stuffs, and, above all, the gold and silver which would allow it to meet its heavy commitments and fight its foreign wars. In the earlier years of the century, gold and silver remittances, while offering a dazzling new

source of income to a hard-pressed Charles V, had fluctuated sharply
with the discovery of easily worked veins and caches of hidden treasure. But these sources of revenue were a diminishing asset, and a large
and continuing supply of precious metals was only assured when the
silver mines of Potosí (in modern Bolivia) were found in 1545, and
those of Zacatecas in Mexico in 1546. These discoveries of the 1540s,
however, did not of themselves ensure a rapid and regular expansion
of silver remittances for Spain. The mines had to be worked, and
effective large-scale working only became possible around 1560,
with the introduction of a new method for extracting silver from the
ore by use of an amalgam of mercury. Even then, it took time for the
new system to get under way. In the first half of Philip II's reign, as
under Charles V, America's contribution to the royal treasury,
although immensely valuable because it came in the form of silver,
was still relatively small when compared with other sources of revenue. It was only in the 1580s that the stream of silver became a flood,
allowing Philip to spend money with an abandon that would have
been unthinkable in earlier years.[1] But already by 1560 Spain and its
colonies had become mutually interdependent, and a Spanish-Atlantic
economy had become an established fact.

At the heart of this economy was the port of Seville, which enjoyed
monopoly rights over Spain's American trade. The monopoly, while
vigorously upheld by one of the most powerful pressure-groups in
sixteenth-century Europe – the Consulate of the Merchants of Seville
– had both experience and logic on its side. Seville was the best placed
and best equipped of all the ports of Spain for trade with the Indies,
and the cargoes of precious metals needed careful surveillance on their
journey, and official registration at a single port when the ships came
home. Seville's ability to meet these varied needs of the American
trade brought with it a privileged status, a sometimes feverish prosperity, and a rapid increase in population, which made it one of the
largest cities of its time, with over 100,000 inhabitants in the closing
decades of the century. The vast and imposing cathedral, the House of
Trade (the *Casa de la Contratación*), where the cargoes were itemized
and registered and the sailing of the fleets prepared, the *Lonja* or
palace of the Consulate of Merchants – all of these bore witness to
the wealth and prestige of one of the most Spanish, and yet most
international, of cities, whose streets swarmed with merchants, sailors
and dock-hands of every ethnic group and nationality: Flemings, Germans and Portuguese, Genoese, Ragusans, Africans and Moriscos.
Their life, like that of their city, was geared to the departure and
arrival of the fleets which linked the Old World to the New by a
tenuous silver thread.

It was in the 1560s that the system of navigation between Spain and
America acquired its definitive form. The month of May saw the

departure from San Lúcar, the port of Seville, of the *flota*, the fleet destined for Vera Cruz in Mexico. In August it was the turn of the *galeones*, a second fleet, probably again of some sixty to seventy vessels, destined for Nombre de Dios (Portobello) on the isthmus of Panama. After unloading their cargoes at the end of the five or six-week transatlantic crossing, the *galeones* would retreat for the winter months to the sheltered harbour of Cartagena, on the South American mainland. Then, in the spring, they would return to the isthmus to pick up the silver consignments laboriously carried by land and sea from Potosí and Peru, and would sail on to Havana for their *rendez-vous* with the returning Mexican *flota*. The combined fleets, sailing in well-guarded convoy, would hope to be back at Seville by early autumn at the latest.

The elaborate mechanism of the Indies trade, while of immediate and overwhelming concern to Spain's American colonists and the merchants of Seville, proved to be of no less importance to the economic life and well-being of Europe as a whole. Although the trade between the Baltic and western and southern Europe was considerably greater in volume than the transatlantic trade, certain features of the Indies traffic gave it a unique position in European life. Most important of all, it brought to Europe a regular flow of the silver which Europeans needed so desperately for their own commercial transactions and to make up their adverse balance of trade with the Far East. It replenished the coffers of the kings of Spain, who used it to meet their commitments to their bankers, to pay their armies in foreign parts, to grease the palms of foreign clients, and to buy abroad the military provisions or naval stores that the peninsula itself could not provide. It also paid the merchants for the goods they had shipped to the New World, and enabled them in turn to pay their debts to the manufacturers, whether Spanish or foreign, of the articles they had bought. A highly complex network of mutual obligations therefore stretched all the way across the continent from its starting-point in Seville; and the arrival of the fleet would bring a sudden upsurge of activity in the fairs of Medina del Campo, the counting-houses of Genoa, the international bourses at Lyons or Antwerp, for it meant a new influx of silver with which to lubricate a European economic system all too likely to creak to a standstill in the absence of regular supplies of fresh bullion.

Europe, therefore, became heavily, and indeed dangerously, dependent on the smooth working of the transatlantic trading system and the punctual arrival of the fleet at Seville. A serious delay in the return of the galleons could trigger off a series of bankruptcies among Sevillian merchants, which in turn might have international repercussions as the ripples spread further outwards through Spain and western Europe. Similarly, the fitting out of the Indies fleets acquired a momentum of its own, for the only means of obtaining more silver from America was to sell more goods to its inhabitants; but more goods demanded more shipping, and more shipping demanded heavier investment in the Indies fleets, which itself meant a pressing need for still higher returns. But there was a limit to the quantity of European goods which the Indies could absorb at any given time, so that goods intended for export could easily pile up on the wharves at Seville, while the ships to carry them piled up in the Indies, awaiting sufficient bullion and freight to justify their next trip home. When this happened, the whole delicate machinery was thrown out of gear, and a Europe starved of silver stood facing an America glutted with goods across an ocean that now divided instead of uniting two interdependent worlds.

The extent to which Europe had come to be affected by fluctuations in the American trade is suggested by the great depression of the 1550s. Many of the troubles of the 1550s – the years which saw the bankruptcies of the French and Spanish Crowns – were the outcome of specifically European conditions, notably the expense and devastation of the Habsburg-Valois war. But they coincided with a sharp recession in the transatlantic trade. This was caused partly by the activities of French pirates in the Caribbean and along the Atlantic trade-routes, but also by the inevitable process of adjustment in the New World itself, as the robber economy of the first decades of the century gave way to a new and more solid economic system based on the exploitation of agricultural and mineral resources. The transformation took time, and it brought in its train a ten or twelve-year slump in the transatlantic trade, reflected in a sharp fall in the value of freight and the number of ships crossing the Atlantic between 1550 and 1562. Now that silver was momentarily less easily obtained in America, and the activities of French pirates endangered security on the seas, the merchants of Seville nervously reacted by refusing to ship their cargoes, and for twenty-two months between 1554 and 1556 no fleet sailed from San Lúcar for the ports of the New World. In turn, silver remittances dwindled, the confidence of bankers and financiers sagged, and it became hard, and finally impossible, for Charles V to obtain further credit for a war on which he had already heavily over-spent.

From 1559, however, confidence began to return. The restoration of peace and the rapid expansion of American silver production, bringing with it a renewed demand for European goods and an increased capacity to pay for them, did more than anything else to revive Seville's American trade. Around 1562 there began a great upswing in the volume and value of shipping between Spain and America – an upswing which continued, with some interruptions and fluctuations, almost to the end of the sixteenth century. The

period between the 1560s and the 1590s, then, represented the first
great age of the Atlantic world, an age of expanding trade between
Spain and its overseas possessions which brought prosperity and
increased economic activity not only to Seville itself but to regions
far away.

Inevitably this growth of an Atlantic economy brought further
changes in the balance of European life. In particular, it helped tilt
the continent towards its periphery, away from a central Europe
whose silver mines could no longer compete with those of Zacatecas
and Potosí; away, too, from a land-based to a sea-based economy, to
the benefit of the Channel and Atlantic ports of England and France.
Seville had replaced Antwerp as the hub of the western world, but
Seville itself was no more than one link, although a crucial link, in an
intricate chain. It was this which enabled regions that might otherwise
have suffered from the changing patterns of trade to participate in the
Atlantic economy, if only at second hand.

At first sight it was the Mediterranean that stood to lose most.
Apparently by-passed by the opening of new trade-routes, first to
Asia and then to the New World, it could hardly avoid losing its
former primacy to the new, European, Atlantic. But at least throughout the sixteenth century its fortunes were far less gloomy than might
have been expected. It had seemed for a time that the first casualty
would be Venice, which, in the first decades of the sixteenth century,
had begun to look less like the Queen of the Adriatic than a declining
dowager duchess amidst a shrinking circle of admirers and friends.
But the old lady had not yet lost her capacity to surprise. At a time
when other parts of Europe were devoting more of their attention and
resources to maritime trade, Venice chose to move in exactly the
opposite direction. The Venetian fleet began to decline in the years
after 1560, and Venetian shipping retreated from northern waters, and
even those of the western Mediterranean, to confine itself more
strictly to the harbours of the Adriatic and Levant. But, this maritime
retreat coincided with a great shift of Venetian capital from seafaring
to the mainland. Here it was used, not for trade, but for the acquisition of land and the building up of a large-scale textile industry,
capable of competing successfully with the North Italian and Netherlands textile industries, both of which had suffered from the European
wars. This policy, at least in the short run, yielded rich rewards. For
the rest of the century, with only brief interruptions, the Venetian
broadcloth output remained at a high level, and the city of as many
as 170,000 inhabitants before the plague of 1576, basked in an
opulent splendour which made it seem for a time as if the days of its
former glory had miraculously returned.

While Venice ostentatiously turned her back on the Atlantic,
although eagerly pocketing all the American silver that came her

way, her rival, Genoa, chose a different and more enterprising course. Genoese merchants had long ago glimpsed the prospects of great profits to be made in the West: already by the later Middle Ages they had defeated their Catalan rivals in the struggle for control of west Mediterranean markets and had entrenched themselves in the leading commercial towns of Castile and southern Spain. It was natural that they should seize the opportunity of the discovery and conquest of America to extend their activities to the farther side of the Atlantic, and to prise their way into Seville's American trade; and the agreement of 1528 by which Andrea Doria placed the Genoese galleys at the service of Charles V represented a tacit recognition by Genoa of where her future lay. Henceforth, the Genoese would be the loyal, but also the indispensable, allies of Spain, offering the Spanish Crown their services, both naval and financial, and expecting in return a preferential status which would facilitate their exploitation of Spain and her possessions.

They were not disappointed. Genoese bankers moved in alongside the Fuggers as creditors of Charles V, and, as the influence of the Fuggers declined after the royal bankruptcy of 1557, so that of the Genoese grew. The names of Justiniano, Spinola, Negro and Doria appear with increasing frequency in the *asientos* of Philip II – the formal contracts drawn up between the king and the financiers for loans to be repaid by the king in specific places at a specific date under equally specific and generally onerous conditions. These men received due reward for their services, in the form of monopolies and special grants and a succession of privileges, which gradually enabled them to acquire a commanding control over the economic life of the Spanish peninsula. Indeed, by the later years of the century, it is possible to speak of a 'Hispano-Genoese' system as one of the dominating elements in the European economy. This system helped to ensure that the Mediterranean world would not be entirely excluded from the benefits of the transatlantic trade, for some of the silver which flowed from Seville to Genoa would then flow outwards again to Venice and the ports of the Levant. If the rise of an Atlantic economy primarily brought new life and vitality to the western fringes of the continent, its prosperity in the expansive years of the later sixteenth century was such that it could still afford to scatter its largesse indiscriminately through Europe as a whole.

3   Silver and Prices

Although the expansion of trade between Europe and America was reflected in an increase in every kind of economic activity – in shipbuilding, in the production of textiles, metal goods, and wine, corn

and oil for a growing American market – its most spectacular mani-
festation was obviously the silver extracted from the American mines.
The second half of the sixteenth century was pre-eminently the silver
age of Europe, as the white metal flooded into the continent, and gold
in its turn grew more rare. The quantities of silver entering Europe
were very considerable, as the figures for the registered arrivals at
Seville suggest:[2]

Period	For the Spanish Crown	For private individuals	Total
1556–1560	1,882,195 ducats	7,716,604 ducats	9,598,798 ducats
1561–1565	2,183,440	11,265,603	13,449,043
1566–1570	4,541,692	12,427,767	16,969,459
1571–1575	3,958,393	10,329,538	14,287,931
1576–1580	7,979,614	12,722,715	20,702,329
1581–1585	9,060,725	26,188,810	35,249,534
1586–1590	9,651,855	18,947,302	28,599,157
1591–1595	12,028,018	30,193,817	42,221,835
1596–1600	13,169,182	28,145,019	41,314,201

By no means all this silver came permanently to rest in European
hands, for some of it flowed eastwards to pay for Europe's purchase of
Asian luxury products. Nor was all the silver that stayed in Europe
automatically converted into coinage to swell the continent's depleted
stores of liquid capital. The sixteenth century was, after all, the
century of Benvenuto Cellini, and large quantities of silver and gold
passed into the skilled hands of jewellers and silver-smiths, whose
production of intricately-worked chalices and crucifixes, candlesticks
and salt-cellars helped to stimulate but never to satisfy the insatiable
appetite of the European élite for the more spectacular and extravagant appurtenances of a civilized way of life.

The increasing taste for luxury no doubt helped to keep silver
relatively rare as a form of currency at a time when it was more
profusely distributed through Europe than ever before. The mass of
Europe's rural population would rarely if ever set eyes on a gold or
silver coin, for transactions at village level, when they were not conducted by credit and barter, would be carried out in small coins of
copper and alloy whose numbers were rapidly increasing while their
intrinsic value shrank. Such silver as circulated in the form of coins
was likely to be concentrated in the larger towns, and was used in
particular for the purposes of the State and for the purchase of
luxuries from abroad. It was present, however, in sufficient quantities
to suggest to a small but growing number of observers that it was at

least a contributory cause of the most baffling phenomenon of the age – the rise in the cost of living.

By the middle of the sixteenth century the high level of prices had become a subject of lively and anxious discussion in many parts of Europe. The debate was particularly intense in Spain, where prices in the 1550s were more than double what they had been at the beginning of the century. Not only was the high cost of living a source of constant complaint in the Cortes of Castile, but there was also widespread concern that home-made goods had become relatively much more expensive than similar products imported from abroad. University circles in Salamanca were already beginning by the middle of the century to make a tentative connection between the declining exchange value of Spanish money and its relative abundance in the peninsula; and in a treatise of 1556 one of the most distinguished of the Salamanca professors, Martín de Azpilcueta Navarro, directly linked the Spanish price-level with American silver: 'We see by experience that in France, where money is scarcer than in Spain, bread, wine, cloth and labour are worth much less. And even in Spain, in times when money was scarcer, saleable goods and labour were given for very much less than after the discovery of the Indies, which flooded the country with gold and silver.'[3]

These first inklings of the quantity theory found a more celebrated exponent in 1568, when Jean Bodin published his *Response à M. de Malestroit*, on the causes of the price-rise in France. Bodin's ideas had begun to gain currency in England by 1581 at the latest, and from the late sixteenth century the relationship between American bullion and the inflation in Europe became a commonplace. The argument, however, only acquired statistical precision in 1934 with the publication of Earl J. Hamilton's *American Treasure and the Price Revolution in Spain*, which suggested a correlation between registered silver imports to Seville and the movement of Spanish prices too close to be coincidental.

Neither Azpilcueta nor Bodin, however, argued that American silver was the *sole* cause of the price-rise, and any such assumption runs into a number of serious difficulties. In Italy, for instance, the steepest price-rise of the entire century occurred between 1552 and 1560, at a time when American silver was apparently entering the peninsula in too small a quantity to have a spectacular impact on prices. In the years after 1570, when large amounts of silver were flowing into Italy from Spain, Italian prices actually fell.[4] It would therefore be perfectly possible to explain the Italian price-rise of the 1550s without reference to American silver, simply in terms of the coming of peace, the recovery of population and the boom in reconstruction after the devastations of war.

Comparable explanations could also be provided for other parts of Europe. One of the most striking features of the great inflation of the sixteenth century is the tendency for food prices, and especially those of grain, to rise more sharply than those of manufactured goods. This is what might be expected of a society in which population is increasing at a faster rate than the capacity of the land to feed it. Unfortunately, however, population statistics for the sixteenth century remain highly speculative, and there is a natural temptation, in the absence of firm evidence, to produce a circular argument that population growth is the prime cause of rising prices, which themselves are clear proof that population is growing. The growth of population in the cities can be reasonably well documented, but it is much more difficult to discover reliable statistical evidence for the movement of population in the country side. The general balance both of inference and evidence, however, indicates a substantial increase in the total size of Europe's population between the middle of the fifteenth century and the end of the sixteenth – perhaps from fifty or sixty million to around ninety million people in 150 years. The national distribution of this population around 1600 appears to have been of the following order:

England and Wales	4.5 million
Scotland and Ireland	2 million
Netherlands	3 million
Scandinavia	1.4 million
Poland and Lithuania	8 million
Germany	20 million
France	16 million
Italy	13 million
Spain and Portugal	8 million
Turkey (Europe and Asia)	18–30 million

While all these figures represent an increase on estimated figures for the beginning of the century, there were inevitably wide variations in the speed and the degree of population growth. In some regions, such as Languedoc, the rapid growth of the earlier sixteenth century died away around 1560–1570. Elsewhere, as in Catalonia, across the border from Languedoc, growth seems to have been sustained into the early seventeenth century. But, whatever the local variations, the sixteenth century was pre-eminently a century of population increase – a century in which the gaping holes created by the Black Death were filled, and there were once again too many people in Europe, too many mouths to feed.

The growth of Europe's population inevitably had profound social and economic consequences. It placed increasingly heavy pressure on food supplies and land. It swelled still further the miserable ranks of Europe's largest army – that of the hungry and unemployed. It provoked bitter competition for jobs and offices, to which guilds and corporations responded by closing their doors to newcomers and raising their entry dues. It sharpened the lines of distinction between the privileged and the under-privileged, exacerbating social antipathies and creating new social frustrations. And it turned men into nomads – whether as mercenaries in the pay of foreign captains, or emigrants in search of new opportunities, or merely as vagabonds. The cities, the armies, the colonies of sixteenth-century Europe bore eloquent witness to a population on the move.

It helped, too, to depress wages and to push up prices, although the extent of its responsibility for the great inflation is impossible to determine. Bodin himself singled out the increase in population as one of the causes of rising prices in France. But he did not consider this as significant a cause of rising prices as the influx of precious metals. This influx he attributed to the growth of foreign trade, the development of an international bourse at Lyons, and the seasonal migration of workers from southern France into Spain, where they could earn higher wages to be spent on their return. He pointed, too, to the growth of conspicuous consumption – the increasing expenditure by princes, nobles, merchants and wealthy citizens on their houses, their clothes and their food, and on all those luxuries which had recently come to be regarded as essentials for men of rank and quality.

For Bodin's opponent, Malestroit, the debasement of the currency was the villain of the piece. Certainly, in some countries, such as France itself, devaluation of the silver coinage caused violent price disturbances; but in Spain, on the other hand, Philip II successfully resisted any temptation to debase silver, and explanations for the rise in Spanish prices must be sought elsewhere. The very variety of circumstances, from one season to another, from one country to the next, suggests that no one explanation is either wholly right or wholly wrong. At one time or another most of the causes adduced by Bodin and his contemporaries are likely to have come into play in some form or permutation, and the search for a unified explanation which will cover every local variation, from Madrid to Frankfurt and Cracow, remains a hopeless quest. But in general it would seem reasonable to assume that, after a long period of relatively stable prices in the late Middle Ages, prices began moving upwards under the stimulus of increased demand – a demand prompted by the growth of population, the expansion of commercial activity, and changes in the spending-habits of princes and aristocracy. Silver, first from the mines of central Europe, and then more and more from the Indies, partially helped to relieve the desperate shortage of liquid capital created by the growth in demand. But at the same time it also caused sharp local price increases when suddenly injected in large quantities into areas previously starved of silver; and, as it spread through Europe it had a more general impact in stimulating activity during moments of expansion, and in preventing the fall of prices below a certain level at times when trade was slack.

In comparison with the price increases of the twentieth century the inflation of the sixteenth was not, in fact, very great; but it attracted a vast amount of contemporary attention, partly because it was a novel phenomenon after a long period of price stability, and partly because it was accompanied by spectacular changes in the distribution of incomes, which seemed to dramatize the fragility and precariousness of human affairs. Some sections of society in the 1560s were substantially worse off than their grandfathers, and were seen to be so. In particular, wage-earners, whether rural labourers or urban artisans, were very badly hit. Throughout Europe, wages limped haltingly behind prices, although now and again they would make a sudden spurt, when for some reason the demand for labour became intense, as in Antwerp in the late 1550s. The big European cities in the later sixteenth century therefore swarmed with semi-skilled or unskilled artisans and casual labourers, whose employment fluctuated sharply with the general level of prosperity, and whose low level of wages could not possibly absorb a sudden rise in the price of bread caused by a bad harvest or by the failure of grain-supplies to arrive on time. As municipal authorities knew to their cost, this great mass of unemployed or underemployed citizens living on or near the breadline represented a standing threat to the public peace. Town councillors would therefore make anxious provision for bulk-purchases of grain to be stored in municipal granaries against a sudden emergency, knowing that the alternative was riot and looting by a hungry mob.

If wage-earners were the principal casualties of the sixteenth-century price-rise, its main beneficiaries were – or at least should have been – the owners of land and the producers of food. With grain prices rising steeply, the peasant, the farmer, the landowning noble apparently stood to gain. But while the sixteenth century was an age of agricultural profits, there was certainly no automatic guarantee that these profits went into the pockets of those who actually owned, or worked, the land. More often than not it was the middle-man – the steward, the rent-collector, the tenant-farmer – who benefited most from agrarian prosperity. The small peasant often found himself squeezed out as the result of harvest-failure and a crushing burden of debt. The noble or gentleman proprietor found himself hamstrung by rent-agreements fixed by his ancestors in days when money was worth more than it was now.

Even where landlords did succeed in raising their rents and dues, the gain was all too easily wiped out by increases in the cost of living, and by their inability or refusal to trim their needs to suit their budget. The poverty of the French nobility was primarily to be ascribed, according to the Huguenot leader François de La Noue,[5] to 'the mistakes it has committed in the spending of its wealth'. Vast sums were squandered on clothes and buildings ('for it is only in the last sixty years that architecture has been re-established in France'), on food and furniture, and on all the outward symbols of status and rank. Now that a legal or university training was coming to be an indispensable passport to office under the Crown, nobles found themselves with heavy educational expenses for their sons. There was also the expense of military service, which La Noue himself did not consider ruinous, on the curious assumption that serving nobles would be adequately rewarded by a grateful king. Many lesser nobles and gentry, however, whether French, Flemish, or Castilian, did find in service under arms one means of escape, however temporary, from the troubles that beset them. For these impoverished captains, peace held no benefits. Many a gentleman from France and the Netherlands found himself left suddenly high and dry by the disbanding of the armies after Cateau-Cambrésis, at a time when the pressures to spend were growing and costs continued to rise.

The economic problems which followed in the wake of rising prices had therefore become by 1560 a source of potential discontent. A new phase of economic expansion may have begun with the end of the Habsburg-Valois conflict – an expansion stimulated by the growth of demand in Europe, and the development of West European trade with the lands of Eastern Europe and the New World across the ocean. But the benefits of expansion were not equally distributed. There was, no doubt, plenty of money to be made – in commerce, in agriculture, in banking, in government and the law. But there was also misery and impoverishment and hunger on a vast, and growing, scale. The debt-ridden gentleman, the depressed wage-earner, the small peasant who had fled for refuge to the town – these were the casualties of the century, and the embittered potential recruits for the armies of unrest. In the religious and social climate of the 1560s, it would not be excessively difficult to mobilize these armies, which were held in check by little more than the always fragile authority of the European State.

3

The Problem of the State

I Monarchy

Sixteenth-century Europe was essentially a Europe of 'composite monarchies'. By this is meant that most States under the sovereignty of a single ruler consisted of a number of territories acquired over the course of time by conquest, dynastic union or inheritance. The supreme example of a composite monarchy was the *monarquía española* inherited by Philip II, who found himself master of a wide variety of lands, each with different laws, institutions and customs, which he swore to maintain and uphold. But the Tudors, too, ruled over a composite monarchy consisting of the kingdoms of England and Ireland and the principality of Wales, while Valois France, although the most integrated of the monarchies of western Europe, still had a considerable way to go to assimilate relatively recently acquired territories like the duchies of Brittany and Burgundy, with their own distinctive historical traditions and their representative assemblies, or Estates.

In spite of the constraints inherent in the composite character of their monarchies, however, West European monarchs had in general succeeded during the first half of the sixteenth century in increasing their power. Stronger armies, improved financial facilities, more efficient administrative organization, and the exercise of a tighter control over the national church – all these had enhanced the personal authority of kings and the coherence of their States. While the lawyers deployed sophisticated arguments on behalf of the royal prerogative, no effort was spared to emphasize the supreme majesty of kings as at once the vicegerents of God and the perfect embodiments of the national will. The style and trappings of kingship thus tended to be characterized by increasing formality as the century advanced. The title of 'Majesty', which had traditionally been reserved for the Emperor, was adopted by Henry II of France and Philip II of Spain, and was used with growing frequency in England, alongside or instead of 'Your Highness' and 'Your Grace'. In 1548 the Spanish court adopted the elaborate traditional ceremonial of the House of Burgundy. In France, in the second half of the century, the *'lever'* and *'coucher'* became formal ceremonies for which a special invitation was required. And even foreigners accustomed to the style of Habsburg and Valois were amazed at the elaborate formalism of the Elizabethan Court.

The development of this stiff and measured ceremonial was, no doubt, a fitting recognition of the enhanced power and majesty of sixteenth-century kings. It was certainly intended as such. Yet those bizarre rituals, the oddest of which was surely the French practice of serving ceremonial meals to the funeral effigy of a deceased monarch until his successor was crowned, were perhaps as much a sign of royal weakness as of royal might. Pageant and ceremonial, as Catherine de Medici was quick to perceive, were a useful means of asserting what was not automatically taken for granted. Skilfully deployed they could be used to impress upon naturally fractious subjects the unique authority and splendour of the crown; and, by emphasizing the majesty of the institution they might help to conceal the weakness of the man.

For, whatever gains may have been made in the earlier part of the century, monarchy still remained pathetically vulnerable to the vagaries of chance: the chance of personality, of uncertain succession, and, most of all, of sudden death. In no decade could men have been more uneasily aware of this than in the 1550s – a decade which saw not only the accidental death of Henry II of France, but also

---

New Accessions, 1550–1560

(the end of the reign appears in brackets after the ruler's name)

1550	Duke Albert of Bavaria (1579)
	Duke Christopher of Württemburg (1568)
1553	Duke Augustus I of Saxony (1586)
	Mary I of England (1558)
	Duke Emmanuel Philibert of Savoy (1580)
1556	Emperor Ferdinand I (1564)
	Philip II of Spain (1598)
1557	Sebastian of Portugal (1578)
1558	Elizabeth I of England (1603)
1559	Frederick II of Denmark (1588)
	Frederick III, Elector Palatine (1576)
	Francis II of France (1560)
1560	Eric XIV of Sweden (1568)
	Charles IX of France (1574)

widespread natural mortality among Europe's ruling houses. Indeed, by the end of the decade there was scarcely a single important ruler in northern, central or western Europe who had been on the throne in its opening year.

Innumerable doubts and uncertainties surrounded this new generation of princes as they assumed the reins of power. Mary and Elizabeth of England, and Mary Queen of Scots, were all considered to be grievously handicapped by reason of their sex. Sebastian of Portugal and Francis II and Charles IX of France were no less handicapped by reason of their youth. Charles IX was ten and a half years old when he succeeded his brother; and it was only by cooperating with Antoine de Bourbon, the first prince of the blood, that the queen-mother Catherine de Medici secured the regency powers that were to make her, a foreigner and a woman, the dominant figure in French life for over twenty years. Sebastian of Portugal was mentally unstable. So also was Eric of Sweden, although in his case the instability was partially redeemed by flashes of the hereditary Vasa genius. Even in those countries where the monarch proved a capable ruler, uncertainty was often perpetuated by doubts concerning the succession. Until the birth of Charles Emmanuel in 1562 there was no heir to Savoy. Elizabeth of England would neither marry, nor designate a successor in the event of her death. Philip II's only son, Don Carlos, displayed a growing abnormality which made him quite unfitted for the throne; and after his death in 1568 Philip had to wait another ten years for the birth of a son who survived infancy.

Any momentary weakening of royal power, such as could easily happen with the accession of a new and untried king, might hazard in a few months the laborious work of years. The sixteenth-century monarch was, after all, little more than *primus inter pares*, his authority constantly open to challenge by nobles who might well consider their own claims to the throne superior to his own. Even if his rights were uncontested, he needed the loyalty and goodwill of his magnates to help maintain his power. In England, where the Crown had lost ground since the death of Henry VIII, Elizabeth's fate at the beginning of her reign hung on the loyalty of a handful of peers – Pembroke and Norfolk, Northumberland and Shrewsbury, who between them dominated Wales and East Anglia and the always dangerous North. The France of Catherine de Medici was effectively divided into spheres of influence controlled by three great family networks – the Bourbons in the South and West, the Guises in the East and in Normandy, and the Montmorency-Châtillon connection in the centre of the country. Since the Guises enjoyed virtually undisputed control over the eastern provinces, any move by the Crown which alienated the duke of Guise and his friends could jeopardize royal authority in a third of the nation. Philip II, on the whole, was better placed than Elizabeth and Catherine, for the transfer of central and local government into the hands of paid royal officials had progressed farther in Castile than in England and France. But even Philip found it useful to turn for help to a magnate with widespread local influence, like the Andalusian duke of Medina Sidonia; and he was never allowed to forget the competing claims of the great noble families for places of profit and power in the Spanish Monarchy.

In such circumstances, it is not surprising that some of the new rulers of the 1550s displayed a marked caution and conservatism in their early years. Elizabeth was reminded, no doubt quite unnecessarily, of 'how dangerous it is to make alterations in religion, specially in the beginning of a prince's reign.'[1] As new rulers, Philip, Elizabeth, and Catherine de Medici, while occasionally yielding to temptation in matters of foreign policy, were generally careful to avoid unnecessary risks both in domestic and international affairs. On the whole, it was enough – and hard enough – to preserve the *status quo*. For Emmanuel Philibert of Savoy, heir to a shattered State, it was a different story. Here, with the ruling classes disintegrated and demoralized after half a century of foreign occupation, there was no alternative to a policy of radical reconstruction, personally directed by an energetic duke. But Piedmont was an exception. Elsewhere it was wiser to watch, and to wait. Those who did not were liable to pay a heavy penalty. Mary Queen of Scots fatally antagonized nobles and people by her personal behaviour and matrimonial proclivities, and was driven to abdication in 1567. Eric XIV of Sweden, who harboured a chronic suspicion of the high nobility, deliberately alienated them by his highhanded system of government, and paid the price with deposition in 1568. In both Scotland and Sweden, circumstances were no doubt exceptionally difficult. In Scotland, the Crown was faced by a well-organized Protestant revolt; in Sweden, the very success of Gustavus Vasa in enhancing royal power invited a reaction when his firm hand was removed. But exceptional circumstances demanded exceptional skill. Nobles were dangerous objects, to be handled with care.

The power of the magnates, whether in England, Spain, or France, stemmed from their territorial possessions and their extensive local influence, which in turn gave them a commanding position at the centre of national life. In place of the old feudal structure, based on homage and the fief, there now existed throughout Western Europe a complicated network of clientage, held together by the more subtle ties of loyalty, interest and friendship. Friendship – a heavily charged word in the sixteenth century – usually developed between equals, while clientage reflected a relationship based on inequality. The impoverished country gentleman, anxious to place a son, would seek an aristocratic patron to further his career. 'From this', as François de La Noue found it necessary to explain, 'there follows on the part of father and son a great obligation towards him who does them this courtesy' – an obligation expressed by their willingness to be known as his 'creatures' and to foster his interests in those communities where they in turn had influence and clients of their own.

This reciprocal relationship of obligation and favour reached from the top to the bottom of the social scale. Patronage undoubtedly gave cohesion to societies sharply divided into horizontal strata by the concept of 'Estates', and firmly grounded on the principles of hierarchy and degree. But the clientage system, while playing a crucial part in the vertical articulation of society, could also on occasion prove cruelly divisive. For potentially there were several clientage systems within a single State. The Guises, the Montmorency, the Bourbons in France, the Toledos and the Mendozas in Spain, were rival clans attempting to outbid each other for influence and power. Since each family had its own network of clients scattered widely through the country, a clash either at Court or local level could rapidly lead to repercussions with national overtones.

It was at this point that the power and character of the monarch became decisive in relation to the cohesion of the community at large. The king was at the apex of the national pyramid. He was the supreme source of patronage and favour: it lay in his hands to raise a Montmorency or depress a duke of Guise. But in view of the great following, and still greater expectations, of the leading noble houses, to favour one excessively at the other's expense was to court disaster on a national scale. The successful sixteenth-century ruler was the one who deployed his reserves of patronage and power to moderate the perennial rivalry of opposing factions, while exploiting their systems of clientage to further the interests of the Crown. For aristocratic clientèles were a permanent fact of life, and without their cooperation there was little hope of royal commands being obeyed in the provinces. There was, therefore, no question of ruling above faction. The art of government lay in ruling *through* it, as Elizabeth demonstrated in England. 'The principal note of her reign', remarked a contemporary, 'will be that she ruled much by faction and parties, which she herself both made, upheld, and weakened as her own great judgment advised.'[2] Philip II, confronted by the rivalry of the duke of Alba and Ruy Gómez de Silva, prince of Eboli, used the same technique. So also, with less success, did Catherine de Medici, walking her tight-rope between Bourbon and Guise.

In performing their balancing act, princes enjoyed substantial advantages, even though many never learnt how to exploit them to the full. The conferring – or withholding – of patronage was a powerful political weapon, which a past-master like Philip II could deploy with consummate skill, as he showed in his handling of the Italian house of Farnese. The Farneses had attained their present eminence through the Farnese pope Paul III, who had ceded them in perpetuity the duchies of Parma and Piacenza, as hereditary fiefs of the papal see. Philip's half-sister, Margaret, married in 1538 Paul III's grandson, Ottavio Farnese, and their son Alexander, the future prince of Parma, was born in 1545. As a potentially important Italian prince, it was essential to tie him securely to the Spanish interest, and a dispute in 1557 between the Farneses and Henry II of France provided the occasion. Philip at once hastened to confer his protection on the family, in return for two conditions which were to dominate its life for many years to come. The young Alexander was to be brought up at the Spanish Court, where indeed contemporaries openly spoke of him as a hostage for the loyalty of his mother, Margaret of Parma; and a Spanish garrison was installed in the fortress of Piacenza. Margaret and Alexander thereafter rendered loyal service to Spain, while Philip dangled Piacenza before them as a tempting bait, only to jerk it away again when it seemed within their grasp.

Philip's cat-and-mouse game with the Farneses was being played, with innumerable variations and at innumerable levels, in every European State. But indispensable as was patronage as a device for political control, it was not by itself enough. To be fully effective, it needed the backing of royal authority, as measured by administrative and judicial competence, and the ultimate sanction of military power. In the generation or two before Cateau-Cambrésis, monarchical power had gained in authority as bureaucratic and administrative procedures were extended and overhauled by professionally-minded administrators, often trained in the universities or the law. These men impressed their own stamp on everything they did. The sixteenth century was the first great age of government by paper. Everywhere the stacks of documents piled up, as more and more government business was consigned to carefully-written records kept by a growing army of clerks. Government by paper was the preserve of the professionals – the clerk, the secretary, the trained civil servant, whose philosophy of life was never better expressed than by that paragon of civil servants, Antoine Perrenot, cardinal Granvelle, in 1567: 'I am content to get along well with my master, and I am no more Flemish than Italian. I am from everywhere, and my creed is to look after my own affairs and employ myself in those of my master and of the public, in so far as is required, and no farther.'[3]

Of all the European monarchies that of Spain had developed the most elaborate machinery of government by the middle of the century. The distances within the Spanish Monarchy were so large, its constituent territories so widely dispersed, that it presented the Crown with administrative problems unequalled in other parts of Europe. In an attempt to solve these problems, the Spanish Habsburgs had elaborated a system of government which combined central control by councils and local rule by viceroys and *audiencias* (judicial tribunals which had come to assume advisory and even administrative powers). Under Philip II there were nine viceroyalties in the Spanish Monarchy: in the peninsula itself, Aragon, Catalonia, Valencia, Navarre; in Italy, Sardinia, Sicily and Naples; and in the Indies, New Spain (Mexico) and Peru.[4] Each viceroy's activities were surveyed, and his correspondence studied, by the relevant council – whether of Aragon, Italy, or the Indies – which was nominally attendant on the person of the king. Over and above these territorial councils stood the council of State, flanked by councils with specialist concerns such as finance, or war.

In spite of the nominal pre-eminence of the council of State, neither Charles V nor Philip II held it in very high regard. For them it served as a useful sounding-board and as a forum in which personal and aristocratic animosities could be harmlessly discharged. The serious work of government was done elsewhere – at the various council tables, in the homes of the secretaries, and by the king himself. The secretaries, whether attached to the king's person or serving a council, were figures of great, and growing, importance in the administrative machine, as the middlemen between the king and his councils on the one hand, and the councils and the viceroys on the other. At the time of his accession Philip depended on the services of a single secretary of State, but on the death of Gonzalo Pérez in 1566 his secretariat was divided into two departments, of which one was given to his more famous son, Antonio.[5] Antonio Pérez and his colleagues never quite achieved the status of ministers, for Philip himself, preferring to be his own secretary and minister, closely supervised their work – when he did not do it for them. But inevitably they wielded great power behind the scenes, insinuating, suggesting, and actively advising a king who, however conscientious, was at times nearly overwhelmed by the stacks of papers piled high on his desk.

The elaborate machinery by which the Spanish Monarchy was administered evoked admiration and exasperation in roughly equal parts. It was routine-bound, it was cumbersome, its delays were notorious, but on the whole it worked. Now and again it even received the compliment of imitation. It was after one of Henry II's secretaries, Claude de Laubespine, had watched his Spanish counterparts at work during the Cateau-Cambrésis negotiations that the title of 'secretary of State' apparently gained currency in France. But in general it would seem that similar problems were leading the States of Western Europe to similar solutions, and there was little need for more than a quick look over the shoulder at what was done elsewhere. The rise of the office of secretary of State, in particular, was a characteristic sixteenth-century solution to a universal problem. Kings needed discreet and reliable officials, whose loyalties were to the

Crown rather than to any social group or faction in the State. They needed men who could master the new bureaucratic processes, and possessed special skills in the drafting of documents and the handling of papers. They must be men, too, who could cope with the business of councils, and were capable of acting as intermediaries between the central government and its local officers.

All these functions could be filled, to a greater or lesser degree, by the secretary. In France four special secretaries were appointed in 1547. They attended with the king the sessions of the *conseil des affaires*, which, along with the larger *conseil privé*, was the principal organ of government in the reign of Henry II. They not only served, as in Spain, as the essential link between king and councillors, but also as the link between the central government and the thirteen local *gouvernements* into which the country was divided. The same held true of England, where the secretaryship, as exercised first by Thomas Cromwell and later by William Cecil, entailed close personal supervision of the major affairs of government, and the maintenance of close contacts with Lords Lieutenant and Justices of the Peace. But, as in every sphere of sixteenth-century life, it was ultimately the man who counted rather than the office. The secretaryship was potentially a post of enormous influence. But it was made so by distinguished individual holders of the office – Cecil in England, De Laubespine or Villeroy in France – and it would quickly lapse into mediocrity in mediocre hands.

By the use of secretaries and professional bureaucrats who were generally laymen drawn from among the gentry and the middling ranks of society, early sixteenth-century rulers succeeded in strengthening the authority of royal government in the face of those traditional rivals of monarchy – church and aristocracy. In this sense it is reasonable to regard the first half of the century as a period of State-building, although 'State-building' has connotations which would be largely unfamiliar to sixteenth-century minds. Government was the king's government, and royal officials thought of themselves essentially as servants of the king. One or two of them, like Cecil or Granvelle, may have had a sense of service which extended beyond the king to the State, but the word 'State,' used to describe the whole body politic, seems to have acquired a certain currency only in the closing years of the century. Even then, in some quarters it was badly received – not least by the queen of England. 'At the latter end of Queen Elizabeth, it was a phrase to speak, yea for to pray for the Queen and the State. This word "State" was learned by our neighbourhood and commerce with the Low Countreys, as if we were, or affected to be governed by States. This the Queen saw and hated.'[6]

Whatever the ambiguities and uncertainties which prevented a clear formulation of the idea of the 'State', there could be no doubt that the

sheer professionalism of the new class of State officials was strengthening the efficiency of governments, and thereby enhancing the
possibilities of authoritarian rule. By the middle of the century this
had become a source of widespread uneasiness among the traditional
governing classes in many parts of Europe. They saw their privileges
encroached upon by officials of low birth, who displayed all the
symptoms of the arrogance of power. They saw themselves excluded
from offices which they had considered theirs of right, and they feared
the imposition of arbitrary government by 'new men' serving as the
instruments of an unchecked royal will.

These fears, which were to be a potent source of domestic unrest in
the second half of the century, were not entirely groundless. Eric XIV
of Sweden seems to have seen in the rule of secretaries an ideal means
of promoting absolutist designs, and his deposition was the act of an
aristocracy legitimately afraid that they were in danger of tyrannical
rule. But whatever the aspirations of sixteenth-century rulers, their
actual achievement was likely to be contained within relatively
narrow limits. Quite apart from the insuperable problems of
communication and distance, they lacked the physical means to
enforce their will in face of the resistance or non-cooperation of the
local governing class. They were hampered, too, by the divided loyalties of the men they chose as their servants. In a society where the
individual took second place to the family, and where title and rank
were regarded as the prime criteria of success, the royal official
naturally thought of his office as a means of social advancement,
which might eventually place his family among the great houses of
the land. If he looked to his sovereign's interest, he must look also to
his own, and this led him into an equivocal relationship with the great
nobles who surrounded him at court. On the one hand he must
protect the Crown's interests against those of private individuals; on
the other, he would wish to avoid displeasing the nobility whose ranks
he hoped to join.

Some degree of corruption was unavoidable so long as an office was
regarded as a piece of private property, rather than being associated
with the idea of public service. But corruption was exacerbated by the
inability of sixteenth-century monarchs to pay their officials either
regularly or well. Living on inadequate salaries paid in arrears, officials would naturally look to gifts and perquisites to supplement their
meagre incomes. In a sense these perquisities were no more than fees,
and tended to be regarded as such by both donor and recipient. But
their acceptance meant that the official's dependence on the Crown
was less than complete, and the fabric of royal government was
correspondingly weakened.

Monarchs did what they could to reduce the temptations. They
attempted to compensate for their inability to pay their servants

regularly at a reasonable rate, by granting occasional favours and by promising the reversion of offices to sons or nephews of the holders. But this also to some extent weakened the royal control over the machinery of government, by turning offices into family patrimonies and creating regular dynasties of officials or secretaries, like the Pérez in Spain or the De Laubespine in France. This was only one of the many ways, however, in which the efficiency of royal government was impaired by that perennial problem of sixteenth-century monarchies, the shortage of cash. Increasingly it became the practice to create and sell new offices as a means of enlarging the royal revenue. In Spain, although the Crown managed to retain in its hands the disposal of the principal administrative and judicial offices of State, it was forced into the creation and sale of increasing numbers of lesser posts in local and municipal government. In France, the Crown suffered from fewer inhibitions. In 1554 it ordered the sale of each new office to two purchasers, who would hold the office alternately for six months at a time. By the later years of the century French administration had virtually slipped from the hands of the Crown into those of a large caste of office-holders, who regarded themselves as a privileged corporation in the body politic, and their offices as valuable pieces of family estate.

The aspirations of monarchs towards more effective authoritarian government were therefore checked both by the unreliability of many of their officials, and by their own inability to pay for what they wanted. There was little chance of extending royal power at the expense of the nobles if the Crown was forced by financial stringency, as it was in Sicily, to alienate lands and to sell fiefs to which rights of private jurisdiction were attached. Finance was the key to effective government, and everywhere by the middle years of the century the state of Crown finances was reaching crisis-point. Monarchies had over-extended themselves with their long and costly wars, and their revenues had failed to keep pace with rising prices in an inflationary age. By the time of Cateau-Cambrésis it was clear that action was needed, and needed soon, if the gains of the first half of the century were not to be thrown away.

2 Estates

How could kings restore their solvency and increase their revenues? The conventional answer was still that they should appeal to their subjects, assembled in Estates. Admittedly the representative assemblies of Europe had suffered a number of casualties since the later Middle Ages. In France in particular, the Estates-General had not been summoned since 1484, although the various provincial Estates still continued to meet. So also did the *parlement* of Paris and the seven provincial *parlements*, which were nominally sovereign courts upholding the royal authority, but which had acquired in course of time their own particularist tendencies. But when Francis II sought the advice of Charles de Marillac, archbishop of Vienne, he urged him to follow the example of other European monarchs and to summon a national assembly which would provide a solid basis of support for the financial and religious policies to be adopted by the Crown. His advice was accepted and the Estates-General met at Orleans in December 1560 after a lapse of over seventy years. The decision of the French monarchy to wave its magic wand over the recumbent body of the Estates-General was not, however, universally acclaimed. In his opening address the chancellor, L'Hôpital, found it necessary to counter the argument that 'the king diminishes his power in taking the advice of his subjects when he is not obliged to do so; and he also becomes too familiar with them, which engenders contempt and lowers the dignity and majesty of kingship.' On the contrary, he considered 'there is no act so worthy of a king, and so befitting him, as to hold Estates, to give general audiences to his subjects, and to render justice to each of them.'[7]

Unfortunately the sleeping beauty proved less beautiful that L'Hôpital had hoped. The deputies of the Estates-General were willing enough to recognize Catherine de Medici as regent, but they baulked at considering new taxes on the grounds that they had been given no powers by their constituents to discuss the financial affairs of the Crown. Catherine, undeterred, gave orders in March 1561 for the summoning at Pontoise of a fresh assembly of the Estates-General; and this time she not only offered the redress of grievances in return for financial aid, but also proposed that the Estates themselves should control the machinery of tax-collection. But the proposal, which would have placed a powerful weapon in the hands of the deputies, was ignored, and the Third Estate refused to offer any money to the Crown. The clergy, on the other hand, meeting separately at Poissy, were terrorized by dark warnings of the spread of heresy into offering to pay the mortgage on the royal domain, and into voting a grant of 17 million *livres*. The differing response of the two Estates set the pattern for the rest of the reign of Charles IX. The clergy, as might be expected, were frequently summoned, and clerical subsidies did much to keep the monarchy afloat during the years of civil war. The Estates-General, on the other hand, were not re-convoked until 1576. Moreover, the Crown had no hesitation in imposing a tax on wine in September 1561, although it had failed to obtain the deputies' approval.

The French Crown's difficulties with its Estates-General were much greater than those of Philip II with the Cortes of Castile. Castile's representative assembly, unlike that of France, had continued to meet during the first half of the century, but had steadily lost ground before the royal power. After the aristocracy had led the resistance to tax increases in the Cortes of Toledo of 1538–1539, the nobility and clergy were no longer summoned, and the Castilian Cortes were reduced to a single chamber, composed of thirty-six representatives drawn from eighteen towns. The small size of the assembly and the limited scope of its representation made it highly vulnerable to royal pressure – all the more so as it had never managed to secure legislative powers or to establish the principle that redress for grievances must precede supply. In 1561 Philip II persuaded it, without excessive difficulty, to vote a large rise in the figure for which the *alcabala*, or sales tax, was compounded; and he was able at the same time to increase very considerably the yield of his extra-parliamentary revenues, in the form of customs dues, export duties and monopolies. The financial position of the Spanish Crown therefore began to show signs of improvement from the early 1560s, at a moment when increased revenues were needed for the construction of new galleys for the naval war against the Turks.

But Philip II was less fortunate in his other kingdoms and provinces, and even in Castile the Cortes world acquire a new assertiveness in the later years of the reign as his tax demands escalated. The parliament of Sicily, it was true, voted regular subsidies, though even with special grants and extra-parliamentary taxation, the rise in government revenues barely kept pace with the rise in prices during the second half of the century. Nearer home, Philip fared even worse. The three Cortes of the States of the Crown of Aragon – the kingdoms of Aragon and Valencia and the principality of Catalonia – had a long tradition of independence behind them, and had developed institutional safeguards which effectively made them the masters in matters of finance. Charles V had adopted the practice of summoning them simultaneously, and had succeeded in obtaining regular, if not very large, grants. But each fresh subsidy was gained only at the price of new royal concessions, which steadily diminished the Crown's control over jurisdiction and government. Since the revenue provided by the Crown of Aragon was barely worth the cost, Philip II summoned the general Cortes only twice – in 1563 and 1585 – and otherwise contented himself with appeals for voluntary cooperation.

In the Netherlands, where more was at stake than in the Crown of Aragon, the difficulties had in recent years become acute. Not only were there here, as in France, a number of provincial Estates (Flanders, Holland, Brabant, Artois and Hainault), but there was also – again as in France – a States General, which was essentially an assembly of delegates from the provincial Estates. Although the States General were ardent defenders of the liberties and privileges of the Netherlands, Charles V had made no attempt to dispense with their services, partly because they provided useful machinery for dealing jointly with political units that were otherwise hopelessly fragmented. But as the condition of the Netherlands deteriorated during the 1550s under the pressure of war and economic strain, the deputies of the States General became increasingly articulate spokesmen for general grievances. They agreed in 1557 to the vote of an annual grant of 800,000 florins for nine years, but only on condition that their own representatives should control the machinery for raising and spending the money. By winning in this way the power of the purse, the States General made themselves a formidable body – so formidable, indeed, that Philip would be likely to have recourse to them only when all other fiscal devices had failed.

Philip's difficulties in the Netherlands and Catherine's in France were typical enough of the problems created by Estates. All over Europe, princes found themselves face to face with parliaments whose powers may have varied considerably from one State to the next, but all of which were likely to impinge at some stage on the political calculations of the Crown. In Sweden, the *Riksdag* – remarkable for having a fourth chamber of peasants, alongside those of clergy, nobles and burgesses – successfully survived Gustavus Vasa's administrative revolution to provide some counter-balance in the later years of the century to the enhanced powers of monarchy. In England, where Henry VIII had associated parliament with his reformation of the church, Elizabeth found it necessary as well as expedient to follow his example in 1559. In Saxony, Brandenburg, Württemberg and the duchies on the Rhine, the Estates all succeeded, like the English House of Commons, in maintaining or strengthening their political influence, helped by the accident of royal minorities and by the customary embarrassments of the royal treasury. The same was also true of the Habsburg lands – Austria, Bohemia and Hungary – where the Emperor had been hampered in his dealings with the Estates by his own financial weakness and by the dangerous proximity of the Turk.

Confronted on the one hand with acute financial problems, and on the other with truculent Estates, the princes of mid-sixteenth-century Europe might well have been tempted to dispense altogether with these tiresome assemblies and to raise new taxes by royal decree. One of them, Emmanuel Philibert, did precisely this. His unhappy experiences in the government of the Netherlands had naturally left him disinclined to share his power with his subjects when he was restored to his duchy in 1559. The following year, when enthusiasm for the restored House of Savoy was still running high, he summoned the Estates of Piedmont and obtained from them a large and unconditional grant, sufficient to maintain a standing army of 24,000 men.

Thereafter he never summoned the Estates again, having made himself strong enough, with the support of his army, to levy taxes at will.

If Piedmont in the later sixteenth century was a miserable country, its peasantry crushed beneath the burden of taxes, this was perhaps beside the point. The 'iron-head' duke had raised his revenues from under 100,000 to half a million ducats a year, and his contemporaries were duly impressed. But it was one thing to admire, another to imitate. In Piedmont, after the long years of foreign occupation, there was no solid centre of opposition to absolutist rule. The new duke could begin almost with a *tabula rasa*, although even he found it necessary to conciliate the nobles by refraining from interference in their relations with their peasantry. But elsewhere it was a different story, and the Estates were generally too well entrenched to be quietly suppressed. Nor, even if this had been politically possible, would it necessarily have been regarded as a desirable end. Kings had their obligations and parliaments their uses, and neither, in sixteenth-century circumstances, could be lightly dismissed. When L'Hôpital said at Orleans in 1560 that 'there is no act so worthy of a king, and so befitting him, as to hold Estates', he was doing no more than utter a commonplace of the times. A continuing dialogue between king and people was regarded as a normal part of political life, and the meeting in solemn conclave of the monarch and the Estates of the nation was held to reveal in its highest degree the harmonious functioning of that delicate organism, the perfect commonwealth.

There were practical benefits, too, which could not be ignored. The calling of a representative assembly was, after all, a very convenient means of associating the mass of the nation with fiscal or religious policies which might well prove unpopular. Estates could be used as a means of levying new taxes, of bringing pressure to bear on the clergy or other sectional interests, and of rallying the nation behind the Crown for purposes of domestic or foreign policy. Their existence did not imply the sharing of government between king and subjects (although it might well lead to this during royal minorities), for it was universally agreed that government and the dispensing of justice were prerogatives of the king. But it did imply that the king was ready to hear and to remedy the grievances of his people, and that the people in turn would be ready to help him with their persons and their cash.

A prudent king would hesitate to throw these advantages away. Estates, on the whole, were desirable – but they should be submissive Estates, like the Cortes of Castile in the early years of Philip II. Unfortunately this was easier to hope for than to achieve. The more frequently Estates were summoned, the more likely they were to increase their sense of corporate identity and to gain in self-confidence and procedural skill. This was happening with the English House of Commons and some of the German Diets, and inevitably it called for increasing expertise in the art of parliamentary management on the part of the prince. But parliamentary management was a difficult enough art at the best of times, and in the 1560s it was made more than usually difficult by two exceptionally grave developments – the growth of religious opposition and aristocratic discontent.

The representative assemblies of sixteenth-century Europe provided religious dissidents with opportunities which they were quick to exploit. In the first parliament of her reign Elizabeth I was compelled by conservative opposition in the House of Lords to water down the Protestant settlement she had originally envisaged, while in later parliaments she found herself confronting a well-organized Protestant lobby in the House of Commons, determined to push her farther and faster than she was willing to move. In Scotland, the parliament of 1560 carried through a religious revolution in defiance of the wishes of Mary Queen of Scots and her husband Francis II. In Bavaria during the 1550s the Lutherans used their influence in the Estates to extract concessions from the new duke, Albert V. But this time it was the prince, not the parliament, who won. By buying off some of the leading nobles and dividing the opposition, he crushed the Lutheran 'conspiracy' in 1564. The Bavarian Estates never recovered from this decisive blow. Cowed and submissive, they abandoned their challenge to the ducal authority, and Bavaria became in due course the prototype of the 'Counter-Reformation State' – a country stifled beneath the heavy hand of a vast clerical establishment and an absolutist prince.

By the 1560s, therefore, it was clear that the growth of religious dissidence had enhanced the possibilities of conflict between princes and Estates. The same was true of aristocratic discontent. A noble chamber in the Estates was an ideal forum for the expression of deeply felt resentments against the rule of secretaries and the encroachment of royal prerogative on aristocratic rights. The Estates provided, too, a safer and more sophisticated means of opposition to royal policy than baronial revolt. A representative assembly was endowed, after all, with the unique respectability that only time could confer. It possessed 'immemorial' rights and privileges – the right, perhaps, to advise on the government of the realm during a royal minority, such as the nobles claimed in the Estates-General of Pontoise in 1561.

Even if the claim were specious, it might still be justified by historical 'proof'. For the growing uneasiness of the European nobility at the apparent consolidation and extension of royal power coincided with, and to some extent nurtured, a historical and legalistic movement of increasing importance and scope. In France, in particular, a reaction against Roman Law was gathering force, and it was coupled with a revival of interest in the customary laws of the realm. In applying to Roman law texts the new critical and philological techniques taught by the humanists, French academic jurists had become increasingly aware that the Roman Law taught in medieval universities was by no means necessarily the Roman Law as Justinian understood it; and they also began to appreciate that Justinian's own codification of the Law was neither perfect nor complete. During the 1560s no less than three eminent French jurists – Baudouin, Hotman and Bodin – published important treatises suggesting that a systematic jurisprudence could not be set up on the basis of Roman Law alone, and displaying a new respect for customary law, as a natural expression of the historical and political development of the French nation.[8] The political implications of these conclusions were not likely to be overlooked. Where Roman Law tended to benefit the prince by providing a general code which could ride roughshod over regional and local traditions, the customary law benefited privileged groups and corporations within the State by establishing their privileges on a basis of indefeasible right. And even when the basis was fundamentally unsound, a sufficient display of erudition might help to conceal this inconvenient fact.

The legal and historical revolution of the mid-sixteenth-century was therefore in process of forging a powerful weapon for the use both of nobles and Estates. Whether in France or Sweden, the Crown of Aragon or the Netherlands, the aristocracy was able to claim a prescriptive right, based on the customary law and constitution, for liberties and privileges which were under attack. This 'aristocratic constitutionalism' of the later sixteenth century was regarded, at least initially, as a means of defence. But historic rights were capable of almost indefinite extension once the initial point had been gained. Representative assemblies could be endowed with a mythical past which justified the fullest participation in the government of the State. The magnates could find, in the customary laws and constitutions of their nation, a prescriptive right to act as the advisers of the Crown. From here it was only a short step to oligarchy. Sixteenth-century Venice, after all, was a working model of successful and stable government under aristocratic control, and few European nobles could be expected to regret the transformation of king into doge.

3   National Unity and Religious Diversity

In ordinary circumstances, kings could probably have managed to contain an aristocratic attack conducted through the Estates, for other social groups could be expected to rally to the Crown in self-defence against any further extension of seigneurial power. But the circumstances of the 1560s were far from ordinary, for in many States the tasks of princes, already made exceptionally difficult by their

financial troubles and by the stirrings of aristocratic constitutionalism, were complicated by a third problem – religious disunity.

Religion was universally regarded as the basis of a well-ordered
society, and the preservation of religious unity was considered essential to the survival of the State itself. The French adage popularized in
the 1560s – *un roi, une foi, une loi* – was a natural enough sentiment
in an age when uniformity alone appeared to guarantee public order
in States that had barely been brought under the control of one central
power. Already the unity of Christendom had been destroyed by
religious dissension. Now it began to look as if the precariously
achieved unity of national States would be similarly destroyed. Most
people in the 1560s, whatever their faith, would have agreed with the
later verdict of a Spanish priest: 'Never has a republic been well
governed or peaceful where division and diversity of faith prevail,
nor indeed can it be. The reason for this is that . . . everyone considers
his own God to be the only true God . . . and everyone else to be blind
and deluded . . . And where there is such rancour and inner fire, there
cannot be good fellowship or lasting peace.'[9]

It was to be in the name of 'good fellowship' and 'lasting peace' that
men of the later sixteenth century perpetrated the most barbarous
inhumanities against their fellow-men. But, for a time at least, the
cruel irony of the situation went almost unobserved. As the religious
temperature rose, as Catholic and Protestant began to turn on each
other in mutual hatred and fear, society began, as if by an automatic
reflex, to insist with mounting hysteria on the preservation of a unity
that was slipping from its grasp. Minor deviations, which might have
been tolerated or ignored in ordinary times, now became the source of
profound and frenzied suspicion on the part of governments and their
subjects alike. The polarization of belief round Geneva and Rome left
no room in the middle for the tolerant, the indifferent, the sceptics.
Conformity had now become the price of survival. The persecuting
activities of State and Inquisition, the widespread and frightening
revival of witch-hunts,[10] and finally the wars of religion themselves
– these were the symptoms of a divided society so terrified at the
prospect of its own dissolution that it no longer dared tolerate those
elements which it had failed to absorb.

Against this background of deep social fear, such rulers as remained
unaffected by the prevailing hysteria were confronted by an almost
impossible task. It was not easy to resist, as Elizabeth was determined
to resist in England, the insistent demand to make windows into men's
souls. Nor was it by any means necessarily safe. For one of the great
tragedies of the later sixteenth century was that the fears of political
and social subversion proved all too often to have a basis in fact.
Fanatical minority groups, whether Catholic or Protestant, posed a
genuine threat to the stability and cohesion of the State. In the face of

this threat, 'one king, one faith, one law' seemed to offer some guarantee – perhaps the sole guarantee – of survival. But it proved a harsh and ultimately self-defeating doctrine, and it led many innocent men and women to their deaths.

While the growing virulence of religious animosities inevitably jeopardized national unity, the supreme threat to the monarchies of mid-sixteenth-century Europe lay elsewhere. Princes had been confronted, for many decades now, by varied manifestations of religious dissent. They had been confronted even longer by aristocratic opposition, both overt and in constitutional guise. The real novelty of the middle years of the century was the fusion of the two – the alarming convergence of religious and aristocratic protest to create a combined movement of formidable power.

The fusion was achieved in little more than a decade, for it was during the 1550s and early 1560s that the European aristocracy began to move over in significant numbers to the Calvinist faith. All across Europe, from Scotland to Poland, nobles and gentry were openly rallying to the Protestant cause. In the Netherlands, where Protestant movements had tended, as in England, to be confined to the lower orders of society, the first significant conversions came at the end of the decade, when the two brothers Jean and Philippe de Marnix were converted to Calvinism after a visit to Geneva in 1560. Their example was followed by a growing number of gentry, who began sending their sons to the Geneva Academy to complete their education. But it was among the French nobility that Calvinism achieved its most remarkable success. In the late 1540s Protestantism could claim only a handful of French nobles. By the 1560s, perhaps as much as half the aristocracy had abandoned their allegiance to Rome, as against a conversion rate in the country at large of ten to twenty per cent.

The reasons for this mass conversion of nobles and gentry are, in the nature of things, both complex and obscure. As a small child the future Huguenot publicist, Philippe Du Plessis-Mornay, was given a Lutheran tutor by his semi-Protestant mother, and firmly chose Protestantism at the grave age of ten. The conversion of that volatile character the prince of Condé was apparently effected during the course of an illness in 1558, by his wife, Eléonore de Roye, one of the many distinguished feminine converts among the higher nobility. Of the three Châtillon brothers, the youngest and most impetuous, François d'Andelot, was the first to change his faith. The middle brother, Coligny, moved slowly towards Protestantism in 1556–1557, and was apparently confirmed in his new faith by an intense study of the Bible during his period of captivity after St Quentin. The eldest, Odet de Châtillon, a cardinal who had never been ordained a priest, followed his brothers' example in 1561, without, however, abandoning his title or his princely ecclesiastical revenues.

Personal decisions, reached on personal, and no doubt very various, grounds... Conviction and expediency, painful wrestlings of the spirit and sudden movements of the heart, all contributed to the renunciation of old religious loyalties which had come to irk or offend. Many nobles and gentry of a liberal and humanist turn of mind, who in normal circumstances would have chosen a middle course, may well have come to feel by the 1560s that Geneva offered the best port in a storm. Clericalism in all its forms was anathema to them, as to vast numbers of the European laity. But the times demanded firm commitment to a cause; and the clericalism of Geneva may well have seemed less obnoxious, and ultimately more amenable to lay control, than the massive hierarchical organization of the Roman Catholic church.

Calvin himself was in no doubt as to the supreme importance of winning the nobility to his cause. Both he and his lieutenant, Theodore Beza, were well aware that the conversion of a single great noble might lead to multiple conversions among his relatives and dependents, and that nobles could offer both respectability and protection to their infant church. 'He has promised us marvellous things,' wrote the pastor who reported Condé's conversion to Calvin. 'Please God he keeps the half of his promises.' Beza, as the son of a minor noble family from Vézelay in Burgundy, was ideally equipped both by background and temperament to appeal to the members of his own social class. On his visits to France be proved a highly successful and persuasive exponent of his faith, and achieved some spectacular conversions, including that of the future Protestant heroine Jeanne d'Albret, the wife of Antoine de Bourbon, king of Navarre. He also succeeded in attracting recruits for the ministry from among good families: of the eighty-eight pastors sent into France from Geneva between 1555 and 1562, ten are known to have been of noble birth, and there were probably more.[11]

No doubt the sincerity of many of the noble converts is open to question. There were, after all, many good reasons, besides religious conviction, for becoming a Calvinist during these years. Fashion and example played an important part. The conversion of the Bourbons and the Châtillons inevitably accelerated the rate of conversion among those of the provincial nobility who were not wedded to the rival – and unswervingly orthodox – faction of the Guises. Moreover, there were many impoverished and unemployed gentry in France, especially after the disbanding of the army in 1559. Some of these had come into contact with Protestant soldiers during their military careers; all of them cast covetous eyes on the wealth and the estates of the church. 'Several', according to the chancellor, L'Hôpital, 'take shelter beneath the cloak of religion, even though they have no God and are more atheist than religious: among them there are lost souls, who have consumed and wasted their all, and can only survive on the troubles of the realm and the possessions of other men.'[12]

The inevitably mixed motives behind this mass conversion of the nobles and gentry are in the long run of less importance than the fact that it occurred. Its outcome was a radical transformation of the balance of political power in the State. A group of nobles, many of them already opposed to various aspects of royal government and policy, were now bound together, and to other groups in society, by the common bond of their chosen faith. This group would naturally exploit every means at its disposal, including the opportunities afforded by meetings of parliaments, to influence the religious policies of the Crown, and to win, if possible, the commanding positions of power in the State. It is not therefore surprising that the 1550s and early 1560s should have seen the formation of Protestant 'parties' in several European countries, and the organization of Protestant lobbies, backed by aristocratic support, in their parliaments and Estates.

The combined political and religious pressure exercised by an influential section of court and provincial nobility created new and dangerous problems for hard-pressed monarchs. Elizabeth was fortunate in that the cause of Rome had been too discredited in England by the events of Mary's reign for there to be any effective and organized resistance to such concessions to the radical Protestants as she felt it necessary to make. But even she was unable to avoid alienating an influential group of nobles still attached to the old religion, who retired to their tents to bide their time. In at least two continental States, however, – Poland and France – there was an imminent prospect of conflict between the rival religious parties if the Crown showed any sign of inclining to either; and in a third, the Netherlands, there was an ominous growth of religious and political opposition to the Spanish régime.

The princes concerned – Philip II, Catherine de Medici and Sigismund II Augustus of Poland – adopted different approaches to the problem that faced them. Philip II, determined never to rule over heretics, pursued in the Netherlands a vigorous policy of repression from the first.[13] Sigismund, although no less sincere a Catholic than Philip, realized that repression in Poland was out of the question. The *Sejm* or diet, dominated by the gentry, was Protestant, or at least strongly anti-clerical, in outlook. A rash attempt by the dilapidated Roman Church in Poland to enforce the heresy laws raised a storm in the diet of 1552, and the king was only able to assuage it by agreeing to a temporary compromise under which the clerical courts should be suspended for a year, while the gentry in return should continue to pay tithes. Although Sigismund felt strong enough to resist fresh Protestant demands in the following years, he found it necessary to prolong the compromise of 1552. As a result, Roman Catholicism and the various Protestant sects began, however uneasily, to learn the difficult art of co-existence; and at a time when most of the continent was dividing into two armed camps over matters of the faith, the Poles were already beginning to move hesitantly towards the acceptance of toleration as a maxim of State.

The choice appeared to lie between repression and some form of toleration, however tacit. Either, or neither, might prove workable. But by the 1560s there seems to have been no real alternative, although Catherine de Medici still clung to the hope that there was. Herself indifferent to the subtleties of theology, which she regarded as matters of baffling incomprehensibility, she found it hard to believe that others might see them in a different light. The cardinal of Lorraine had long entertained ideas of a French national council, as the means of providing an appropriately Gallican solution to the problems of a Gallican church always suspicious of Rome. In the cardinal's suggestion Catherine glimpsed the possibilities of a doctrinal reconciliation such as had proved totally elusive at an international level; and she now began to pursue the idea of a national council with all the formidable energy at her command.

Catherine's setbacks and misfortunes in the pursuit of her aim suggest something of the supreme difficulty involved in devising a generally acceptable religious formula, especially when the balance of political forces was itself unfavourable to the attempt. By the early months of 1560 the situation in France was already critical. Since the first French Calvinist national synod had met at Paris in May 1559, the Guise-dominated government of Francis II had adopted a series of increasingly repressive anti-Calvinist measures. As persecution intensified, the more impetuous Calvinist nobles began to conspire. Condé remained in the shadows while a member of the lesser nobility, Jean de Barry, seigneur de La Renaudie, laid the plans for a *coup* in which the king would be captured, the Guises arrested or killed, and their régime replaced by a new government of nobles sympathetic to the Protestant cause. But the *coup*, which was planned for March 1560, misfired; and Condé disavowed the conspirators, who were tracked down and killed.

The conspiracy of Amboise made a royal attempt at conciliation all the more necessary if France were to be saved from a bloody civil war. Already by the summer of 1560 Condé was conspiring again, and a national uprising of Protestants appeared to be imminent. On 31 October the Guises had Condé arrested and sentenced to death for treason, but the sudden death of Francis II on 5 December saved Condé's life, and completely transformed the political scene. Where the Guises had been able to dominate Francis II, they failed to secure a comparable hold over his younger brother, who now came to the throne as Charles IX. The death of her eldest son therefore gave Catherine a chance to loosen the grasp of the Guises on the crown. Seizing her opportunity, she assumed the powers and the duties of regent for the young king, and proceeded to associate with her in the government Condé's elder brother, Antoine de Bourbon, king of Navarre. As first prince of the blood, Navarre was entitled to a position of pre-eminence during a royal minority, and the Estates duly recognized him as lieutenant general of the realm.

Catherine, as regent, was now well placed to embark on her great schemes for political and religious reconciliation. But the antipathy of Guise and Bourbon, exacerbated by their different religious allegiances, divided the political nation into two hostile camps. Even if a conciliatory religious formula could be devised, a strong third party would be required to help Catherine impose it. The obvious, and indeed the only, leader of such a party was the Constable Montmorency, linked by kinship to the Protestant nobles and by his religion to the party of the Guises. Now that the Guises had lost some of their power, Montmorency partially recovered his influence at court. But the Constable, always stronger in loyalty and sense of service than in political imagination, proved unequal to his opportunity, which perhaps he never even clearly saw. Much as he hated the Guises, he was at one with them in his anger at the recent success of Antoine de Bourbon in acquiring a pre-eminence which he and the duke of Guise had been accustomed to share between them in the past. He remained adamant, too, in his detestation of heresy, and was not the man to countenance a religious compromise. Instead, therefore, of occupying an intermediate position he gradually moved towards a *rapprochement* with his old rivals, the Guises.

This striking realignment of political forces was completed in April 1561 when a triumvirate was formed, consisting of the duke of Guise, the Constable Montmorency, and Montmorency's colleague at Cateau-Cambrésis, the Maréchal de Saint-André. Created in order to save France from falling under Protestant control, the triumvirate, by its very existence, brought the country several steps closer to civil war. The chances of her being able to build a third force were now so slight as to be negligible, but Catherine remained determined to have her national council, and still hoped to reconcile Condé and Guise. At the end of August 1561 Theodore Beza, who had been chosen as the Protestant spokesman, arrived in France from Geneva, and was summoned to an interview at Saint-Germain with the queen-mother and the cardinal of Lorraine. A few days later, on 9 September, the colloquy of Poissy was opened in the presence of the king.

The colloquy was organized less like a council than a tribunal sitting in judgment on the Protestants. But Beza, a clever if often vituperative polemicist, deployed his arguments with skill, and succeeded in winning a favourable hearing until the moment when he hit on an unfortunate image to explain the Calvinist conception of the Real Presence. 'Blasphemavit!' cried the scandalized Catholic bishops, and Catherine had hastily to interpose that she intended no innovation in matters of faith. The incident revealed the extreme fragility of any basis for compromise, and although the discussions continued over the next few weeks, they failed to bring the two parties any closer together. On the contrary, cardinal de Tournon, the spokesman of the forces of conservatism, appealed to the king to refuse the heretics the right of reply, in accordance with the formula *un roi, une foi, une loi.*

The cardinal of Lorraine was himself now under strong suspicion for his conciliatory attitude, and orthodoxy secured its final triumph when the Jesuit General Laynez intervened on 25 September to denounce the whole purpose of the colloquy, and to insist that the only true council was in session at Trent.

Laynez's intervention, which reduced Catherine to tears, meant in effect that the colloquy was doomed. The faculty of theology at the Sorbonne rejected the proposed compromise settlement on 9 October, and the colloquy itself was formally closed on the 14th. Its closure was followed by the retreat of the Catholic magnates from court – the duke of Guise and the cardinal of Lorraine on 19 October, Montmorency on the 23rd. But Beza stayed on, preaching at Saint-Germain and advising the Protestant leaders, whom Catherine now saw as possible defenders of the monarchy against a Guise revolt. The departure of the Guises enabled her and her advisers to resume a moderate policy which culminated in the famous January Edict of 1562. By the terms of the edict, the Huguenots were granted full freedom of worship outside towns, and the right of private worship within them. They were also allowed to hold synods, and their pastors were officially recognized as long as they took an oath of loyalty to the crown. The edict was a triumph for Beza and Coligny, but it came too late. The Guises were determined to resist moderation. On 1 March 1562 the duke of Guise, on his way to Paris in arms, allowed his followers to attack a group of Protestant worshippers at Vassy in Champagne. Seventy-four were killed, and a hundred or more wounded. Guise had shown what he thought of the edict, and there was no escape from civil war.

Catherine's desperate attempt to achieve doctrinal reconciliation had in fact been doomed to failure well before the colloquy of Poissy was ever convoked. The time for confessional reunion had long since passed. Repression or some form of toleration – these were now the stark alternatives. But repression was likely to prove abortive, where dissident aristocrats came out in defence of heretics. Toleration, too, had powerful enemies, as the behaviour of the duke of Guise had shown. Whichever was chosen – repression or toleration – would therefore require skilful management and basically favourable political conditions to achieve any significant degree of success. Yet success was essential; for failure to end discord by one means or the other would lead to the gradual disintegration of the State. The mid-sixteenth century State was, after all, a vulnerable institution, lacking a sound financial basis, and inadequately served. Its integrity was endangered by religious dissidents and by unruly nobles, who glimpsed in 'constitutionalism' and religious dissent the opportunity for furthering their own private aims. In times like these there was reason enough for princes to fear the union of aristocratic, popular and religious unrest. They would need a high order of helmsmanship if they were to steer successfully past the reefs of rebellion and escape the shoals of confessional strife.

PART II

1559–1572

4

Protestantism and Revolt

1   Wars of Religion?

The 1560s were a decade of revolt. In France, there was civil war from
1562. In the Netherlands, a movement of protest by the high nobility
was followed by a popular rising and revolt in 1566. In Scotland, the
queen was deposed in 1567 and fled defeated to England in 1568. In
England, there was a rising of the northern earls in 1569. In Spain, the
Moorish population of Granada took to arms at the end of 1568 and
was defeated only after two years of savage war. All these insurrections were either closely connected with, or directly inspired by,
religious discontents. Revolt in the first three countries was Protest-
ant-inspired. The northern rebellion in England was a Catholic insurrection. The Granada revolt was the last desperate protest of a racial
and religious minority against a Christian, and Catholic, domination
which had become intolerably oppressive.[1]

That these risings should all have assumed a strong religious
colouring was, in the circumstances of the 1560s, natural enough.
Rome against Geneva; Christian against Moor... The mounting religious intolerance of these years inevitably bred suspicion and hatred,
and exacerbated political and social discontents. But the relationship
between religion and politics is never clear-cut. To many, both at the
time and later, the wars of the second half of the sixteenth century
were pre-eminently 'wars of religion'. 'This war', wrote the French
Protestant pastor Pierre Viret, 'is not like other wars, for even the very
poorest man has an interest in it, since we are fighting for freedom of
conscience (*la liberté de nos consciences*).'[2] On the other hand, the
Venetian ambassador was able to discuss the wars in terms of purely
secular motivation: 'In like manner as Caesar would have no equal
and Pompey no superior, these civil wars are born of the wish of the
cardinal of Lorraine to have no equal, and the Admiral (Coligny) and
the house of Montmorency to have no superior.'[3]

Whether or not these were really 'wars of religion' must to some extent depend on whose war is being discussed. A Calvinist pastor was unlikely to view the conflict in the same light as a Condé, nor a Condé as an artisan. If, for some, the salvation and triumph of their faith was the sole purpose of the struggle, for others this may have served as no more than a convenient pretext. Yet those who fought in the Protestant ranks all subscribed, even if only through the fact of comradeship in arms, to a common vision of the world. It was a world in which the Christian was engaged in ceaseless struggle against the power of Satan; in which the pope himself – the child of Satan – was the anti-Christ, and his works were the works of idolatry, of darkness and superstition. The forces of darkness wrestled with the forces of light, but ultimately the kingdom of God must triumph over that of men, and Satan be overthrown.

Similarly, on the Catholic side, the impending struggle was also set in a cosmic context. The sixteenth century – the century of Nostradamus (1503–1566) – was an age of prophecy. Prophets and astrologers were constantly predicting the impending coming of Christ and the ending of the world. Where the Calvinists saw themselves as ending the reign of the Roman anti-Christ and cleansing the church of its pollution by the smashing of images and the overthrow of idolatry, many Catholics were held in the grip of a deep fear generated by the imminence of the Last Judgment. Violence provoked violence, and they saw themselves as embarking on a crusading war in which their own fury reflected, and was justified by, the wrath of God descending in judgment on a sinful world. The Wars of Religion, therefore, were already being fought out in the imagination before the struggle was joined. Inevitably this created a climate of catastrophic expectation in which violence was anticipated, and therefore all the more certain to erupt.

It was at the point at which this cosmic vision impinged on human affairs, that the differences of emphasis and opinion began. What attitude should the faithful adopt in the face of this awful conflict? How should they regard the civil power? What was their proper duty, both to God and man? To its opponents, whether Roman Catholic or Lutheran, Calvinism was by its very nature conducive to civil disorder. 'Their religion' declared a typical Roman Catholic pamphlet of the period, 'tends to exempt them from subjection to men, so that they may live in the liberty of the Swiss, and turn themselves into cantons.'[4] There is no doubt an element of truth in this – there were bound to be certain 'democratic' tendencies inherent in a religion which demanded so much of the individual layman, and provided him with so many opportunities for active participation in the life of the church. But, where this 'democratic' element touched on political life, events showed that its effects were by no means always predictable. There was a constant tension within the Calvinist movement between the ministers and some of the laity. John Knox and his colleagues were determined to carry through a democratic religious revolution, which would achieve the (somewhat improbable) feat of approximating the kingdom of Scotland to the kingdom of heaven on earth. The earl of Moray, on the other hand, would not have the kirk for his master. This resistance of influential laymen, and particularly of the lay nobility, to clerical domination and 'democratic' control ran right through the history of Calvinism in the later sixteenth century. Occasionally a Calvinist leader – notably Coligny in France – would share so many of the ideals of the ministers as to be able to work in close harmony with them. But more commonly the lay leadership looked askance at the ministers for their radical tendencies, for their dangerous disregard of social and political realities, and their clerical authoritarianism, while the ministers reproached the leadership for neglecting the things of God and preferring those of mammon.

It would, however, be misleading to assume that the pastors were inexorably cast in the role of radicals. Calvinism could be, and often was, an activist religion. But any faith founded on the doctrine of predestination was bound to place a heavy emphasis on the need for patience and Christian resignation. An alliance between Calvinism and the forces of political or social protest was therefore by no means a foregone conclusion. It depended, in the first instance, on a victory of the activist element within the Calvinist church itself. Driven together by mutual need, militant Calvinism and militant political and social discontent might then make common cause. But, even at the height of the wars, there was never a fixed and unvarying relationship between the three most dynamic elements among the forces of protest – Calvinism, aristocratic opposition and popular unrest. The three became interdependent, but their relations were subject to constant changes of emphasis, according to the times and the men.

At the beginning of the 1560s there were marked similarities between the situation in France, Scotland and the Netherlands, but the revolutionary movement in all three countries evolved at different rates of progress and in rather different ways. In Scotland, the revolt developed and triumphed rapidly because Mary Queen of Scots managed to alienate all sections of opinion, and lacked the military strength to fight back. But in France and the Netherlands the story was very different, because the rebels met effective resistance, and the struggle proved prolonged.

It was the situation of the churches in France which first compelled Geneva to redefine its attitude to the secular authorities and to factions within the State. Calvin's policy, like that of Luther before him, was effectively one of non-resistance in the face of persecution. In

1559, when the harrying of French Calvinists was becoming increasingly severe, Calvin's lieutenant Beza wrote to Bullinger at Zurich: 'We are often asked whether it is permitted to take up arms against those who are the enemies not only of our religion but also of the kingdom... Up till now, our answer has always been that the tempest should be faced only with the arms of prayer and patience.'[5] This doctrine, however, was more easily preached in Geneva than practised by adherents in the field. Nor did it commend itself to some of the hot-headed young nobles who had recently joined the Calvinist ranks in France. La Renaudie and his supporters were plainly deviating from Geneva's declared policy when they planned the conspiracy of Amboise in March 1560. On the other hand, there were signs that the mood in Geneva itself was now beginning to change. A Geneva tribunal explicitly absolved Calvin and Beza from charges of complicity in the Amboise conspiracy, but a certain degree of general approval might reasonably be deduced from the fact that Beza sent La Renaudie a little book by François Hotman which denounced the Guises and accompanied the gift with his own translation of the highly pertinent Psalm 94: 'O Lord God, to whom vengeance belongeth, show thyself...'

The truth was that, if Calvinism were to survive, Geneva's traditionally passive attitude was becoming increasingly difficult to maintain. La Renaudie's plot was ill-conceived and ill-organized, but sooner or later force would have to be met with force. Now that the churches were emerging into the open under aristocratic protection, and Calvinist nobles were becoming deeply involved in the feuds and faction-struggles of the court, religion was inevitably caught up in high politics, and found itself resorting to political weapons – intrigue, conspiracy, and finally revolt. After the failure of the conspiracy of Amboise, Condé joined his brother, the tepidly Protestant king of Navarre, on his estates at Nérac. At Navarre's request, Beza left Geneva for Nérac on 20 July 1560 to take part in their discussions, which ranged over the whole question of the state of the reformed churches in France, and the attitude to be adopted to the Guise-dominated government in the light of recent events.

The first decision taken at the Nérac meeting seems to have been to establish contact with Protestant leaders in Europe as a whole. During 1561 a series of secret embassies set out from the court of Navarre to the Swiss cantons, to England, and to Germany, where the French jurist François Hotman conducted secret negotiations with the Protestant princes who were to attend the Imperial Diet. At the same time, some at least of the Huguenot leaders appear to have been taking military precautions against the eventuality of war. It would hardly seem an accident that a large consignment of gun-powder, manufactured in Geneva by close associates of Calvin, was sold at

Lyons in July 1561 – presumably to nobles in south-eastern France who would later hold command in the Huguenot armies.

It was in the months following the breakdown of the colloquy of Poissy in October 1561, however, that Beza and the Calvinist leaders finally accepted commitments which would lead inescapably to a recourse to arms. Catherine de Medici's position during these months was exceptionally difficult. Her attempt to bring about a reconciliation at Poissy had failed – partly because the religious differences were irreconcilable, and partly because the two great factions of Guise and Bourbon had already assumed postures which they were not prepared to abandon. Clashes between the two parties were becoming increasingly frequent, and it was clear that both were preparing for war. If the activities of the Bourbons were becoming increasingly menacing, so also were those of the Guises, who withdrew from the court without royal permission before the end of October.

Guise power was formidable, not only because of the wealth and large following of the family, but also because of its vast clerical influence and its international links. Through the acquisition of archbishoprics and bishoprics, and the skilful deployment of ecclesiastical patronage, the Guises had secured for themselves a commanding position in the Gallican church. Through their marriages they were connected with the ruling dynasties of Scotland and Lorraine, and were able to negotiate on an equal footing with the leading princes in Europe. While Condé was seeking allies at foreign courts, the Guises were doing the same. They strengthened their connection with the Spanish court; they detached the king of Navarre from his Protestant friends; and by exploiting the mutual antipathy of Lutherans and Calvinists, they reached an understanding with the Lutheran duke of Württemberg which would thwart Condé's plans for an alliance with the German Protestant princes.

But, most dangerous of all for Catherine, was the fact that the Guises controlled the royal army and the royal artillery, perhaps the best in Europe. Without troops of her own, and with no money to raise them, her only recourse in the face of intimidation from the Guises was to turn to their opponents for help. At the end of 1561 or the beginning of 1562 she secretly summoned Beza and Admiral Coligny and asked them how many soldiers the Huguenots could put at the Crown's disposal in case of urgent need. Coligny informed her that there were 2,150 Protestant communities which would be willing to come to her assistance on condition that they could worship undisturbed. The January Edict of 1562, that expression of moderate court policy which granted the Calvinists conditional freedom of worship, was to turn them into the defenders of the legally established order. Consequently, when France drifted into civil war in March 1562 after the massacre of Vassy, the Calvinists had been given an

excellent pretext for military preparations, and had achieved respectability as supporters of the royal cause. Even the most delicate of
Calvinist consciences might find reassurance in Condé's assertion that
he and his followers were defending the 'authority of the king, the
government of the queen, and the tranquillity of the realm.'

Condé, however, proved unequal to the opportunity that had come
his way. 'The taking of the king or Paris', wrote a contemporary, 'is
half the victory in civil war.' Condé lost them both. The Huguenots
suffered throughout the civil wars from the weakness of Protestantism
in Paris, and the consequences of this weakness were revealed from
the moment the first shot was fired. On 15 March the duke of Guise,
defying royal orders, entered Paris with two or three thousand men.
Feeling himself at a disadvantage in the capital, Condé left it on the
23rd for Meaux, where, four days later, Coligny reluctantly joined
him. Condé might have gone, bidden or unbidden, to the assistance of
the queen-mother, who was at Fontainbleau with the young Charles
IX, but he failed to grasp this supreme opportunity to seize the
political initiative. This failure to join Catherine at Fontainebleau is
as inexplicable as it was disastrous to his cause. For if he had taken the
royal family under his protection, he could convincingly have associated Calvinism with the maintenance of royal authority. As it was,
the queen, as a Catholic, could hardly move from Fontainebleau to
throw herself on the mercy of her Huguenot subjects. So she remained
where she was, awaiting the inevitable – the demand of the Triumvirs
that she should return to Paris, where they were now in full control.
Eventually, under pressure from Guise and his armed cohorts, she and
the king set out on their slow, reluctant journey to the capital, which
they re-entered on 6 April. Henceforth, Guise and the Catholics
would be the guardians of the Crown.

While the success of the Triumvirs in securing the persons of Catherine and Charles IX deprived the Huguenots of the two most valuable
pieces on the board, it did at least leave them with some justification
for their resort to arms. On 8 April Beza published a manifesto which
claimed that military action by Condé was necessary to free the queen
regent and the king from Guise control. Already on 2 April Condé had
occupied Orléans, which now became the headquarters of the Huguenot cause. During the course of the month, the Huguenots rose in the
provinces, ostensibly to send help to Condé at Orléans, but more
often, in practice, to pay off local scores. Armed rebellion, therefore,
had become the order of the day, and it fell to Beza, first as the aide
and accomplice of Condé and then as Calvin's successor on his death
in May 1564, to formulate for the faithful a theory of armed
resistance.

While the convenient fiction of a defence of the royal authority
served its turn for a time, it began to look increasingly threadbare

under the pressure of events. But the development of a fully-fledged doctrine of resistance proved a slow and hesitant process, for the whole weight of tradition favoured the forces of authority. Beza himself abhorred the iconoclasm that was sweeping through French churches in the regions under Huguenot control, and he was anxious to avoid offering the more zealous among the faithful a justification for religious or political excess. Theory therefore limped haltingly behind action, but the fact remained that the decisive step had been taken in 1562. The Calvinist church, both at the national and international level, was now prepared, under certain circumstances, to associate itself with armed revolt. Once this step had been taken, it was open for Condé's rebellion to assume at least some of the characteristics of a religious uprising, and for its leaders to make use of such help as the church and the faith could provide.

2   The Huguenots at War

The assistance given by Geneva and the national churches to the leaders of the Bourbon-Châtillon insurrection was decisive in many ways – and not least in preventing it from being merely another abortive and easily suppressed attempt by a group of disaffected aristocrats to seize power in the the State. As members of an international religious movement, Condé and his friends found that many doors were now opened to them beyond the borders of France. At first there was some hesitation about assisting armed revolt. Frederick, the Elector Palatine, who was later to be so active in the Calvinist cause, expressed his disapproval of rebellion, and urged resort to prayer. But Beza, an internationally known and respected figure throughout Protestant Europe, successfully negotiated with the German Protestant princes for the troops of *reiter* which would become in the following years the nucleus of a mobile Protestant army, ready to accept employment in either the Netherlands or France.

It was Beza also who acted as the link between Condé and Geneva during the first crucial months of the war. Geneva helped to supply arms and munitions for Condé's forces, and played its part in negotiating the loans raised at Lyons, Basle and Strasburg for the financing of his campaigns. The financing of the Huguenots thus became an international operation, in which England, afraid of the consequences of a Guise victory, was also prepared to join, at a price. By the treaty of Hampton Court of September 1562, Elizabeth offered a substantial loan in return for the immediate cession of Le Havre, which was to be exchanged for Calais at the end of the war.

The surrender of French territory to England did Condé's cause great harm, but in other respects his international connections proved highly advantageous. It was, however, the support of the local churches which transformed both the character and the prospects of Condé's insurrection. Traditionally a rebellious noble relied for support on his own clientage and retainers, and on any malcontents whom he could induce to rally to his cause. Like his predecessors, Condé hastened to call out his vassals and clients, who took a formal oath to 'render him faithful service'. But alongside this traditional body of adherents drawn from the ranks of the Bourbon and Châtillon connections, he was able to turn to another potential army of even greater extent – the membership of the Calvinist churches and communities which together constituted the French Reformed Church.

The organization of these churches and communities followed a well-defined pattern. Each local church had its own 'consistory' of minister and lay elders, and – if it were large enough – its own company of pastors. The consistories of a number of neighbouring churches were grouped together into a 'colloquy', which exercised a general oversight over the religious affairs of the region. Above these, at the provincial level, were the 'synods', and finally, at the summit, the national synod, which met for the first time at Paris in 1559. By the end of the sixteenth century, eleven such national synods had been held, and it was at one of them, that of La Rochelle in 1571, that the French Reformed church adopted its definitive confession of faith – the *Confession de la Rochelle* or *Confessio Gallicana*.

This system of ecclesiastical organization proved to be ideally designed for the tasks which it was now called upon to assume. It provided a coherent network of highly disciplined bodies reaching across the country to include Frenchmen of every social degree; and it dovetailed very neatly with Condé's own clientage system. During 1560 and 1561 the majority of the churches, especially those in the regions most affected to the Huguenots – Dauphiné, Languedoc, Guienne and Provence – placed themselves under the formal 'protection' of local magnates or country gentry who committed themselves to defend them in the event of an attack. These 'protectors' themselves formed part of a social hierarchy headed by the figure of Condé, 'protector general of the churches of France' from 1562.

Between 1560 and 1562, therefore, the Condé faction superimposed its own military organization on the purely religious organization of the French Calvinist churches. This naturally transformed the character both of French Calvinism and of its relationship to the Crown. Instead of turning instinctively to royal officials, who in any event were increasingly incapable of protecting them, the churches now looked to Condé and his client nobles for support. This in turn weakened the influence both of the ministers and of Geneva, which fought a long but losing battle to prevent all authority from slipping from its grasp. The ministers, who had no doubt failed to foresee the consequences when they first appealed to the nobles for help, now saw themselves increasingly pushed aside in the government of their churches, which were becoming the instruments of a dissident noble faction. This capitulation of the churches to the Bourbon connection might have culminated in the total subordination of religious to political ends, had it not been for the religious integrity of a section of the nobility, and especially of Admiral Coligny, who never lost sight of what was to him the prime purpose of the revolt – the salvation of God's church. It was Coligny, more than any other man, who held the political and religious movements together, and prevented secular ambitions from irrevocably distorting an authentic religious cause.

In the long run, for all Coligny's efforts, the close association of the churches with an armed aristocratic faction did irrevocable harm to the Calvinist movement in France. The churches depended on the towns rather than the aristocracy for the bulk of their supporters, and the capture of the churches by nobles – some of them little better than gangsters – inevitably lessened the Calvinist appeal to men of sincerity and conviction, and helped to check the movement towards conversion which had been gathering momentum in the later 1550s. But in the short run the alliance of the Calvinist churches with Condé proved of undeniable benefit to both. The churches gained military protection on a national scale at a moment when the power of the Guises threatened them with extinction. For his part, Condé gained an instrument of extraordinary civil and military effectiveness for the advancement of his aims.

It soon became clear that the close-knit organization of the Huguenot churches made them ideally suited to the work of subversion and revolt. While the governors of the provinces, lacking any consistent instructions from the court, watched the development of events with indifference or prudently hedged their bets, the Huguenots had ample opportunity to infiltrate and subvert. By systematically gaining control of public offices they were able to build up a hierarchy of Huguenot office-holders alongside that of the Crown. Wherever possible, also, they seized control of municipal and provincial government. A classic example of their technique is provided by the seizure of Lyons at the very beginning of the war. This was planned and organized, to Calvin's distress, by the local ministers. Once the city was in their hands, they systematically set about the stripping of the churches, the expulsion of monks and nuns, and the installation of Huguenot officials in the municipal administration. Whatever the propriety of the methods, there could be no denying the value of the results. The possession of Lyons, a leading centre of international finance, did much to facilitate the raising of loans for the Huguenot campaigns. Condé could count, too, on financial support from Calvinist bankers and merchants, and on the voluntary contributions of the churches.

The militant spirit of the churches was never better expressed than by the Calvinist community of Valenciennes, over the border in Hainault. 'We are determined', they declared in 1562, 'to endure and remain constant in and for the name of Jesus Christ; otherwise, if we turn against the faith, we shall never enter the kingdom of heaven.'[6] The French Calvinists shared this passionate determination to remain constant to the end in the defence of a cause to which they felt themselves summoned by God; and they proved themselves adept in finding practical means to further His special purposes. In particular, it was by the intelligent exploitation of their religious organization that they were able to mobilize with exemplary speed an army for Condé's use. The royal army, which was under Guise control, was essentially a mercenary army, with the characteristic defects of such a body. Condé's army, on the other hand – although reinforced by foreign mercenary regiments – was primarily dependent on the troops provided by the churches.

These troops were soon being levied on a systematic basis.[7] While ministers would exhort their flocks from the pulpit to rally to Condé's forces, a system of conscription was devised which took into account the size of a population. Each parish was expected to furnish its quota of troops, known as an 'ensign', and the ensigns recruited from the parishes forming a 'colloquy' were combined in regiments, of which some joined the army while others were detailed for home defence. These regiments, drawn largely from the ranks of the urban artisans, were of high quality, and their leaders had none of the hesitations about arming them which were customary in sixteenth-century Europe. Ordinarily, the development of a national infantry force tended to be inhibited by fears of the dangerous consequences that might follow from the indiscriminate arming of the lower orders of society. It was typical, for instance, that in the royal armies one half of the troops were cavalry. In the Huguenot armies, on the other hand, there were three infantrymen to every cavalryman, and the commanders depended primarily on the fire-power of their light infantry regiments, armed with arquebuses. They had at their disposal a large force of men – their army in 1569 was 25,000 men strong, of whom 14,000 were native Frenchmen – and these men were fighting for a cause in which they passionately believed. It was a formidable army which marched into battle singing the Psalms as translated by Marot and Beza, and especially that most famous of all Beza's Psalms, 'Que Dieu se montre seulement'.

The same spirit was shown by the Huguenot fleet which was created at La Rochelle during the course of the 1560s. Many of the sailors in the French Atlantic ports had developed their navigational and fighting skills, and sharpened their hatred of Catholicism, in sorties into the Spanish Atlantic and Caribbean during the years of the Franco-Spanish conflict. These men provided the recruits for the fleet of forty sail under the command of Jacques de Sores. The fleet patrolled the coast from Cap Gris-Nez to Bayonne, and it played a vital part in the Huguenot war effort by disrupting the enemy's maritime routes, protecting Protestant shipping and the salt supplies for the Netherlands, and keeping open the lines of communication between La Rochelle and Protestant England.

Between 1562 and 1570 these military and naval forces helped to maintain the Huguenot cause during three periods of open warfare, in which it became increasingly apparent that Calvinism did not command, and had less and less hope of commanding, the allegiance of the majority of Frenchmen. The first war, beginning in April 1562 and ending with the Pacification of Amboise of 19 March 1563, was fought primarily in the valley of the Loire between the troops of Condé and Coligny, based on Orléans, and those of Guise and Montmorency, with their headquarters at Paris. Fortunately for Catherine, the war neatly disposed of some of the faction-leaders most responsible for her political embarrassments. The king of Navarre died of his wounds in November 1562. Condé and Montmorency were taken prisoner at the battle of Dreux.[8] The duke of Guise, more ominously, was assassinated by a Protestant fanatic while besieging Orléans in February 1563. In the years to come, the murder of Guise would prove a potent new source of bitterness and tension, for Coligny, although officially exonerated in 1565 of complicity in the crime, had rejoiced at the event, and continued to be held responsible by Guise's family and supporters. But, in the short term, the death of Guise and the removal of so many leaders smoothed the way for a settlement. Catherine seized the opportunity to carry through the Edict of Amboise, which – while recognizing freedom of conscience to all her subjects – drew a distinction between nobles, who were allowed absolute freedom of worship, and the rest of the Huguenots, whose worship was restricted to one town in every *bailliage*.

The Peace of Amboise was followed by a period of supposed national reconciliation, during which both parties united to recover Le Havre from the English. But the truce remained uneasy, and Catherine, with typical flair for dramatizing the majesty of kingship, set out in May 1564 on a great royal progress through France with the young Charles IX, whose majority had been declared nine months before. The queen-mother moved slowly, in great state, and deliberately used spectacular masques and festivals to bring the rival factions together and preach the virtues of peace. The climax came at Bayonne in the summer of 1565, where Catherine was reunited with her daughter Elizabeth of Valois, the queen of Spain, whom she had not seen since her marriage to Philip II in 1559. As a spectacle, the meeting of the Spanish and French courts was an unparalleled success. But politically it was a disaster. Instead of coming himself, Philip II sent the duke of Alba to represent him. Not only did Alba's meetings with Catherine fail to re-establish the close Franco-Spanish relationship momentarily achieved after the signing of Cateau-Cambrésis; they also led to dark suspicions among the Huguenots that the Catholic monarchies were hatching a plot against them and against their brethren in other parts of Europe.

The worst Protestant fears about the interview of Bayonne seemed fully confirmed when the duke of Alba himself headed the army sent by Philip to stamp out religious dissidence in the Netherlands. Anxious to seize the initiative before it was too late, Condé took to arms again in the late summer of 1567, and attempted, without success, to capture Catherine and the king at Meaux. This time the Huguenot forces were joined by a formidable body of German *reiter* under the command of John Casimir, the second son of Frederick the Elector Palatine, whose original scruples about aiding rebellion had been banished by what seemed to be mounting evidence of a grand popish design. Already, then, the French civil wars were showing signs of developing into an international conflict. But this second religious war, during which the old Constable Montmorency was killed, came to a swift conclusion with the peace of Longjumeau of March 1568.

The peace, however, proved even shorter than the war that preceded it. Catherine had been finally alienated from the Huguenots by Condé's attempted *coup*, and was becoming disillusioned with her policy of conciliation. Under the growing influence of the cardinal of Lorraine the king dismissed his chancellor L'Hôpital, the symbol of moderation. The Guises were back in power; the king's younger brother, the duke of Anjou, was urging tough action against the rebels; and in September 1568 both parties took to arms again. In the third and fiercest of the religious wars, which lasted until August 1570, Anjou defeated the Huguenots at two major battles, Jarnac and Montcontour, and gained in the process a spurious reputation as a great commander.

The Huguenots had never suffered such reverses as those of 1569. Condé himself was killed at Jarnac in March, and the leadership of the Huguenot movement devolved on Coligny. But, under Coligny's direction, the movement weathered the storm, and acquired a new unity and cohesion. This nearly great man – symbolized for contemporaries by the inseparable toothpick, stuck in his beard or behind his ear[9] – succeeded in capturing popular respect and admiration as Condé never could. No doubt he was lacking in subtlety, and in a certain political sense. He was prone to meet difficulties by directly confronting them, where others would have tried to outflank them. But this was perhaps a defect of his qualities, as a man of rock-like constancy, a thoughtful, austere and slightly solitary figure, who lived for his faith and his country, and was incapable of guile.

Coligny was a natural leader, with the unique gift of being able to win and to keep the confidence both of the gentry and of the churches. He had also achieved a close working relationship with Beza and with Jeanne d'Albret, the widowed queen of Navarre. As a commander, he proved singularly incapable of winning large-scale battles, but displayed outstanding gifts as a strategist. During 1569, when the Huguenots were heavily pressed, he conducted a skilful and highly mobile campaign in Languedoc, while the best of his lieutenants, François de La Noue, succeeded in consolidating the Huguenot position in Poitou. Between them, Coligny and La Noue saved the Huguenots from defeat. By the summer of 1570, it was clear that the royal armies – badly led, and, as usual, short of money – had dismally failed to exploit the victories of 1569, and both sides were now desperate for a settlement. The peace of Saint-Germain, concluded on 8 August, was by no means unfavourable to the Huguenots, and it introduced the novelty of allowing them to garrison four towns as a security (*de sûreté*) – Cognac, La Charité, Montauban and La Rochelle. As the Guises departed from court in disapproval of Catherine's return to a moderate line, it seemed that, after eight years of alternating war and truce, the Huguenots, if they had not achieved victory, had at least not fought in vain.

3 The Revolt of the Netherlands

The experiences of the Huguenots in the France of the 1560s showed how much more could be achieved by minority religious and political movements working in unison than by either acting alone. The aristocratic opposition to the Guises had cast a protective cloak over the persecuted Calvinist churches, while the churches in turn had given the Condé faction a broad basis of popular support and the great benefit of being able to draw on the varied resources of a national – and international – organization. In the Spanish Netherlands, however, the alliance between aristocratic opposition and militant Calvinism was much slower in the making than in France, and, even when achieved, it wore its similarities with a difference. This was only to be expected, for although there were some curious parallels between the situation in France and the Netherlands at the beginning of the 1560s, the resemblances were often no more than superficial.

Politically, it was an odd coincidence that both France and the Netherlands were governed in the early 1560s by women regents. Margaret of Parma, who had been left in charge of the government on Philip's departure from the Netherlands in 1559, found herself faced by much the same kind of problems as Catherine: a decline in the authority and prestige of the Crown, an empty treasury, fractious and difficult Estates, and a divided upper nobility anxious to capture control of the royal administration. There was, however, one essential difference between the régimes in France and the Netherlands which profoundly affected the respective characters of their political opposition. Catherine herself was half foreign, but she headed a royal government which remained a symbol of national unity in a divided country. Margaret, as the daughter of Charles V and a Flemish woman, was a Netherlander by birth; but she headed a royal government which was increasingly regarded as alien. This proved in the long run to be a fact of incalculable importance, for it allowed the opposition to appear – as it could never convincingly appear in the France of the 1560s – as the defender of national traditions against foreign innovations.

The religious situation, too, seemed at first sight strikingly similar. The governments of both countries had been thrown onto the defensive by the spread of heresy, and particularly in the last few years, by the increased activity and success of the Calvinists. Again, however, there were differences. Already by 1560 Calvinism in France was well established and had developed a nation-wide organization. But in the Netherlands it was still at this moment at an unformed stage, and highly localized. The total number of active Protestants remained small – perhaps not much more than 5% of the population – and of these the Calvinists, for all the activity of Guy de Brès and his friends, were as yet but a tiny minority. Anabaptism, which had won many adherents in the early 1530s, still had a sizeable following, especially in the northern provinces of Holland, Zealand, Groningen and Overijssel. In these provinces, which were one day to be the bastions of revolt, the influence of Calvinism was for a long time remarkably slight. Its impact was largely confined in the opening years of the decade to the towns of the industrial south – the region which, by one of the great ironies of the revolt of the Netherlands, would end by affirming its allegiance to Spain and to Rome.

The progress of Calvinism in the Netherlands may to some extent have been hindered by the fact that other forms of Protestantism, especially Lutheranism and Anabaptism, had already succeeded in entrenching themselves, in spite of persecution. The Calvinists were being held in check, too, by the repressive measures of the authorities. But, in spite of this, their preachers in the southern towns were beginning to attract support by playing on the anti-clerical sentiments of the urban population. There was no comparison, however, between the solidly-based Calvinist church organization in the France of the early 1560s and the still embryonic movement in Hainault, Brabant and Flanders. Nor was there yet any parallel in the Netherlands to the mass conversion of nobles and gentry which had transformed the character and prospects of the Calvinist churches in France. The governing classes in the Netherlands were strongly imbued with humanist and anti-clerical traditions; and although Calvinism was soon beginning to win converts among them, there were many who seem to have found the new faith excessively intolerant and authoritarian, and eventually adopted it only under the pressure of circumstances – and then with reservations.

In so far as the higher nobility held views about the worsening religious situation in the Netherlands, these tended to be in favour of moderation. Many of them had close ties with the nobility of the Empire, and the German solution of *cuius regio eius religio* was naturally attractive to them. But in the early 1560s they were less concerned with religious than political affairs. The wealthiest and most influential of the magnates, William of Nassau, prince of Orange, was no doubt disturbed by the religious tensions in his country, but he made no public protest against persecution until the end of 1564. Whatever their private views, he and his fellow-magnates seem to have been devoting their principal energies at this moment to imposing their wishes on a government which was proving much less amenable than they had originally hoped and expected.

The Council of State set up by Philip in 1559 to give advice to Margaret of Parma, included the prince of Orange, the count of Egmont, a Frisian lawyer, Viglius, a penurious Walloon noble, Berlaymont, and Antoine Perrenot, bishop of Arras, who was raised to the purple as cardinal Granvelle in 1561. Although Margaret herself was no cypher, Perrenot was the dominant figure in this company. It was he who made the important decisions, either on his own, or in consultation with Viglius.

There was no denying Granvelle's outstanding abilities, or his unfailing loyalty to his master, Philip II. No doubt, like his contemporaries in high places, he knew how to take advantage of the opportunities that came his way. Always uneasily aware of his social origins (his great-grandfather was a blacksmith of Besançon, his grandfather a notary, his father at first a notary and later the principal councillor of the Emperor Charles V) he was determined to live, and be seen to live, like a lord. He owned fine town houses and country palaces in the Netherlands and in his native Franche-Comté, collected pictures and books and statues, and entertained on a lavish scale out of his copious ecclesiastical rents. His interest in religion seems to have been decidedly temperate; he disliked all forms of fanaticism, believed that the best means of defence against Protestantism lay in a spiritual regeneration of the Roman Church, and was closer in spirit to Erasmus than to the violent religious partisans of his own generation. This itself was typical of the man. By temperament and training he belonged to an age that was past – the age of Charles V – and he never quite succeeded in adapting himself to the spirit or the methods of Philip II. His outlook on the problem of the Netherlands was Burgundian rather than Spanish, and his ideal was the firm but by no means inflexible system of government pursued in the Netherlands by Charles V's sister, Mary of Hungary – a system which was designed to reduce by cautious stages the autonomy of the seventeen provinces and to build up the royal administration as an effective centralizing power.

To provide vigorous and efficient government in the conditions of the early 1560s was by no means an easy task. There was resentment that the king had abandoned the country, while the *tercio* of Spanish soldiers, brought to Flanders in 1553, was left behind. Financial and religious difficulties were growing, and the government was being undermined by the faction struggles of the higher nobility feuding to gain control of the offices of State. Margaret and Granvelle enjoyed the support of the duke of Aerschot, the head of the Walloon house of Croy; but a rival group consisting of Orange and Egmont, count Horn and the baron of Montigny, was displaying increasing signs of antagonism to the régime of cardinal Granvelle.

Whatever their political relationship, Orange and Granvelle remained on good personal terms until 1561. Their two families had a long-standing association, based on common interests in the Franche-Comté and at court, and it took a number of events, both political and personal, to end the friendship between them. Orange, for all his charm and exquisite courtesy, was a complex personality, whose intelligence and ability Granvelle consistently underrated. Highly sensitive to his own dignity and reputation, he resented Granvelle's methods of personal government and his own exclusion from vital decisions of State. Gradually, as the two men came into conflict on a widening range of issues, he began to identity Granvelle as the symbol of an absolutist system of government which would by degrees erode the rights and privileges of the Netherlands nobility and people.

What exactly precipitated the final break has never been entirely clear. Orange was annoyed by the cardinal's open disapproval of his marriage in 1561 to Anne, the daughter and heiress of that celebrated Lutheran, the Elector Maurice of Saxony. He also came into open conflict with Granvelle in the same year over a vacancy in the governorship of the Franche-Comté, where both men had important interests. Since 1559 an egregious character, Simon Renard – like Granvelle a Burgundian, and a former Imperial ambassador to England and France – had been conducting in the Franche-Comté a private campaign against Granvelle, who had formerly been his benefactor but had failed to get him appointed to the council of State. In the course of his intrigue he cultivated and won the friendship of

Egmont and Orange, whose influence he saw as a possible counter-balance to that of the Granvellistes in the Franche-Comté administration. On the governor's death in 1561, Orange, at Renard's instigation, demanded the succession for himself, knowing that it would otherwise go to a local noble belonging to the Granvelle connection. Although a compromise was eventually reached under Margaret's influence, the whole affair helped to widen the rift between Orange and the cardinal.

The event in 1561 which overshadowed all others, however, was the publication of a papal bull which made clear Philip's determination to proceed with plans for a radical ecclesiastical reorganization in the Netherlands. As long ago as 1525, and then again in 1551–1552, proposals had been made for an increase in the number of bishops and a reduction of foreign ecclesiastical authority, in order to strengthen the Netherlands church against the rising tide of heresy. When Charles V transferred government in the Netherlands to his son in 1555, nothing had yet been done, but Philip made it clear from the first that he intended to continue and expand his father's war on the heretics. The Jesuits were allowed to establish themselves in the Low Countries in 1556. The Placards, or edicts, against the heretics were rigorously enforced by the local Inquisition – in some ways more obnoxious than the Spanish variety, because it condemned to death even the penitent heretic. In 1559 a papal bull was secured for the foundation of a new university at Douai, which would in due course play a great part in the revival of Netherlands Catholicism. And a further bull in the same year prepared the way for the reorganization of the bishoprics.

By the terms of the 1559 and 1561 bulls, fourteen new dioceses were to be added to the four already in existence. Instead of forming part of the ecclesiastical provinces of Rheims and Cologne, the Netherlands would in future be divided into three independent provinces under the archbishops of Cambrai, Utrecht, and Malines. The new sees would be endowed out of the revenues of a number of wealthy abbeys, and the bishops and the principal canons would be chosen by the king from among qualified theologians and canon lawyers. The scheme was eminently rational, and like many such schemes it at once ran into every kind of difficulty. The nobles saw their younger sons ousted from lucrative ecclesiastical sinecures by lawyers and low-born clerics. Egmont and Orange saw Granvelle, as archbishop of Malines and a cardinal of the church, take precedence over them at the council table, instead of occupying the fourth place, as hitherto. The Estates of Brabant saw their three abbots being replaced by three royalist bishops, headed by the bishop who became abbot of Affligem – none other than cardinal Granvelle. Here surely was proof enough of the sinister intentions of the government – its determination to interfere with sacrosanct property rights, to exercise arbitrary power and to ride roughshod over privilege.

The unfortunate Granvelle, who held no brief for the ecclesiastical reorganization and had done what he could to delay it, now found himself made the scapegoat for the sins of his royal master. It was a normal enough practice to blame the king's evil counsellors, rather than the king himself, for unpopular decisions and policies; but the tendency may well have been intensified in the Netherlands by the fact that the king was an absentee. In an age when kingship was still intensely personal in character, an absentee king was a contradiction in terms, and his absence demanded of a traditionally-minded nobility difficult psychological adjustments. Almost as if in compensation for his absence, the Netherlands nobility – and not least Orange himself – displayed, and seem to have felt, an intense personal loyalty towards Philip II. But there remained a vacuum which Margaret, who anyhow lacked regal dignity, proved incapable of filling. Now, in 1561, the bitterness of a deprived and disillusioned aristocracy, and the anger of the Estates, overflowed into vituperation against all things Spanish, and a campaign of hatred and vilification against the absent king's principal minister.

Granvelle himself manoeuvred as best he could to further his master's policies while preserving his own position. He induced Philip to withdraw the Spanish *terico* from the Netherlands, but still found himself denounced and caricatured for his pains as a 'red devil' and a 'Spanish pig'. The great nobles themselves, under Orange's leadership, formed a league against him, and sent one of their number, Montigny, to the Spanish court in the autumn of 1562 to petition for his removal. When Montigny returned from his mission empty-handed, Orange and Egmont withdrew, in March 1563, from meetings of the Council of State. But their public expressions of disapproval for Granvelle might not have achieved very much had these not been supported by some active lobbying in Madrid by the ubiquitous Simon Renard, now the grand manager of a great anti-Granvelle campaign that was being simultaneously conducted in the Franche-Comté, the Netherlands and the court. In the end, despite the duke of Alba's pleas that he should hold firm, Philip yielded to the pressure and decided to part with his minister. A secret letter of 22 January 1564 gave Granvelle permission to leave the Netherlands 'for some time' (it proved to be for ever) in order to visit his mother at Besançon. The Granvelle régime was over; the victory of the Estates and the magnates complete.

The great aristocrats of the Netherlands had achieved the ambition of all great aristocrats – control of the royal administration. They were not, however, notably successful in the exercise of their new-found power. Faction-feuds continued unabated, and the Estates proved no more willing to vote taxes for the new régime than the old. Their position was made more difficult by the fact that a recent suspension of imports of unworked cloth from England had raised the level of unemployment and given rise to growing social distress. Popular unrest and religious enthusiasm traditionally went hand in hand in the Netherlands, and 1564 was no exception. Encouraged by the weakness of the new government, the Calvinist ministers began holding open-air meetings to which large crowds were attracted.

The emergence of militant Calvinists urging active resistance to the Placards and the Inquisition placed the Council of State in a very delicate position. If it enforced the anti-heresy legislation it would alienate the people; but if it relaxed the persecution it would antagonize the king. It seems to have been at this point that Orange, still nominally a Roman Catholic (unlike his younger brother, Louis of Nassau, who had been brought up as a Lutheran),[10] first began to see himself cast in the role of protector of the Protestants. It might perhaps be possible to introduce into the Netherlands some form of toleration; but in August 1564 orders arrived from Philip II for the promulgation of the decrees of the Council of Trent. If the Tridentine decrees of the were enforced, toleration would be out of the question. The execution of Philip's orders was therefore deliberately delayed by the Council of State, while the various provinces insisted that there should be no enforcement without express safeguards for their privileges. Egmont was now sent on a mission to the Spanish court to plead for a moderation of the king's religious policies, and a great debate on the question of toleration began both in the Netherlands and Madrid. The theologians advising Philip II were apparently not as hostile to the idea of toleration as might have been expected, but the king remained unconvinced; and a second meeting of theologians held in Brussels after Egmont's return rejected toleration on the grounds that the existence of two religious in a single State must lead it to disaster.

Throughout 1565 and 1566 Orange and his partisans continued to press, by means of petitions and pamphlets, for some form of religious liberty. While there was a strong liberal tradition in the Netherlands, the demand for toleration at this moment seems to have owed more to immediate tactical considerations than to a belief in its intrinsic virtues. Already in France, about the year 1564, the term *'politique'* had come into use to describe the growing body of middle-of-the-road opinion which, while holding no brief for the new religious doctrines, considered that repression would only precipitate the very disasters it was designed to avert. Catherine de Medici and her chancellor L'Hôpital, by permitting Huguenot worship in a Catholic State, were in effect drawing the distinction between citizenship and religious orthodoxy which lay at the heart of *politique* thought. In appealing for toleration, Orange was profoundly influenced by the French example – notably by the Edict of Amboise of 1563 – and also by the Augsburg formula, which he thought might be extended to the Netherlands through the influence of his friends in the Empire.

Unfortunately for Orange, however, Philip's reactions were very different from the reactions of Catherine and L'Hôpital. In his famous letters written from his country house in the woods of Segovia in October 1565, Philip instructed Margaret that the Placards against the heretics should be enforced, and that the Inquisition should punish offenders rigorously. It was not surprising that a distressed and worried Margaret should have taken a week to summon up the courage to reveal the king's instructions. Her fears were fully justified, for the news of the orders from Spain sent a shock-wave of indignation and anger through an already restive country. The rising hatred of Spain and the Inquisition was vigorously exploited by the Calvinist preachers, and may have drawn fresh strength from gruesome tales of the Spanish Inquisition sedulously propagated by the small group of *Marranos* – Iberian Jews – who had made their home in the Netherlands.[11] For the first time, too, the lesser nobility, as distinct from the magnates, made their presence effectively felt. During the festivities held in Brussels in November for the marriage of Margaret's son, Alexander Farnese, to Maria of Portugal, a group of nobles, including the Calvinist brothers Jean and Philippe de Marnix, and that blustering buccaneer the count of Brederode, met together in company with Louis of Nassau to plan their programme of action. The result of this and further meetings was the formation of a Compromise, or league, of nobles – Catholic as well as Protestant – who demanded in an open letter to the king an end to the Inquisition's activities, and a change of religious policy.

The combination of popular discontent and organized aristocratic protest made Margaret's position critical. At the end of March 1566 she summoned a great meeting of notables to seek their advice. On 3 April the confederate nobles, some two hundred strong, rode together into Brussels; and on the 5th a group of them went in procession to the palace to present their formal request to the Governess. As Margaret, troubled, received them, her councillor Berlaymont hastened to reassure her. There was, he said, no need to fear these beggars – 'ces gueux'. Although most of the nobles were Dutch-speaking, the French name stuck. At the fateful banquet held on 8 April to celebrate Margaret's agreement to suspend the persecution until the arrival of fresh instructions, the confederate leader Brederode gave the toast: 'Vivent les Gueux'. Egmont, Orange and Horn, all of whom had held aloof from the Compromise, unwisely dropped in on the noisy celebrations, and heard their own names coupled with the toast. 'Vive le prince d'Orange! Vive Egmont! Vivent les Gueux!' At this moment their own fate was sealed, and the myth of the *Gueux* was born.

When Granvelle, now in Rome, heard the news of the Compromise, he drew a natural deduction. 'The style,' he wrote, 'is borrowed from that of the League which the Huguenots have made in France, and for the same ends.' The comparison was just, in so far as the royal authority was being openly challenged in both countries by an organized movement of opposition consisting of nobles from widely different regions. But there was also an important difference, in that the French aristocratic opposition was composed of nobles most of whom were at least nominally Calvinists, whereas the Netherlands League contained members of every faith, and had no formal association with the Calvinist cause. The crucial question in the Netherlands in the tense spring and summer months of 1566 was therefore whether the aristocratic opposition would make common cause with the religious opposition, as in France. Already there were indications that the more radical section of the League would be willing to join forces with the Calvinist communities. If this policy should command general support, Margaret would find herself in as serious trouble as Catherine and Charles IX.

The crisis of royal authority was now unmistakable, and it was at this moment that the populace rebelled. Economic conditions in the Netherlands during the past three years had been bad. The outbreak of the Northern Seven Years War in 1563[12] had hurt the Baltic trade and closed the Sound to shipping, while commercial and political difficulties with England had disrupted the trade in English cloths and thrown many wage-earners out of work. On top of this came hunger. The winter of 1565–1566 was unusually severe. Bitter frosts continued into February, and the Swedish–Danish conflict kept two hundred grain ships tied up in Danzig, waiting for permission to pass through the Sound. By the spring of 1566, when the grain-ships had at last arrived and the price of bread began to fall, the misery of the winter months had produced much bitterness and suffering in the textile towns of the southern Netherlands, and had provided Calvinist preachers with ready-made and receptive audiences.

The protest, when it came, however, seems to have been born less of total and unbearable misery than of a deep fear for the loss of recently hard-won gains. The famine of 1565–1566 was less sharp than that of 1556–1557, which had been followed by a general rise in wages. At least in Antwerp the acute labour shortage had prevented any reduction of wages at the end of the 1550s; and since corn prices at this time were low, there was a substantial improvement in living-standards, which was maintained at least to the end of 1562. Employers were by now complaining of the high wage-rates, but as economic troubles and unemployment mounted in the following years, the position began to change. In good times, expenditure on food consumed something like 30–40% of an Antwerp wage-earner's income. In bad times, the figure could rise to over 80%, and butter and meat gave way to a less varied diet of cheaper foods, like vegetables and rye.[13] Now, in 1566, skilled artisans saw their wages falling and their new living standards threatened. They were still better off than their fathers in the reign of Charles V; but perhaps for this very reason they were not prepared to accept without protest a fall in their standard of living.

The political and religious situation, too, was very different from that at the time of the Anabaptist troubles in the early years of Charles V. Then, an under-nourished, under-employed and under-paid populace, led by visionaries with apocalyptic yearnings, had found themselves confronted by the power of the State, supported by a united ruling class which would on no account tolerate any violent alteration of the existing order. Now, the populace was led by trained Calvinist ministers, with immediate objectives that could be secured by practical means; the authority of the State had virtually ceased to exist; and the governing class itself was in open opposition to the religious and political policies of the Spanish Crown.

The moment was therefore highly propitious for a Calvinist attempt to overthrow the old religious order – an attempt which, in spite of Orange's warnings, would certainly command the support of at least a section of the nobility. But there seems to be no evidence of collusion at this moment between the Calvinists of France and the Netherlands. How far, then, the events of August 1566 were the outcome of organization, and how far of a spontaneous movement among the people, will probably never be known.

Everyone knew that trouble was coming. In June and early July the crowds which turned out to hear the preachers in Flemish towns and villages were swelling day by day. While armed men kept guard against a possible intervention by the magistrates, the preachers excited their hearers with fiery denunciations of clerical riches, and of the idolatry practised in the churches. Margaret of Parma sent urgent messages to the towns to organize their defences and place a guard on the churches, but the response in town after town was lukewarm. In Ghent, which seems to have been reasonably typical,[14] the magistrates were drawn from a closed and exclusive caste, which commanded no sympathy among the citizens at large. The members of the special militia recruited from the craft guilds were ready enough, at the magistrates' request, to take an oath of loyalty to the government, but as soon as they were asked to commit themselves to defending the churches, the prevarications and excuses began. Out of 1767 men whose response is known, only 332 – 18% – declared themselves ready to do everything in their power to defend the Catholic clergy in the event of an attack. It seems clear enough that the Roman Church had lost the allegiance of the mass of the population in the towns and villages of Flanders, before the Calvinists ever arrived.

The overwhelmingly anti-clerical sentiments of the population made Flanders fertile ground for the preachers. They were beginning to win converts, especially among the middling and upper ranks of the citizens: skilled craftsmen, shopkeepers, lawyers and wealthy merchants. Of the 12,000 households in Ghent, some 1500 – or 13% – could be classed as Calvinist by 1566–1567. But in addition to the hard core of converts, the preachers could count on the sympathy and goodwill of a large proportion of the population, which was either hostile to Catholicism or religiously indifferent, and which hated the clergy, as it hated the magistrates, for their arrogance and their wealth.

At the lowest level of this population were the outcasts, the paupers and the unemployed. These too had been touched by the words of the preachers, which gave them a glimmer of hope. In August, as corn prices started rising again, their anger was suddenly unleashed. On 10 August at Steenvoorde in west Flanders, a frenzied mob surged into the churches, smashing the abominable images and looting the gold and silver ornaments. The iconoclastic fury spread onwards and outwards, from village to village and town to town, reaching Antwerp on 20 August, Ghent and Amsterdam on the 23rd. There were convinced Calvinists and agitators among the iconoclasts, but they were acting against the orders and wishes of the ministers. This was essentially a spontaneous revolt of the people outside the structure of corporate municipal life, of casual labourers in the building and textile industries, and of the exploited and the oppressed.

While the frenzied mobs sacked and desecrated the churches, the magistrates in many towns looked on, too frightened to intervene, although resolute action by a united city government sensitive to popular aspirations might help to save a town from the iconoclastic fury, as it did in Lille. Nor could Margaret of Parma, without troops, and uncertain of the loyalty of the ruling classes, take any immediate action. But it was clear that many of the more moderate members of the Compromise were terrified by the violence of the popular insurrection. In order to gain time, and to rally moderate opinion around her, Margaret agreed on 23 August to an 'Accord' with the leaders of the Compromise, by which persecution would be suspended if Catholic worship was left unmolested and the people laid down their arms.

William of Orange, who had been sent by the Governess, with some hesitation, to help keep order in Antwerp, knew that the time was short. His immediate aim was to widen the Accord into a formal religious peace between Calvinists, Catholics and Lutherans. The inclusion of the Lutherans was essential, partly because it would encourage the Lutheran princes of Germany to throw their weight behind his compromise solution, but also because the increasing tension between Lutherans and Calvinists in the Netherlands was threatening to dissolve the fragile unity of the movement against the régime. In Antwerp during the autumn, Marcus Pérez, a wealthy *Marrano* merchant who had become a Calvinist convert, worked desperately with a number of liberally-minded fellow Calvinists to maintain a dialogue with the Lutherans. But the continuing violence of the radical Calvinists and their intolerance of worship in any churches other than their own made his task impossible.

On hearing the news of the Accord, cardinal Granvelle wrote to the king in September warning him that 'the French expedient of allowing two religions' in one State would destroy the Roman Church in the Netherlands. Neither Philip nor Margaret, however, attached much weight to an agreement extracted under duress, and they knew that the violence of the Calvinist supporters was playing into their hands. Margaret, after a momentary panic, was recovering her courage under the steadying influence of a member of the older generation of Burgundian nobles, count Mansfeld, a devout Catholic who now became her most trusted adviser. With the arrival of money from Spain she was able to raise troops to deal with the armed bands of insurgents under Brederode's command. As the Governess reasserted her authority, the ruling classes rallied round – especially the Walloon nobility, who assisted in hunting down the roaming bands of iconoclasts and rebels, and in laying siege to the Calvinists of Valenciennes. In the meantime, the opposition was being isolated and divided, as Margaret and Mansfeld had planned. Moderate opinion was outraged by the continuing Calvinist excesses. Orange, unwilling to identify himself with the Calvinists, would make no move unless he could be sure of help from the German princes. Egmont, too confident of royal good faith, was veering back to the régime. With the movement so divided and leaderless, its defeat could only be a question of time.

In February 1567 the rebels made their last desperate bid for success. But Orange refused to open the gates of Antwerp to them, and the Lutherans and Catholics in the city joined forces against the Calvinist insurgents. On 13 March Jean de Marnix's rebel forces were cut down by government troops and their Antwerp supporters in open country outside Antwerp, at Osterweel. Soon afterwards, Valenciennes surrendered after enduring a three months' siege, and Guy de Brès, who had inspired its resistance, was hanged.

William of Orange's personal position was now exceptionally dangerous and difficult. His equivocal attitude had made him appear a traitor both in the eyes of the Governess and of the Calvinists. He felt unable to take a fresh oath of loyalty to the Crown. And rumours were rife that Alba would soon be sent with an army to the

Netherlands to put down the revolt. In February the dying landgrave of Hesse had sent urgent warning to William and Louis of Nassau to put no trust in the Spaniards, and least of all in the duke of Alba, whom he had seen at work in Germany in 1547. William took the hint, and prudently retired in April into voluntary exile at his German home in Dillenberg.

Orange was not the only man to leave the country. A number of armed bands continued to hold out, concealed in the forests, but Brederode fled to Germany, where many of his supporters joined him. During the spring and summer of 1567 a stream of refugees flowed out of the Netherlands, to seek shelter in Emden, Cologne, France or England. Drawn from all classes of Netherlands society, they had either been actively involved in the rebellion or were convinced Calvinists who feared for the future of their faith and their country. Their emigration was vivid testimony to the decisiveness of their defeat. It seemed that the revolt of the Netherlands was over, almost before it had ever begun.

The reasons for the failure of the opposition movement in the Netherlands were to be found at the very point where the movement in France had achieved success – at the point where aristocratic and religious opposition met. In France, the Calvinists and the nobility had been welded into a single movement of revolt, largely because each had need of the other in the face of determined opponents. But in the Netherlands, the religious movement had slipped at an early stage from the grasp of the nobility; an isolated régime had given way at the crucial moment; and militant Calvinism had become so wildly uncontrollable as to forfeit public sympathy, and so deprive itself of any chance of success. Only very severe repression was likely to bring the patricians and popular Calvinism together again in an alliance based – however precariously – on the recognition of mutual needs. But severe repression was hardly necessary; Margaret had done what had to be done. Despite her success, however, Alba left Spain for Italy in April 1567. His mission was to assemble the *tercios* at Milan and lead them up to Flanders. Philip, it seemed, was not prepared to run the risk – however slight – of seeing one of his own dominions turned into another France or Scotland. The iconoclasts were to be punished, and rebellious and heretical subjects would be treated to the fate that they deserved.

5

Catholicism and Repression

1   The Council of Trent and the Catholic Reformation

'The Catholic religion should defend itself unstintingly, but it will achieve better results by preaching, by the reform of discipline and the good example of the clergy, than by force of arms.'[1] Cardinal Granvelle wrote these words in 1583, long after the duke of Alba's policy of repression in the Netherlands had collapsed in ruins. But in the early 1560s, when both France and the Netherlands were falling prey to heresy, the Roman church was simply not equipped to defend itself in the way that Granvelle suggested. Admittedly, the winds of reform had begun to blow, even in Rome itself. The new religious orders had already begun to make their mark, and the Jesuits in particular had become a powerful force for religious revival by the time of Loyola's death in 1556. The church had made some progress, too, in defining at the first sessions of the Council of Trent the dogmas which divided it from the Protestants. But when the Council re-opened on 18 January 1562, a vast amount still remained to be done, and the prospects were not very hopeful.

There were 109 bishops present at the opening session, and these were almost exclusively of Italian or Iberian origin (86 Italians, 13 Spaniards, 3 Portuguese), for it was not until November that the cardinal of Lorraine arrived like a Renaissance prince with his phalanx of French bishops, acting for all the world as if he had won instead of lost his battle against the resumption of the Council. The cardinal's arrival merely served to sharpen the divisions in a Council that was already bitterly divided. Ranged against the little group of moderates who had first begun the battle for ecclesiastical reform during the long pontificate of Paul III (1534–1549) there stood cardinal Simonetta's strongly traditionalist curial party. While the influential Spanish contingent under archbishop Guerrero of Granada demanded that the new assembly should be regarded as a continuation of the old, the

Imperial party wanted the church to make a fresh start. Their disagreement pointed to a fundamental division of opinion about the whole nature and purpose of the Council. The Germans, later joined by the French, were obsessed by the need to preserve religious peace at home, and they still hoped that Protestant representatives could be induced to attend the Council and participate in discussions that would lead to a Christian reunion. The Spanish bishops and the Louvain theologians, on the other hand, were convinced that the days for reunion were past, and that the immediate task was to bring reform to those regions of Europe still loyal to Rome.

The prime concern of the Spanish bishops – untroubled by the presence of Protestants in their native land – was to see that the dogmas of the church were propounded in their purest form, and that ecclesiastical reform was finally achieved, even at the cost of affronting the pope and the curia. It was generally held that the key to reformation lay in the question of episcopal residence. As late as 1560, in spite of numerous attempts to ensure that bishops resided in their dioceses, no less than seventy Italian bishops were living in Rome, and conditions were similar elsewhere. Since all attempts to curb episcopal absenteeism had hitherto failed, the Spaniards now began to insist that the residence of bishops in their dioceses was a divine obligation. But the curial officials detected in this claim a threat to papal supremacy, for it raised the delicate question of whether bishops exercised their authority as delegates of the pope or received it directly from God. Since this could lead the Council into treacherous quicksands of debate about its own relationship to papal power, there was reason for alarm. The unfortunate cardinal-legate Seripando was subjected to the papal wrath for imprudently laying the article on residence before the Council, and heavy pressure was applied to the Spaniards to moderate their line.

The problem of episcopal residence, however, was not the only one to agitate the Council, for the representatives of the Emperor were determined to secure major concessions in ritual and doctrine which would ease the problem of relations with the German Protestants. Both the Emperor Ferdinand and duke Albert of Bavaria believed that concessions on clerical marriage and on the use of the chalice by the laity would induce many erring sheep to return in due course to the Catholic fold. The Spanish bishops were bitterly opposed to any concession on the chalice, but the arrival of the French delegation brought welcome reinforcements to the Imperialists. The question was eventually referred to the pope, as being a matter of practical discipline relating to the life of the church in Germany. But the wider problem remained, and the alliance of the ultramontane nations inevitably extended beyond the question of the chalice to embrace the entire field of reform.

During the winter months of 1562 the papacy's position became critical. While the forces of opposition gathered round the person of the cardinal of Lorraine, the battle over episcopal residence broke out again, this time directly raising the whole problem of the powers of the pope and the church's constitution. Feeling was now running high against the papal legates, and if the cardinal of Lorraine had chosen to press for a vote by nations instead of by heads, the papacy might have suffered a series of humiliating defeats. Ferdinand received a visit at Innsbruck from the cardinal of Lorraine and sent a letter to Pius on 3 March 1563 expressing his deep dissatisfaction with the Council and the pope. A schism at this point seemed very close.

It was left to cardinal Morone, appointed legate and president of the Council after the death in March of cardinals Seripando and Gonzaga, to see that the key to the solution of the papacy's difficulties was to be found not at Trent but at Innsbruck. Trent was no longer an assembly of prelates and theologians, but a great international council, in which national delegations voted in accordance with the instructions of their princes. What was therefore required was direct negotiation with the princes; and the first prince to be won must be the Emperor himself. In April, Morone set off for Innsbruck, where he found Ferdinand in a truculent frame of mind. But Morone was a skilful diplomat, and by promising papal recognition of Ferdinand's son Maximilian as king of the Romans and conceding the use of the chalice by the laity in the Emperor's dominions, he succeeded in winning the Emperor for the papal cause. There was still the cardinal of Lorraine, but he too might be open to persuasion. The assassination in February of his brother, the duke of Guise,[2] had reduced Guise power at the French court, and the cardinal was anxious to restore the diminished influence of the House of Lorraine. By the autumn, with an offer of the legation to France in his pocket, he had ceased to oppose the wishes of the pope.

Philip II was not to be won by such methods as these, but he was now an isolated figure among the princes, and he was anyhow deeply concerned that a conclusion should be reached. With the opposition divided and weakened, much of the business which had for so long delayed the Council was quickly despatched; and reports of a grave papal illness and the consequent possibility of a new conclave helped wonderfully to concentrate the minds of delegates who had long grown weary of the interminable proceedings. On 4 December 1563, in the presence of 254 cardinals, bishops and theologians, the Council of Trent was formally closed. But reform itself had still to begin.

The Council's decrees were published with papal approval in January 1564. They covered an enormous range of problems in the fields both of dogma and discipline, as the Venetian bishop Jerome

Ragazzoni acknowledged in an enthusiastic discourse to his colleagues at the final session of the Council: 'You have proscribed all superstition and avarice, and all irreverence in the celebration of the mass...You have removed sensual songs and music from the temples of the Lord...Great ecclesiastical offices will in future be filled by those in whom virtue prevails over ambition...and bishops will remain in the midst of their flocks...'

Lyrical words – but how far were they justified? Certainly the decisions of the Council were of exceptional importance, providing firm answers to problems that had provoked long and acrimonious religious debate. They made it clear, for instance, that the post-Tridentine church would be totally subordinate to the decisions of the pope, for the papacy had emerged with its power unscathed and enhanced. It would be a church dedicated to the struggle against the Protestants, its dogmas now defined in accordance with the spirit and the letter of scholastic theology. Moreover, its servants would be far better equipped for the battle than their pre-Tridentine colleagues, for bishops would henceforth reside in their dioceses, and seminaries would be founded in every diocese for the education of the clergy.

It was one thing, however, to publish the decrees, and quite another to enforce them. Those relating to discipline were dependent on the goodwill of the secular princes, and this was by no means necessarily forthcoming, even in the most Catholic of States. Philip II was prompt in announcing his acceptance of the Tridentine decrees, but continued to maintain his vigilant regard for the rights of the Crown. Venice, Portugal and seven Swiss cantons accepted them at once, as did the Emperor and several German princes. But the Imperial and Polish Diets refused to accept them; and the French crown and the *parlement* of Paris, true to their Gallican traditions, proved equally recalcitrant. In so far as dogma was concerned, however, the decrees had better success. The new Roman Catholic orthodoxy gradually eliminated the more obnoxious deviations, including the communion in both kinds which the pope had conceded for Germany. Dispensations for the use of the lay chalice were being refused by the papacy within ten years of the closing of the Council.

Yet even the decrees on dogma raised problems which it would take at least a generation to solve. The limits of the new dogma were theoretically defined by the papal Index. But Paul IV's Index of 1559 was characteristically so severe as to drive most versions of the Bible out of the market, together with many famous editions of the classics and the early Fathers. The Council of Trent recommended a modification of the Index; but the work, which was placed in the hands of a special congregation, was arduous and slow, and the Index finally published in 1596 proved to be double the size of the Tridentine list of prohibited books of 1564. The Index, however, was at best no more than a negative response to the Protestant challenge, and there was a growing awareness of the need for something more positive. In 1559 the Dalmatian Protestant Flacius Illyricus had published the first volume of *The Centuries of Magdeburg* – a great collective work, finally completed in 1574, which was designed to prove by historical argument that the Lutheran church, and not that of Rome, was the true heir of the church of the apostles. This argument could only be adequately answered on the historical plane, and it soon became apparent that Roman Catholic scholarship was ill-equipped for the task. There was a death of scholars in the church with the historical knowledge and the critical and linguistic apparatus to set the newly defined dogma on a firm foundation. Nor, even if they had existed, could they have published their books at Rome. A Venetian printer, Paolo Manuzio, had been brought to Rome in 1561 at the suggestion of cardinal Seripando to set up a Roman press; but scholarly works were hard to come by, and Manuzio left the city disillusioned when the death of Pius IV restored power to the conservatives who had always distrusted his schemes.

It was not, in fact, until 1587 that a Vatican press was founded; not until 1592 that the much-debated new edition of the Vulgate at last appeared; not until the later years of the century that Rome began to produce men like cardinal Bellarmine who were capable of challenging Protestant scholars on their chosen ground. No doubt the years immediately following the conclusion of the Council saw the appearance of some notable works. Cardinal Borromeo's famous Catechism appeared in 1566, the new Breviary in 1568, and the Missal in 1570. But these were works produced for the faithful. To reply to the Protestants and win back those who had been lost to the church demanded an enormous work of education – and especially of self-education – which as yet had hardly begun. If the Roman Catholic clergy and laity were to defend themselves successfully against the Calvinist graduates of Heidelberg or the Lutherans of Wittenburg, they must be armed with the most modern weapons of theological debate. These could only be supplied if new schools and seminaries were founded, and universities reformed. It was here that the Jesuits had a special contribution to make. When Pius IV founded the Roman seminary, it was to the Jesuits that he turned; and it was through Jesuit schools and colleges that many of Europe's youth would be won back to Rome.

Throughout Catholic Europe the fate of the movement for reform was determined by a host of local circumstances, and was heavily dependent for its success on the capacity of a few individuals to provide leadership and inspiration in an environment that was often indifferent or downright hostile. One of the most charismatic of these individuals was Charles Borromeo, appointed archbishop of Milan in

1564, and, when he entered the city in triumph in 1565, the first archbishop to take up residence in eighty years. Milan was the largest archdiocese in Italy, with over 2,000 churches, 3,000 clergy, a hundred conventual establishments, and 800,000 souls. From the start, Borromeo made it clear to the civil authorities, who had grown accustomed to legislating on manners and morals in the absence of their archbishops, that reform was to lie exclusively in his own hands and those of his agents. During his nineteen years in Milan, which ended with his death in 1584, his combination of personal piety and reforming zeal had a galvanizing effect on clergy and laity alike. In those nineteen years he convoked six provincial councils and eleven synods, designed to implement the Tridentine reforms and lay down new standards of pastoral care; made regular visitations to parishes and monasteries; preached innumerable sermons; established three seminaries; and set up a printing press in Milan for the publication of the new breviary, missal and catechism. He also did much to encourage the use of a new piece of church furniture that would later be taken as emblematic of post-Tridentine Catholicism – the confessional-box. Initially no more than a grill separating the confessor from the confessant, the confessional was intended to prevent sexual solicitation by the clergy. But the privacy and anonymity that it offered may well have had the effect of shifting the emphasis in Catholic Europe away from public penitential performances and the concern with social sins towards a more interiorized religion, and a sense of greater individual responsibility and personal contrition.

If so, however, this was a slow and long-term process, as indeed was the process of spiritual reformation as a whole. Borromeo himself ran into intense opposition from laity and clergy alike; his ideal of a virtually autonomous bishop controlling every aspect of diocesan life was to be frustrated by the centralizing inclinations of the papacy; and the reforming movement in his archdiocese died away once he was no longer there to drive it forward by exhortation and personal example. Milan was not after all to become a Catholic Geneva.

The difficulties encountered by Borromeo, and the numerous problems involved in the defence and promotion of post-Tridentine Catholicism, suggest something of the magnitude of the task that confronted the church. They point also to the extreme complexity of the movement known (although only since the nineteenth century) as the *Counter-Reformation*. The Council of Trent and its programme of reform were intended to counter the Protestant threat. Inevitably this gave them a defensive, and even negative, appearance. An embattled church naturally resorted to such defensive weapons as the Inquisition and the Index; and it was driven to an almost compulsive reaffirmation of its belief in those articles of faith – such as the cult of the Virgin Mary – which constituted the principal targets of Protestant attack.

But the Tridentine reformers also had the more positive task of restoring content and vitality to a weakened faith. In attempting to fulfil this task, they were led far beyond the limitations inherent in a movement which is no more than a response to the challenge of another. For the reform of the Roman church, however much it was conceived as an answer to the Protestant challenge, flowed from that same broad stream of spiritual renewal which had revitalized Europe since the later years of the fifteenth century.

The subtle and complex inter-relationship of *Counter* and *Catholic* Reformation is to be found in every sphere of the church's life, and not least in the realm of art. The Roman church saw itself confronted by two major enemies – Protestantism and paganism. Protestantism attacked the most cherished dogmas of the church, and displayed its hatred for the objects of Catholic veneration in the iconoclastic outbreaks which were stripping bare the churches of Scotland, the Netherlands and France. Paganism, while no less determined an opponent, was also in some ways more subtle. The fashionable artistic style in mid-century Europe was Mannerism: a style which had developed as a logical extension of certain aspects of High Renaissance artistic achievement – especially that of Raphael and Michaelangelo – and which cultivated the virtuoso, the stylized, the artificial. 'Mannerism' is a word that has also been used, with varying degrees of conviction, to describe other arts of the period – polyphonic music and madrigals, and the literary style known as 'Bembismo' in Italy and 'Euphuism' (after John Lyly's *Euphues*) in England. Whatever the merits of transferring a stylistic description from the visual to the non-visual arts, one feature was common to all 'Mannerist' works, whether artistic, musical or literary: their emphasis on the manner at the expense of the matter.

The implications of this tendency for religious life are obvious enough, and were spelled out in a work called the *Dialogo degli errori della pittura* by Andrea Gilio da Fabriano, published in 1564 just after the conclusion of the Council of Trent. Gilio criticized modern artists for preferring artistic effect to honest representation of sacred themes, for twisting the human body into elegant distortions, and for depicting it naked instead of decently clothed. What was needed, in Gilio's view, was a return to the strict iconography of the pre-Michaelangelesque generations, although with the incorporation of the technical and stylistic improvements of more recent times. The result would be a judicious mixture (*regolata mescolanza*) of the old and the new, which would produce a form of purified religious art appropriate to the needs of the age.

Gilio's views reflected those of the fathers assembled at Trent, although the Council's artistic pronouncements were somewhat limited, and essentially negative in character. All sensuality should be forbidden; the dishonest and profane should be avoided; and there should be no excessive elegance in the adornment of images. Propriety, decorum and verisimilitude were the qualities expected of works of religious art in the post-Tridentine years. The same puritanical spirit was displayed in the discussion on music. One party, to which Pius IV himself inclined, favoured the suppression of all music in the church, but the Spaniards in particular insisted on the antiquity of the Gregorian chant, and its efficacy as an aid to devotion. The partisans of church music won the day, and a commission was set up under cardinal Borromeo to consider suitable reforms. The Vatican was fortunate in having at its service a great musician in Palestrina, who showed in his *Missa Papae Marcelli* how the demands of Tridentine spirituality and music might be satisfactorily combined. It was in the pursuit of this ideal that Gregory XIII would order the return to the purity of the Gregorian chant, and that in due course composers would evolve the oratorio.

Although the Council of Trent imposed no specific style on artists and architects, certain artistic consequences logically flowed from the needs of the post-Tridentine church. Churches must be well illuminated, so that the faithful could follow the offices in their books, and therefore the stained glass window began to disappear. The Council had insisted on the need for preaching to combat heresy, and therefore the pulpit must be placed in a prominent position, so that the preacher could be properly seen and heard. Since the Protestants challenged certain fundamental dogmas of the church, these must be given a special emphasis in newly commissioned paintings and images. Did heretics reject the sacrament of penitence, and dismiss the confessional as useless? Then artists should depict Mary Magdalene and a penitent St Peter. Did they challenge the necessity of good works for salvation? Then saints must be displayed doing all manner of charitable deeds. Did they deny the Immaculate Conception? Then the Virgin Mary must be glorified by every means at their command. The artist as much as the priest must become an active participant in Rome's battle against heresy.

It would seem, from Gilio's *Dialogue* and from the Council's artistic pronouncements, that Mannerism was no longer in favour, at least for religious works. But the movement of opposition to Mannerism cannot be ascribed simply to the Council of Trent, for well before the conclusion of the Council some painters had already reacted against the pagan themes of High Renaissance art, and had begun to move towards the production of more specifically devotional works. Artists, therefore, were already being affected by the climate of spirituality – the aspiration for a *Catholic* Reformation – which itself did so much to influence the proceedings of the Council. At the same time, while the Council undoubtedly encouraged certain anti-Mannerist tendencies already in existence, there was no clean break between the artistic styles of the pre-Tridentine and post-Tridentine eras. In the secular arts, in particular, Mannerism remained the fashionable style until the end of the century. In religious painting there was from the 1560s a shift towards simplicity and a greater degree of piety. But old artists do not easily adopt new ways. Mannerist influences remained pervasive in religious art for many years after the ending of the Council, and the dominant artistic style might best be characterized by Gilio's expression – *regolata mescolanza.*

It was eminently appropriate that Gilio's work should have been dedicated to that prince of patrons, cardinal Farnese, for the taste of patrons was at least as influential in the determination of styles as the taste of the artists themselves. Cardinal Farnese (1520–1589), the grandson of pope Paul III, was incomparably the most influential patron of artists and scholars in sixteenth-century Rome. In his person he bridged the worlds of the Renaissance and the Counter-Reformation, and by his sensitivity to the aspirations of both, he perhaps did more than any man to ensure that the art and culture of the post-Tridentine church incorporated, instead of dismissing out of hand, many of the humanist values that had prevailed in his youth. There had always been something intelligently eclectic about Farnese's tastes, and artists who pursued the *regolata mescolanza* – the judicious blending of the old and the new – appealed strongly to his temperament. He supported them with all the vast resources of patronage at his command, and the commissions which he gave helped to set the imprint of the new thinking on Rome. It was Farnese, also, who took the Jesuits under his special protection when they and their founder became the objects of Paul IV's hostility. As their protector and patron, he gave them something of his own instinctive feeling for culture and scholarship. He gave them, too, their famous church of the Gesú in Rome, whose carefully contrived stylistic eclecticism so typical of Farnese's personal taste, would set the pattern for some of the most influential artistic tendencies in the post-Tridentine church.

The Jesuits are traditionally credited with establishing the Baroque as the chosen style of the Counter-Reformation church. But in fact the Jesuits favoured no specific style, and their order was still at this time a poor one, dependent on the goodwill, and the taste, of its patrons. Baroque itself was the response of a new generation of artists and patrons to the needs of an increasingly self-confident Catholicism and to the artistic limitations and possibilities of Mannerist art. The puritanism and austerity of the Tridentine popes and cardinals proved to be only a passing phenomenon. The next generation of popes shared the extravagant tastes of their contemporaries among the secular princes, while the church as a whole became more indulgent towards artistic display. Why should not the temples of God be more ornate than the palaces of men? So the great Counter-Reformation churches were designed as manmade reflections of celestial beauty – a profusion of light and colour and ornament, of marble pillars and ornate gilt *retablos*, rejoicing in the new freedom which Mannerism had brought to art, but triumphantly displaying those elements of dynamism and unity which Mannerism had so conspicuously lacked.

The whole artistic development of the Roman church, through a purged and refined Mannerism to the spectacular assertions of the Baroque, suggested how much more was the Catholic Reformation than a mere defensive reaction against the forces of Protestantism and paganism. Participating in that same movement for spiritual regeneration which had given birth to Protestantism itself, the Catholic Reformation faced many of the same problems and was subjected to similar strains. Both religions were confronted with the fundamental problem of their relationship to the achievement and the values of the Renaissance. Both of them were at least partially inspired by a revulsion against Renaissance ideals, as was shown by their first austere reaction to the sensualism of Renaissance art, and by their emphasis on the depravity and the dependence of man, where Renaissance humanists had proclaimed his autonomy and his endless possibilities. An influential section of conservative opinion in both religions saw the only hope of salvation in the total rejection of everything for which the Renaissance had stood. But against this was ranged a more moderate body of opinion, which hoped to incorporate at least some of the conquests made by the Renaissance into a cultural life purified and renovated by religious reformation.

In the second half of the century, the struggle was fought out all over Europe, Protestant and Catholic alike. It was fought, for instance, in Spain, where writers and scholars, in the face of bitter conservative opposition, struggled to apply the tools of Renaissance scholarship to the traditional theology, or attempted to find some compromise between the neo-Platonic idealism of the earlier humanists and the new despairing sense of the sinfulness of man. Compromises were often impossible to find, but the very strain involved in the attempt to reconcile the irreconcilable could itself produce tensions that were artistically creative. In the widest sense the art and culture of the Counter-Reformation were the art and culture of a Catholic Reformation, inevitably sharpened by the conflict with paganism and heresy, but responding to a deeper impulse which sought to bring the human world into closer alignment with that of the spirit. The balance between the two worlds was often unevenly held. The human world might itself be decisively rejected in the more extreme forms of mysticism; or it might crowd out the spiritual, in the very excess of Baroque embellishment. The successes, the failures, the endless variations, all serve, however, to suggest the extraordinary complexity of the Catholic and Counter Reformation – a movement which both inspired, and was inspired by, the deliberations at Trent.

2   The Counter-Reformation and the Secular Power

It was symptomatic of a movement which was fighting its own internal battles as well as the great battle against Protestant heresy, that even the character of succeeding pontiffs should constantly have alternated, as if reflecting the divergent tendencies within the church itself. Paul IV (1554–1559) had been the very image of a Counter-Reformation pope, the militant defender of an embattled church against the forces of darkness. Pius IV (1559–1565), on the other hand, had about him something of the easy-going manner of the popes of the Renaissance. He had done the church an incomparable service in steering the Council of Trent to a successful conclusion, but a pope so anxious for the welfare of his numerous relatives could hardly be said to epitomize the spirit of reform. It was, however, a crowning irony that the last flowering of the discredited system of papal nepotism should now have produced a papal nephew who was genuinely both a nephew and a saint. Cardinal Borromeo symbolized, as his uncle never could, the hopes and aspirations of the post-Tridentine church, and it was fitting that Pius should entrust him with the ungrateful task of bringing reform to the curia. But there was always something a little incongruous about Borromeo's heroic reforming efforts at the behest of a pope whose Renaissance-style court had swollen to over 1,400; and it was typical of Borromeo that when his uncle died on 9 December 1565, he should have cast his vote for Michele Ghislieri, whose election as Pius V brought to the papal throne a man whose character was the very antithesis of that of his predecessor.

Pius V (1566–1572) seemed closer in spirit to Paul IV than to Pius IV, and his election was greeted with acclamation by the partisans of Paul. But if Pius possessed a firmness and intransigence comparable to that of Paul IV, he also possessed far more of the spirit of the Catholic Reformation. A man of extreme personal austerity, he cherished an idealized vision of the spiritual purpose and functions of the church, which he would never allow to be tainted or compromised by the intervention of merely material contingencies. This made him a good pastor of souls, but a poor diplomat; a man determined to further the work of ecclesiastical reform and the recovery of Christendom for Rome, whatever the obstacles and whatever the price.

This uncomfortable and uncompromising man had no use for the servants of his predecessor, but was prepared to adopt any of his policies as long as they could be shown to promote the interest of the church. Pius IV had already done something to improve and modernize the institutions of papal government. In particular, he had begun to bring papal administration into closer alignment with contemporary secular practice by appointing Ptolemy Gallio, his former private secretary, to the office of domestic secretary to the pope. Although Gallio lost his post with the new pontificate, and retired to his diocese of Como to await better days, his years in office had helped to establish the practice of appointing a cardinal domestic secretary, who would gradually take over the traditional functions of the cardinal nephew in the papal administration, and would carry special responsibility for the conduct of foreign affairs.

The rise of the papal secretary of State was only one aspect of the process of modernization which was taken in hand by Pius V and continued by his successors. It was Pius who, in creating the first two special congregations – those of the Index and the Council – set the precedent for the organization of groups of cardinals into boards of ecclesiastical civil servants. He also made considerable use of special nuncios for the conduct of papal diplomacy, although it was left to his successor, Gregory XIII, to formalize the system of papal representation by nuncios at the courts of Catholic kings.

Yet, in spite of these improvements, the general impression created by the church in the 1560s is one of extraordinary administrative and diplomatic inadequacy for the great task on which it was engaged. This was a church which had lost, and hoped to regain, the British Isles and Scandinavia, most of Germany, half Poland and Switzerland, and considerable parts of France. But its ignorance of the character of these lands was sometimes abysmal. It even managed to address the bull of summons to the Council of Trent to 'Suetiae et Norvegiae Rex', apparently unaware that, since 1450, Norway formed part of the Crown not of Sweden but of Denmark. It was hardly surprising if the first Scandinavian exiles to take refuge in Rome should have felt it necessary to begin the campaign for the reconversion of their native lands by giving the curia a few basic lessons in geography.

Much could be, and was, done by remarkable legates like cardinal Stanislas Hosius, who played a decisive part in the recovery of Poland for Rome; and the intense activity of the Jesuits was beginning to loosen the hold of Protestantism over wide areas of central and eastern Europe. But the fact remained that the church was still desperately weak, and that until it could substantially improve its own agencies for conversion, it would be as dependent as the Protestant churches in the early stages of the Reformation on the favour and assistance of the secular power.

Although a devout Catholic prince, like Albert V of Bavaria, could give the church invaluable assistance, it was clear that the main burden must fall on the shoulders of Philip II of Spain. Maximilian II, who had succeeded Ferdinand as Emperor in 1564, was believed to be a crypto-Lutheran, and was clearly unreliable. Philip II, on the other hand, was a prince of irreproachable orthodoxy; and Philip alone possessed sufficient military resources to fight the church's battle against Protestantism and Islam. Philip's enemies, too, were the enemies of the church – the Turks in the Mediterranean, the Protestants in the Netherlands. Since Philip for his part needed the moral support of Rome, and the substantial clerical subsidies that Rome must authorize, it seemed that an alliance between Spain and the papacy would be of benefit to both.

Alliance, however, was one thing, and subordination another. Philip showed himself determined from the outset to be the master in his own house, and to keep a firm hold on the extensive prerogatives and patronage belonging to the crown. Admittedly he was compelled in 1566 to allow the transfer to Rome of the unfortunate archbishop of Toledo, Bartolomé de Carranza, who had been arrested by the Spanish Inquisition on suspicion of heresy in 1559. But Spain's ambassadors to Rome managed to ensure that Carranza's case was interminably protracted, and it was another nine years – and only two months before Carranza's death – before a final, and somewhat ambiguous verdict, was reached.

In his struggle to maintain his regalian rights, Philip could count on the Spanish Inquisition, and on the somewhat embarrassed support of the episcopate, which knew that its prospects of promotion depended entirely on the king. In 1572 papal briefs citing Spaniards to appear before foreign courts in ecclesiastical cases were declared null and void; and Philip was always careful to insist on the crown's right to scrutinize all papal bulls and to refuse their publication if they contravened the laws and customs of Spain. In this way he managed to ensure that the Tridentine decrees were implemented in his kingdoms on his own terms and at the pace that he himself chose to dictate. His chosen agent for the task was the cautious and conservative Gaspar de Quiroga, whose career as Inquisitor General and as archbishop of Toledo from 1577 to 1594 was hardly distinguished by that burning zeal for the faith which is usually associated with Counter-Reformation Spain. It was in Toledo that El Greco produced his great works of Counter-Reformation spirituality for a group of enlightened lay and clerical patrons. But Quiroga, while charitable and devout, was essentially an administrator, more interested in the raising of clerical standards and the enforcement of the ceremonial and disciplinary provisions of Trent, than in the intense spiritual upsurge of contemporary Spanish Catholicism.

Philip's control over the process of ecclesiastical reform in Spain led to constant friction with the papacy, which was exacerbated by

conflicts of jurisdiction both in Spain and in the king's Italian dominions. In Naples and Sicily Philip maintained a tight royal grasp on the
church, and usually had his way. But the worst clashes between king
and pope occurred in Milan. A clash over jurisdiction between Borromeo and the Spanish governor in 1567 led to a long and acrimonious dispute, which even the appointment of Borromeo's friend, Don
Luis de Requesens, as governor of Milan in 1571, proved unable to
resolve. 'I am no longer defending the jurisdiction of the king', wrote
Requesens after being excommunicated in 1573, 'but am attempting
to prevent the total loss of this State, for which cardinal Borromeo is a
greater danger than an army of a hundred thousand Frenchmen at the
gates.'[3] For a man in the heat of the battle, the agitation is understandable. But in the wider perspective of the 1560s and 1570s, the
differences between Spain and Rome over questions of jurisdiction
were of minor significance in comparison with the dangers that
threatened them both.

The continuing irritants may have disturbed, but could never
destroy, that essential community of interest between Spain and
Rome, which inexorably cast Philip in the role of secular champion
of the church. This role did not, however, imply the subordination of
Philip to the dictates of Rome in a common crusade against the forces
of heresy. On the contrary, Philip pursued his own foreign policy, just
as he pursued his domestic policy, without any excessive concern for
the susceptibilities of the pope. The papacy suspected, as did the
Protestants, that Philip was furthering his own political interests
under the convenient cloak of religion, and up to a point the suspicion
was correct. Yet the fact remained that Philip's natural enemies happened, as often as not, to be the enemies of the church; and he could
reasonably claim credit for his great services to the church, even if
success in the struggle redounded at least as much to his own benefit
as to that of Rome.

It was one thing, however, to march alongside the papacy, and
quite another to keep in step. Popes, after all – and especially popes
of the character of Pius V – could allow themselves to survey the
wider horizon, and to dismiss the most formidable obstacle with a
wave of the hand. But Philip, as a mere king, was bound to concern
himself with such mundane questions as the availability of troops
and cash. This difference in the respective positions of king and
pope could not fail to lead to wider divergences over major matters
both of policy and timing, which in turn increased the mutual exasperation and the areas of conflict. Pius V, for instance, was almost
obsessively concerned with the struggle against the Turks. This, too,
was Philip's overriding concern in the 1560s, and he did much to
intensify the war in the Mediterranean.[4] But, for Pius, it was never
enough.

In the Netherlands, however, after an initial divergence. Pius and Philip were in general agreement. The breakdown of authority in the Netherlands and the iconoclastic troubles of 1566 had faced Philip with the agonizing necessity of making up his mind. Margaret of Parma wanted a conciliatory policy. So also did the group in the Spanish council of State headed by Ruy Gómez, prince of Eboli – a group which seems to have had close ties with the Netherlands nobility, and which favoured some kind of federal solution to the complex constitutional problems of the Spanish Monarchy. It was widely felt at this time that the best of all answers to the question of the Netherlands would be a personal visit by the king. The Dutch nobles themselves hoped for this, and a visit to the Netherlands was urged on Philip by Pius V and by cardinal Granvelle. But something always seems to have held the king back. He may have been influenced by unhappy memories of his earlier stay in the Netherlands; but more probably he was concerned at the increasingly strange behaviour of his son and heir Don Carlos, who was temperamentally too unstable to be left in charge of the government in Spain, while his father was away.

In the event, Philip let himself be persuaded by the duke of Alba that the sedition and heresy of the rebels more than justified the use of force, and that any royal visit must first be preceded by the despatch of an army to the Netherlands. Given the king's inability to make a personal visit in 1566, Alba's arguments were undoubtedly cogent. It was an axiom of sixteenth-century statecraft that incipient rebellions must be speedily suppressed, and France and Scotland stood as awful warnings of what could happen if the axiom were ignored. Moreover, the geographical position of the Netherlands greatly added to the normal dangers of revolt. Philip and Alba could never afford to forget that long stretch of frontier between the Netherlands and France. Unless the frontier were strongly defended, the heretics in France would give aid and shelter to their brethren in Flanders, and the French theatre of conflict would inevitably be extended to include the Netherlands.

There was considerable force of logic, therefore, in the decision to send Alba with an army to the Netherlands; and the arrival at Seville of the treasure fleet with a record sum of silver in the autumn of 1566 made military action feasible. At Alba's insistence, this action was to be regarded as a campaign to crush rebellion, and not, as Pius V wanted, as a holy war on heretics. To represent his expedition to the Netherlands as a religious crusade would, in Alba's eyes, entail the risk of intervention by the German Protestant princes and England. It would also, very tiresomely, deprive him of the opportunity of recruiting for his army German Lutheran mercenaries. But Philip spared no pains to impress upon the pope the religious motivation which had prompted his decision. The king told Requesens, at that time his ambassador in Rome, that 'to negotiate with those people is so pernicious to God's service...that I have preferred to expose myself to the hazards of war...rather than allow the slightest derogation from the Catholic faith and the authority of the Holy See.'[5] These words were no doubt intended for the ears of the pope, but they represented accurately enough the king's personal belief. Whatever the ostensible objects of Alba's expedition, the enemy were, for Philip, 'rebels and heretics', and his army became the Catholic army – the *ejercito católico*.

Alba's final interview with the king took place in the middle of April 1567, and he sailed for Italy at the end of the month. After assembling an army of 9,000 men in Milan, he began his northwards march in June. He went by way of the Mont Cenis, past Geneva and then up through the Franche-Comté, Lorraine and Luxemburg.

Alba's march had a traumatic effect on the Protestants of Europe. No one could be sure of the exact objectives of the army, and it was suspected that the first objective was Geneva itself. The destruction of Geneva was a cherished project of pope Pius V, and he urged Philip to undertake an action that would redound to his own glory and that of his faith. But Philip was not prepared to compromise the success of his plans for the Netherlands by an enterprise that would seem both untimely and inadequately prepared. While the Geneva garrison, hastily reinforced by French Huguenot contingents, manned the city walls, Alba's imposing army passed by and disappeared into the distance without a shot being fired. Geneva, for the moment at least, was saved. But the passage of the *tercios* had reawakened all the latent fears of Rome and of Spain that had agitated the Protestants since the meeting at Bayonne.[6] There could now be no doubt that the arrival in the north of this formidable engine of war was the first part of a grand Spanish design to reconquer Europe for the church. In France, the Huguenots, determined to strike first, took to arms in September. In the Palatinate, the Elector Frederick, convinced of the reality of a Spanish conspiracy, began planning with his Calvinist advisers a grand anti-Spanish alliance of the Protestant powers. Everywhere, as the result of Alba's march, the identity of papal and Spanish was automatically assumed. Catherine de Medici was troubled, the Protestants were frightened. In consequence, international tension rose sharply from 1567, as the shadow of the duke of Alba fell menacingly across the face of northern Europe.

Alba's objectives were, in reality, far more limited than the Protestants assumed, since his sole immediate concern was with the problem of the Netherlands. On 22 August he made his entry into Brussels, and went to the palace to salute Margaret of Parma. In Margaret's eyes his presence was unnecessary and his arrival unforgiveable, as she made clear in her letters to the king before leaving the Netherlands for

Parma at the end of the year. But Margaret's counsels were no longer heeded in Madrid, and Alba pressed ahead with his plans for the total submission of the Netherlands. These plans included the punishment of the rebel leaders, the centralization of government, a general fiscal reorganization, and the imposition of effective religious discipline. In effect, this was to be a reconquest of the Netherlands – a *Reconquista* in the Spanish style – replacing provincial liberties with a central royal authority, and substituting for the tolerant Erasmian Catholicism of the Low Countries the intransigent Tridentine Catholicism of the Mediterranean world.

On 9 September Alba arrested Egmont and Horn, both of whom were knights of the privileged and exclusive Order of the Golden Fleece; and he set up the 'Council of Troubles', which was designed to hunt down and punish all those considered responsible for the disorders: Calvinist ministers and members of consistories, together with iconoclasts, and rebels who had taken up arms against the king. Alba's intention, in his own words, was not to 'uproot this vineyard, but to prune it', and he apparently hoped to limit the shedding of blood. But the establishment of a special tribunal was inevitably seen as marking the inauguration of a régime of terror. In May 1568 the exiled William of Orange, making use of German troops released from service by the ending of the second French civil war, organized an invasion of the Netherlands, launched from Germany. But the country was too frightened to respond and the invasion proved an ignominious failure. Not a single major town rose spontaneously in support of Orange, who merely succeeded in giving Alba a pretext for fresh repressive measures. On 1 June there were eighteen executions, mostly of signatories of the Compromise of the nobles; and on 5 June, Egmont and Horn were publicly executed in the market place of Brussels. The ill-organized army of Louis of Nassau was defeated a few weeks later, and a final attempt at invasion crumpled in November. William himself, still dreaming of resistance, chose to fight with the Huguenot army while he awaited better days.

The news of the execution of Egmont and Horn created a profound impression in the Netherlands. But in Rome it was received with satisfaction and confirmed the pope in his belief that the government of the Low Countries was at last in safe hands. It did indeed seem that Alba's triumph was complete. Resistance had collapsed, and the Council of Troubles – the 'Council of Blood' – was systematically pursuing its grim work. Between 1567 and 1573 if dealt with 12,203 cases. Of these, some 9,000 seem to have been convicted, and just over 1,000 executed. The butchery was not therefore as savage as it has sometimes been represented; but against this must be set the fact that many of those most implicated in the troubles had succeeded in fleeing the country, and that perhaps as many as 60,000 people – or

2% of the total population – emigrated from the Netherlands during the six years of Alba's rule.

With the policy of repression nearing a successful conclusion, the time had come to reorganize the fiscal system in the Netherlands, so that the royal government and the army could be paid without recourse to Spanish subsidies. Alba's plan was to raise a once for all tax of 1% – the hundredth penny – on real property, a 5% permanent tax – the twentieth penny – on sales of real estate, and a ten per cent permanent tax – the tenth penny – on articles for export and on the sale of goods. But the levying of these taxes required the assent and cooperation of the Estates; and although the States General, meeting in March 1569, was willing to approve the first tax, if would have nothing to do with the others, which seemed ominously reminiscent of the Spanish sales tax, the notorious *alcabala*. The duke then attempted with some success to put pressure on the provincial Estates, but failed completely with the Estates of Brabant.

The opposition to the tenth penny, especially among merchants and artisans, was violent and intense – so intense, indeed, that it was never collected, at least in Flanders and Brabant.[7] It was hated both because of its permanent and unparliamentary character, and because it seemed to threaten the Netherlands with economic ruin. Although Alba reacted to the pressure of public opinion, first by temporarily contenting himself with the offer of two grants of two million florins a year, and then in 1571 by modifying the incidence of the tenth penny and reducing the figure on exports from 10% to 3.3%, the political and psychological consequences of his proposal were profound. It hardened popular feeling against the already very unpopular municipal oligarchies, except in those few towns, like Amsterdam, where they had stood firm under pressure from Alba. It intensified hatred of the government, at a time when the religious persecution and the behaviour of the Spanish *tercios* billeted on the country had created a climate of bitterness and sullen resentment. Now that the Calvinist organization in the Netherlands had been destroyed or paralyzed by Alba's repressive measures, the tenth penny provided the obvious rallying point for national opposition to an alien and oppressive régime.

Opposition, however, signally failed to turn into open revolt. It seemed that the Netherlands were now permanently cowed, and the threat to Spanish domination of the Low Countries looked increasingly as though it would come from without rather than from within – from France, from the activities of Netherlands, French and English privateers, and from the policies of the queen of England, who in November 1568 had seized in Plymouth harbour four Spanish ships laden with £85,000 for the payment of Alba's troops. But Philip, encouraged by the news of Alba's successes in pacifying the

Netherlands, was beginning to think that the time had come for a change of policy and perhaps of governor. In 1568 he had rebuffed proposals by the Emperor Maximilian that he should end the rule of terror and extend the religious peace of Germany to the Netherlands. He remained adamant in his refusal to treat with heretics; but cardinal Granvelle and the prince of Eboli were now joining their voices to that of the Emperor in urging the adoption of a more conciliatory approach. Early in 1569 the king decided on a general pardon – although it was to be considerably less general than its name suggested. But the pardon was considered premature by Alba, and it was not until July 1570 that it was finally published amidst official rejoicings and public indifference.

With the publication of the amnesty, Alba's task seemed officially completed. He had frequently asked the king for permission to retire, and Philip at last felt able to accede to his wishes. Towards the end of 1570 the duke of Medina Celi was appointed to succeed him, although he did not arrive to take up his new post until 1572. The news of Alba's impending departure from the Netherlands greatly disturbed the pope. The peace of Saint-Germain, which ended the third French religious war in August 1570, had horrified him by its concessions to the heretics, and filled him with foreboding about the future of the church in northern Europe. Alba might have saved Catholicism in the Netherlands but there remained more – much more – for him still to do. Was it, for instance, conceivable that Spain should withdraw from the battle as long as a heretic sat on the English throne?

Philip II was well used by now to papal agitation about the queen of England. He had twice, in 1561 and 1563, intervened at Rome to prevent Elizabeth from being excommunicated – not because he approved of her or her ways, but because the maintenance of an Anglo-Spanish understanding was essential for the success of his policies towards France and in the Netherlands. But in the later 1560s it was becoming increasingly difficult to maintain good relations with England. Alba's arrival in the Netherlands had alarmed England, as it had alarmed every Protestant State, and English fears were much increased by the events of 1568. The flight of Mary Queen of Scots to England in May opened up dangerous possibilities of a rebellion by English Catholics in conjunction with foreign military intervention designed to set Mary on the English throne. Alba's successes in the Netherlands in the summer and autumn obviously increased the danger, and helped persuade the English government to indulge in a few well-applied pin-pricks against Spanish and Catholic power – a little help for the Huguenots at La Rochelle; tacit approval for the seamen who joined the Dutch and French privateers in the Channel; and then, in November, the seizure of the payships.

The affair of the payships, followed by the news of John Hawkins's slaving expedition to the Caribbean, where it had been badly mauled by the Spaniards in September in the Mexican port of San Juan de Ulúa, brought a sharp deterioration in Anglo-Spanish relations. Mutual hatreds were now beginning to undermine the counsels of restraint. Encouraged by the prince of Eboli and his friends, Philip was listening more sympathetically to the views of his ambassador in London, Don Guerau de Spes, who insisted that little was to be expected of Elizabeth, and that more could be gained by supporting Mary Queen of Scots. Under the pressure of events, therefore, Philip's policy towards England was moving closer to that of the pope. In February 1569 he wrote to Alba that he felt he had a special obligation to preserve and restore the faith in England, but he left the initiative entirely to the duke.

In November 1569 came the event for which Don Guerau de Spes had been waiting – the rising of the northern earls against the Protestant government of the upstart William Cecil and his friends. But Alba did nothing. His failure to intervene was partly caused by an instinctive dislike, which he shared with his master, of all insurrections against legitimate authority – a dislike which prevented him from establishing direct contact with the rebels. But it also sprang from the well-founded conviction that the situation in the Netherlands, and his own lack of money, simply did not allow him to embark on so hazardous an enterprise as the invasion of England. His reaction to the Ridolfi plot in 1571 was equally unenthusiastic. He knew that little faith was to be put in the English Roman Catholics, and that only a massive and well-organized invasion stood any hope of recovering England for the church.

The twists and turns of Philip's policy in his dealings with England vividly illustrate the complexity of his relationship with Rome. On the one hand, his distrust of France and his preoccupations in the Netherlands made him desperately anxious to retain Elizabeth's goodwill; on the other, the pope's constant insistence on the need for military intervention, together with the growing embarrassment of English privateering activities, pushed him reluctantly towards a more aggressive policy. Yet as late as 1570, when Pius finally issued his bull of excommunication against Elizabeth, Philip expressed his grave displeasure at what seemed to him a most untimely act, and refused to allow its publication in his own dominions. He may have authorized Alba in 1569 and again in 1571 to intervene in England; but he knew his man, and he knew the difficulties, and he drew the right conclusion. Such caution and hesitations did not of themselves make Philip any less dutiful a son of the church. He remained, and intended to remain, the champion of the faith, but he would champion it on his own terms, and in his own good time.

Philip's behaviour aroused deep misgivings and suspicions in the mind of Pius V. But he knew, as Philip must have known, that events were gradually pushing Spain towards an open confrontation with the Protestant North. Increasingly, Philip found himself challenged at every turn by enemies who were in equal measure enemies of his faith. In the Netherlands his authority had been defied by Calvinist rebels. In the New World, Spain's sovereign rights had been challenged first by the Huguenots, who attempted to colonize Florida in 1564–1665, and then by Protestant Englishmen, Hawkins and Drake, in 1568. In the Channel and the Bay of Biscay, Spain's vital lines of communication with the Netherlands had been disrupted by the activities of heretical privateers. Sooner or later the confrontation of Catholic South and Protestant North must come – a confrontation for which the northward march of Alba's army had spectacularly set the scene. But at this moment the north was not the only, nor even the most important, battlefront; nor were Protestant heretics the only enemies of the church. With the blessing of an impatient pope Philip was deeply engaged in another, and still more urgent crusade: the crusade in the Mediterranean against the forces of Islam.

6

The War with Islam

1 Prelude to Conflict

The revolt of the Netherlands appears, in retrospect, so momentous in its consequences that it needs an effort of the imagination to appreciate that, for most of the 1560s and 1570s, the Low Countries came a poor second to the Mediterranean among Philip II's priorities. The successes of Protestantism in Northern Europe were deeply disturbing. But if it came to a choice between Italy and the North for the allocation of troops and money, Italy must win. For Italy was the bastion shielding Spain from the Turk; and no ruler of sixteenth-century Spain could afford to neglect the defence of Spanish interests and security when faced with the terrifyingly unpredictable intentions of Ottoman power.

Philip II learnt his lesson very early in his reign. The enterprise against Tripoli, which he had authorized perhaps too carelessly in 1559,[1] ended in disaster in May 1560. The Christian expedition of forty-seven galleys and some twelve thousand men met with no opposition when it seized the isle of Djerba, guarding the approaches to Tripoli. But a Turkish fleet of eighty-five vessels under the command of Piali Pasha set sail from Constantinople almost as soon as the news arrived. Taking only twenty days to reach Djerba, it attacked on 12 May. The Christian forces panicked and made a mad rush for the galleys, which failed to reach open water before the Turks bore down on them. Twenty-seven galleys fell into Turkish hands with scarcely a shot being fired; and the six thousand men left behind in the fortress were driven to surrender ten weeks later by thirst and starvation.

The Djerba fiasco showed well enough that the Ottoman Empire now enjoyed naval supremacy in the Mediterranean – and if further evidence were required, it came in 1561 when a Turkish fleet was sighted as far west as Majorca. But Djerba was a salutary misfortune in that it forced Philip to make provision for the strengthening of his fleet. After Djerba he could count on only some sixty-four galleys for Mediterranean operations, including those of the Knights of Malta, and of his Italian allies – Genoa, Florence and Savoy. A large galley-building programme was essential, whatever the cost. The Castilian Cortes proved amenable; extra-parliamentary sources of revenue were substantially increased; and the annual *subsidio* paid by the clergy was fixed in 1561 at 300,000 ducats, and then raised to 420,000 in the following year.

From 1561 the dockyards of Spain and Italy were hard at work, but galley-building was a slow and laborious process, which involved the felling of forests often far removed from the coast, the transport of the timber overland or by river to the yards, and then a further delay as the wood was left to season. By 1564, however, Spanish naval power was reviving, and Don García de Toledo, who had been appointed from the viceroyalty of Catalonia to the post of 'Captain General of the Sea', was able to put to sea with a fleet of one hundred ships, of which seventy were Spanish. His objective was the Peñón de Vélez, a notorious hide-out for corsairs between Oran and Tangier. The expedition met with complete success. In the western Mediterranean at least, the initiative had been recovered by Spain.

But it was in the central Mediterranean, where Philip was still at a disadvantage, that the Turks were now planning their next full-scale campaign. It had been known for some months in the capitals of Europe that a great fleet was being fitted out at Constantinople, but it was not known whether its objective was the Venetian island of Cyprus, or Malta, the last stronghold of the Knights of St. John. The mystery was solved when it suddenly appeared off the Maltese coast on 18 May 1565. The Grand-Master of the Knights of Malta, John de la Valette, had done his best to strengthen the island's defences with the help of Don García de Toledo, now viceroy of Sicily. But La Valette had less than 9,000 men at his disposal, and on 18 and 19 May 23,000 Turks were landed on the island. For twenty-three days the little garrison of the bastion of St. Elmo, the key to Malta's defences, threw back a series of Turkish assaults. Their extraordinary resistance gave La Valette time to strengthen the fortifications of Il Burgo, the island's principal fortress, and to send out urgent appeals for help.

Effective help could come only from the Spaniards, and it took painfully long to arrive. The reasons for the delay were less sinister than contemporaries believed. For all Don García's energy, it took time to assemble troops and a fleet at Messina; and it would be folly to send an ill-prepared fleet to Malta, and run the risk of a defeat which would leave the entire western Mediterranean helpless before an Ottoman assault. It was not, therefore, until 26 August that the relief expedition sailed from Sicily, and it sailed with strict instructions from the king to avoid a battle with the superior naval forces of the Turks.

After being driven back to Sicily by storms, the fleet at last reached Malta on 7 September, at a moment when both besiegers and besieged were nearing exhaustion. Don García executed his orders brilliantly, and landed 10,000 men without engaging his ships in battle. The long-awaited arrival of these reinforcements brought the siege to an end. Piali Pasha gave the orders to his troops to embark, and by 12 September the last Turkish vessel had disappeared over the horizon. The raising of the siege was celebrated throughout Europe as a great triumph for Christian arms, but it was generally felt that Philip II had been grudging and dilatory in his help, and Pius IV ostentatiously avoided all reference to Spain in his expressions of gratitude for the victory. Yet the fact remained that it was the Spanish fleet which had saved Malta and the central Mediterranean from the Turks, and that Spanish naval power was the only effective obstacle to the Ottoman advance.

The ageing Sulaiman the Magnificent sought his revenge for the humiliation of Malta in a land campaign against central Europe, rather than another naval assault in the Mediterranean. Although the Sultan and the Emperor had officially been at peace since 1562, the death of the Emperor Ferdinand in 1564 had provided the Turks with a useful pretext to demand payment of tribute in arrears. The new Emperor, Maximilian II, was anxious to avoid war, but had become hopelessly entangled in conflict with the prince of Transylvania, who turned to his patron at Constantinople for help. By the beginning of 1566 it was clear that a new Turkish invasion of Austria was on the way. Maximilian II, with financial help from his cousin Philip, scraped together a motley army of 40,000 men; but Sulaiman had set out from Constantinople on 1 May at the head of an army said to be 300,000 strong. It was not until the Ottoman forces had been on the march for ninety-seven days that they ran into serious resistance from the fortress of Szigeth in south-west Hungary. Here they were held up for thirty-four days, until 8 September. By this time the campaigning season was almost at an end; and two days before the fall of Szigeth, Sulaiman died in his camp.

The grand vizier Mehmed Sökölli managed to conceal for three weeks the news of the sultan's death. This allowed time for the peaceful accession of Sulaiman's son, Selim II, and for the new sultan to travel from Constantinople to Belgrade to be acclaimed by his army. For the time being, at least, the danger to Austria was over; and although the war in Hungary continued in a desultory fashion for a further year, it soon became clear that neither party was anxious to prolong it. An Austrian embassy arrived in Constantinople at the end of 1567, and Selim agreed in Feburary 1568 to an eight-year truce.

The truce was conditional on the annual payment by the Emperor of a 30,000 ducat tribute, which – to save Maximilian from excessive humiliation – was euphemistically described as a gift.

Although the death of Sulaiman had brought the Austrian campaign to an abrupt conclusion, there were other, and profounder, reasons for the slackening of the Turkish offensive against the heartlands of Europe. For much of Sulaiman's long reign, the Turkish army had been a more formidable engine of war than the fleet. In its European campaigns this army had primarily been used during the past forty years for large-scale raids rather than for massive territorial conquest. These raids, however, had been conducted so far from the army's base at Constantinople as to deprive Ottoman power of much of its effectiveness. The campaigning season proved all too brief when some ninety days were required to move the vast trains of men, camels, and supplies up through the Balkans into Hungary; and the Christian commanders soon devised an effective response to the Turkish thrust by setting up a string of fortresses which proved strong enough to halt the army in its tracks, and frequently to tie it down until the campaigning season was past. The prolonged resistance of Szigeth in 1566 showed how well this strategy worked: even if Sulaiman had lived, his army could not have achieved much in the short time that remained between the fall of Szigeth and the onset of winter. The whole campaign, indeed, vividly illustrated how the Turkish attack on central Europe had by this time become fatally blunted, and how the land-war between Christendom and Islam was reaching stalemate.

But if Ottoman effectiveness in land-warfare against Europe was visibly declining, the events of the 1560s made it clear that Ottoman strength at sea was by now very formidable. This made it probable that, in spite of the repulse at Malta, the weight of the Ottoman onslaught against Christendom would be shifted back to the Mediterranean, and directed either against Cyprus or Italy, or even, conceivably, against Spain itself. Selim II, to Europe's intense relief, was more of a poet than a warrior; but it was customary for the Turks to mark the opening of a new sultanate by some spectacular campaign. A Mediterranean enterprise could hardly fail in the long run to provoke a firm response from Spain, for religion, history, and Spain's own security all combined to make it the natural enemy of the Turks, and the inevitable champion of Christendom against Islam. Spain itself had been forged in the white heat of conflict with the Moors. It alone, of west European States, had a large Moorish population, left high and dry in the wake of the triumphant advance of the *Reconquista*. As a legacy of the *Reconquista* it also had a precarious hold on Moorish North Africa. And its vital interests were threatened by the alliance between Constantinople and the North African corsairs, who persistently endangered the lifelines of the Spanish Monarchy – the sea-routes that linked the peninsula to its Italian possessions and the granaries of Sicily.

Of all the Mediterranean States, Spain alone had the capacity to contain an Ottoman attack. But in organization and resources it was in some respects inferior to the Turks. The Ottoman Empire was a vast military machine, with apparently inexhaustible reserves of money and men. In a Mediterranean world approaching sixty million inhabitants, perhaps thirty million were subjects of the Porte. Although there were wide racial and religious differences among these thirty million, the Ottoman Empire had acquired through its State apparatus and its system of recruitment for government service, a cohesion and a unity which could not be equalled by the Christian West. The Imperial ambassador in Constantinople was deeply impressed by the opportunities for advancement enjoyed by even the humblest subjects of the sultan, and compared this with the European practice, where everything depended on birth and there was no room for merit.[2] It was the conquered races – Greeks and Albanians, Armenians and Slavs – who provided the sultans with their soldiers, their advisers and officials: of forty-seven grand viziers between 1453 and 1623, only five were Turkish by birth. The contrast was striking with the Spanish Monarchy, whose viceroys and governors were primarily drawn from among a few great families of Castile. Philip's empire was a semi–closed Castilian empire. That of Sulaiman and Selim was an open empire, drawing its officials indiscriminately from among the subject races, and offering opportunities of high office without regard for origin.

Although the subjects of the sultan were not, by contemporary western standards, heavily taxed, Sulaiman enjoyed in his later years an annual income of some eight million ducats. Just as Philip had his German and Genoese bankers, so the sultan had his Greeks. He also had, in the mysterious Portuguese Jew, Joseph Nasi or Micas, (later known by the flamboyant title of the duke of Naxos) the most spectacular financier of the later sixteenth century. Admittedly the Ottoman Empire lacked a system of public credit comparable to the elaborate Spanish system of *juros*, or credit-bonds, which enabled Philip II to raise enormous sums in long-term loans. But the first and most important use of credit among Christian kings was to subsidize war; and the Ottoman Empire was so much better organized for war than Christendom that it was capable of fighting at far less cost. Where European armies were dependent on the expensive and wasteful system of mercenaries, the Ottoman army formed an integral part of society and the State. The Sipahi warrior class lived off fiefs in conquered territories; and as long as the Ottoman army could pillage the borderlands of the Empire – as it could with profit in the first half of the century – warfare on land could be made to pay for itself. The fleet, it was true, posed more serious problems. Timber, naval stores and oarsmen could be supplied from the sultan's dominions, but the hiring of skilled western technicians was very expensive. Yet in the great days of the Turkish fleet, between the battles of Prevesa in 1538 and Lepanto in 1571, sea-warfare, like land-warfare, was made self-supporting by systematic pillage and the capture of prizes.

The capacity of the Ottoman Empire for war therefore made it a dangerous adversary, even for a Spanish Monarchy that was beginning to reap substantial benefits from its conquest of America. There were undoubted weaknesses in the Ottoman system – its need for continuing conquests to maintain its coherence and momentum; its dependence on the person of the sultan, who after 1566 was rarely equal to the heavy demands of his office. Yet an able grand vizier, such as Mehmed Sökölli, could go a long way towards remedying his master's deficiencies. He controlled, too, a remarkable military and administrative machine, whose efficiency contrasted sharply with the varying degrees of confusion to be found in the administrative systems of European States. Philip II was no doubt fortunate in that the Ottoman Empire's Asian and African interests frequently diverted its attention from the Mediterranean, although he also had his commitments elsewhere. He was also fortunate in that western Europe was at this time building up a technical lead in ship-construction, which would give a decisive edge to the Christian forces when the fleets of East and West eventually met at Lepanto. But, with his finances insecure and with trouble gathering in the Netherlands, he showed a proper caution in the mid-1560s in refusing to be drawn prematurely into a full-scale Mediterranean conflict. The confrontation must be deferred as long as it could.

2   The Confrontation of Empires

If that single-minded ascetic, Pius V, had had his way, the new pontificate in 1566 would have been magnificently inaugurated by the formation of a Holy League of Spain, France, Venice and the Italian States, to fight Islam. Throughout his six years on the papal throne, Pius cherished the vision of a great Christian crusade against the infidel; and if the vision finally came to pass, it was to him more than any other man that the credit was due. He was for ever chiding and chivying the ambassadors of the Catholic powers. But in the opening years of his pontificate all he could get was evasive answers, whether from the Spaniards, whose attention was distracted by the problem of the Netherlands, or from Venice, desperately concerned not to jeopardize the precarious relationship with the Turks on which the prosperity of the Levant trade depended.

The papal overtures might have received a warmer welcome if the Ottoman threat had at this moment been acute. But the two or three years after Sulaiman's death were years of a strange and ominous calm in the Mediterranean. The inner workings of Ottoman policy are still unknown. The unexpected respite may have been caused by harvest failures in the eastern basin of the Mediterranean, or it may have derived from more acute preoccupations elsewhere. The Turks had been deeply concerned by the southwards advance of Muscovy, which had annexed Kazan and Astrakhan in the mid-1550s. It was clear that a great new power was rising on the north-eastern border of the Ottoman Empire, threatening the pilgrim route and the central Asian trade, and disturbing the power-balance between the Turks and their traditional rivals, the Persians. It was apparently under Mehmed Sökölli's direction that the Turks turned their attention in the later 1560s to the Muscovite threat. Their grandiose schemes for redressing the balance included an abortive attempt in 1569 to construct a Don – Volga canal, designed to link the Black Sea and the Caspian, and to facilitate attacks on Muscovy and Persia and the liberation of Astrakhan.

Whatever the reasons for the respite in the Mediterranean, it could only be welcomed by a harassed Philip II. 1566 was the year of the Netherlands revolt. Much of 1567 was occupied with preparations for the duke of Alba's march. The following year, 1568, was, from both a personal and national standpoint, a terrible year for Philip – perhaps the worst of his reign. Conscientiously he had taken the government of Spain in hand, and his style of kingship was by now well established. Unlike his father he was a sedentary monarch, who had chosen to govern his kingdoms from a desk. In 1561 he had given Spain a permanent capital in Madrid; and in 1563 he had begun to construct in the Guadarrama hills the monastery and royal residence of the Escorial, which would be an absorbing interest and pastime until its completion in 1583. In the seclusion of his study he would pore far into the night over government papers and despatches, making endless marginal comments in his spidery hand. The attention to detail was close and obsessive – everything must be perfectly ordered and every formality observed. No king was ever more conscious of his duty to God and his subjects. Government must be good (although, regrettably, its workings were slow); justice must be dispensed without regard for person or rank; and all decisions, however laboriously reached, must be personal decisions, for Philip trusted his own judgment more than he trusted his advisers, though in matters of conscience he would invariably seek theological guidance.

Overshadowing all Philip's labours in the early years of his reign, was the terrible problem of Don Carlos, his only son and heir. Not only was Don Carlos's personal behaviour growing increasingly strange and abnormal, but he was also beginning to indulge in dangerous political fantasies. These brought him into contact with the Flemish Baron de Montigny, who had come to Spain as the representative of the Netherlands nobility in the summer of 1566; and they seem to have involved the idea of flight to the Low Countries to escape from the constraints that he felt in Madrid. When Egmont and Horn were arrested in September 1567, Montigny was taken into custody in Spain. Montigny's arrest is likely to have increased Don Carlos's desperation, and his desire to get away at all costs from the presence of a stern and disapproving father. Philip was perfectly aware of his son's intentions, and reluctantly decided that, both for personal reasons and for the safety of the State, it was essential that Don Carlos should be kept in confinement. On the night of 18 January 1568, a party which included the king and the prince of Eboli entered the prince's bedroom, and the unfortunate youth was placed under an armed guard. Six months later he died in the Alcázar of Madrid.

The mystery surrounding the imprisonment and death of Don Carlos gave birth to a host of rumours – eagerly seized on by Philip's enemies – that he had been put to death by the king. The secret strangling of Montigny two years later in the castle of Simancas suggests that judicial murder was not an action from which Philip would shrink if he considered it necessary. But Don Carlos's personal behaviour in confinement would be sufficient on its own to account for his death. For Philip II both the life and the death of his son were a terrible tragedy, and the tragedy was doubled by the death in October 1568, three months after Don Carlos, of his queen, Elizabeth of Valois.[3]

A year of personal bereavement and tragedy ended in a national misfortune with the rising of the Moriscos of Granada on Christmas night. The Morisco revolt was the outcome of long-standing racial and religious problems in Andalusia, and in that sense was an event unconnected with the conflict between the Ottoman Empire and Spain. But the very fact that this was a Moorish rising within the Iberian peninsula meant that it at once assumed a place in the wider context of the great struggle between Christian Spain and Islam. The Spaniards could not fail to see the revolt as further proof of the dangers that threatened them as long as the crusade against the Moors remained uncompleted. The Turks for their part were bound to look sympathetically on the struggle of their brethren against Christian domination. The events in southern Spain between 1568 and 1570 therefore had inevitable repercussions on the Mediterranean conflict, and lent credibility in Philip's eyes to the urgent warnings from Rome of the need for a Holy League.

The revolt could hardly have come at a more awkward moment for Spain, denuded as it was of experienced troops for Alba's march to the

Netherlands. Essentially this was a revolt born of despair, and it might with better management have been averted. Ever since the conquest of Granada in 1492, the Moorish population had constituted a large and unassimilated minority within Spanish society, and a nagging reminder of work left undone. Nominally, the Moors of Granada had been Christians since 1499. In practice, the lax and ill-organized church in Granada had taken little trouble to teach Christian doctrines to its Morisco flock. Benefiting from the negligence of the clergy, the Moriscos surreptitiously continued to follow the faith of their fathers, to observe their traditional customs and to wear their traditional dress. While this brought them into sporadic conflict with the church, the Inquisition, and the *audiencia* of Granada, they could always turn for protection to the hereditary captains-general of Granada, the marquises of Mondéjar, who sought to preserve their own position by holding the rival Christian authorities in check.

By the 1560s, however, the precarious equilibrium of fifty years was on the point of being upset. In a sense, the Moriscos were victims of the Counter-Reformation: the post-Tridentine church in Spain was becoming impatient of Morisco practices, which were increasingly hard to tolerate at a time when any religious deviation seemed to jeopardize the struggle against heresy at home and abroad. On 1 January 1567 a pragmatic was issued ordering the Moriscos to abandon the use of Arabic, together with their racial and religious customs, and to adopt Castilian dress. Similar pragmatics had been issued and ignored in the past, but this time there was a real danger of enforcement because the influence of the Moriscos' natural protector, the marquis of Mondéjar, was being eroded by the intrigues of his enemies at court.

The Moriscos were now deeply concerned for their future. The Inquisition had intensified its activities. The *audiencia* was packed with Mondéjar's enemies, from whom no mercy was to be expected. And the silk industry, on which they depended for survival, had been badly hit by drastic tax increases since 1561. In the circumstances, it was natural that they should turn to their fellow-Moslems for help. At the time of the siege of Granada, three Moriscos had been arrested as spies, and had revealed the existence of Turkish plans for a Turkish conquest of the Granada coast. A corsair raid on the coast in the winter of 1565 increased Philip's fears of a Morisco insurrection synchronized to coincide with a Turkish invasion. These fears were reasonable enough at a time when all European princes were haunted by the vision of foreign intervention in aid of domestic revolt, and Philip was persuaded by his most influential adviser, cardinal Espinosa, that the best hope of averting the danger lay in a rigorous enforcement of the pragmatic against Moorish practices. The marquis of Mondéjar, who knew his Moriscos better, warned the king that this might produce the very consequences it was designed to prevent. Mondéjar was right, and the Moriscos revolted.

The failure of the rebels to seize the city of Granada did much to reduce their chances of success, but the reports that reached Madrid caused justifiable alarm. The Moriscos had turned savagely on the Christian population, and were desecrating churches and slaughtering the priests. Philip was fortunate in having, in the marquis of Mondéjar, a very capable commander, who was quick to counter-attack with the levies which the cities of Andalusia sent to his aid. But the country was mountainous; progress was slow; and the king, susceptible to the insinuations of Mondéjar's enemies, was unable to leave well alone. The unfortunate marquis was first ordered to share his command with a rival magnate, the marquis of Los Vélez, and then, when the two men fell out, the supreme command was given to the king's half-brother, the twenty-two years-old Don John of Austria.

For month after month the cruel war dragged on in the mountains of Granada. There were too few galleys to protect the long Andalu-sian coast-line, and a Turkish landing in support of the rebels would have been relatively easy. But although the governor of Algeria responded to Morisco appeals for help by sending arms, ammunition and a small force of soldiers, the Turkish fleet failed to appear. The Moriscos fought with great courage, and their struggle served as a source of inspiration to that other rebel, William of Orange, watching from afar. If these Moors, who after all were poor people, 'like a flock of sheep', could achieve so much against the great king of Spain, what could not be achieved by the people of the Low Countries, 'strong and robust, who can count on help from every part of the world?'[4] But gradually, and with great brutality, the rebels were crushed. In May 1570 the Morisco captain-general agreed to Don John's terms of surrender, although sporadic warfare continued in the mountains for a long time to come.

Having won his victory, the king chose a drastic solution for the problem of Granada. The kingdom was to be emptied of its Morisco inhabitants, who were driven from their villages and dispersed north-wards through Castile. Although a substantial number of Moriscos managed to evade the deportation orders, the expulsion of the major-ity of them – perhaps 80,000 all told – effectively ended the danger posed by Granada as the soft under-belly of Spain in its conflict with the Turk. There would be no future repetition of the horrors, or the fears, of 1568–1570. But the security that followed from the paci-fication of Granada had been gained only at the price of turning a local Andalusian problem into a national problem affecting all Castile. The Moriscos, scattered through the towns and villages of Castile, no longer constituted a serious military danger. But their very ubiquity created new racial and social problems which would haunt the government for another forty years, until Philip III decreed their expulsion from Spain, and cut the Gordian knot.

In failing to send large-scale help to the Moriscos, the Ottoman Empire lost an obvious opportunity for a decisive blow at Spain. It is still not clear why the chance was missed. There is talk of disagreement among Selim's advisers, but perhaps it was simply that the difficulties were too many, and the distances too great. With the failure of the Don-Volga project in 1569 the sultan's attention was turning back to the eastern Mediterranean, and to the opportunities for Ottoman expansion in areas at present dominated by the Portuguese – eastern Africa and the Indian Ocean. Constantinople had long had its eyes on Cyprus – an embarrassing Christian outpost which lay across the vital sea-route from Constantinople to Alexandria, and whose conquest was seen as the essential prelude to an Ottoman thrust towards the south. Cyprus surely presented an easier, and more vulnerable, target than Spain.

The Venetians had hitherto managed to avert an Ottoman attack on their richest possession by means of skilful diplomacy and by heavy reliance on the good offices of those traditional allies of the sultan, the French. But the civil wars in France and the consequent waning of French influence in Constantinople, left the Venetians dangerously exposed, and by 1569 there was little to deter the sultan other than the fear of provoking a maritime alliance between Venice and Spain. That same year, Venice's arsenal blew up, and the reports reaching Constantinople suggested that the major part of the Venetian fleet had been destroyed. With Spain's resources simultaneously stretched to the limit by the war in Granada, the moment seemed ideal for an attempt against Cyprus.

As naval preparations went ahead in Constantinople, the Venetians, lulled into a false sense of security by thirty years of lucrative peace, refused to believe the evidence before their eyes. But their last illusions were dispelled at the beginning of February 1570 when a Turkish envoy arrived to demand the immediate cession of Cyprus. Opinions in the city were sharply divided. The surrender of Cyprus would mean the sacrifice of Venice's wealthiest colony and the centre of its Levantine trade; and it might well lead in turn to the loss of Venice's other overseas possessions like Corfu and Crete. But the alternative was war with the Ottoman Empire, which could well end with the destruction of Venice herself. One group of senators, primarily concerned with the preservation of Venice's trade, favoured appeasement, even if this entailed the cession of Cyprus; the other, eagerly supported by the papal nuncio, considered war the only honourable response. When the question was put to the vote, the Turkish ultimatum was rejected by 220 to 199.

For a city which had neglected its military and naval defences, the decision was brave to the point of foolhardiness. Everything depended on whether Philip II could be induced to abandon his distrust of the Venetians and send the Spanish fleet to their aid. This was Pius V's opportunity, and he seized it with characteristic determination. Don Luis de Torres, a Spanish official in the papal service, was at once sent to Spain to urge on the king the supreme necessity of participation in a Holy League with Venice against the Turk. Within eight days of giving audience to Torres, Philip agreed in principle to the papal request.

The reasons for Philip's change of front after four years of evasion must be sought in the profound changes in Spain's national and international position since the opening of Pius's pontificate in 1566. The year 1570 was in reality the first year in which Philip II's Spain had the opportunity, the will, and something approaching the capacity, to embark on a full-scale Mediterranean war. The opportunity was provided by the apparent success of the duke of Alba in quelling the revolt of the Netherlands. The Granada war had brought home the gravity of the threat from Islam – a threat which actually moved Philip, in a moment of panic, to order the evacuation of the Balearic Islands in 1571. Moreover, Spanish military prestige, already damaged by the delay in suppressing the Morisco revolt, had been dealt a fresh blow in January 1570 when the corsair king of Algiers, Euldj Ali, profited from Spain's internal embarrassments to seize the Spanish puppet State of Tunis. Spain's mood in 1570 was therefore compounded of anger, wounded pride, religious enthusiasm, and a fierce desire for revenge. Pius V seized the right moment to exploit this mood, and at the same time gave to the idea of a crusade the impress of his own extraordinary personality, which – for all the irritations of his day-to-day conduct – held Philip II in a kind of fascinated awe.

Although the Turks landed in Cyprus in July 1570, and had soon occupied most of the island except the fortress of Famagusta, the negotiations between Spain, Venice and the Papacy were endlessly protracted, and were clouded, as always, by bitter mutual suspicion. Philip II not unreasonably insisted that Spain should have a commanding voice in the military and naval operations to which it would be making the largest contribution. It was only on 20 May 1571, therefore, that the Holy League at last came into being. Spain was to contribute half the funds, troops and ships, the Venetians a third and the pope a sixth; and Don John of Austria, the victorious general of the Granada war, was to be appointed commander-in-chief.

Famagusta fell to the Turks on 1 August 1571, when Don John's fleet was still no nearer than Naples. The news of its fall took two months to reach Venice, which had already decided that it was too late in the season to attempt a recovery of Cyprus. Instead, Don John and his colleagues boldly agreed to search out and give battle to the

Ottoman fleet, even if this took them into the alien waters of the eastern Mediterranean. The combined Christian fleet which was now assembled at Messina consisted of some three hundred ships and eighty thousand men, of whom fifty thousand were sailors and oarsmen. This meant that it was roughly equal in size to the Turkish fleet, although the latter contained a larger proportion of galleys, and carried more soldiers on board. The Christian fleet suffered some disadvantage in its heterogeneous composition, but compensation was provided by the dashing personal leadership of Don John, who showed a genius for uniting men of differing nations as warriors in a great crusade.

On 16 September 1571 the great armada, duly blessed by the papal nuncio, set sail from Messina and headed for Corfu. Here it was learnt that the Ottoman fleet, under the command of Ali Pasha, was anchored off Lepanto, far into the gulf of Corinth. There were obvious risks in seeking it out for battle, especially so late in the season, and there were bitter disagreements in the council of war. But it was finally decided, as Don John had urged, that the Christians should move into the attack, and at dawn on 7 October the two fleets – the largest opposing fleets that had ever met in battle – sighted each other at the entrance to the gulf of Patras.

The ships on both sides were drawn up in line, with the Venetians on the left of the Christian fleet, the papal and Genoese galleys on the right, Don John's flagship in the centre, and a reserve of thirty-five Venetian and Spanish galleys under the command of the marquis of Santa Cruz in the rear. As battle approached, Don John, his armour glinting in the autumn sunlight, transferred to a fast galley from which he could harangue the Christian forces as it ran along in front of the line. On every ship a crucifix was raised, and crews and soldiers knelt on the decks in prayer.

The attack was launched by the Venetian galleasses, floating fortresses whose heavy guns, mounted on a high gun-deck, sank several Turkish galleys and broke the force of the first attack. While the two wings of the Ottoman fleet attempted an outflanking movement, and scored considerable successes against the Genoese and Venetian galleys, it was in the centre that the decisive struggle was fought. Although Turkish arrows were deadly, their cannon fire proved less effective and less accurate than that of the Christians, which did heavy damage to the Turkish flagship before Don John gave the order to board. The first two boarding attempts were repulsed, but the third carried the poop, where Ali Pasha was cut down. His head was promptly mounted on a spike set up on the prow of the Turkish vessel, and the banner of the Cross was raised in place of the Crescent.

The death of Ali Pasha and the capture of his flagship decided the struggle of the central squadrons, and with it the battle. The Turkish centre and right had been almost entirely destroyed, but on the Turkish left Euldj Ali, the victor of Tunis, evaded the pursuit of Santa Cruz and escaped with some fifteen galleys. Of the original Turkish fleet of about three hundred ships, 127 fell into Christians hands, and some 30,000 Turks were killed. The Christians lost fifteen or twenty ships and perhaps 8,000 men; and there were 15,000 wounded, among them Miguel de Cervantes, who lost the use of an arm. It was a costly enough victory, but one apparently so complete and overwhelming that it seemed as if the humiliations of centuries had been wiped out in a single decisive blow.

3   The Aftermath of Lepanto

The victory of Lepanto was the greatest victory won by Christian arms against Islam since the capture of Granada in 1492. It showed conclusively that the Turks were not invincible, and that the Christians possessed both the morale and the technical resources to hold the Ottoman Empire at bay. This new-found confidence of Christendom, which celebrated the triumph in services of thanksgiving and in a lavish production of pictures, medals and mementoes, was perhaps in the long run the most important result of the battle. For the military and political consequences of Lepanto proved sadly disappointing.

Although the Turks never fully recovered from their disastrous loss of skilled manpower, the strength and resources of the Ottoman Empire were such that they were able to rebuild their fleet with extraordinary speed. Moreover, the practical limitations on galleys – the fact, for instance, that they could not carry more than twenty days supply of drinking water and therefore had a cruising radius of ten days at most – meant that no Mediterranean naval battle in the sixteenth century was capable of giving the victors 'command of the sea'. Irrespective, therefore, of the capacity of the Turks to make a rapid recovery, the immediate military consequences of Lepanto were likely to be small. The battle, too, had come late in the year; supplies were running low; and Don John was back in Messina by 1 November with the campaigning season at an end. As an Austrian noble, Hans Khevenhüller, observed with disappointment in his secret diary, Lepanto failed to win for the Christians a single yard of land.

How could the victory most effectively be exploited? Don John, in his own way as much of a visionary as Pius V, was dreaming of Constantinople and Jerusalem. The Venetians were interested only in the recovery of Cyprus and their lost possessions in the Adriatic. Philip II, for his part, wanted any future campaign to be conducted in North Africa, where it would be of immediate benefit to Spain. Pius V died on 1 May 1572, but his successor, Gregory XIII, was determined to keep the Holy League in being. At the urgent insistence of the new pope and of Don John, Philip reluctantly agreed that the Spanish galleys should be mobilised for an expedition against the Morea. But little of consequence was achieved that autumn, and the Venetians were showing themselves increasingly restless allies. Their trade was being destroyed by the war, and they were deeply suspicious of Spanish intentions. On 7 March 1573 Venice signed with the sultan a peace treaty so unfavourable that Lepanto might never have been fought and won. The Republic renounced its claims to Cyprus and to its lost territories in Dalmatia, handed back to the Turks its own conquests in Albania, and paid an indemnity of 300,000 ducats. These humiliating terms may have offered Venice some prospect of commercial revival, but they killed the Holy League stone dead.

Released from any sense of obligation to its difficult allies, Spain was now free to turn to its own plans for the reconquest of Tunis. An expeditionary force of 20,000 men under the command of Don John sailed from Sicily and captured the city in October 1573. Don John, the bastard son of an emperor, spent much of his brief and poignant life scheming for a crown, and he may for a moment have toyed with the idea of becoming king of Tunis. But in the end he left the city with a Spanish garrison and a native governor, together with the unsolved problem of how to defend itself in the probable event of a Turkish counter-attack. This was not long in coming. Selim II and his viziers were determined to restore imperial prestige by recovering the initiative in the western Mediterranean. Massive resources were mobilized across the Ottoman Empire, from eastern Anatolia to North Africa, and in July 1574 a large Turkish expedition under the irrepressible Euldj Ali arrived off Tunis before the garrison could be adequately strengthened. Within a few weeks, to the surprise and consternation of Christendom, both Tunis and the fortress of La Goleta had fallen, and the kingdom of Tunis had joined the rapidly lengthening list of Don John's shattered dreams.

With the fall of Tunis, Philip II had had enough of Mediterranean campaigns. Money was running short, and events in Northern Europe were demanding increasing attention. The Turks, for their part, were not sorry to be relieved of war in the Mediterranean at a moment when, on their eastern frontiers, the Persian Empire seemed on the verge of disintegration. A truce was signed, therefore, in 1578 and was periodically renewed thereafter. The two giant powers of the Mediterranean were disengaging, their mutual hostility tempered by a growing awareness of their commitments elsewhere.

The slackening in the 1570s of the Turkish impetus to expansion, both on the plains of Hungary and on the waters of the Mediterranean, has tended to suggest that the Ottoman Empire in these years was already starting on its long decline. Certainly, the great generation of

Turkish leaders was passing away, and Mehmed Sökölli was assassinated in 1579. Important structural changes, too, were gradually alter-
ing the character of the Empire. Ottoman society was becoming less
mobile and flexible as the army struck roots in the conquered territories, and as the idea of hereditary succession gained strength among
the military caste. New concepts of property and privilege, which had
seemed to be distinctive peculiarities of Christendom in the great days
of the Ottoman Empire, were beginning to undermine the efficiency of
Turkish administration. Financial difficulties increased as western
silver percolated into the Ottoman economy, and the rulers found
themselves wrestling with those problems of inflation which had
done so much to complicate the lives of their counterparts in the
West. There was a hardening of the arteries of empire, a failure to
respond to new military and technical challenges, which was itself
exacerbated by the rigid structure of government, and by its dependence on the personal and capricious rule of feeble-minded sultans.

Yet, in spite of these signs of change and of structural deficiencies, it
is too easy to judge the Ottoman Empire – so mysteriously different
from European States – by the criteria of western experience. Apart
from an unconvincing and abortive renewal of the war with the
Austrian Habsburgs between 1593 and 1606, the Ottoman Empire
was turning its back on Europe during the last quarter of the sixteenth
century. Warfare with Christendom was no longer as profitable as it
had been in former times, either on land or by sea. Turkish pressure on
the eastern fringes of Europe therefore slackened, and the border
territories began hesitantly to blossom out in precariously independent lives of their own. But far away to the south and the east, in
regions of which Europe knew little or nothing, the story was different. In 1571 Hejaz in southern Arabia fell into Ottoman hands. On
the east coast of Africa, the Turks hastened to exploit the weaknesses
of Portugal after its great defeat in North Africa, at Alcázarquivir.[5]
Above all, they were seeking to take advantage of the troubles of their
two powerful neighbours – of the anarchy in Persia after 1576 and the
crisis in Muscovy in the later years of Ivan IV. From 1577 they were at
war with the Persians, and made fresh conquests in Georgia and
Azerbaijan. The balance of military and technical expertise might be
slowly tilting in favour of Christendom, but there was life in the
Ottoman Empire yet.

No doubt, if Spain had been willing or able to follow up Lepanto
with energy, the Turks would have responded with equal force. The
struggle for Tunis was proof enough of this. But even if this had
happened, it is hard to believe that the eventual outcome in the
Mediterranean would have been very different, while Spain's capacity
for war in Northern Europe would have been profoundly affected. In
all probability, the Mediterranean would have remained a divided sea,

with the Turks controlling the eastern half, the Spaniards the western, while the centre would still have been – to the despair of Venice – the home of the Moorish and Christian corsairs. As it was, other commitments and interests brought a premature end to a struggle that could hardly have ended in a clear-cut victory for either side. The Ottoman Empire was turning east, and in doing so allowed the Spanish empire to turn north and west, to face an enemy that was beginning to look still more dangerous than Islam. Already, within a year or two of Lepanto, the focus of conflict was beginning to shift – from the struggle between non-Christian East and Christian West, to that between Catholic South and Protestant North.

PART III

1572–1585

7

Crisis in the North: 1572

1 The Capture of Brill

When Pope Pius V died on 1 May 1572, it was still barely apparent that his successor would be confronted with a very different world. The old pope had impressed his own austere image on the post-Tridentine church. He had inspired a great Mediterranean crusade, which had brought undying glory to Christian arms at Lepanto. He had watched with satisfaction as the grip of the duke of Alba closed on the heretics in the Netherlands; and he had fulminated – although admittedly in vain – against the heretical queen of England. The way ahead was therefore clearly marked out for the pope who followed him. Cardinal Farnese, that liberal patron of the arts, had few doubts that he was the destined successor, but the king of Spain had other ideas. The size of the Spanish faction in the conclave made Philip's veto decisive, and the cardinals' choice fell on Hugo Buoncompagni, who ascended the papal throne as Gregory XIII. He was seventy years old at the time of his election; an obstinate, capricious but energetic old man, who combined a legalistic outlook on life proper to a Bologna-trained jurist, with a fitting realization of the standards expected of him as the heir to so holy a pontiff as Pius V.

His programme, he announced, would be to maintain the league against the Turk, to pursue the work of reform, and to secure acceptance of the Tridentine decrees. There was to be no change, then, from his predecessor's aims and priorities. But the world itself was undergoing change; and a pontificate which would last for thirteen years, from 1572 to 1585, saw a decisive shift in the direction and the emphasis of papal policy. This shift became necessary as a result of what happened in northern Europe in the spring and summer of 1572. On 1 April the Dutch Sea Beggars captured the little port of Brill; and early on 24 August, St Bartholomew's day, three thousand Protestants were murdered in Paris.

It is one of the ironies of historical writing that both the capture of Brill and the massacre of St. Bartholomew have been represented as carefully premeditated events. But the debate that once surrounded them has died away, and both are now seen as the outcome of short-term accident rather than long-term design. Yet, for all the fortuitous element involved, the course of events since 1570 together with the characters of the principal participants made them something more than a matter of chance. Admiral Coligny, Catherine de Medici and Louis of Nassau all thought to catch that tide in the affairs of men, which, taken at the flood, led on to fortune. They took the current when it served. One gained, two lost, their ventures.

Catherine de Medici was never one to give up hope. The conclusion of the third French civil war with the peace of St. Germain in August 1570 suggested that the time had come for a fresh attempt at reconciliation. The new balance of forces in France itself indicated the lines to be followed. The Huguenots, in bargaining for and obtaining four 'places de sûreté', had treated with the monarchy as if they were virtually an independent power. For the moment, at least, they must be humoured, and Coligny must be brought back to the council table. This would certainly accord with the wishes of the increasingly influential group of *politiques*[1] which was forming around François de Montmorency, the son of the late Constable. Moderation and conciliation were now the order of the day, as Charles IX delicately indicated by creating a royal academy of poetry and music in which the discordant notes of Protestant and Catholic should blend together in a new-found harmony.

The move to unity, based on limited religious toleration, was to be reinforced by a series of alliances which would show the world that France had recovered both its internal cohesion and its external credibility as a counterweight to Spain. No one was more skilled than Catherine at devising alliances, especially where marriages for her own children were involved. Between 1570 and 1572 she spun an elaborate spider's web of matrimonial designs. At home, the civil wars should be permanently ended by the union of Bourbon and Valois, to be symbolized by the marriage of her daughter Marguerite to Henry of Navarre, the son of the late king of Navarre and of his ardently Protestant widow, Jeanne d'Albret. Abroad, France's position would be fortified by the marriage of Charles IX to the daughter of the Emperor Maximilian whose sympathy for the Lutherans made him a significant figure in that curious demi-world of hopes and schemes for religious toleration. One further marriage would complete the intricate design. Catherine's second surviving son, Henry duke of Anjou, would become the husband of Elizabeth of England.

It took the duke of Anjou a year to discover for himself what others had found before him: that the queen of England was more easily wooed than won. But the protracted, if entertaining, negotiations for an English alliance were accompanied by more successful negotiations elsewhere. Charles IX was duly married to Elizabeth of Austria in June 1570, and the Bourbon-Valois marriage was agreed in principle by the end of the year.

These arrangements corresponded well with the grand design which was forming in the mind of Coligny, now the most powerful man in France. Coligny's world was a battlefield in which the armies of light and the armies of darkness strove for mastery. As an ardent Protestant and an ardent Frenchman, he saw the forces of darkness symbolized by the pope of Rome and the king of Spain – the oppressor of the Protestants in the Netherlands, the murderer of the Huguenots in Florida, and the ruler of a Monarchy bitterly hostile to France. Ranged against these were the Lord's Elect, led – however unworthily – by himself, by William and Louis of Nassau, and by the two Protestant queens of Navarre and England. At the centre of the struggle, pulled this way and that, was to be found the young king Charles IX, dominated by a mother whom Coligny distrusted, but did not distrust enough. The answer was clear. Once abstracted from his mother's influence and following the guidance of the Admiral, Charles could bring his country back to the path of national greatness. As a warrior king he would lead his army of Protestants and Catholics to the rescue of the persecuted Christians of the Netherlands. France would acquire new territories; Cateau-Cambrésis would be avenged; and the warring religious factions would be reconciled in the after-glow of victory over Spain.

Such a heroic, if simple, vision was bound to have its attractions for the impressionable character of the young Charles IX. This ferocious hunter of rabbits and stags was beginning to hanker after bigger game; and his aspiration after military glory made him listen with interest to certain proposals put forward in July 1571 by Coligny's confidant and ally, Louis of Nassau. Since 1570 Louis had been living in La Rochelle, where he had been hard at work organizing support for his brother, William of Orange. He had already done much to further the aims of the revolt in his capacity as commander of the Dutch and French corsairs who preyed on Spanish shipping from the Meuse to the Loire. But massive foreign help would be needed if William were to fulfil his great ambition of overthrowing Alba and freeing his country. William himself was in Germany, where he was attempting, as always, to enlist the active support of the Protestant princes. Louis's hope was to include France and England alongside the German princes in a general coalition against the king of Spain.

Louis's design harmonized perfectly with Coligny's plans, and elicited sympathetic noises from the queen of England, until she discovered how much it would cost. But French help was even more necessary than English, and Louis outlined his proposals at two very successful meetings with Charles IX, in which he offered France the southern half of a partitioned Netherlands in return for military assistance.

The warm response of Charles and his advisers made the summer and autumn of 1571 a hopeful time for Coligny and Louis of Nassau. Even Catherine was showing interest in the revival of an anti-Spanish policy, and a rapprochement between Coligny and the queen-mother now became possible on the basis of the Bourbon-Valois marriage plan and a campaign in Flanders. When Coligny came to Blois in September, casting aside his suspicions of the queen-mother's intentions, he found himself showered with favours, and soon acquired an extraordinary ascendancy over the person of the king. Charles, fatherless for so long, greeted him as 'Mon père', and could refuse him nothing. Perhaps the euphoria of the moment made Coligny and his friends oblivious to a certain menace in the air; perhaps the menace was only noted and remarked upon later, when it seemed as if the king's affection for the Admiral had been a deliberate piece of deceit. But few would have denied that in the autumn of 1571 Coligny and his Huguenot friends were riding high with the king.

Coligny's grand design, however, was impeded – as tends to happen with grand designs – by a shortage of cash. The resulting delay in the start of preparations for a Flanders campaign gave Catherine an inconvenient amount of time for second thoughts. Her son's extravagant enthusiasm for the Admiral was undermining her maternal authority. But, above all, she remained uneasily aware of one of her principal maxims of state, that France should steer clear of war with Spain, unless she could call on English help. While Anglo-French negotiations were mildly prospering and might end in a treaty, if not in a marriage, she was unable to share Coligny's belief that Spain's power was on the decline. The news of Lepanto in November 1571 confirmed her belief. It was a victory, reported the Huguenot Philippe Du Plessis-Mornay, which had 'frightened many people, who imagine that it has considerably increased the power of Spain'. For Catherine at least this was no time to court a break with Philip by drawing up plans for an attack on the Netherlands.

The news of Lepanto did, however, serve to remind both Catherine and Elizabeth of the desirability of an Anglo-French rapprochement to provide a counter to Spanish power. Elizabeth and William Cecil (now Lord Burghley) had no wish to see Spanish domination of the Netherlands replaced by that of France. On the other hand, an agreement with the French which fell short of a commitment to aid them in the Netherlands, would have obvious advantages, especially if it could deter them from fresh interference in Scotland. Catherine had some scruples about abandoning support for Mary Queen of Scots, but she was not a woman who found excessive difficulty in shedding either her scruples or her friends, and in April 1572 France and England signed the treaty of Blois. Each power promised help to the other in the event of an attack; but the treaty contained no provision for that offensive league against Spain with which Coligny and Louis of Nassau had hoped to crown their grand design.

The spring of 1572, however, was a time when events were overtaking the plans and preparations of men. On 1 March Elizabeth had ordered 'all freebooters of any nation' to leave English harbours. The decree was aimed at the swarms of corsairs who were now infesting the English Channel. After the failure of Louis of Nassau's invasion of Groningen in 1568, some of his supporters who possessed their own ships based themselves on Emden and plundered the coasts. The numbers of these 'Sea-Beggars', as they came to be called, were rapidly swollen by fresh recruits from the Netherlands – by Calvinist exiles, by nobles and gentry with a price on their head, and by fishermen and unemployed workmen from Flanders and Brabant. This motley crowd of exiles and desperadoes were nominally dedicated to the overthrow of the tyrant Alba, but proved a more or less indiscriminate menace to Channel shipping of every flag. Orange, however, saw that they could help his cause, both by cutting Spain's maritime routes to the Netherlands and by providing prize-money to finance his campaigns. He therefore gave them a semi-legal status in 1570 by issuing them with letters of marque, while Louis of Nassau began to organize them from the Huguenot base of La Rochelle.

In her campaign to spite the duke of Alba after his adoption of reprisals for the affair of the payships, Elizabeth chose to recognize the legality of the letters of marque, on the grounds that William and Louis possessed sovereign powers as princes of the Empire. But the Privy Council failed to foresee the results of its action. The Sea Beggars flocked to English ports; their commander, La Marck, found it impossible to control them; and their acts of piracy against ships of all nations became a serious embarrassment to the English authorities during the autumn and winter of 1571. The queen's proclamation of March 1572 was therefore the punitive act of an exasperated government.

In response to the proclamation, La Marck and his ships vanished over the horizon. They were later sighted between Dover and the Downs, waiting, it seemed, for reinforcements for an attack on the Netherlands coast. There appears to have been no suspicion, even in the minds of the participants, that this was to be anything more than another tip-and-run raid on a coastal town in search of plunder. But at this point the Channel winds intervened. La Marck's twenty-five ships were in need of shelter, and the English ports were closed to them. Driven towards Brill, the Sea Beggars found to their surprise that the

Spanish garrison had left in order to deal with unrest at Utrecht. On the evening of 1 April six hundred men landed, and sacked the undefended port. Then, as they were preparing to put their booty on board, one of their number pointed out that there was no reason why they should not remain where they were. So it was that, almost as an afterthought, the Sea Beggars secured their first foothold on their native soil.

It was predictable that Alba should have brushed aside the capture of Brill as of no consequence – '*no es nada*' ('it is nothing'). More surprising was the reaction of William in Germany and of Louis, then at Blois. They both displayed a marked lack of enthusiasm on hearing the news, for the Sea Beggars had moved too fast and too soon, and threatened to jeopardize all their plans. The obvious embarrassment and uneasiness of the two leaders of the Dutch revolt are themselves an indication of the unplanned, haphazard character of the capture of Brill, and of the extent to which the control of events had been removed from their hands. But Louis, with his sharp strategic eye, quickly grasped the possibilities of this premature move. If the technique used at Brill could be repeated at Flushing, the enterprise would have justified itself, for Flushing – the key to Zealand – commanded the entrance to the Scheldt.

There was only a token garrison in Flushing, and within a week Orange's tricolour had been run up in the town. Reinforced by English and Huguenot recruits, the Sea Beggars now advanced through Zealand, seizing town after town and plundering the churches as they passed. It had always been intended that any sea-based attack on the Netherlands should be supported by invasions from France and Germany. Louis of Nassau was mustering Huguenot companies in France, but there was no time for Orange to recruit troops in Germany, for Alba's counter-attack against the Beggars was expected from one day to the next. On 15 May Louis of Nassau took hurried leave of Jeanne d'Albret, queen of Navarre. He never saw her again – she died (of poisoning, alleged the Huguenots) three weeks later.

Louis joined François de La Noue and the other Huguenot captains on the Hainault frontier, and on 23 May he captured Mons, while La Noue's little company seized Valenciennes. At the very moment, then, when Holland and Zealand were slipping from Alba's grasp, he had lost the two towns which commanded the entry into Flanders from France. But the invaders had few troops; the local population proved markedly unfriendly; and when Valenciennes was lost again six days later, Louis was left anxiously waiting at Mons for Coligny to arrive with the French army, and for his brother to launch the long-awaited invasion from Germany. But neither Coligny nor William was yet ready to move, and it was not until 8 July that William crossed the Rhine at Duisberg and advanced into Gelderland.

Neither Louis's nor William's invasion was in itself immediately serious, for one was short of men and the other of money. But in Holland and Zealand the Sea Beggars were enjoying an extraordinary success. By July both provinces had almost completely fallen under rebel control, and Antwerp – the port on which Alba depended for his sea-borne supplies – was being subjected to an intensive blockade.

The explanation of the rebel successes in the northern Netherlands is not as simple as it might appear at first sight. It is easy but misleading to depict the Beggars as marching to victory on a wave of popular enthusiasm, to the triumphant strains of the *Wilhelmus* song. But in practice the rebel successes were the outcome of skilful, and often ruthless, tactics by an activist minority, which knew how to make the most of a favourable moment. The Calvinists, after all, represented only a tiny fraction of the population, especially in the northern provinces, where their influence had been much less than in the south. But in every town there was a handful of Calvinists and of active Orangist sympathizers, with friends and relations among the exiles who made up the invading Beggar forces. As the Beggars approached a town, they would make contact with their friends inside the city walls, and draw up plans to gain an entry. For instance at Gouda, at four o'clock on the morning of 21 June, an armed band of sixty-nine men was waiting by arrangement outside one of the city gates which was closed but not guarded. All but fourteen of the sixty-nine were natives of Gouda or near-by Oudewater – some of them exiles returning home. The gate was opened by their friends inside, and they made their way without resistance to the market place. Here a section of the city militia was stationed in front of the town hall, but was taken completely by surprise. One of the militiamen was about to shoot, but was deterred by a shout that they were 'our own fellow-citizens'. After this the danger of conflict was over, and the city fell into Beggar hands.

The capture of Gouda was repeated, with innumerable local variations, throughout Holland and Zealand during these summer months. Towns were taken by armed bands from outside, operating in conjunction with well-wishers within. Then a church was taken over for Calvinist worship; oaths of loyalty to William of Orange were demanded; churches were stripped of their images and their gold and silver ornaments; and the town council was purged if it showed any signs of resistance. William himself hastened to strengthen his position by arranging in July for a session of the Estates of Holland. Following the lead given by Philippe de Marnix de Sainte Aldegonde, William's confidant and adviser, the eight towns unanimously recognized the prince of Orange as the Stadtholder of Holland, and dedicated themselves to the defence of the Netherlands against 'all invasions and oppressions'. Roman Catholics and Protestants were to enjoy freedom of worship, and a large sum of money was voted for William's campaign. By these decisions of 19 and 20 July 1572, the Estates of Holland took their first steps along the road which would one day lead to rejection of the man they still regarded as their natural sovereign – Philip of Spain.

Yet although the conquest of Holland and Zealand represented a skilfully engineered take-over by a group of activists, they could never have achieved their startling success without at least the passive acquiescence of the population. It was here that the course of events since 1566 proved decisive. Although William of Orange could count on the support of a number of magistrates and patricians, the great majority of this class were opposed to a movement which threatened their power and their privileged position. But the mood of the mass of the citizens was very different. Strong tensions had built up since 1566, when the most substantial section of the citizenry had been frightened by the violence of the iconoclastic excesses. Alba's measures of repression, the scandalous conduct of royal officials and the Spanish soldiers, and finally the demand for the tenth penny, had all helped to complete the disenchantment with the royal government. The régime was hated as both Spanish and oppressive, and the church, which was closely identified with it, was still further discredited. On top of this, tradesmen and artisans, textile-workers, sailors and fishermen had all been badly hit by the deteriorating economic situation. Since 1568, as a result of the Anglo-Spanish dispute over the seizure of Alba's payships, commercial relations with England had been suspended. The activities of the Sea Beggars had badly damaged trade, and had interrupted the supply of Iberian salt for the crucial herring industry. There are some signs, too, that employers had taken advantage of Alba's strong government to keep down wages. Misery and unemployment were therefore rapidly increasing, and the winter of 1571–1572 was one of deep discontent.

It was an indication of the change of popular mood that whereas, in 1567, the 'regent' class of magistrates had carried out royal orders through fear of Alba, it was unwilling in 1571–1572 to collect even the modified tenth penny, because it now feared the people even more than the duke. It also seems as if those regents who had put up some opposition to the demand for the tenth penny had a better chance of carrying their cities with them against the Beggars than those who had surrendered with scarcely a protest. Amsterdam, where the magistrates had resolutely resisted the tenth penny, held firm against the Beggars in 1572 and only abandoned its loyalty to the king in 1578. On the other hand Dordrecht, whose magistrates had yielded to Alba's threats, was carried without difficulty into Orange's camp. In most towns the extreme unpopularity of the privileged magistrate class – increased by the pusillanimity under Alba's rule – left the town councils hopelessly isolated and exposed, when confronted with an angry crowd demanding that they should give entry to the Beggars. The civic militias proved consistently unreliable. They had shown their indifference for the church in 1566; they showed their indifference for the magistrates in 1572.

It was the climate of popular opinion, ranging from indifference to open enthusiasm, which prepared the way for the Beggars' success. The behaviour of the Beggars, once they had occupied a town, was often sufficient to alienate those moderates or neutrals whose acquiescence had made possible their original success. But the remedy might prove still more unpleasant than the disease, for if there was one thing worse than an armed band of Beggars it was a regiment of Spaniards. Therefore cities which had accepted the Beggars out of indifference often acquiesced in their continuing presence out of fear – fear of the Spanish soldiery and the reputation of Alba.

There was, however, one other crucial reason for the Orangist successes in the summer months of 1752. If the towns of Holland and Zealand had been well defended by Spanish garrisons, the Beggar army could have achieved very little. But Alba was short of men and money – the war in the Mediterranean had swallowed them up, and the failure to collect the tenth penny had ruined his carefully prepared scheme for paying for the Netherlands army out of local resources. Confronted with a shortage of men and a simultaneous invasion in the north and the south, he decided that the greater danger came from the frontier with France. He therefore pulled his best troops and his artillery out of the northern provinces, and it was their disappearance which gave the Beggars their chance.

There was every justification for Alba's decision. It should not be difficult in due course to deal with a few ill-disciplined bands of Beggars. But if Coligny should come with the French army to the aid of Louis of Nassau, the Netherlands might very easily be lost. Already a relief force of some 6,000 Huguenots under the seigneur de Genlis was approaching Mons. Towards the end of July, however, Spanish troops, aided by local peasants, surprised and defeated Genlis's men. Their booty included a letter from Charles IX which proved beyond doubt his complicity in plans for the invasion of Flanders.

The defeat of Genlis had serious consequences for the Protestant cause. Orange, having advanced into Brabant, now felt it wise to pull back to the Meuse near Roermonde and wait on events. In France, Coligny was becoming increasingly anxious, for Catherine's long-standing fear of Spanish power was revived, and she was convinced that Alba himself was planning an invasion. At all costs, therefore, the Admiral must get a decision from the king. During the first weeks of August, Coligny and Catherine fought their battle for the vacillating will of the wretched Charles IX. One day he would promise to declare war on Spain. The next, confronted by his mother, her face streaming with tears, he would change his mind and take back his promise. Perhaps after all she was right, when she warned that war with Spain would only deliver him and his kingdom into the hands of the Huguenots. If only England would come to his help, victory was assured. But Elizabeth and Burghley were not to be drawn. The duke of Alba's régime was intolerable, but, from the standpoint of England's security, French control over the Netherlands would be even worse. The government's fear of France, indeed, was so great, that Burghley recommended in a secret memorandum in June that England should go so far as to offer all help to Spain, if Alba proved unable to protect the channel ports from the French. *Raison d'état*, not religion, dictated England's policies towards the Netherlands in 1572.

Coligny waved Charles IX's hesitations aside. Even without English or German help, he assured him, the Huguenots could put enough men in the field to defeat the Spanish army. It was Coligny, not Catherine, who at last won the battle. On 11 August Charles wrote to William of Orange that an army of 15,000 men under his own leadership would shortly be taking the field. William's forces were at this moment close to Brussels, but he decided to wait for the entry of the French army into Flanders before beginning a siege. But the next message to reach him from France brought the shattering news that the Huguenots had been massacred in Paris and that his ally Coligny was dead.

2   The Massacre of St Bartholomew

Looking back on the terrible events of the night of 23–24 August 1572, the Huguenots found it easy to believe that the massacre of their brethren was the culmination of a carefully contrived and long-prepared plot. They saw it as the logical end to the story that had begun with the infamous meeting at Bayonne in 1565.[2] Alba, they were convinced, had proposed to Catherine de Medici that she should exterminate the Huguenot leaders; and since then the queen-mother, making use of all the arts taught by her fellow-Florentine Machiavelli, had been carefully baiting the trap. At the time of Charles IX's marriage in 1570 it had been suspected that she had been plotting with the cardinal of Lorraine the murder of Coligny and his friends. Certainly the Guise faction had made no secret of its determination to have its revenge for the assassination of Francis, duke of Guise in 1563.[3] Now, in August 1572, when the Huguenot nobility had gathered for the wedding of Henry of Navarre, the Guises had obtained their revenge and the trap had been sprung.

Ironically, the very expectation of some terrible deed itself made the deed more easily accomplished. Whatever Alba may have said to Catherine at Bayonne, she was shrewd enough to appreciate that the elimination of the leaders of one of the factions would deliver herself and the monarchy into the hands of the other. Her policy had always been to hold the balance between the two, playing on their strengths and weaknesses to the advantage of the crown. The massacre of the Huguenots in 1572 was thus a departure (and a fatal one) from a tenaciously pursued policy, for reasons that have never been fully elucidated. The evidence for Catherine's complicity in the initial act which triggered the events leading up to the massacre – the unsuccessful attempt on the life of Coligny – remains inconclusive, but there is no doubt of the part she played in the subsequent decision to eliminate the Protestant leadership.

There were certainly good reasons for Catherine to want Coligny out of the way, and the account which follows is an attempt to explain the attempted assassination of the Admiral in terms of why the Queen Mother might have been driven to undertake such a desperate act. It assumes premeditation, but it is also possible that Catherine was no more than privy to an act which can also be seen as a revenge murder by the Guises, who believed that Coligny was responsible for the assassination of Francis duke of Guise during the siege of Orleans in 1563. If so – or if, more implausibly, the attempt on Coligny's life came as a total surprise to Catherine – this version of events would either need to be modified or rejected, but it seems unlikely that clear proof will ever be forthcoming, one way or the other.

If premeditation is assumed, the reasons for Catherine's decision, reflecting as it did a radical departure from her previous policy, would seem to lie both in her own character and in the tensions set up at court by the actions of Coligny. By August 1572 the Admiral had secured an apparently unshakeable hold over the affections of the king. Moreover, he had used all his formidable powers of persuasion to press for a French invasion of the Netherlands – an action which, in his view, would put an end to the civil strife in France, whereas to Catherine it openly invited disaster. When Coligny and Du Plessis-Mornay put forward their plan, they were in effect only producing a new version of an old policy, and following an ancient maxim of state. In earlier years the cardinal of Lorraine had made a similar proposal, but with England instead of Spain as the object of attack. In an age when factious nobles and gentry were a perennial source of domestic unrest, it seemed no more than intelligent statecraft to divert surplus energies from internecine into international wars.

It may well be questioned, however, whether the domestic disputes in France had not become too complex to be resolved in this way. The French wars were, after all, something more than the feuds of noble factions, and passionate religious hatreds could not be summarily exorcised by a foreign campaign. Nor indeed could there be any guarantee that the French army would emerge victorious. The duke of Alba would certainly be gravely embarrassed by a full-scale invasion of France, and William of Orange might succeed in conquering the provinces of the north. But was France really strong enough to challenge Spain with success, especially without the assistance of England?

The opposition to Coligny's plan by Catherine and many of the royal councillors was therefore very solidly founded. But, the stronger the opposition, the more determined Coligny became; and this in turn forced Catherine into a position where she enjoyed less and less room for manoeuvre. The situation was still further exacerbated by the fact that Coligny's frantic efforts to win his point were leading him to trespass into the dangerous area bounded by Catherine's tenacious concern for her children. The three royal brothers – Charles IX, Anjou and Alençon – were by now at daggers drawn. The fratricidal rivalries of this miserable trio naturally played into the hands of faction. Coligny had already won the king, and he seems to have been drawing Alençon into the Huguenot camp. Anjou, for his part, reacted by moving closer to the Guises and the Catholics; but the death of the king of Poland in July aroused Huguenot hopes that he might be soon removed from the country as the elected king to a vacant throne.[4]

In exploiting the feuds of the royal brothers, Coligny was playing with fire. He must have known that, in alienating the queen-mother, he had embarked on a perilous course. His willingness to run the risk is open to various explanations. His staunch blend of patriotism and Protestantism no doubt helped to convince him that war with Spain was both honourable for France and divinely ordained. He also believed that a successful campaign would transform him into the indispensable right-hand-man of a victorious king. It was therefore worth playing for the highest stakes. But it remains open to question how far the initiative lay in his hands. For all his unique prestige among the Huguenot nobles and churches, even he could not hope to restrain indefinitely the passions and hatred of some of his followers. Perhaps, after all, only a foreign campaign could avert an explosion.

The very stridency of Coligny's demands may therefore have sprung, at least in part, from an awareness of how fundamentally weak was his own position. Patiently and persistently he had to curb those of his partisans who were spoiling for a fight. Simultaneously he had to win and retain something that was vital for his own future and that of his cause – the confidence of the king. Paradoxically, it was his very success in this which contributed most to his final downfall; for it brought upon him the hatred of Catherine, and gave him an unjustified confidence in his own ability to remain the master of events. Coligny's behaviour in the summer of 1572 suggests an unhappy combination of desperation and aggressive confidence which made him curiously blind to the dangers around him.

By the second week of August, these dangers were becoming very real. In a carefully calculated blaze of anger Catherine had left Paris for the castle of Monceaux, where she could meditate undisturbed on her future plans. Everything now pointed to the elimination of Coligny as the best, and perhaps the only, hope for preserving peace at home and abroad. Her resolution was probably fortified by the promptings of the duke of Anjou, jealous and frightened of an elder brother who, as Coligny's dependent, was asserting a new-found independence of his own. By the time Catherine was back in Paris for the royal wedding festivities of 16 to 21 August, the decision had been taken and the plans prepared. The Guises had often and publicly announced their determination to have Coligny killed. In the event of an assassination she could conceal her own complicity behind the convenient façade of faction feuds. Nor would she be unduly distressed if the Huguenots, seeing their leader struck down, should decide to take revenge on the Guises. A few bold strokes by each side in turn, and the monarchy would be safe from the domination of those over-mighty subjects who were pressing so close around the throne.

Henry of Navarre and Marguerite of Valois were duly married on 18 August. The festivities were splendid but too protracted for Coligny, who was anxious to be away on the Flanders campaign. But on the morning of 22 August he was struck, but not killed, by a shot from an arquebus as he was walking home from the Louvre.

That the assassin might botch his job had apparently not occurred to Catherine when she laid her plans. She was now in the worst possible position, with her victim still alive and her own complicity all too likely to come into the open. The Huguenots would surely take their revenge, which could well extend to herself and Anjou. It was not therefore surprising if at this moment she panicked. Her only hope now was to strike first, and this required the assent of the king. Charles's fury at the attempt on Coligny's life made him momentarily deaf to his mother's pleas. But later she returned to the attack. The Huguenots, she insisted, were planning a *coup*; Coligny was a traitor, and the safety of the throne and of France was at stake. She appealed to his honour, and, more shrewdly, to his courage: was he afraid of the Huguenots? This time she struck home.

The royal council, terrified of a massive reprisal by 4,000 Huguenot troops stationed outside the capital, fully supported the king's decision. A pre-emptive strike was needed to save the day. A list was prepared of the Huguenot leaders, headed by the Admiral, confined to bed by his wounds. The executions were to be limited in number, and carefully arranged. But again Catherine had miscalculated, under-estimating both the Guise desire for revenge, and the anti-Huguenot instincts of the Paris populace. If she had second thoughts as the tocsin rang out in the early morning hours of 24 August they had come too late. Within a few hours, Coligny and two or three thousand of his fellow-Huguenots had been butchered in the capital, and it was not long before the anti-Protestant frenzy was spreading through France. Massacres occurred in a dozen provincial cities, including Rouen, Orleans and Lyons. These were all cities controlled by Catholics, but in which the presence of substantial Huguenot minorities created a climate of persistent sectarian tension. As in Paris, the Catholic pop-ulace, convinced that it was acting on behalf of God and the king, turned violently on its Protestant neighbours, mutilating corpses and committing unspeakable barbarities in a mass upsurge of frenzied hate. All the fears and predictions of violence, which themselves helped to feed it, had been horribly fulfilled.

St Bartholomew, then, was a classic example of a process of escala-tion, the final consequences of which Catherine had neither desired nor foreseen when she first gave the order for the killing of Coligny. Faced with the unwelcome consequences of her own decision, her natural instinct – as might have been expected of a woman of her character – was to feel regret for a blunder rather than remorse for a crime. It was no less true to character that, even as she threw herself into the task of steering the monarchy back on to course, she should have made such capital out of the situation as she could. Alternative versions of the story of St Bartholomew were therefore prepared for the different courts of Europe. In Spain, it did Catherine no harm to hint that the massacre had been carefully prepared. In Rome, too, a story of premeditation was assiduously fostered by the cardinal of Lorraine, who hoped by this means to enhance the credit of the Guises, while tying Catherine closer to the Catholic cause.

Gregory XIII was duly delighted, and had a special medal struck to commemorate the great event. In the circumstances, it was hardly surprising that Protestant princes and their subjects should have been confirmed in their suspicions that the massacre was the outcome of a plot carefully hatched between Catherine, Philip and Rome. Catherine's ambassadors to Protestant States therefore had to work hard to provide more respectable explanations for what had occurred. Coligny, they suggested, had been plotting against the life of the king, and the massacre was a necessary counter-measure taken only in the nick of time. Alternatively, the massacre was presented as an unfortunate incident in the notorious feud of Coligny and Guise, which had nothing to do with Charles IX. Nobody could be expected to take these explanations very seriously in the Protestant North. It was easier, and more attractive, to see Catherine as the arch-conspirator and Charles IX as a man of blood; and if this remained the general impression, Catherine, in her deviousness, had only herself to thank.

However hard Catherine attempted to play down the massacre, the fact remained that what had happened could never be wholly undone. The first outcome of St. Bartholomew was, inevitably, widespread terror and confusion. There was butchery in town after town during the course of September, and many Huguenots who had survived the killing fled for refuge to Geneva or Strasburg. Others, especially among the nobility, felt it prudent to abandon a faith which seemed threatened with extinction, and they returned, at least nominally, to allegiance to Rome. This aristocratic defection in the months follow-ing the massacre drastically changed the character of the Huguenot movement, just as the adherence of the nobility had previously trans-formed its character a decade before. Deprived of aristocratic protec-tion and leadership, the movement turned back to the pastors for guidance, and recovered some of the spirit which had animated it during the later years of Henry II. Once again Protestantism in France became a genuinely popular and religious cause. Under the impact of St Bartholomew, the Huguenots of the south and the west rallied to the defence of their faith, and rose in revolt against a king who had ordered the murder of their brethren, and had even joined in the killing himself.

So far, then, from bringing the wars to an end, the massacre merely began them again. Everywhere the Huguenots were taking to arms. La Rochelle refused in September to admit a royal governor, and prepared itself to withstand a siege which began in December and continued unsuccessfully for seven months. The Huguenots were now fighting in order to survive, and the knowledge of this stiffened their resistance, which for the first time began to be presented as open resistance to the power of the crown. Until 1572 they had consistently maintained that they were fighting to protect the interests of a king subjected to the malign influence of the Guises. But after St Bartho-lomew it became impossible to maintain this convenient fiction, and Calvinists everywhere were forced to come to grips with a problem which they had done their best to evade – the problem of the legitim-acy of resistance to lawfully established authority.

Although some sanction could be found in Calvin's *Institutes* for the organizing of resistance to tyrants, Calvin had insisted that any decision on so crucial a question must be determined by reference to the laws and constitution of the State concerned. Beza had always been less legalistic in his approach, and in 1573, under the impact of St Bartholomew, he wrote a treatise on the general problem of obedi-ence and resistance. The city fathers of Geneva, however, had recently found themselves in trouble with the French Crown over the publication in their city of the *Franco-Gallia* of the Huguenot François Hotman – an examination of France's ancient constitution, which propounded the subversive thesis that the final authority rested with the Estates and not with the king. They therefore refused a licence for publication, and Beza's work appeared anonymously at Lyons in 1574, in a French version entitled *Du Droit des Magistrats sur leurs Subjects*.

John Knox had already argued in the late 1550s, for the right of resistance in its most radical form. But Beza's book was the first clear statement, from an official Calvinist standpoint, of the proper limits to monarchical power. Absolute power belonged only to God; kingship was based on a covenant with the people; and if the king became a tyrant, it was the duty of the magistrates (in France the Estates-General) to curb, and in the last resort, to depose him. Although the absence of Beza's name deprived the book of some of its authority, it represented an important addition to the theories of resistance which had been appearing in France since St Bartholomew's day. The massacre had prompted a flood of Protestant pamphlets, some of which merely recounted the horrible story, while others – like the notorious *Réveille-Matin* – advanced certain democratic ideas of popular revolt. But Beza's work presented the doctrine of resistance in the form most likely to be acceptable to the political nation in France. By laying the responsibility on the magistrates rather than the people at large, he conferred a degree of respectability on a highly explosive theory. It was this 'aristocratic' formulation of the theory of resistance which was adopted in the best known of all sixteenth-century works on the obligations of kings and the rights of subjects – the *Vindiciae contra Tyrannos* of 1579, probably written by Du Plessis-Mornay in collaboration with Hubert Languet. Here Beza's theories reached their logical conclusion: there was a formal contract between king and people, and it was for the magistrates to authorize resistance to a tyrannical ruler, and to seek help, if necessary, from foreign powers.

In forcing a reappraisal of the fundamental question of rights and obedience, the massacre of St Bartholomew rendered a signal service to the cause of political liberty. But the Calvinist constitutionalism of the post-massacre period also had its limitations. It placed a powerful weapon in the hands of the victimized and the persecuted, but it did the same for the mere opportunist, who constituted a less genuine case of need. Nobles would be able to resume their permanent vendetta against royal power in the comfortable assurance that they were acting as the divinely appointed guardians of the people's right. It was for this reason that the new constitutionalism was unlikely to appeal to the growing number of *politiques*, who saw in the restoration of strong monarchical power the only hope for the future of

France. Contractual arguments and doctrines of tyrannicide were anathema to men who ascribed more importance to political than religious unity, and entertained a deep veneration for the royal prerogative. It was Jean Bodin who, in his *Six Books of the Republic* of 1576, best formulated the *politique* ideal of the just society. Justice represented for Bodin an ideal order, in which men obeyed a prince who governed according to the laws of God. This unexceptionable ideal was one to which all parties would be able to subscribe. But Bodin's emphasis on the nature and resources of true majesty, and his insistence that passive disobedience was the sole recourse against tyranny, divided him sharply from Huguenot theorists, and provided an alternative political doctrine which corresponded closely to *politique* ideas.

Yet however much *politique* conceptions of the State may have differed from the more extreme contractual theses of the Huguenots, the condition of France after St Bartholomew made a Huguenot-*politique* alliance inevitable. Many of the leading *politiques* had themselves been in danger as enemies of the Guises, and had lost friends and relatives on St Bartholomew's day. One such was Montmorency-Damville, second son of the Constable Montmorency. As a Catholic who was a cousin of Coligny, he was ready to support any movement which would destroy the power of the Guises and bring the religious wars to an end. Making use of his strategic position as governor of Languedoc, he began to lay the foundations for a semi-independent Huguenot-*politique* state in the south of France. Other nobles shared Montmorency-Damville's ideas; and since Henry of Navarre and the young Condé were at present closely confined at court, they sought the leadership of the duke of Alençon, Catherine's youngest and most unsatisfactory son. This neurotic prince, with his wild ambitions, was delighted to acquire a personal and political following of his own.

It was easy enough for this group of disaffected nobles and genuine *politiques* to make common cause with a Huguenot noble like François de La Noue, now the commander at La Rochelle. Catherine therefore found herself, as the result of her foolish and terrible action, in exactly the position she had always sought to avoid. Once again the crown was the prisoner of faction – that of the Guises – and it was faced by an increasingly formidable coalition of Huguenot and anti-Guise nobles. The Huguenots were, if anything, more determined and united than ever before, and their organization was now more solid and extensive, stretching as it did from Dauphiné in the south-east through Provence, Languedoc and Béarn in the south, and then up through Guienne to La Rochelle. But it was not only at home that Catherine had done herself incalculable harm. Her foreign policy had always been designed to counter-balance the power of the Emperor and Philip II. But St Bartholomew had brought her into disrepute among exactly those States on whom she most depended – England, Poland, and the Protestant principalities of Germany.

It was, indeed, not Catherine but Philip who proved to be the real beneficiary of the massacre. Between the capture of Brill on 1 April and the events of 24 August, Alba's position in the Netherlands had deteriorated rapidly. Holland and Zealand had fallen to the Sea Beggars, and Brussels was threatened on one side by William of Orange invading from Germany, and on the other by Louis of Nassau and the French. It was a startling transformation after all Philip had been told about the success of Alba's policy of pacification; and the duke of Medina Celi, who had arrived to replace him in June, made the most of the disasters in his reports to Madrid. The real cause of the trouble, he wrote to his friend Ruy Gómez, was not heresy but the cupidity of Alba's officials and the appalling behaviour of his troops. Having diagnosed the disease to his own satisfaction, Medina Celi declined the governorship and departed for Spain, leaving Alba to find the cure.

It was the massacre of St Bartholomew which saved Alba, and transformed the military situation overnight. 'What a stunning blow (quel coup de massue)', wrote William of Orange to his brother, when he heard the news. 'My only hope lay with France.' Now there would be no French army to relieve Louis of Nassau at Mons, and William lacked the resources to come to his help. On 21 September Louis was allowed by the Spaniards to leave Mons with the honours of war, while William drew back disconsolately from Malines. The duke of Alba, fortified by papal encouragement, proceeded to make the most of the dramatic change in his fortunes. Malines was taken and sacked by his troops, and the iron hand of his government was felt again in Hainault, Brabant and Flanders. There remained only the northern provinces, and Alba was in no mood for mercy. One force, commanded by his son, Don Fadrique de Toledo, made towards the Zuyderzee while another was sent to reconquer Zealand. Everywhere the Spanish troops behaved with extraordinary brutality. The sack of Zutphen on 16 November was followed by the burning of Naarden and the butchery of its inhabitants. It was as if Peter Breughel, in his 'Massacre of the Innocents' had foreseen the miseries of his native land.

Early in December Toledo's forces advanced on Haarlem. The city was well protected by water, its garrison was strong, and the population was driven to a desperate resistance by the reports of Spanish arrocities. A first assault failed on 21 December, as did another in January. Haarlem's resistance forced Toledo to settle down to a long and costly siege, which ended only in July 1573, when starvation finally compelled surrender.

The year 1572, then, ended in the Netherlands as in France amidst the miseries and frustrations of a siege. La Rochelle and Haarlem: two Protestant strongholds under attack. At first sight, it might have seemed as if Protestant revolt in both countries was destined to fail. But the picture was perhaps rather less dark than it looked at the time. Although a year of terrible tragedy, 1572 had also been a year of success. The optimism of the summer had been brutally dispelled by St Bartholomew, but even the massacre could not totally obliterate the triumph of Brill. The very fact that the régimes both of Alba and Catherine had been reduced to undertaking long and tedious sieges was itself a sign of their political and military bankruptcy. Protestant resistance had hardened under fire. The Calvinists in both France and the Netherlands were now firmly established in a territorial base, and in both countries the attempt to reduce it proved in the long run self-defeating. In the Netherlands, Alba's savage campaign of reconquest had effectively alienated from Philip II the sympathies of those who had no liking for Orange and his Beggars. In France, the massacre had similar consequences – and Catherine, unlike Alba, did not even believe in what she was doing. Somehow, after the aberration of St Bartholomew, she must get the monarchy back on to course, for protracted war with the Huguenots could only deliver her into the hands of the Guises and Philip II. Besides, she had a new ambitious project on hand. Buoyant and resourceful as ever, she wanted the vacant crown of Poland for her favourite son, the duke of Anjou.

8

A Middle Way?

1   Poland and the West

The policy of religious repression in France and the Netherlands was visibly failing. War and massacre had brought no nearer a solution to the most acute political problem of the age: how to preserve the authority of the crown and the cohesion of the State in an epoch of confessional strife. Philip II in the Netherlands and Catherine in France may have been more starkly confronted with this problem than some of their colleagues, but a queen of England and a prince of Transylvania were no less alive to its complexities. Throughout the Europe of the 1570s kings and their ministers were searching, with varying degrees of skill and success, for that elusive point of balance between the competing claims of conscience, authority and public order which might give them a little respite from the troubles of their time.

The failure of repression in 1572–1573 inevitably quickened interest in possible alternative solutions to the great dilemma. In some circles, particularly at the Imperial court, the movement for confessional reunion, which reached back to the days of Erasmus, still had its fervent devotees; and at certain moments in the later decades of the century their irenical aspirations flickered into unexpected life. But, as the German and Swedish experiences were to show, the climate was unpropitious for an effective ecumenical movement. It seemed that syncretic religion, while exercising a will-of-the-wisp enchantment over a handful of rarefied spirits, left the mass of the European clergy and laity unmoved. The only alternative to confessional reunion – other than repression – was coexistence. But was this even desirable? And, even if it was, could it ever be achieved? There was one country which could perhaps supply the answer – a country which, through a dynastic accident, had suddenly caught the attention of Europe. Perhaps, in the example of Poland, there lay some lesson for the West.

The event which suddenly precipitated western interest in Polish affairs was the death in July 1572 of Sigismund II Augustus, leaving no heir. Although the Polish throne was elective, the crown had passed without serious difficulty during the last two centuries from one member to the next of the Jagiello dynasty. But now the dynasty was extinguished in its male line, and the election could not fail to be something more than the usual formality. It would also be an event of more than merely domestic interest, for candidates of no nationality were debarred, and the 1570s happened to be a period with more than its fair share of footloose young princes – Anjou, Alençon, Don John of Austria, and the archduke Ernest, the Emperor's son – ambitious for a crown and for a piece of land they could call their own.

There was, then, no shortage of candidates, and the choice was wide open. Internal rivalries among the Polish magnates soon eliminated any possibility that the next king of Poland would be native-born, but the problem of the religious affiliation of the new monarch was not so easily resolved. Poland's religious condition during the past few years had become exceptionally delicate. Although Protestantism had achieved some spectacular successes, it was not as firmly established as its adherents would have liked. It had made many converts among people of rank, especially among the upper and middling nobility, and among the gentry in certain regions. But its impact on the towns was less, and it had barely touched the countryside. It was, too, a Protestantism divided into many sects – Lutherans, Calvinists, Bohemian Brethren, Anabaptists and anti-Trinitarians.

The Roman counter-attack began in earnest in 1563 with the arrival in Poland of cardinal Commendone, sent as a papal nuncio to urge on the king and senate the acceptance of the Tridentine decrees. Although he failed in this particular mission, he persuaded Sigismund Augustus in 1565 to consent to an action that was to prove crucial for the future of Polish Catholicism – the admission of the Jesuits. By 1571 four Jesuit colleges had been founded in Poland, and the Order had made some significant conversions among the great aristocratic families. The Protestants, whose interminable feuds were a source of unconcealed delight to the native Polish cardinal Hosius, suddenly awoke in the late 1560s to the fact that the tide was beginning to turn against them. A new attempt to end their bickerings led in 1570 to the Consensus of Sandomir, an agreement between Lutherans, Calvinists and Bohemian Brethren. The Consensus, which represented a serious effort to preserve religious peace among Protestants on the basis of a mutual guarantee of confessional rights, raised the hope that, in Poland at least, men of differing faiths might learn to live side by side within one State. No doubt this was toleration by default – a renunciation of the quest for religious unity imposed by the sheer necessity of survival. On the other hand, the very peculiarities of

Polish life – the long experience of co-existence between the Roman and Orthodox churches, the multiplicity of sects, the deep influence of humanist education on the aristocracy – all helped to produce a climate in which the tender plant of toleration might hope to flower. Already in the 1560s the king's humanist secretary, Andrew Modrzewski, had attempted to persuade his master of the futility of compulsion in matters of faith – 'what belongs to the mind and the spirit cannot be forced out of anybody by torture or threats'. This sentiment began to appeal to increasing numbers of nobles and gentry – both Protestant and Catholic – during the last clouded years of Sigismund's reign.

When the king suddenly died, however, nothing had yet been decided or agreed. Toleration was still unrecognized in the constitution, and derived simply from the formal suspension by the Diet of 1562–1563 of all sentences passed by ecclesiastical tribunals. For the Protestant nobility it was therefore essential that the new king, if not himself a Protestant, should at least guarantee their religious rights, and that these should, if possible, acquire a constitutional sanction. For Rome, it was no less essential that the successful candidate should be a faithful son of the church, since the election of a Protestant might well undo all the work of Commendone and Hosius, and perhaps permanently remove Poland from its allegiance to the Holy See.

The Polish Election of 1572–1573 therefore became, like every other major political event in later sixteenth-century Europe, a trial of strength between the competing faiths. The candidate favoured by Rome was the archduke Ernest, second son of Maximilian II, since it was hoped that the presence of a member of the Imperial family on the Polish throne would help to engage the Emperor's flagging interest in the holy war against the Turk. Maximilian, however, suffered from a congenital incapacity to seize his opportunities. There were deep-rooted objections in Poland to a Habsburg succession, partly from anti-German sentiment, and partly from a suspicion among many of the nobles and gentry that a Poland under Habsburg rule would go the way of Bohemia and Hungary and lose its liberties one by one. But Maximilian was far better prepared at the time of Sigismund's death than any of his rivals, and a well-timed show of force, such as cardinal Commendone recommended, might have won the crown for his family, just as it later won the crown of Portugal for Maximilian's cousin (brother-in-law and son-in-law) Philip II of Spain.[1] But Maximilian characteristically hesitated, and the unfortunate Ernest was appropriately initiated on his *manqué* career as a man who never quite made a throne.

Maximilian's strength lay in the absence of any very obvious alternative candidate. There was no suitable Protestant prince who could hope to carry the day. Poland's foreign policy under Sigismund had been based on friendship with Sweden and Turkey against the common Muscovite enemy; and although Ivan IV had his supporters among the Lithuanian gentry, there were obvious objections to the candidature of the Tsar. Sigismund had also courted the friendship of France, and Catherine de Medici had for a long time had her eyes on the Polish crown for her second son. But Sigismund's death caught her unprepared. The devious, egoistical and effeminate Anjou would hardly have seemed a very convincing king for a nation which prided itself on its military virtues, but Anjou was misguidedly known in the east, in so far as he was known at all, as the victor of Jarnac and Moncontour. France, too, was a country which had its fascination for the Poles, and which, unlike the Empire, was conveniently remote. All this, when coupled with the inept behaviour of Maximilian and his diplomatic representatives, made it natural enough that the Valois candidature should quickly gain in strength.

But Catherine nearly wrecked Anjou's chances at the very start of the game. The news of St Bartholomew shocked Poland, as it shocked most of Europe, and threatened to deprive the French candidature of the Protestant support which was essential for success. It took all the diplomatic finesse of Catherine's adroit envoy Montluc, bishop of Valence, to undo the damage done to France's prestige by the events of that fateful day. In the autumn and winter months of 1572 in Cracow and Warsaw, Anjou's chances turned on the capacity of a highly sophisticated diplomat to bridge the credibility gap between Catherine de Medici's words and her actions. By a judicious combination of propaganda and persuasion he succeeded in building up a pro-French party among the nobles and gentry which appeared strong enough by the time of the Convocation Diet in January 1573 to carry the day. Realizing that their chances of excluding Henry of Anjou were fading, the Protestant nobles wisely decided to concentrate on securing constitutional changes which would preserve Polish liberties after his election, and which would render impossible a Polish version of St Bartholomew.

In representing themselves as the champions of Polish liberties, the Protestant magnates had achieved that combination of aristocratic constitutionalism and religious dissent which had done so much to undermine royal power in France and the Netherlands during the preceding decade. A vacant throne to be filled by election offered irresistible opportunities to an ambitious aristocracy, Catholic and Protestant, to realize its dream of an aristocratic 'republic' with a royal doge – the same dream as had been cherished by Condé, or by William of Orange when he secured the dismissal of Granvelle in 1564. The Convocation Diet of 1573 duly adopted certain measures which would still further reduce the already limited powers of the crown in Poland. The principle of dynastic hereditary succession was formally abolished, and election procedures were agreed; no new king was to be crowned before swearing to observe Poland's laws and liberties; Anjou, if chosen, would have to accept the so-called *pacta conventa* and the *articuli Henriciani*, which fixed the form of government and imposed strict limits on monarchical power. Poland in future would be governed by the Senate, which itself would be responsible to Diets meeting regularly every two years.

In addition to these governmental provisions, the Convocation Diet also agreed on the idea of a 'confederation' for the preservation of religious liberty – the celebrated Confederation of Warsaw of 1573. 'As there is great discord in this kingdom touching the Christian religion, we promise, in order to avoid sedition such as has come to other kingdoms...that all of us of differing religions will keep the peace between ourselves and shed no blood.' This remarkable compact, which the new king was to promise to preserve, had no exact parallel anywhere else in the Europe of its day. The Augsburg Peace of 1555 had been confined to Roman Catholics and Lutherans, and had rested on the principle of territorial division. There had been certain acts of toleration for individual sects, like the conditional edicts of toleration for the Calvinists in France, or Maximilian II's grant of toleration to the Lutheran nobles of Austria in 1568. Perhaps the act most comparable in its scope was the recognition by the Transylvanian Diet of 1571 of equal religious rights for Roman Catholics, Lutherans, Calvinists and Unitarians. But the Confederation of Warsaw extended the principle of religious liberty to nobles of *any* faith.

As far as can be judged from a rather ambiguously worded text, toleration was intended solely for the upper orders of society, although many individual nobles no doubt refrained from interfering with the religious practices of their tenants and serfs. In spite of all its defects and ambiguities, however, the Confederation of Warsaw did hint at some way of escape from the religious dissensions of the age. Its acceptance by the Roman Catholic lay nobility (although not by the primate and most of his bishops) was sufficient to secure from the Protestant nobles approval for the Valois candidature. At the beginning of April 1573 some 40,000 nobles and gentry – all electors to the Polish crown – assembled on the Warsaw plain. The result of the voting, which began on 4 May, was a foregone conclusion, for the earlier decision of the Convocation Diet to hold the Electoral Diet at Warsaw rather than in the Protestant centre of Lublin meant that the electoral proceedings would be dominated by the mass of the impoverished, pro-French and predominantly Roman Catholic lesser nobility, who could hardly have met the travelling expenses to attend a Diet any farther from home. On 11 May Henry of Valois was duly elected, and the Confederation of Warsaw was formally confirmed.

The news of the election, which reached Paris in June, had an immediate impact on the French domestic scene. The duke of Anjou was at this time personally conducting the siege of La Rochelle; but it was unthinkable that the monarch-elect of a nation dedicated to the principle of religious toleration should continue to persecute Protestants in his native France. On 24 June, therefore, a settlement was reached, and the siege of La Rochelle was raised. To the Huguenots it seemed a miraculous deliverance: 'God wished to spare His church, and delivered La Rochelle by calling the duke of Anjou to the Polish throne.'² From La Rochelle Anjou returned to Paris, to prepare a reception for the delegation on its way from Poland to offer him the crown.

The arrival in August of the Polish embassy – twelve ambassadors, Protestant and Roman Catholic, accompanied by two hundred and fifty Polish gentry in exotic attire – was something more than a sartorial sensation. For the symbolism which was expressed in the mixed religious character of the delegation was unlikely to be lost on the growing number of French *politiques*, who were suddenly presented with a living example of fraternal unity among adherents of widely differing faiths.

The unity was not in fact quite as profound as the more hopeful French observers liked to believe. Henry was quick to detect and exploit the confessional differences which lay beneath the surface, and he hoped in this way to free himself from the unpleasant obligation of taking the oath. But the ambassadors closed their ranks in time, and Zborowski's stern *'Jurabis aut non regnabis'* gave Henry no option but to yield. On 10 September 1573 he bound himself to do everything within his power to maintain religious peace in his new kingdom. The natural corollary to his oath was a return by the French monarchy to some measure of tolerance for its own Protestants, on whose behalf the Polish ambassadors had petitioned Charles IX. Slowly, under the impact of domestic necessity and the demands of her foreign policy, Catherine was bringing the repressive era of St Bartholomew to a close.

Anjou had an obvious role to play in the new age of mutual understanding, but no king could have displayed less enthusiasm for the tasks ahead. It was only with the greatest reluctance that he could be persuaded to leave the civilized delights of France for the discomforts of a barbarian land. In the meantime, boundless new possibilities were suggesting themselves to the fertile mind of Catherine. France was once more influential in Constantinople, which had given useful support to the Valois candidature; a French prince was now established in Poland, where his immediate task would be to overthrow the Tsar; Charles IX, as the son-in-law of the Emperor Maximilian, might in due course present himself as a plausible successor on the Imperial throne; and Alençon, with better luck than his brother, might one day become king-consort of England. Then French influence would span the continent from London to Moscow, Spain would be left without an ally, and each of Catherine's sons would wear a crown.

Before these glittering visions could be translated into fact, there remained a certain amount of diplomatic reconstruction to be done. Paris must mend its traditional alliance with the Protestant princes which had been temporarily shattered by St Bartholomew. This task was initiated on 4 December 1573 at Blamont in Lorraine, where Catherine and Alençon had come to take leave of Henry on his departure for Poland. In addition to the French royal family and a vast Franco-Polish entourage, Louis of Nassau also turned up in Blamont, accompanied by duke Christopher, the son of the leading German Calvinist, the Elector Palatine. Louis brought with him instructions from William of Orange to reopen negotiations with France. At highly secret discussions – a kind of Protestant equivalent of the meeting of Bayonne – it was agreed to form an alliance between France, Poland and the German Protestant princes. Henry of Valois would send William of Orange Polish reinforcements for a new campaign in the Netherlands.

The secret meeting of Blamont looked like inaugurating a new and happier era, in which France, inspired by the Polish example of religious co-existence, would combine toleration for its own Protestants with a return to active cooperation with the Protestant powers. As Henry took his oath at Cracow in February 1574 to preserve '*pacem inter dissidentes de religione*', and Louis of Nassau mobilized his troops in Germany, the hopes of Protestant Europe were rising fast. But they failed to survive the spring. In April, Louis of Nassau's invading army met the Spaniards at Mook, near Nijmegen. The day ended in complete disaster for the Dutch rebel cause. Louis of Nassau was killed in the battle, together with his younger brother Henry, and duke Christopher of the Palatinate.

The outcome of the Polish venture proved in its own way as disillusioning to Protestant hopes as the battle of Mook. Henry's interest in the Polish crown – never very great at the best of times – faded rapidly as reports began to reach him that his brother Charles IX was dying. His position was anyhow very unenviable, as the *roi fainéant* of an aristocratic republic, whose problems bore alarming similarities to those he had left behind in France. Instead of the Catholic Guises and the Protestant Bourbons there were the Catholic Zborowskis and the Protestant Firleis, and Henry was soon back at the old Valois game of dividing in order to rule. He deeply offended the Protestants by conferring offices and favours on the Zborowskis, and suspicions grew that he was attempting to restore monarchical power with the support of the Roman Catholic magnates. But Henry was primarily playing for time, doing what he could to avoid any confirmation of Polish laws which might weaken his position when he came to deal with the Huguenots at home. On 14 June 1574 the long-awaited news reached him at Cracow of his brother's death at the end of May. Four days later the new king of France slipped away from Cracow by night, and was almost out of the country before the indignant Poles could give chase.

The tragi-comic episode of a Valois king on the Polish throne had proved a bitter disappointment to many – to the Poles themselves, who had looked for a warrior and been saddled with an aesthete; to Catherine, who had dreamt of a second Valois monarchy away in the east; and to the Huguenots and *politiques* who had seen in the Polish connection and the Polish example a way of escape from the impasse of the French civil wars. A strange moment in east–west relations faded rapidly into history, but the memory of it was not entirely forgotten. For Poland had become to the Protestants of the west a symbol of moderation and tolerance – a symbol to which William of Orange would make a delicate allusion by the gift of a specially designed set of tapestries, when he tried again in the early 1580s to interest Henry and Catherine in his plans for a *politique* alliance against the king of Spain.[3]

How far, though, did the image accord with the reality? Civil war had been avoided in Poland in 1572, during the first interregnum, and a Protestant revolt was probably prevented by Henry's ignominious flight. When it became clear that Henry had no intention of returning, there was no choice but to summon another Election Diet. This time, tempers were shorter and divisions ran deeper, and it seemed that only a miracle could avert the shedding of blood. Once again Maximilian entered the lists, and again he managed to muff his chances. In December 1575 he was proclaimed king of Poland by the primate, in the Senate's name; but the Diet had other ideas, and chose the prince of Transylvania, Stephen Báthory.

The choice proved to be outstandingly good. Báthory was a highly intelligent and civilized man, who had completed his education at Padua, and retained a life-long interest in humanist studies. With the sultan's support he had been elected prince of Transylvania on the death of Sigismund Zapolyai in 1571. Himself a Roman Catholic, his own temperament combined with the complications of religious life in his own principality to give him a tolerant outlook well adapted to Polish needs. As soon as the news of his election reached him, he moved with characteristic vigour to take possession of his new kingdom. By the time Maximilian had decided to assert his own right, it was already too late. On 1 May 1576 Báthory was crowned at Cracow after agreeing to observe the *pacta conventa*, and was duly married to Anne Jagiello, the elderly sister of Sigismund Augustus II.

In due course Maximilian was ready to invade, but he suddenly died on 12 October. His genius for mistiming had remained with him to the end. From this moment until his own death in 1586 Báthory was the uncontested king of a nation which, under his leadership, enjoyed a final spectacular epoch of glory and military success.

Báthory realized that the first essential was to remove the spectre of civil war which still hovered over Poland. As a faithful son of the Roman church, he pressed ahead with ecclesiastical reform on Tridentine lines; but he remained true to the spirit of the Confederation of Warsaw, and insisted that the faith should be propagated 'not by violence, fire and sword, but by instruction and good example.' When the predominantly German and Protestant city of Danzig rose in support of Maximilian at the start of his reign, Báthory was careful, at the end of a six months' siege, to confirm the city's religious as well as its civil liberties.

It was Báthory's grand chancellor, John Zamoyski, who made the celebrated remark: 'I would give half my life to bring back to Catholicism those who have abandoned it, but I would give my whole life to prevent them from being brought back by violence.' So long as this spirit prevailed among the Polish nobility, religious peace could be preserved. But it was under constant strain, and Báthory – like Coligny – saw the best hope of conjuring away the demon of sedition in the diversion of national energies into foreign war. Traditionally, Muscovy was to Poland what Spain was to France. But the circumstances of Báthory and Coligny were only superficially alike. In Poland, there seems to have been less religious animosity than in France among the population at large, and among the nobles and gentry there was a well-established tradition of mutual tolerance on which Báthory could expect to build. Moreover, the Russian conquest of north Livonia in 1575 could be represented as a more immediate danger to the national interest than could the presence of the Spaniards in the Netherlands. Báthory, too, was a better general than Coligny, and possessed in the riches of his native Transylvania adequate resources for waging a successful war.

By 1578, with the Danzig question settled, Báthory was ready to launch his counter-offensive against Ivan the Terrible. Four years of brilliantly successful warfare, beginning with the rout of Ivan at Wenden in 1578, forced the Tsar to agree in 1582 to a humiliating truce, ceding to Poland all those parts of Livonia which were not in Swedish hands. Ivan's death in 1584, followed by the gradual descent of Russia into its 'Time of Troubles', ended the Muscovite threat to the Baltic and Poland for the best part of a century. As a result of the Polish conquests in Livonia, Báthory now found himself face to face with the Sweden of John III. But Báthory by this time was engaged in a grandiose project for a crusade against the Turk, to be followed by the incorporation of Poland, Hungary and Muscovy into a great east European empire. He therefore avoided a conflict with Sweden; and when he suddenly died in 1586, his crusade not yet begun, the Swedes and Poles would seek to reconcile their differences by the election of a Vasa prince to the Polish throne.[4]

In his ten years' reign, Báthory had done well by his Polish subjects. He had defeated their enemies, extended their frontiers, and preserved them from civil and religious war. Good leadership at a crucial moment in its history, together with a reasonably humane tradition and a basic community of interest among an aristocracy determined to maintain and extend its privileges at the expense of the crown, had saved sixteenth-century Poland from the fate of France. Báthory, an ardent Catholic and patron of the Jesuits, did much to promote the recovery and eventual success of the Roman church in Poland, but he always played the game according to the rules. There were obvious defects and shortcomings in the Polish compromise: fundamentally, it was no more than an agreement among the nobles and gentry to avoid recourse to the sword in disputes over matters of the faith. But in the heated religious atmosphere of the later years of the century, even this represented a considerable achievement, and was certainly far better than no toleration at all. Nor, for all its limitations, were its benefits solely confined to a single privileged class. There were not many countries in which a ruler, whether Protestant or Roman Catholic, would have allowed Socinus to propagate his anti-Trinitarian beliefs.[5] But whether the Polish model of religious co-existence was capable of satisfactory transposition to other parts of Europe – as Orange and the *politiques* had hoped in 1573 – was a matter open to doubt. There was no response in 1578 to an appeal by the Polish Protestants to the various Protestant churches of Europe to follow the example of conciliation set by the Consensus of Sandomir. It looked as though each nation would be forced to discover through trial and error its own individual road to salvation.

2   Sweden and Germany

There was, it seemed, no universally applicable solution to the politico-religious problem of the age. There were, of course, certain constants in the religious life of the later sixteenth century, of which every ruler had to take account. One was the post-Tridentine Catholic revival. By the 1570s this was affecting more and more nations in a widening radius from Rome, as Gregory XIII turned his attention to the re-conversion of central, northern and eastern Europe.[6] The other was the internal crisis of Protestantism, characterized by bitter internecine feuds as Calvinism became increasingly militant, while

Lutheranism lost its impetus and began to stagnate. But alongside these constants there were numerous variables, determined by local and national conditions and the endless interplay of personalities. What Stephen Báthory could achieve, Catherine de Medici could not. Princes were all too likely to find that their room for manoeuvre was sharply restricted, and that the best intentions received short shrift at the hands of their religiously committed subjects. The successful ruler, in this age as in any, was one who – like Elizabeth of England – possessed a well-developed sense of the politically possible, an instinctive feel for timing, and a fair share of luck.

These were hardly the characteristics of the Emperor Maximilian II, or of that self-opinionated royal scholar, John III, who had replaced his deposed brother Eric XIV on the Swedish throne in 1568. At the time of John's accession, the situation of the Swedish church was not dissimilar to that of the church of England in the early years of Elizabeth's reign. Originally created, like the church of England, as a deliberate act of the royal will, its doctrines remained imprecise and its organization left much to be desired. By the 1560s it was beginning to experience those strains and stresses which were affecting Lutheran churches everywhere in the middle years of the century. Exiles from France and Germany were introducing Calvinist doctrines, and the Swedish church was inevitably affected by the bitter feud in Germany between the orthodox Lutherans, championed by the redoubtable Flacius Illyricus, and the 'Philippists' (so-called after Philip Melancthon) who were denounced by their opponents as crypto-Calvinists. On the other hand, there was unlikely to be any effective demand from within Sweden for the restoration of the Catholic church. Swedish Catholicism, deprived of its leadership and cut off from the outer world, had dwindled more rapidly than its English counterpart. Any reconquest of Sweden by Rome would have to be mounted from outside, under the leadership of Scandinavian exiles like the young Jesuit convert, Laurentius Norvegus.

John III, however, had various reasons for wishing to steer a rightwards course. He was married to a Roman Catholic wife, the sister of Sigismund II Augustus of Poland, and the daughter of Bona Sforza, from whom she had inherited a considerable fortune. Unhappily, much of this Sforza fortune consisted of assets frozen in Naples by Philip II, and John would need the help of the pope to make Philip change his mind. There was, too, the question of the Polish succession. Either John or his son Sigismund stood a fair chance of eventual election to the Polish crown, but for this they would need the Roman Catholic vote. John's own religious inclinations coincided with the requirements of his foreign policy. Himself a learned theologian, he had been attracted when in Poland by the theology of George Cassander (1513–1566), a Flemish humanist of Erasmian outlook who had advocated a reconciliation of Catholic and Protestant on the basis of common articles of faith. John III made Cassander's ecumenical aspirations his own, and – as a first step to reunion – introduced in 1576 a new liturgy, the 'Red Book', which cleverly blended the Roman and Lutheran orders of service.

While busily reforming Swedish ceremonial and doctrine, the king was also responding to overtures from Rome and Spain. Philip II, hampered in his struggle against the Dutch rebels by his weakness on the sea, had his eyes on a hundred warships of the Swedish fleet. In order to secure the loan of these ships he dangled before John III the tempting bait of the Sforza inheritance. Negotiations between the two rulers were initiated in 1574 by a Polish Jesuit, who was able at the same time to test for himself the king's religious views. The results seemed sufficiently encouraging for the pope to send a secret Jesuit mission to Sweden, led by Laurentius Norvegus, disguised as a Protestant cleric. He was followed in 1577 by a papal legate, Antonio Possevino, and in the spring of 1578 the king was secretly converted to Rome. He seems to have agreed to conversion, however, on the assumption that the pope would make special concessions for Sweden on the marriage of the clergy, mass in the vernacular, and communion under both kinds. The assumption proved to be quite unfounded: John III's syncretic religion was totally unacceptable to Counter-Reformation Rome. Already the king's attempts at liturgical reform were leading him into difficulties with his own subjects, and especially with the anti-liturgical party led by his neo-Calvinist brother, Charles, duke of Södermanland. Disillusioned with Rome, and confronted by a demand from the Riksdag that he should sever relations with the papacy and expel the Jesuits, John III bowed to the inevitable. In 1580 the *missio suetica* was liquidated. It had made no more than a handful of converts, and the king himself was soon reacting violently against Rome and all its works.

John III's abortive attempt to reconcile the churches showed how easily the best-intentioned plans could go awry. John was shrewd enough to grasp that his country was not prepared to follow him, and that an open declaration of his conversion would undoubtedly cost him his throne. He had, in any event, grossly underestimated the theological obstacles to a reunion of the churches – a mistake that was also made by the Emperor Maximilian II. Maximilian had been educated by Lutheran tutors, and it is possible that he remained throughout his life a Lutheran at heart. But his position as Emperor, and his exquisitely delicate relationship with Philip II, whose throne might revert to the Austrian branch of the family if he died without an heir, made it inconceivable that he should go so far as to break with Rome. Consequently, throughout his twelve years on the Imperial throne he found himself awkwardly condemned to the role of honest broker, desperately mediating between Catholics and Protestants, while trying to avoid offence to either.

The religious situation in Germany would in any event have tested to the limits the political skills of an abler man. By the time of Maximilian's accession in 1564 the balance of forces registered by the Augsburg settlement was already beginning to be seriously disturbed. Most of the major lay princes and the free cities were now Protestant, and the Lutherans had their eyes on the wealthy ecclesiastical principalities. A further complication was added by the conversion of the Elector Palatine Frederick to Calvinism. Once the Diet in 1566 had failed to support Maximilian's request for common action to exclude Frederick from the benefits of the Augsburg settlement, the religious dyke was effectively breached. During Frederick's reign, Calvinism spread northwards from Heidelberg into the Rhineland and Westphalia, and was adopted in the early 1570s by the homeland of the Orange dynasty, the county of Nassau.

Faced with the religious babel in Germany – Lutheran against Catholic, Lutheran against Lutheran, and Calvinist against them all – Maximilian attempted to find some middle way, which would bring the warring churches together again. Like John III of Sweden he too looked to the works of Cassander for some miraculous solution to the enigma of confessional dispute. But he looked in vain. The failure of Maximilian's efforts at reconciliation dampened but did not extinguish the ecumenical aspirations of the Austrian Habsburgs. Maximilian was succeeded in 1576 by his extraordinary son Rudolph II, who differed from his father in being a devoted son of the Roman church. But in the strange world which Rudolph created for himself in the Imperial court at Prague, surrounded by men of letters and charlatans, astrologers and alchemists, he too pursued the family quest for the elusive religious synthesis. Partly this reflected the natural bent of a speculative and dilettante mind; but it also testified to the potency of the new sense of mission among the Austrian Habsburgs – a mission which, by restoring unity of faith, might also restore cohesion to their shattered Empire.

Unable to win sympathy for their dreams of confessional reunion, both Maximilian and Rudolph found it politic to bend before the prevailing winds. Protestant nobles, acting through the Estates, were subjecting them to heavy pressure in their own hereditary lands. Maximilian responded by conceding in 1568 and 1571 to the Lutheran nobles of Lower and Upper Austria the right to free exercise of their faith on their own estates. Rudolph in turn had to accept some form of toleration in both Hungary and Bohemia, where the price of his election to the crown in 1575 was the acceptance of a 'Bohemian confession', to which Lutherans, Calvinists, Utraquists and Bohemian Brethren all – by some miracle – found it possible to subscribe.

Toleration in the Habsburg lands was a temporary necessity, which reflected the relative strength of German Protestantism and the weakness of Catholicism at the time of its concession. But by the mid-1570s the situation was gradually beginning to change. German Catholicism was at last showing certain signs of revival. The Jesuits had been making converts under the energetic leadership of the Dutchman Peter Canisius, director of the upper German province of the Jesuit order from 1556 to 1569. Meanwhile, duke Albert of Bavaria, in reconverting his duchy to Rome with Jesuit and Capuchin support, showed what could be achieved by a determined ruler, if he could once manage to break the hold of his Estates. There was little hope of this in the Habsburg lands, but Rudolph II took the first tentative steps to check the spread of Protestantism. In 1578 he ordered the expulsion of Protestant preachers from Vienna, and then from other parts of Austria.

The visible progress of the Roman church in Germany during the 1570s was sufficiently alarming to give a fresh impetus to the Lutherans to sink their internal differences. In 1574 that coldly calculating patriarch, the Elector Augustus I of Saxony (1553–1586) abruptly changed course on discovering – at least to his own satisfaction – that Philippist[7] theologians at his court were attempting to Calvinise his Lutheran Electorate. His discovery led to a ferocious persecution of the crypto-Calvinists, and the firm planting of his Electorate in the orthodox Lutheran camp. The religious realignment of Saxony and the death in 1575 of that stormy petrel of Lutheran politics, Flacius Illyricus, gave new strength to the movement for Lutheran unity. In 1580 a 'Formula of Concord' was agreed among the Electors Augustus of Saxony and John George of Brandenburg, the Elector Palatine Louis (the Lutheran son of a Calvinist father), and twenty princes, twenty-four counts and thirty-eight cities. While the Formula helped to check the demoralization and disintegration of German Lutheranism, it also sharpened the divisions between the Protestant churches, for the Philippists were left out in the cold. This meant the disappearance of any chance of reconciliation between Lutherans and Calvinists, which the queen of England had hoped to bring about when she despatched Sir Philip Sidney on a mission to Protestant Germany in 1577.

The hardening of religious divisions in the Germany of the 1570s between a resurgent Catholicism, a redefined Lutheranism and an activist Calvinism inevitably increased the tensions and sharpened the conflicts. The most sensitive of the danger-points were the ecclesiastical principalities, the subject of the 'reservation clause' of the Augsburg settlement, which stipulated that any prelate who ceased to be a Roman Catholic should resign his see. The Protestants had never formally accepted the 'reservation', although it had been tacitly agreed that the *status quo* of 1555 should be maintained. The test came in 1577 when the archbishop of Cologne, an Elector to the Empire, very properly resigned in order to marry. Cologne occupied a vital position among the Catholic States of north-west Germany near the Netherlands border, and was a tempting prize for the Protestants. Their supporters in the cathedral chapter succeeded in carrying the election of a conveniently dissolute character of impeccable Roman Catholic background, Gebhard Truchsess. In 1582 Truchsess indicated that he would imitate his predecessor in taking a wife. Persuaded by the Protestants that he could nevertheless retain his see, he announced his conversion to Protestantism and his determination to preserve his ecclesiastical state. He was duly deposed by the pope, who put in his place a brother of the duke of Bavaria – a man whose morals were no better but whose religion was safe. Truchsess discovered too late that the Bavarian Wittelsbachs were prepared to risk a good deal more than the Protestants for the sake of Cologne; and after some vigorous military skirmishing, which kept north-west Germany in a state of unrest for three or four years, the lucrative and influential Electorate of Cologne passed into the eager hands of the Wittelsbachs, who successfully clung to their valuable prize.

The Cologne affair, which marked the turning of the Protestant tide in Germany, revealed all too clearly the deficiencies of the Augsburg settlement, and the increasing probability of armed conflict between the rival faiths. Stronger Imperial leadership might perhaps have secured a realistic revision of the 1555 settlement, which was, after all, no more than a truce. But the leadership was not forthcoming, or was diverted into ecumenical generalities; and the feeble constitutional structure of the Empire reduced the possibility of any emergence in Germany of a *politique* party, prepared to subordinate religious convictions to the needs of the – non-existent – State. If Germany escaped civil war in the second half of the century, this was largely because the constitutional issue had already been fought out and decided under Charles V, while the Imperial authority was too weak to prevent each prince from going his own religious way.

3   France and the Netherlands

Poland and Germany had both succeeded in achieving some form of coexistence, however precarious, between the adherents of rival creeds. The Germans relied on the Augsburg formula of territorial division, *cuius regio eius religio*, while the Poles had managed at least a degree of toleration. But the principle of toleration remained anathema both to Geneva and Rome. In spite of this, however, there were men in both France and the Netherlands who were prepared to defy the official lines of their own churches, in the belief that some form of religious coexistence had become indispensable for the survival of civil and political life. In both countries the 1570s were a decade distinguished by strenuous, although unsuccessful, efforts to secure civil peace by means of a religious truce.

On his dilatory return to France by way of Germany and Italy in the summer of 1574, Henry III had ample opportunity to collect ideas about possible methods of restoring peace and unity to his shattered kingdom. In Germany, everyone from the Emperor downwards seems to have advised him that the Huguenots must be given full toleration. But a much greater impression was made on the new king of France by his meeting in Milan with that supreme representative of Counter-Reformation spirituality, cardinal Borromeo. The impact on Henry of the cardinal's personality, with its intense religious sensibility and its austere devotion to charitable works, was overwhelming and profound.[8] It apparently gave him a vision of a sinful world that could be redeemed only through expiation. He would become a royal penitent, who would seek with a few chosen companions to expiate through spiritual exercises and mortification his own and his subjects' sins.

As a practical solution to his country's problems, this approach left something to be desired. Catherine wanted her son to be a leader, and to assume the full majesty of kingship. But Henry, as she knew in her heart, lacked the qualities that make a king. This last ruler of the Valois line was a strange compound of contradictions. Periods of rigorous mortification would alternate with bouts of dissipation with his fellow-penitents, his so-called *mignons* – the group of refined and elegant young men, drawn from the middling ranks of the provincial nobility, whom he banded together to form the nucleus of a potential king's party, and who became the objects of universal dislike and derision because of their success in obtaining the royal favour and their allegedly effeminate ways. Henry was shrewd and subtle, and infinitely superior in intellectual ability to his worthless brothers, but temperamental stability was not to be found among his many gifts. He lacked physical and mental stamina, the capacity to act on a decision and follow it through to the bitter end. Trusted by no one, and trusting no one in his turn, this clever, twisted, unhappy man – crowned at Rheims with all the pomp and pageantry that it took a Medici to devise – was condemned by the defects of his own character to watch his kingdom waste away through a sickness which he could perfectly diagnose but for which he was unable to provide the cure.

Catherine had saved the kingdom for him against his return. This itself was a considerable achievement, for Alençon was doing his best to supplant his brother on the throne. But in the process she had

antagonized Montmorency-Damville, the leader of the *politiques* and
the uncrowned king of the south. Damville reacted by strengthening
his ties with the Huguenots and calling a general assembly of *politiques* and Huguenots at Nîmes in December 1574. This assembly led
to the transformation of southern France – Languedoc, Provence and
the Dauphiné – into a virtual State on its own, with its own
institutions and financial machinery, and a firm agreement among
its members to allow each other freedom of conscience and to unite
as 'true-born Frenchmen'.

Faced with *de facto* toleration in the southern half of France, Henry
had no choice but to capitulate. Alençon and Navarre had escaped
from their captivity at court to join Montmorency-Damville's revolt.
Henry had neither money nor friends, and in May 1576 he accepted
the humiliating terms of the peace of Monsieur.[9] This peace, which
was confirmed by the edict of Beaulieu, represented the most favourable settlement which the Huguenots had so far achieved. It allowed
them complete freedom of worship in French towns, with the one
major exception of Paris; eight 'places de sûreté'; and admission to all
offices, including half the seats in the *parlements*.

The terms of the edict of Beaulieu give the impression that France
was at last on the point of resolving its domestic troubles on the basis
of equality between the two religions. But any such hope proved
illusory. Civil war was becoming a way of life, and the king, surrounded by his lap-dogs and *mignons*, lacked the gift of leadership.
The initiative therefore fell to the Guises, who joined with the more
extreme Catholics in finding the settlement totally unacceptable. The
cardinal of Lorraine had died in 1574, but the young Henry, duke of
Guise,[10] was now old enough to become an effective faction-leader,
and the Catholic opposition formed itself under him into a 'Holy
Union' or 'League'. There had in the past been local Catholic leagues,
but the League of 1576 was a national organization, depending for its
support on the Catholic and Guise nobility, and on the Catholic city of
Paris. But like the Huguenot national organization, to which it bore a
marked resemblance, it also counted on mass support – that of the
Catholic laity; and, just as the pastors played an active part in rallying
the Huguenots, a similar role was played in the League by the parish
priests and the monks and friars.

The first action of the League was to demand the summoning of the
Estates-General, which met at Blois in December 1576. The League
had managed the elections for the assembly, and the Huguenots and
politiques refused to attend. The Estates of Blois were therefore an
almost entirely Catholic assembly, subjected to heavy pressures from
the League, which had already shown itself a formidable political
organization. Its nominal purpose was to maintain the authority of
the crown as well as the unity of the faith, but its own character as a

nation-wide movement with its own leadership made it from the first a potential challenge to the royal power. Henry III, knowing that he was too weak to beat it, decided instead that it was wiser to join it, and turn the oaths of loyalty to his own account. In his address to the Estates of Blois he announced that he would in future tolerate only one religion in the kingdom, and cleverly placed himself at the head of the League. The Estates in turn pronounced themselves in favour of a restoration of religious unity, although a majority of a divided third chamber, while voting for the suppression of the Reformed Religion, added the rider that this should be achieved by 'gentle and holy means'.

Even if the country was tiring of war, the sentiments of the Estates of Blois made it clear that the principle of toleration as expressed in the edict of Beaulieu was unacceptable to a broad range of public opinion in France. Without a broad consensus in its favour, and without strong royal leadership to enforce it, it was inevitable that the recent peace should fail. Hostilities were resumed again, and then once more brought to a temporary halt by the edict of Poitiers in October 1577. This was less favourable to the Huguenots than the edict of Beaulieu, because Protestant worship was now restricted to the suburbs of one town in every *bailliage*, and to those towns where it had been practised before the latest resumption of war.

The edict of Poitiers was followed by the formal dissolution of all Leagues, Protestant and Catholic. But the period between the League's extinction in 1577 and its resurrection in 1584 proved to be one of sporadic and uncertain peace. While the edicts of Beaulieu and Poitiers provided the essential basis for a settlement on *politique* lines, of the type finally adopted in 1598, the forces of disruption were too strong and the forces of order too weak for the edicts to offer any way of escape. In his dependents and favourites Henry III had the possible nucleus of a king's party, without which the crown could never recover its power. But he was unable to lead it or use it to any purpose, and his own irresponsible behaviour made him an endless liability to the royal cause. In the meantime, Henry of Guise and Henry of Navarre faced each other as rivals for power, while the duke of Alençon intrigued and conspired. Behind the great families, struggling for control of government at Paris and in the provinces, were ranged the impoverished nobles and gentry, who depended for survival on the profits of war. For as long as three régimes existed in France – a Huguenot, a Catholic, and an enfeebled royal administration – unity and order could never be restored on the inevitable basis of a limited religious toleration, even if the desire for toleration had been sufficiently strong. In his despair at the hopelessness of the situation, the royal secretary Villeroy neatly expressed the dilemma of those who still attempted to maintain the authority of the crown: 'We cannot either make war or peace. That is our trouble, for which there is no remedy without the help of God.'[11]

... 'We cannot either make war or peace.' It could as easily have been the *cri-de-coeur* of a Spanish governor in the Netherlands as of a French secretary of state. The Spanish crown, like the French, found itself saddled with a war that it could neither win nor end; and in the Netherlands, as in France, it was religion that appeared to block the way. The efforts of Alba to provide a military solution had visibly failed. For all the supremacy of Spanish arms on land, Alba had been fatally handicapped by his inability to win control of the sea. The Sea Beggars maintained a constant blockade of the Netherlands coast – a blockade which became total with their capture of Middelburg after a two years' siege in February 1574. The magistrates and citizens of Middelburg had put up a strong defence against the Beggars, and the Spaniards had made frantic efforts to break the blockade. But – as their attempt to contract for the Swedish fleet suggested[12] – they were cruelly hampered by their shortage of ships. Once Middelburg had fallen, the rebels dominated the sea routes between the Netherlands and the Iberian peninsula. This meant not only that they could provision themselves freely from England or La Rochelle, but that they had the Castilian economy at their mercy, for Castile could not dispense with its northern trade and its Baltic grain, even though these had now fallen under rebel control.

Alba's failure to crush the rebels had finally discredited him at court. In the long battle at the council table between the Alba hawks and the Eboli doves, the doves had clearly emerged victorious. The prince of Eboli himself died in July 1573, and the effective leadership of the faction devolved on the king's secretary, Antonio Pérez. But Eboli's views had prevailed with the king well before his death; for at the end of January 1573 Philip had written to his governor of Milan, Don Luis de Requesens,[13] expressing his deep concern at the state of affairs in the Netherlands, and designating him as the duke of Alba's successor. Requesens was an administrator and diplomat, not a soldier, and his appointment was a clear indication of the king's intention to attempt a policy of conciliation now that military measures had failed.

Requesens arrived in Brussels to replace Alba in November 1573. He had secured permission before leaving for Flanders to proclaim an amnesty (with certain exceptions), to abolish the notorious Council of Troubles, and to abandon the project for the collection of the ill-omened tenth penny. But while Philip was ready to make political concessions in so far as the maintenance of his royal authority allowed, he had no intention of yielding an inch on any matter affecting the faith. 'I would rather lose the Low Countries than reign over them if they ceased to be Catholic', he had written in the summer of 1573.[14] The prospects for a negotiated settlement therefore hardly seemed very promising, for Orange's war-aims, as outlined in a letter to his brothers, included important religious concessions by Spain. 'I have only aspired', he wrote, 'for the freedom of the country both in matters of conscience and government... Therefore, the only articles that I have to propose are that the exercise of the Reformed religion in accordance with God's word should be permitted, and that the Republic's ancient privileges and liberty should be restored, which means that foreign, and especially Spanish, officials and soldiers should be withdrawn.'[15]

On arriving in the Netherlands, however, Requesens seems to have had some hope that the king's intransigence on the religious question would not necessarily prevent a settlement. He felt that the revolt of the Netherlands was essentially the revolt of a country provoked beyond endurance by the demand for the tenth penny and by the tyrannical and corrupt government of the duke of Alba. If he was correct in his diagnosis that only the leaders of the revolt were animated by religious concerns, then it followed that a firm determination to abandon the methods of the Alba régime might be sufficient to win back all but a few zealots to the royal cause.

In many ways the spring of 1574 seemed a propitious moment for Requesens to attempt a break with the immediate past and to seek a return to the system of government that existed under Charles V. Although the loss of Middelburg in February 1574 was a major setback for the Spaniards, their crushing victory over Louis of Nassau and his German mercenaries at the battle of Mook in April[16] seemed at the time to provide more than full compensation for their earlier defeat. Orange himself was determined to continue the struggle to the end, and redoubled his efforts to create an anti-Spanish coalition, which he saw as the sole hope for the salvation of Protestantism not only in the Netherlands but throughout Europe; but he was well aware of the fickle character of his compatriots, and feared that the disaster of Mook would weaken their will to resist.

Requesens, sensing the demoralization of the rebels, now had the perfect opportunity to put his theories to the test. But the chance for conciliation from a position of strength was tragically lost almost as soon as it arose. The 'Spanish' army – that great military machine of some 25,000 Germans, 20,000 Walloons and 8,000 Spaniards – was growing restless at its lack of pay. Mutiny broke out in the ranks; the mutineers (including the crack Spanish troops) marched on Antwerp and held it to ransom; and although Requesens succeeded in quelling the mutiny by meeting the soldiers' immediate demands, the damage had been irrevocably done. When he announced his general pardon at the beginning of June 1574, its impact was nullified by the fact that it was announced under the shadow of mutiny and possible military collapse.

William's obvious policy now was to play for time. The Spanish army, with order restored, had settled down at the end of May to lay siege to Leyden. The longer Leyden could hold out, and pin down a substantial portion of Requesens's troops, the less chance would the Spaniards have of following up their victory at Mook. It was clear, too, that Philip's financial difficulties were increasing, and that each succeeding month of war would add to the strain on Spanish resources and enhance the possibility of a fresh wave of unrest in the ranks. Leyden's heroic resistance, and the decision of William and the Estates of Holland to flood the surrounding countryside, saved the day, and perhaps the revolt. As the relief barges approached the beleaguered city on the rising waters, the Spaniards, waist-deep in mud and water, began to retreat. On 3 October 1574 the siege was lifted. William of Orange, a rebel turned statesman, commemorated Leyden's deliverance by founding a university.

Fresh troubles broke out in the Spanish army after its failure to capture Leyden. The indiscipline and excesses of the troops were rapidly antagonizing even the supporters of the royal cause, and Requesens now found himself under heavy pressure from the States-General to withdraw his forces and to restore the ancient privileges of the Netherlands. With no money to continue the war, it was imperative to make a fresh attempt to reach a settlement with Orange. Through the mediation of Maximilian II a conference opened at Breda in February 1575 between representatives of Requesens and the deputies of the Estates of Holland and Zealand. Requesens was prepared to concede that Spanish troops and officials should be withdrawn but only on condition that Catholicism remained the sole religion of the Netherlands. All Protestants would have to leave the country, but they would be given ten years to dispose of their effects.

It was on Requesens's refusal to agree to liberty of conscience that, after five months of discussion, the peace talks broke down. There were strong indications that the majority of Catholics in the Netherlands would not have been opposed to toleration as a necessary means to bring the war to an end. But Requesens would not, and could not, commit his master to a concession which was utterly abhorrent to them both.

The failure of the conference of Breda on the crucial issue of toleration made it clear to Requesens that the religious question had now become a matter of paramount importance in the eyes of the rebels. It may well be that he had underestimated the religious element in the rebellion from the moment he first arrived: it was a natural enough miscalculation when the Calvinists were no more than a tiny minority – especially in the rebellious provinces of the north – and when the entire population, including those whose Catholicism was not in doubt, were seething with indignation against the Alba régime.

But the situation changed radically in the Netherlands in the fifteen months between his arrival and the opening of the conference of Breda. For a revolution was occurring *within* the revolution – a revolution which in Holland and Zealand was carrying the Calvinists to power.

The more zealous Calvinists among the rebels saw the defeat of the Spaniards in Holland and Zealand as no more than an essential preliminary to the achievement of their principal purpose – the establishment in those provinces of the Reformed religion after the manner of Geneva. Wherever possible they had secured the entry of their fellow-Calvinists into municipal government, and had taken all necessary measures to ensure that the populace should become acquainted with the Word of the Lord. A general synod was held at Dort in 1574, and arrangements were made for the establishment of Calvinist churches in every town. Even with all the advantages of official support, however, Calvinism failed to obtain the quick successes that might have been expected – the people remained unaccountably obdurate to the gospel which the ministers preached. It would take forty years of intensive effort, and the immigration of large numbers of Calvinists from the southern provinces, before even half the population of Holland and Zealand had formally abandoned their allegiance to Rome.

Yet, for all the difficulties on the path to conversion, the provinces of Holland and Zealand were on their way to becoming the nucleus of an officially Calvinist State. Given the fact of war with Spain, this was inescapable. William of Orange, although a convert to Calvinism, remained a *politique* at heart; but without the assistance of the Calvinists, he knew that he could never hope to win. Imbued with the belief that they were an elect people, chosen by the Lord, the Calvinists alone possessed both the morale and the organization which were indispensable for success. Since theirs was a militant creed for militant times, Orange had no choice but to take them into partnership. The Netherlands Calvinists therefore secured opportunities to establish and propagate their creed, such as their brethren across the sea in England consistently failed to obtain. In the Netherlands – just as in Scotland during the regency of Mary of Lorraine[17] – the Calvinists were identified with the national cause, and were the only Protestant sect capable of mobilizing the populace for a protracted struggle against an alien régime. In England, on the other hand, the régime since the death of Mary Tudor had neither been Roman Catholic nor associated with a foreign power. Elizabeth herself was fully identified with the national and Protestant cause, especially after her excommunication in 1570. Nor was there any civil war, which would have allowed the Calvinists to seize the initiative as the effective organizers of revolt. Elizabeth was therefore able to keep her presbyterians at arm's length, and to pursue a moderate religious policy, in a way that was impossible for William of Orange at the height of his struggle with Spain.

The necessity for making religious concessions to the Calvinists in exchange for their active support in the war was bound to affect Orange's pursuit of his political goals. His overriding aim was to secure 'liberty' – religious and civil – for all the provinces of the Netherlands. By 1575 this aim no longer seemed hopelessly unrealistic. Although Requesens's army had renewed the offensive with some success after the failure of the Breda discussions, Philip II's suspension of payments to his bankers on 1 September 1575[18] inevitably had drastic consequences for his armies abroad. Requesens himself was a sick man, and he died on 5 March 1576, leaving a vacuum at the centre of government which the Netherlands council of state was incapable of filling. As the leaderless and unpaid army again became mutinous, the provincial Estates began to look to their own defence in the absence of any effective central power.

This was the moment for which Orange had been waiting. As long as the Calvinist zealots could be held in check, he might at last be able to achieve his great ambition of combining all seventeen provinces in a single unified movement of revolt. On 4 September 1576 he engineered the arrest of the royalist members of the council of state, and persuaded the reconstituted council to convoke a meeting of the States General, to be attended by delegates from the Estates of Holland and Zealand as well as the deputies of the southern provinces. The movement in the south was led by disaffected nobles, most of them Catholic, and there was no guarantee that they would see eye to eye with the deputies from the north. But on 4 November the *tercios* ran wild and sacked Antwerp. The horrors of the 'Spanish fury' – eleven days of pillage and massacre, in which more than 7,000 citizens and soldiers lost their lives – were sufficient to unite north and south in a common movement of revulsion against Spain. By the Pacification of Ghent, of 8 November, the States General and the delegates of William of Orange and of the Estates of Holland and Zealand agreed to co-operate in expelling the Spaniards. They also agreed, pending a special session of the States General, that Philip II's edicts against heresy should be suspended, and that Calvinists should be allowed freedom of worship in Holland and Zealand, provided they refrained from interfering with Catholic worship elsewhere.

The Pacification of Ghent of 1576 was in effect a Netherlands equivalent of the peace of Augsburg of 1555 – an attempt to settle the religious differences of the seventeen provinces on a regional basis. Since there were numerous Protestants in the south, and still more Catholics in the north, it was unlikely to prove more than a temporary truce. It did, however, offer some basis for cooperation, as Don John of Austria discovered to his cost when he arrived in the Netherlands as Requesens's successor in November 1576. Immediately he found himself confronted with a general demand that he should confirm the Pacification of Ghent. To the leaders of the north, this meant not only the withdrawal of the *tercios*, but also the acceptance of the religious settlement. To the duke of Aerschot and the predominantly Catholic leaders of the south it meant, essentially, the withdrawal of the troops. Since Don John had arrived with neither soldiers nor money, he had no alternative but to agree. On 12 February 1577 he signed with the States General the Perpetual Edict, by which the *tercios* were to leave the country. But the Edict incorporated a promise that the Catholic religion should everywhere be maintained and restored; and Holland and Zealand duly protested by refusing to recognize Don John as their governor general.

The departure of the troops from the Netherlands in March 1577 removed the prime incentive to continuing cooperation between north and south, although Don John's behaviour a few months later temporarily brought them together again. William of Orange was only too well aware that the preservation of unity now hung on the slender thread of mutual tolerance for each other's religious creeds. But he found it impossible to hold the Calvinists back. In the towns of Brabant and Flanders Calvinism had enthusiastic support, especially among the artisans. There was, too, a long tradition of popular unrest in these cities; and in 1577 and 1578 Calvinism and popular unrest coalesced in a series of risings against the rule of the Catholic magistrates. Using those same techniques which had been perfected in the war with the Spaniards, the Calvinist rebels seized control of the city governments, and took freedom of worship exclusively for themselves.

In a desperate attempt to preserve the fragile union of the seventeen provinces, Orange and his friends presented the States General in the summer of 1578 with plans for a 'religious peace'. Philippe Du Plessis-Mornay, who had written a defence of the *politique* attitude in France at the time of the peace of Monsieur, was now employed by William to write a similar treatise for the Netherlands, which would show that no religious creed could ever be effectively suppressed by violence or force of arms. But the appeals to reason fell on deaf ears. For Peter Dathenus – one of the most vehement of the Calvinist ministers – William of Orange was no better than an atheist, changing his religion as men changed their clothes. It was scarcely surprising, then, that the religious peace was still-born. Vilified simultaneously by the more extreme Calvinist and Catholic partisans, Orange found for himself what so many others were also finding – that Poland, after all, was *sui generis*, and that, for the moment at least, there was no middle way.

9

The Growth of Spanish Power

1   The Problems of Philip II

The mid-1570s were a time of acute difficulty for Philip II of Spain. In North Africa, the hopes and dreams of half a century were shattered by the fall of Tunis to Euldj Ali in 1574.[1] In the Netherlands, Requesens had failed to win back the confidence of a population bitterly antagonized by the policies of the duke of Alba and by the barbarous behaviour of the royal army. But everything was overshadowed in 1574 and 1575 by the most pressing of all Philip's difficulties – the terrifying problem of a rapidly growing deficit.

War in the Mediterranean and the Netherlands was imposing increasingly heavy demands on the financial system of the Spanish Monarchy and on the economy of Castile. Cardinal Granvelle, viceroy of Naples from 1571 to 1575, and the duke of Terranova, the native-born president of Sicily, both made it abundantly clear in their letters to Madrid that the demands of the war against the Turks were creating alarming budgetary deficits in their territories and were placing an acute strain on local resources. This in turn was compelling them to resort to highly undesirable financial expedients, such as the sale of public offices and of royal land and rights of jurisdiction, which inevitably increased the power of the privileged classes at the expense of royal authority. Many of the gains made by the Crown in its Italian territories during the first half of the century were thus whittled away in its second half by the exigencies of war in the Mediterranean and by the inexorable demands of Habsburg foreign policy. But they found it increasingly difficult to meet the costs of their own government and defence; and Madrid, for its part, was never satisfied.

The inability of revenue in the Italian viceroyalties to keep pace with the rise in expenditure merely increased the already very considerable burdens which were being borne by the king's vassals in Castile. By the mid-1570s the total budget of the Spanish Crown was in the region of six million ducats a year. Of this figure, something like one fifth was provided by ecclesiastical contributions from the king's dominions: the *subsidio*, and *tercias reales*, which were taxes on clerical income: the *cruzada* – the proceeds from the sales of bulls for the 'crusade', traditionally conceded by the papacy to the Spanish Crown; and the *excusado*, a new tax consisting of the tithe of the most valuable piece of property in every Castilian parish, first granted to Philip by Pius V in 1567 to help pay for the suppression of heresy in Flanders. Most of the remainder derived from two principal sources: silver remittances from the Indies and taxes paid by Castile. These taxes included the *servicios* voted by the Castilian Cortes, and a number of extra-parliamentary sources of revenue. But the most important tax in Castile was now the *alcabala*, the tax on sales for which the Castilian cities compounded by payment of a lump sum known as the *encabezamiento*.

Since these various sources of income were proving increasingly inadequate to meet the rapidly growing expenses of war, the Crown depended more and more on its bankers to bridge by means of credit the ever-widening gap. These bankers, and especially the Genoese, were indispensable for the Monarchy's survival. Philip's *asientos*, or contracts, with the Genoese alone ensured that cash would be available for the payment of the Netherlands army, in spite of a delay in the arrival of the treasure-fleet, or a shortfall in Castilian payments of the *alcabala*. But the Genoese, very naturally, exacted a high price for their services. They demanded high – and rising – rates of interest for their loans; they obtained from the Crown special licences for the export of bullion from Spain; and they manoeuvred themselves into a position where they could manipulate to their own advantage the elaborate credit system of *juros*, or credit bonds, by which the Crown sought to provide in Castile for its fiscal needs.

By the early 1570s the Crown had run up a vast debt to its Genoese bankers, who in turn found themselves the objects of growing popular hostility in Castile. When the king asked the Castilian Cortes in 1574 for a substantial increase in taxes, the deputies seized the opportunity to unburden themselves on the subject of the hated *asiento* system, which was delivering Castile into the rapacious hands of the Genoese. They did, however, agree to a massive increase in the *encabezamiento* for the *alcabala*, which now became in reality what it had not been for a long time – the equivalent of a 10% tax on sales. But it soon became apparent that the increase was quite unrealistic in relation to Castile's fiscal capacity; and in 1577 Philip was forced to reduce the *encabezamiento* by a quarter, to some 2,700,000 ducats a year. It remained at this high figure for the rest of his reign.

A future increase in Castilian tax revenue, even if it could be collected, offered no relief for present woes. Faced by debts of 36 million ducats – the equivalent of six or seven years of revenue – which he could not possibly pay on time, the king decreed on 1 September 1575 the suspension of all payments of interest to the bankers, and declared illegal all the *asientos* concluded in the last fifteen years. The Crown, in fact, had followed the precedent of 1557 and defaulted on its debts.

If the Crown hoped by the use of this device to meet the demands of the Cortes and break the Genoese stranglehold over its own finances and the Castilian economy, it was promptly disabused. The Genoese could only be dispensed with if there were equally substantial bankers of other nationalities to put in their place. But there were not. Although Castile's own business world included one or two figures of some stature, such as Simón Ruiz, the well-known merchant of Medina del Campo, Castilian capitalism was a modest affair, lacking the expertise and the self-confidence to move boldly into the field of international banking. Beyond Castile itself, Philip was able to turn to Portuguese, Florentines and Lombards, and to those hardly perennials, the Fuggers. But none of these, acting either singly or in concert, proved capable of raising sufficient sums to preserve in full working order the complex financial machinery for the regular payment of the army in Flanders. Consequently, while the Genoese looked on with quiet satisfaction, or surreptitiously intervened to sabotage the efforts of their rivals, the credit structure in the Netherlands foundered and collapsed. The mutiny of the *tercios* and the sack of Antwerp on 4 November 1576 directly followed from the failure of Castilian and international bankers to fill the gap left by the disappearance of the Genoese. There could have been no more decisive testimony to the truth of what the Genoese themselves had always maintained – their own indispensability to the Spanish Crown.

Philip II drew the inevitable conclusion from the Flanders fiasco. On 5 December 1577 an agreement was reached, known as the *medio general*, by which both parties made concessions and the Crown revoked the decree of suspension of 1575. For the following decades, the Genoese reigned supreme. Although Philip engaged, when he could, in hopeful flirtations with the prosperous Grand Duke of Tuscany, Francis de Medici, the credit resources of Florence were unfortunately no match for those of Genoa. The Genoese knew the strength of their position and made the most of it, extracting major concessions from the crown, which included regular licences to export from Spain a substantial proportion of the American bullion unloaded at Seville. This enabled them to dominate Europe's silver-routes and its system of exchange. This system revolved around the 'fairs of Besançon', first established at Besançon, in the Franche-Comté, in

1534, and transferred on a permanent basis to Piacenza in 1579. During the 1580s and 1590s these quarterly fairs became the great European clearing-house for financial transactions. It was at Piacenza that exchange-rates were fixed, old debts paid off and fresh debts incurred, and that Castilian silver *reales* were bought, sold and exchanged for letters of change and for gold needed for certain essential payments, including that of the army in Flanders. From the Genoa-Piacenza complex, new monetary routes wound their way across the continent, linking Spain, Italy and Flanders in a close financial network. In the past, American silver for the Netherlands had been hazardously shipped to Antwerp from Laredo, or had occasionally been sent overland by way of France. But increasingly from the 1570s it took the road from Seville through Madrid to Barcelona, where it was put on board ship for transport to Genoa. In a world in which silver was king, the rise of the Barcelona-Genoa route brought Barcelona back into the mainstream of economic activity, and provided an added enticement for the bandit gangs which were increasingly disturbing the life of Catalonia.

For it was the silver of the Indies which was the bait for bankers and for bandits; and, in the late 1570s, this silver was beginning to flow into Seyille in unparalleled quantities. The intensive exploitation of the American mines and the use of the mercury process for refining Peruvian silver were now beginning to yield significant results. In the quinquennium 1571–1575 some four million ducats reached Seville for the Crown; from 1576–1580, eight million; and from 1581–1585, nine million ducats – or nearly two million ducats a year.[2] The penury which had crippled Philip II in the early 1570s, and had forced him to repudiate his debts in 1575, was therefore beginning to pass as the decade reached its close. As the transatlantic trade attained new heights of prosperity, and increasingly large remittances of silver arrived for both king and merchants, confidence revived. There was a new sense of ease and expansiveness in the world of international finance; a new sense of expansiveness, too, in the projects of Philip II.

Until the mid-1570s, Philip had largely been engaged in a difficult holding operation, designed to contain the Turkish threat in the Mediterranean while simultaneously curbing the rebels in the Netherlands. But the events of the opening years of the decade had starkly revealed the financial impossibility of sustaining large-scale operations simultaneously on two fronts. The mutinies in the army of Flanders between 1574 and 1576 were directly related to the diversion of funds to the Mediterranean front for the war of the Holy League against the Turks. After the signing of the truce with the Turks in 1578 it was again possible to switch men and money to the Netherlands. At the same time, the new availability of credit following the upsurge of silver remittances from the Indies suggested that Philip might at last be able to seize the initiative rather than merely react to events.

New opportunities were beckoning, especially in Portugal.[3] Perhaps after all the situation could be restored in the Netherlands, and the Spanish Monarchy might at last display its full power to the world. Philip had – or might hope to have – the financial resources for more ambitious policies. He could also, as a result of his settlement with the Genoese, count on having the machinery for mobilizing those resources and deploying them at the points where they were most required. But did he also have ministers with the vision to advise him, and subordinates efficient enough to execute his intentions with success?

The quality of Philip II's servants in the mid-1570s was not very impressive, either at court or in the Netherlands. The prince of Eboli had died in 1573, and the duke of Alba had fallen into disgrace. Deprived of Eboli's leadership, Alba's opponents had reconstituted their faction round the persons of Gaspar de Quiroga, archbishop of Toledo, and Pedro Fajardo, the third marquis of Los Vélez. But the animating spirit of the faction was the royal secretary, Antonio Pérez. Vain, smooth and ingratiating, Pérez had acquired a remarkable influence with the king since succeeding his father in the secretaryship in 1566. Philip, for all his indefatigable industry – those interminable days and nights spent toiling over the documents that flowed in from every quarter of the globe – needed counsellors and confidants. He seems instinctively to have shunned and distrusted forceful personalities, like the great duke of Alba. Instead, he turned to more discreet and colourless figures – first the prince of Eboli, and now Antonio Pérez. By the mid-1570s the king and his secretary had established a close working partnership, in which Pérez had begun to take increasing liberties with his master's confidence. Always on the lookout for a little private gain, Pérez knew everything that was happening from Lisbon to Antwerp, through a private network of friends in high places and of ubiquitous informers.

It was on the advice of Pérez and his friends in the council that the king appointed his half-brother Don John of Austria to succeed Requesens as governor of the Netherlands in 1576. The appointment, at first sight, was a skilful move. Don John, as the son of Charles V and the victor of Lepanto, enjoyed a unique prestige. It was on this prestige that the king and Pérez pinned their hopes of a solution to the problem of the Netherlands, for Don John was to go not as a warrior but as a prince of the blood royal bearing the olive branch of peace. His instructions closely accorded with the traditional, policy of the Eboli faction. He was to pacify and conciliate, and to give formal recognition on the king's behalf to the traditional rights and liberties of the Netherlands.

The only drawback to this otherwise admirable idea was that Don John was miscast for this particular role. Madrid needed a peacemaker and it sent a warrior – a warrior without either men or money. Nothing could have been better calculated to add to the frustrations of an already frustrated man. This most insecure of princes, desperate for the rank and respectability of which his illegitimate birth seemed for ever destined to deprive him, spent his life pursuing rainbows that might lead him to the elusive crown of gold. After Lepanto, Tunis and the crown of a conquered Africa... After the Netherlands, England and the hand of a captive Mary Queen of Scots... Each dream was more grandiose than the one before, and each disappointment was correspondingly more bitter. Antonio Pérez, who had no heart of his own but possessed an unerring insight into the hearts of other men, was happy enough to let Don John dream his dreams. But he made sure that he would be the first to learn their content by giving Don John a secretary from among his own confidants, Juan de Escobedo.

Even if Don John had been other than he was, his mission was hopeless from the start. His arrival in the Netherlands in November 1576 coincided with the sack of Antwerp by the unpaid and mutinous *tercios*, and he was at once confronted with the angry demand of a united Netherlands that all Spanish troops should leave the country. The Perpetual Edict of February 1577, which he had no choice but to sign, included among its terms the evacuation of the troops within twenty days by land – a stipulation which effectively prevented Don John from attempting to employ them for his cherished ambition, the conquest of England and the release of Mary Queen of Scots. Without troops he could neither invade England nor impose peace on the Netherlands, and he lacked the authority and the determination to pursue a policy of reconciliation in which he was unable to believe. Soon he was sending urgent pleas to Madrid for men and money with which to resume the war. By now he enjoyed the enthusiastic support of his secretary Escobedo – a watch-dog turned lap-dog, for Escobedo, like so many others before him, had been captivated by Don John's easy charm and his visionary ideas. In the summer of 1577, while Don John champed at his enforced inactivity, Escobedo was sent to Madrid to put his case personally before Pérez and the king. But the moment came when Don John could bear his situation no longer, and on 24 July he rashly seized the castle of Namur.

Don John's precipitate action was an open gesture of defiance towards Madrid's declared policy of conciliation, and as such it greatly increased the king's latent doubts about the trustworthiness of his brother. The appearance in Madrid of Escobedo did nothing to allay these doubts. Don John's secretary was clearly working hand in glove with his master. He was known to have made private approaches to the pope on Don John's behalf for help towards the invasion of England; and he now demanded with insolent eagerness that troops and money should be provided for the Netherlands. Antonio Pérez, who had formerly regarded Escobedo as a useful private agent, now began to think of him as a potentially dangerous rival. Besides, he knew too many secrets – including, perhaps, secrets about Pérez's own relationship with the Dutch rebels, which would destroy Pérez if they ever reached the ears of the king. During the autumn of 1577 Pérez became convinced that his own self-preservation demanded Escobedo's death; and in the king's natural distrust of Don John and his ambitions, he glimpsed the ideal means for effecting his design.

The seeds of doubt in the king's mind were carefully tended by his secretary. Don John, the king well knew, had his eyes on the throne of England. Was it entirely beyond the bounds of possibility that the Spanish throne might also figure in his schemes? And was not Escobedo the evil genius of Don John, subtly encouraging his master's grand designs? But every care was taken to avoid arousing the suspicions of Don John, while the dossier against Escobedo was being studiously compiled. Philip himself had to recognize the failure of his conciliatory policy when the States General of the Netherlands withdrew their allegiance from Don John in December 1577, and proclaimed archduke Matthias, the third of Maximilian II's sons, as governor-general in his place. When Don John, having reconstituted his army in Luxemburg, won a notable victory over the rebel forces at Gembloux in January 1578, the king sent him a letter of fulsome congratulations. But even as he wrote he was becoming convinced that reason of state demanded the death of Escobedo. When he had at last made up his mind, only Antonio Pérez and the marquis of Los Vélez were made party to his decision. On the night of 31 March 1578, after three attempts at poisoning had failed, Escobedo was struck down in a Madrid street by unknown assassins.

The murder of Escobedo was a shattering blow to the prospects and ambitions of Don John, who was quick enough to guess where the real responsibility lay. From now on, he sent no more letters to Antonio Pérez. Inevitably he found that his influence at court was gone: the king showed no further interest in him, and kept him starved of money. Disillusioned, embittered, his confidence broken, Don John saw his fragile world of dreams dissolving. On 1 October 1578 he died of typhus, at the age of thirty-three. On his deathbed he entrusted the command of his army to his nephew, Alexander Farnese, prince of Parma. To his confessor he confided his own bitter epitaph: 'During all my life I have not had a foot of land I could call my own. "Naked came I out of my mother's womb, and naked shall I return thither."'

Don John's death did not, as might have been expected, help to lay the unquiet ghost of Escobedo. On the contrary, the arrival in Madrid of Don John's private papers helped to suggest to an uneasy Philip that he might perhaps have connived at the death of an innocent man. Escobedo's friends and relatives were crying out for justice; and another royal secretary, Mateo Vázquez, guessing at the truth, urged the king to ensure that the guilty were discovered. The uncomfortable suspicion that Pérez might have double-crossed him began to trouble Philip at the very moment when he was embarking on highly delicate negotiations concerning the Portuguese succession. These negotiations were being conducted through Antonio Pérez; and the king's unease was increased by the knowledge that Pérez was suspiciously friendly with the ambitious widow of the prince of Eboli, who had her own private schemes for the future of the Portuguese crown. Each new piece of evidence about the intrigues of Pérez and the princess of Eboli was carefully sifted and stored away for future use, until it became clear to Philip that his secretary had systematically betrayed him.

At a time when the Portuguese negotiations were reaching their climax, the king urgently needed advisers in whom he could place whole-hearted reliance. One name stood out above all others – that of cardinal Granvelle, who had been attached to the embassy in Rome since leaving the vice-royalty of Naples in 1575. The cardinal possessed the integrity and the long experience of politics and diplomacy, which were so badly needed in Madrid at this supremely difficult moment in the fortunes of the Monarchy and the king. On 30 March 1579 Philip wrote to Granvelle, telling him that his presence was urgently required at court. Another man, too, was summoned to join the royal service – Don Juan de Idiáquez, the son of one of Charles V's secretaries, recently appointed from Venice to the embassy in Paris. On the night of 28 July, as Granvelle neared the Escorial, the princess of Eboli and Antonio Pérez were arrested, to their own great surprise and the stupefaction of the court. With Granvelle appointed president of the council of Italy, and effectively first minister, and with Idiáquez as secretary in charge of despatches, the king had the makings of an administrative team worthy of the times. These were the new men he needed around him – men who would help to implement his policies, now that the clouds of bankruptcy were beginning to disperse.

2   Portugal and the Azores

Cardinal Granvelle brought a new energy and an unaccustomed speed to the decision-making processes of the government in Madrid. As a man who had spent long years in the wilderness, waiting for the royal summons which had come so late in his life, he had watched with ill-concealed impatience the mistakes and hesitations of a king who signally lacked the heroic qualities of the great Charles V. Now at last he was in a position to give a firm direction to the vacillating course of the Spanish Monarchy, and to implement the vigorous policies which he had for so long advocated in vain. The times, too, were propitious. The continuing and rapid rise in American silver remittances allowed a new latitude in the framing of policies. The great qualities which Alexander Farnese was already displaying in the government of the Netherlands held out the possibility of a restoration of effective Spanish power, which Granvelle considered the indispensable preliminary to fresh attempts at a settlement. It might be possible, also, to pursue more vigorous and aggressive policies against the French and the English. But the most pressing problem, and the one for which Philip most needed his help, was the safe incorporation of Portugal into the Spanish Crown.

The succession crisis in Portugal had been created by the death at the battle of Alcázarquivir on 4 August 1578 of the young king Sebastian. His death was as unnecessary as his short life was fruitless. Since childhood this unstable youth had been obsessed with the vision of an African crusade against the Moors, and in due course a dazzling opportunity presented itself as the result of bitter dynastic struggle in the Berber Arab kingdom of Fez. In 1576 the shereef, Mulai Mohammed, was chased from his throne by an uncle who had managed to enlist the support of the Turks. The deposed shereef appealed first, and unsuccessfully, to Philip II for assistance in recovering his throne, and then turned to the king of Portugal, whose response was very different. Sebastian's advisers, and his uncle Philip II, did their best to dissuade him from becoming personally involved in a Moroccan dynastic feud, but Sebastian had set his heart on the African adventure, and was not to be deterred. At Alcázarquivir, under a blinding African sun, the Portuguese army went down to disastrous defeat. The flower of the nobility were captured or slain, and both Sebastian and Mulai Mohammed were left dead on the field.[4]

Sebastian's successor was his great-uncle, the aged, unmarried and epileptic cardinal Henry. There was little chance of his living for very long, and still less of his producing an heir; and on his death the future succession was by no means clear. The leading claimants were the duchess of Braganza; Dom Antonio, prior of Crato, the illegitimate son of cardinal Henry's brother, Luis; and Philip II of Spain, through his Portuguese mother the Empress Isabella. There were also a number of less serious foreign claimants, including Emmanuel Philibert of Savoy, Ranuccio Farnese (the son of Alexander Farnese), and, more improbably, Catherine de Medici, through her descent from the medieval Portuguese king Affonso III. Although Philip's claims were stronger than those of his rivals, the number and importance of the claimants immediately made the Portuguese succession a matter for acute international concern, which was vastly enhanced by the value of the prize. For, in spite of the fact that Portugal was a small country fallen on hard times, its potential value to any future possessor was incalculable. Lisbon was the spice capital of the western world, and the centre of a great commercial empire stretching eastwards to the Indian Ocean and the Moluccas, and westwards to Brazil. If the king of Spain added the wealthy possessions of Portugal to his own, then England, France and the Dutch would have every cause for alarm.

Philip's most serious liability in pressing his claim lay precisely in the fact that he was already king of Spain. There was no love lost between Portugal and Castile, and most Portuguese had no wish to see their country included among the many possessions of the Castilian Crown. Philip therefore would have to play his cards with great tactical skill. But he was able to draw on the diplomatic expertise of cardinal Granvelle, and on the extensive knowledge of Portuguese men and affairs possessed by Cristóbal de Moura, a native Portuguese who had risen high in favour at the Spanish court. The prior of Crato, who escaped from Moorish captivity in 1579, was undeniably popular in the country at large. But among certain influential sections of Portuguese society a number of important considerations were working in favour of the idea of a closer association with Spain.

Cardinal Henry himself was infirm of purpose and open to persuasion. The nobility was demoralized by the disaster of Alcázarquivir, and desperately in need of Spanish silver – which Moura was all too happy to supply – to ransom its many members who were still in Moorish hands. The Jesuits, who found themselves cold-shouldered in Spain, began to work for the Spanish cause, possibly in the hope that this would win them the king's protection in the Iberian peninsula and Spain's overseas possessions. Some of the 'New Christians' longed to escape from their Portuguese ghetto to their original homeland of Spain, however much they feared the Spanish Inquisition. Finally, the commercial classes were lured by the prospect of a fuller participation in the lucrative trade of Seville, and of access to the American silver which they badly needed for their own Far Eastern trade.

Philip II and Moura skilfully exploited these opportunities; but the extent of popular opposition and the possibility of foreign intervention on the prior of Crato's behalf, made it advisable at the same time to have an army in reserve. Arquebuses and muskets were ordered from Italy; troops were recruited in Spain and Germany, and brought back from Flanders; and, at Granvelle's insistence, the duke of Alba was recalled from his enforced retirement and given charge of the army. At the end of January 1580 the cardinal-king Henry died, leaving a council of regents to govern Portugal until a successor should be chosen. Granvelle was well aware of the necessity for speed, for the prior of Crato was gathering popular support. There should be no delay, he urged the king, in ordering Alba's army across the frontier. An ultimatum to accept Philip as their king was ignored by the Portuguese, and late in June Spanish forces crossed into Portugal. Dom Antonio's partisans put up no more than sporadic resistance, and within four months the kingdom had fallen under Spanish control.

Granvelle was anxious to reorganize the Portuguese administration and to integrate Portugal into the Spanish Monarchy. But Philip, who by training and temperament was a great stickler for the constitutional proprieties, had already assured his new subjects that he would respect their traditional laws and forms of government. Portugal, then, would become one more addition to that loose federation of semi-autonomous States and provinces known to the world as the Spanish Monarchy. In April 1581 the Cortes of Thomar formally recognized Philip as king of Portugal, in return for the guarantee that their laws and liberties would be preserved. Philip himself remained in Lisbon until 1583, but it was agreed that, during periods of royal absence, the country would be governed by a member of the royal family or a native Portuguese viceroy. It was also agreed that the political and representative institutions of Portugal should be left unchanged, and that Castilians should hold no offices in Portugal and its overseas territories. Castilians, too, should not be allowed to participate in the commercial life of Portugal and her empire. These concessions by Philip meant that, although the Iberian peninsula was now at last formally united beneath a single monarch, Portugal remained, even more than Aragon or Catalonia, a semi-independent State, associated with, but not incorporated into, the Crown of Castile.

The union of the Crowns lasted for a mere sixty years, and was permanently dissolved by the Portuguese revolution of 1640. The later years of the relationship were far from happy, but in the early stages both parties gained substantial advantages. The Portugal defeated at Alcázarquivir needed the shield of a stronger power behind which to recover from its wounds. Philip, for his part, gained a million new subjects, and a valuable new territory with a long Atlantic seaboard, whose ports and dockyards harboured skilled seamen and an ocean-going fleet of some 100,000 tons including ten fighting galleons built in the 1570s.[5] He gained, too, and without a fight, a second overseas empire – Portuguese India and Africa, the Moluccas and Brazil. This represented an enormous accretion of power for the Spanish Monarchy, which now appeared to its rivals an invincible colossus bestriding the globe.

Admittedly Philip still had his difficulties. Sir Francis Drake's circumnavigation of the world in 1577–1580 was an unpleasant reminder that the Iberian monopoly of America and Asia was not yet proof against corsairs. The queen of England's subjects were also giving trouble elsewhere. From 1580 English merchants were opening up the Turkish trade, and Elizabeth entered into negotiations with El-Mansur 'the victorious', to whose kingdom of Fez she exported timber and munitions in return for the sugar and saltpetre that were needed at home. While Spain's rivals sought a potentially useful ally in Fez, they also cherished hopes of reversing the verdict in Portugal. They were encouraged in this by the prior of Crato, who managed to evade capture by the Spaniards and found his way first to France and then to England. Wherever he went he denounced the king of Spain and his wickedness, and managed to enlist widespread sympathy for his claims to the throne.

It had long been appreciated in the capitals of Northern Europe that the weakness of the Spanish Monarchy lay in the fragile lines of communication which linked its widely scattered possessions. It depended for survival on the ocean routes, and most of all on the narrow transatlantic thread which linked the silver-mines of Mexico and Peru to metropolitan Spain. Indeed, William of Orange had suggested to Granvelle many years ago that Spain's enemies could best defeat it by depriving it of the silver of the Indies. With Drake's recent successes and the flight of Dom Antonio an idea which had for long exercised a fascination over statesmen and sailors came suddenly to life.

One of the islands in the Azores – the island of Terceira – had declared its allegiance to the prior of Crato. If this could be used, as Dom Antonio suggested, as a base for the conquest of the Azores, the English and French would be strategically placed astride the silver-routes, and he himself would be poised for the recovery of Portugal. The idea commended itself to Elizabeth's councillors, and plans were drawn up in the first half of 1581 for an expedition to Terceira under the leadership of Drake. Once the island was secured, Drake would be in a position to intercept the silver fleet, or to launch a new attack in the Caribbean. Alternatively, he might use it as the spring-board for England's entry into the spice trade of the East – a dazzling prospect which no longer seemed beyond the realms of possibility since the triumphant achievement of his voyage round the world.

Elizabeth, however, began to raise objections to the scheme, and the prior of Crato felt it advisable to turn elsewhere for support. His ideas strongly appealed to the duke of Alençon, the Huguenots and the Dutch, and received a surprisingly warm welcome in the court of Henry III, although discretion suggested that the king himself should remain scrupulously ignorant of the whole affair. Catherine de Medici wanted her revenge on Philip for depriving her of 'her' Portuguese crown, and was willing to support the prior of Crato's plan for an attack on the Azores. In the spring of 1582 a fleet was assembled in La Rochelle, and was placed under the command of Filippo Strozzi, a Florentine condottiere who stood high in Catherine's favour. But Philip's spies kept him well informed of Strozzi's intentions, and Spain's best naval commander, the marquis of Santa Cruz, was given command of a powerful squadron which defeated the Strozzi expedition at the end of July. Strozzi himself was killed; Dom Antonio fled; and a second French expedition to the Azores in the spring of 1583 met with no more success than the first. The prior of Crato's challenge had been effectively met, and henceforth the Azores became the sentinel outposts guarding the silver-routes of the Iberian Atlantic. For the remaining twelve years of his life, the exiled prior of Crato flitted hopefully from court to court, doing his best to interest the princes of Europe in the recovery of his homeland and his crown. But even his warmest supporters must have entertained some doubts about his prospects, for the Spanish Monarchy was beginning to look too powerful to be challenged with success.

3   Recovery in the Netherlands

However gratifying the annexation of Portugal, the Netherlands were 'twenty times more important than the kingdom of Portugal' in the eyes of cardinal Granvelle. The fate of the Spanish Monarchy would ultimately be determined by its ability to resolve the problem of the Dutch. The king's confirmation of Alexander Farnese as commander of the Flanders army, meant that Spain was now represented in the Netherlands by a man of outstanding ability, who soon revealed, in addition to his military capacity, those gifts of diplomacy and statesmanship which Don John had so signally lacked. In spite of his education at the Spanish court, he remained an Italian prince, a shrewd and supple politician and a generous patron. His munificence, however, was unusual for a sixteenth-century prince in that it came to be accompanied by a remarkable punctiliousness in the payment of his debts – a practice which made it possible for him to secure large loans for the payment of his army at moments when Philip's own credit was temporarily exhausted. Farnese was also an able administrator, and possessed the acute practical sense of his mother, Margaret of Parma, whom Granvelle and the king were anxious to associate with him in the government of the Netherlands. Margaret was now old and ill, and it was only with great reluctance that she agreed to return from Italy to her former post in the Netherlands. Perhaps Philip would at last reward her with the fortress of Piacenza.[6] Her son, however, realized that any division of power in the Netherlands might lead to dangerous consequences. He refused to accept any limitations on his own authority, and a long and painful period of wrangling between mother and son was only ended by Margaret's departure from the Low Countries in 1583.

The gradual revival of Spain's fortunes in the Netherlands from 1578 is to be attributed both to the vision and skill of Alexander Farnese, and also to the growing disagreements among the parties to a united Netherlands. Farnese was at one with cardinal Granvelle in attributing a paramount importance to the question of timing. There was a time for peace and a time for war. Although in 1578 a policy of conciliation was still the order of the day, it was clear to Farnese that the mistakes and failures of Don John had, at least for the moment, wrecked any chance of an honourable peace. Negotiation on a reasonable basis would only become possible again when military and diplomatic victory had begun to restore the shaken prestige of Spain. It was also clear to Farnese that a solution to the problem of the Netherlands could only be found in the Walloon provinces of the south. If these could once be restored to allegiance to the king on mutually satisfactory terms, then in due course the rebellious northern provinces might be tempted to follow suit.

Farnese's chance of recovering the allegiance of the south was much enhanced by the rapid growth of tension between north and south in the period following the Pacification of Ghent of 1576. The attempts of William of Orange to curb the Calvinist fanatics in the southern towns had visibly failed. In Brussels, power fell into the hands of a committee of defence – the Council of Eighteen – chosen by the guilds. In Ghent, a revolution in October 1577 gave the Calvinists and the popular elements control of the city government. A committee was set up on the model of the Brussels Eighteen, and Ghent under the leadership of its burgomaster Jan van Hembyze and the fanatical Calvinist minister Peter Dathenus became the centre of religious and social radicalism in the south. As one town after another fell under Calvinist and popular control, the southern nobility became increasingly alarmed. It was hatred of Orange and his democratic friends which prompted them, under the leadership of the duke of Aerschot, to invite the Austrian archduke Matthias to replace the deposed Don John as governor of the Netherlands. But Orange succeeded in outmanoeuvring his old rival Aerschot. By using the Eighteen to put pressure on the Estates, he got himself appointed as Matthias's lieutenant-general in January 1578.

The same month, however, Don John won the battle of Gembloux. His victory brought into the open the opposition to Orange, which was led by a number of young Catholic nobles – Lalaing, Montigny, Hèze – who commanded the Walloon troops in the armies of the

Estates. These 'Malcontents', as they styled themselves, were concerned for the well-being of their troops, whom the States General
had failed to pay. But they also shared the general concern of the
southern nobility at the spread of popular dictatorship and Calvinist
extremism in the cities of Flanders and Brabant.

In some respects the situation in the summer of 1578 resembled that
in the summer of 1566, when the great iconoclastic fury opened the
eyes of the nobility to the dangers of a social revolution that seemed
alarmingly close. But where in 1566 the nobles could rally to Margaret
of Parma, there was no chance of their rallying in 1578 to so discredited
a figure as Don John of Austria. The archduke Matthias, for his part,
proved a broken reed. The Malcontents therefore turned hopefully to
the duke of Alençon, for whom the Netherlands had always represented a possible outlet for his thwarted ambitions. At the invitation of
the States General, Alençon accepted in August 1578 the grandiloquent
title of 'defender of the liberties of the Low Countries against the
tyranny of the Spaniards and their adherents'. He also agreed to provide French troops for the Netherlands at his own expense.

The Malcontents' appeal to Alençon and the French was repugnant
to the more extreme Calvinists, for whom the true spirit of the
rebellious Netherlands was represented by the city government of
Ghent. It was to John Casimir of the Palatinate that Ghent now
appealed, as a Calvinist answer to the duke of Alençon. But the
Calvinists' position was becoming dangerous. On 1 October 1578,
the day of Don John's death, the Malcontent baron Montigny and his
Walloon troops seized the town of Menin in preparation for an attack
on Ghent. At the moment, then, when Alexander Farnese was assuming the command in the Netherlands, his opponents were on the verge
of civil war, with one side appealing to French troops and the other to
Germans. It looked as though the united Netherlands of Orange's
creation was falling apart, in spite of Orange's desperate efforts to
hold north and south together. In a last bid to preserve unity as his
policy of religious peace collapsed, he placed his support behind the
Malcontents in their appeal to Alençon. But the excesses of the
Calvinists had by now provoked a vigorous Catholic reaction
throughout the south, and in January 1579 the Walloon provinces
concluded among themselves the Union of Arras. The north, where
the town regents had managed to get the better of the extremists and
were no longer threatened with social revolution like their colleagues
in the south, duly responded with its own union – the Union of
Utrecht. After three difficult years the marriage of 1576 had ended
in divorce. In future the northern and southern Netherlands would go
their separate ways.

Although the Walloon provinces had broken with William of
Orange, this did not automatically entail their return to full allegiance

to Philip of Spain. To the Malcontents, Spanish and Calvinist domination were equally abhorrent, and it was Farnese's difficult task to overcome their antipathy to continuing Spanish rule. He did this by a combination of astute diplomacy and military successes. By the treaty of Arras of 17 May 1579 the representatives of Artois, Hainault and Walloon Flanders agreed to respect the sovereignty of Philip II and to guarantee the maintenance of Catholicism as their exclusive faith. In return, Farnese ratified their privileges, confirmed the Pacification of Ghent and the Perpetual Edict, and promised to remove all foreigners from civil and military posts. He also agreed to the formation of a national army and the departure from these provinces of the *tercios*. The withdrawal of the *tercios* was bound to add to Farnese's military difficulties, but this concession was a necessary price for the reconciliation of the Walloons, and it still left him free to use his troops in those parts of the Low Countries which remained disobedient to the king. He was banking on a fresh military success to reinforce his diplomatic achievement at Arras. He obtained it at the end of June 1579 with the capture of Maastricht after a four months' siege – a victory which, as he had calculated, further undermined Orange's prestige, especially in the provinces of Flanders and Brabant.

Although leisurely negotiations for a general peace-settlement in the Netherlands were proceeding at Cologne under the aegis of the Emperor, Farnese considered it a useless exercise to bargain with anyone as intransigently anti-Catholic as the prince of Orange. The immediate task, in his eyes, was to follow up the victory at Maastricht, and to consolidate the royal authority in the newly reconciled Walloon provinces. This was the greatest and most permanent of his achievements in the years ahead. The difficulties were very considerable, for he was faced on the one hand with the continuing suspicion of the southern nobility, fearful that the autonomy they had won in the treaty of Arras would be gradually eroded, and on the other by the inadequacy of the Walloon troops to reconquer rebel territory without Spanish assistance. To bring back the Spanish troops would be to infringe the treaty of Arras, and so alienate the Malcontents, whose allegiance had only been precariously won.

In the summer of 1580 a Malcontent noble, William of Hornes, lord of Hèze, was discovered to be plotting in favour of Alençon. Farnese had him arrested and executed, but he refrained from confiscating his estates. It was essential to avoid a repetition of the sequence of events in 1568, when Alba's persecution of suspected nobles had fatally antagonized the Netherlands ruling class. This time the nobles were humoured and bribed, and were made to feel secure in their titles and property rights. After their experience of popular power between 1576 and 1579, most of them were not disposed to be unnecessarily truculent. Gradually, and with some reluctance, they acquiesced in the new régime – a régime in which the extension of Spanish influence was made acceptable by a guarantee that privileges would be scrupulously preserved. Their acquiescence helped to determine the character of the new State which was beginning to evolve in the southern Nether- lands under the prince of Parma's rule. Catholic and aristocratic in their temper and outlook, the Walloon provinces of the Spanish Netherlands would in due course take their place among the 'Counter- Reformation societies' of seventeenth-century Europe.

Farnese's success in recovering the allegiance of the Walloon ruling class smoothed the way for his next step – the recall of the Spanish troops. Early in 1582 the Estates of Artois, Hainault, Lille, Douai and Orchies (the constituent members of the Union of Arras) were sum- moned by Farnese to the recently captured town of Tournai, where he explained that victory could never be won by the Walloon national army alone. Under persuasion the Estates finally agreed to a return of the *tercios*. By the end of the year Farnese had some 60,000 men under his command, including 5,000 Spaniards and 4,000 Italians. With an army of this size he could hope to realize his plan for a great offensive which would ensure the safety of the Walloon provinces and cut off the rebels from trade with Germany. All he needed now was money. It was true that more and more silver from the Indies was arriving in Spain; but it remained to be seen whether enough of this would be made available in the Netherlands to keep his army in pay.

The victory of Spanish arms in the Netherlands no longer seemed as inconceivable as it had in 1578. But it was bound to be slow and expensive, as long as Orange lived. Charles V had once placed the ban of the Empire on those disloyal princes the duke of Saxony and the landgrave of Hesse. Why should his son not follow the precedent and put a price on William's head? The idea was Granvelle's, and Farnese considered it inopportune; but his resistance was overborne. In June 1580 William was proclaimed an outlaw, and a price of 20,000 écus was placed on his head.

Farnese's objection to the proscription of Orange proved fully justified. So far from inspiring mass desertions from Orange, it increased popular devotion in the north to a man who had come to symbolize in his own person the defence of Netherlands liberties against the tyranny of Spain. At the same time it also helped to snap the last ties of emotional loyalty that still bound Orange to his sovereign, Philip II. Now that he had been outlawed by his king, it was essential for him to justify his actions to the world. In December 1580 he presented to the States General his famous *Apology*, which was later to be distributed through Europe as the opening broadside in a propaganda campaign against Philip II and the Spaniards. The document bore no signature, but only a device borrowed from the motto of William's house of Nassau – *Je le maintiendrai*. It had been prepared by his chaplain Villiers and by the Huguenot pamphleteer, Hubert Languet, and it constituted at once a moving defence of Orange's political career, and a violent denunciation of the king who had put a price on his head. Out of truths, half-truths and legends the emotive words of the *Apology* triumphantly created the anti-Spanish mythology which would become gospel to generations of Protestants. Here were to be found, vividly depicted, all the constituent elements of the famous 'black legend': the cruelty, fanaticism and tyranny which characterized the Spaniards; their persecution of the wretched Moriscos; their extermination of 'twenty million' Indians;[7] the horrors of their Inquisition and the wickedness of their king, a parricide who had 'inhumanly murdered his son and heir', and had killed his wife (Elizabeth of Valois) in order to marry his niece. But behind the crude denunciations there lay also something of the philosophy which had inspired William in his struggle – his defence of liberty of conscience, his concern for the sanctity of traditional rights and privileges, his belief in an open society whose inhabitants, unlike those of Spain, should be free to study abroad in the university of their choice.

For all his brave words, however, Orange was in an exceptionally difficult and dangerous position. He himself was the obvious target for an assassin's bullet. Even if he survived, what were the prospects of success against the greatest power in the world? He was, after all, no more than the *de facto* leader of a loose confederation of towns which had chosen to defy the authority of their king. Their willingness to continue the struggle was constantly in doubt, and ultimately depended on the determination of a hard core of Calvinists, whose fanaticism was anathema to William's own temperate and tolerant cast of mind. He had failed to preserve the fragile union of the northern and southern Netherlands, and had watched helplessly while the prince of Parma recovered the allegiance of the Walloon provinces and set about the systematic reduction of rebel territory. William had always insisted that the only hope for the revolt lay in help from outside. Now, at the beginning of the 1580s, this was more true than ever before. If Farnese were ever to be halted, this could only be with the active assistance of England and France. But Elizabeth remained unwilling to risk an open confrontation with Spain, and William had no choice but to turn to the unreliable figure of the duke of Alençon, always to be found hovering where the waters were murkiest. In September 1580, with some difficulty, he induced the Estates of the rebel provinces to offer Alençon the sovereignty in place of Philip II.

There was common sense and logic in the recourse to Alençon – or would have been if Alençon had been other than he was. Rebellion was anathema to the princes of Europe, and for William to have taken the sovereignty for himself would have condemned the revolt to continuing illegality in the eyes of the world. It was wiser, and more respectable, to turn to an internationally accepted figure, the younger brother of the king of France. Moreover, Alençon was a Catholic, and might therefore appeal to the southern provinces, which William would not yet bring himself to think of as irretrievably lost. Alençon was also engaged in a surprisingly successful courtship of Elizabeth. William was always quick to detect the hand of God in the unexpected changes of fortune which characterized the wavering course of the Dutch revolt. Might not Alençon be God's chosen instrument for reconstituting, under Anglo-French protection, a Burgundian Netherlands rejoicing in their traditional liberties, and dedicated to those *politique* principles which would allow men of different faiths to live side by side in unity and peace?

Alençon, although indifferent to the aspirations of William, was happy enough to accept an offer which gave him at least something of the sovereign power he had coveted for so long. Naturally he could count on the support of many Huguenots, who saw the project as a means of resuming Coligny's grand design for a great Netherlands campaign which would purge France of its evil humours. Catherine de Medici and Henry III, on the other hand, were less enthusiastic. While Henry would be delighted to see his brother's talent for intrigue fully deployed elsewhere, he and his mother were terrified at the prospect of Philip II's reaction to French intervention in the Netherlands. Alençon, however, was not to be deterred by the threats with which the Spanish ambassador in Paris sought to unnerve his mother. He raised an army in France, and besieged and captured Cambrai in the summer of 1581. But this was his sole success. His troops, having failed to receive their pay, deserted and went home, while Alençon himself took ship for England in October to press Elizabeth for her hand, or, failing that, her money.

Alençon's constitutional position in the Netherlands had by now become somewhat clearer. When the offer of sovereignty was first made to Alençon the unhappy archduke Matthias was still nominally the governor-general of the Netherlands on behalf of Philip II – an office to which the States General of the seventeen provinces had unilaterally and illegally appointed him without Philip's approval or consent. In the northern provinces as much as in the south, the opponents of Philip's policies had never sought to replace the king but only to act in his name. It was only when William of Orange was outlawed by the king of Spain that this legal fiction lost its usefulness. William's *Apology* was in effect a final repudiation of Philip's kingship, although the repudiation still awaited a constitutional sanction. This came at a meeting of the States General of the provinces constituting the Union of Utrecht, convened in the Hague in July 1581. On 22 July Philip II was formally deposed as sovereign of the Netherlands, and this action automatically terminated the duties of Matthias as his unwanted governor-general. On the 24th, William provisionally accepted the title of count of Holland and Zealand, since both these provinces were reluctant to accept the sovereignty of Alençon. Finally, on the 26th, the representatives of Holland, Zealand, Gelderland, Friesland, Groningen and Overijssel, Malines, Flanders and Brabant solemnly ratified the Edict of Abjuration by which Philip was deposed. Of all but the first two, Alençon became hereditary sovereign, bearing the style of duke, count, or marquis by which each of the provinces traditionally knew its lord.

The Edict of Abjuration translated into practice the theories embodied in that great Huguenot treatise, the *Vindiciae contra Tyrannos*.[8] Like the *Vindiciae* it contained the standard sixteenth-century doctrines concerning the prince's obligation to be the shepherd and father of his people. The prince who failed in his duty was no prince but a tyrant, and his subjects had the right to choose another ruler to defend their laws and liberties. The arguments were respectably conservative, but their application to Philip II in July 1581 was a revolutionary event. The medieval contractual theories revived by the Huguenots after the massacre of St. Bartholomew, now received the ultimate accolade of being put into practice by the Dutch. The deposition of Philip II was no theory but a fact; and, misleadingly enveloped in medieval garb, a modern State surreptitiously made its first appearance in the world.

The exact constitutional nature of this State, however, remained something of a mystery even to its creators. A pamphlet of 1580 had considered 'whether the Low Countries can maintain themselves without a prince, or as a popular republic after the manner of the Swiss, or as an aristocracy'. Although the idea of a federal republic on the Swiss model had been mooted in the 1570s, and might have appeared well suited to the peculiar conditions of the Netherlands, it was bound to alienate those foreign princes whose help was essential if the United Provinces were to survive. The same objection applied to the alternative model of a State without a king – a Venetian oligarchy governed by a doge. It seemed that there could be no salvation without a prince in the intensely monarchical world of sixteenth-century Europe. But there was no doubt that the conditions under which Alençon was offered the sovereignty of the United Provinces left them with much of the Swiss and the Venetian in their constitution. The slow decline of the monarchical idea, in the face of repeated failures, would in due course leave them with even more.

The constitutional complexities of his new position would clearly demand the maximum tact on Alençon's part. Further tact would be required to reconcile the Calvinists among his new subjects to the government of a French Roman Catholic prince. Alençon, however, was totally unfitted for the delicate role which he was now called upon to play. It was only under the pressure of pleas and threats from the Dutch Estates that he was finally induced to leave England in February 1582 to take up his residence at Antwerp, under the title of duke of Brabant. William of Orange did his best to provide Alençon with guidance and advice, but neither the duke's behaviour nor that of his French soldiers was calculated to endear him to a people who resented his presence from the first. No doubt the acceptance of Alençon was a necessary price to pay for the friendship of Henry III, but there was a limit to what even Orange's more moderate partisans were prepared to tolerate.

Alençon, for his part, was becoming increasingly ill at ease. The populace, with its memories of St Bartholomew, was quick to assume that he was responsible for an attempt on the life of Orange which occurred shortly after his arrival in Antwerp; and he felt his own position to be exposed and insecure. Fearful, neurotic, resentful of the political impotence to which he found himself condemned, he began to toy with ideas of seizing by force the authority which he considered his of right. On the cold and wintry morning of St Anthony's day, 17 January 1583, French troops camped outside the walls of Antwerp forced their way into the city and attempted to rally its Catholic inhabitants with cries of 'Long live the mass!' But the citizens, Catholic and Calvinist alike, responded by throwing up barricades, and the French were routed in the struggle that ensued. St Anthony's day was not, after all, to be a second Bartholomew.

The farce of the '*furie française*' brought Alençon's political career to an end. Orange, still obsessed by the need for the French alliance, did what he could to gloss over the terrible event, but the duke's reputation was ruined. In the autumn of 1583 he abandoned the Netherlands and retired humiliated to France. Here, a few months later, he was struck down by fever and died on 10 June 1584. In his funeral oration he was described as 'a Caesar in enterprise, an Alexander in aspiration, a Hercules in courage, a Cicero in eloquence, a Jonah in zeal, a Jehu in prudence.' The sonorous phrases may have appeared a trifle inappropriate, even to an age which took panegyrics in its stride.

For William of Orange, Alençon's timely disappearance removed a serious personal embarrassment, but only at the cost of replacing it with a political embarrassment even less to his taste. Alençon had always been a political necessity for Orange's grand design for the Netherlands – a living symbol of the monarchical principle, of religious concord and Anglo-French protection, all of which were essential for the realization of his plans. The idea of Alençon had always been more attractive than the reality; but now, with Alençon gone, there was only a vacuum and a policy in ruins. There was no obvious candidate to fill the void, and the French connection had been fatally discredited by the disreputable behaviour of Alençon. Orange himself had incurred popular odium in 1583 by marrying as his fourth wife Louise de Coligny, the daughter of the Admiral. For Orange, the marriage represented yet one more attempt to preserve the shaken French connection which was central to his policy; but not even the impeccable Calvinist background of his new wife could cancel out the original sin of her nationality.

The general distrust created by his pro-French policy was making life in Antwerp increasingly intolerable for Orange, and in the summer of 1583 he left it for Middelburg before removing to Delft. His departure from Antwerp was not intended to be final, but Farnese's successes were daily reducing the chances of his retaining any part of the south. Orange's presence was anyhow urgently required in the north, where Holland and Zealand were planning to vest in him the sovereign authority with the hereditary title of count. Although Alençon's behaviour had weakened the monarchical idea, it had not yet been entirely destroyed; and William had come to seem the inevitable candidate for the sovereign power which Alençon had done his best to discredit. But William was never to be vested with his new authority. On 10 July 1584, exactly a month after Alençon's death, he was assassinated by a fanatical loyalist from the Franche-Comté, Balthasar Gérard.

The States General, in lamenting his death, described him as 'un père de la patrie'. The word 'patrie', which had often been on Orange's own lips, was singularly appropriate. Through all the vicissitudes of the past twenty years he had held steadfastly to the ideal of a fatherland, which demanded an even higher loyalty than should be accorded to the king. At the beginning, the 'patrie' was perhaps for William little more than a historical entity – the symbol of ancient rights and privileges which the king had mistakenly challenged. In the course of the struggle the original conception acquired more breadth and depth. Liberties became liberty – freedom from arbitrary power and freedom of conscience. Hatred of Spain and what it was doing to his country gave strength and steadiness to William's vision, and helped make it meaningful to broad masses of the people. Because they had glimpsed something of his purpose, men of widely different social classes had been willing to unite beneath his leadership for the sake of a common cause. William had made mistakes; perhaps he had temporized too much, although his hesitations may often be attributed to an exceptionally acute sense of the realities of power, which made the quest for foreign allies the foundation of his policy. But he had always, even in the blackest times, remained faithful to his ideal of the 'patrie', and in so doing he had ultimately elevated it above personalities – even his own. The measure of his achievement was that, although the father of his country died on 10 July 1584, that country itself lived on.

Marnix de Sainte-Aldegonde and William's other confidants saw to it that there was no sharp break in continuity and no sudden change of policy. The States General of the United Provinces turned at once to France and England for help, and offered Henry III the sovereignty, although Elizabeth – jealous as always of excessive French influence in the Netherlands – was determined to see that he should turn the offer down. Yet, for all Elizabeth's anxiety to avoid becoming embroiled in open conflict with Spain, there could, in the end, be no escape. Ever since Alençon had declared his willingness to come to the help of the rebels, the conflict in the Netherlands had been internationalized to such an extent that there could now be no return. Too much was at stake in the Low Countries for their appeals to be ignored; and in the months after the assassination of Orange those appeals were assuming a new note of desperation.

Farnese was now marching from success to success, brought about partly by his own great skill and partly by the weakness and dissensions of his enemies. As the military position of the rebels deteriorated, their internal feuds increased. Hembyze, the uncrowned king of the radicals in Ghent, was discovered to be in secret negotiation with Farnese, and was put to death by his colleagues in August 1584. A few weeks later the besieged city was forced to surrender, and the Calvinist republic came to an end. By the end of the year, Farnese had reconquered Flanders and most of Brabant. Brussels capitulated to his forces in February 1585, and then, after a long and brilliantly executed siege, Antwerp itself on 17 August. On receiving the news of the fall of Antwerp in the middle of the night, the usually impassive Philip II leapt from his bed in excitement and ran to his daughter Isabella's room to tell her that 'Antwerp is ours'. In acknowledgement of his gratitude he gave Farnese the most coveted prize of all – the fortress of Piacenza, for which his family had waited for thirty long years. It was a richly deserved reward, for in the seven years since his arrival Farnese had achieved an almost miraculous success. Spain's spectacular recovery in the Netherlands was a remarkable testimonial to the brilliant leadership of a great commander and statesman. But it also reflected a development which was everywhere giving rise to the most acute concern – an impressive and alarming increase in the global power of Spain.

PART IV

1585–1598

The International Conflict

1 The Problems of Intervention

Both the dead heroes of the Protestant cause, Coligny and Orange, had in their time urgently warned the world of the dangers that threatened it from the combined ambitions of Spain and of Rome. The king of Spain's design, Coligny told the English agent in Paris just before St Bartholomew, 'is to make himself monarch of Christendom or at the least to rule the same.'[1] Orange, for his part, had begged the Protestant princes, and especially those of Germany, to wake up before it was too late. Spanish power was growing; the church was becoming increasingly aggressive; and Christendom might once again be crushed beneath a Roman tyranny.

By 1585 these warnings seemed even closer to the mark than at the time when they were uttered. It was not only that Spain was in process of reconquering the Netherlands, and that its power had been for-midably increased by the acquisition of Portugal and its empire – although this itself was cause for deep alarm. Perhaps even more ominous was the extension through Europe of conspiracy and subver-sion in the name of the Roman Catholic church, and with the support or connivance of Spain. This was nowhere more obvious than in the British Isles, where the councillors of Elizabeth had good reason for anxiety. Ireland, in particular, was a source of constant, and growing, concern. Indeed, Ireland represented an almost classic case of the new problems posed for governments by the clash of competing creeds.

Catholicism in Ireland, like Protestantism in the Netherlands, had drawn new strength from its identification with a national cause. Although Irish society was infinitely less sophisticated than that of the Netherlands, its struggle against English domination was characterized by many of the same features as the Dutch struggle against the domination of Spain. In both societies a religious cause enhanced, and was enhanced by, a sense of national identity. In both, the affiliation of national leaders to an international religious movement provided new opportunities for securing international assistance. When even so primitive a rebel as Shane O'Neill had the wit to appeal for help to Paris, Rome and Madrid in the early 1560s, it was clear that the lessons of the new age of confessional strife were capable of being learnt even amid the Irish bogs. Once learnt, the lessons were not forgotten. In 1578 that remarkable adventurer Sir Thomas Stukely persuaded the pope to provide him with men and ships for the conquest of Ireland; but he then diverted his force to Portugal, and lost his life with king Sebastian at the battle of Alcázarquivir. But in the following year a force led by James Fitzmaurice Fitzgerald, and accompanied by a papal legate, managed with Spanish connivance to land in Ireland, where it was joined by the earl of Desmond and his friends. The rebels held part of Munster for over a year, and it was not until the autumn of 1580 that English troops finally crushed the insurrection.

Even though the rebels were unsuccessful in 1579–1580, Ireland was obviously becoming a new, and potentially dangerous, battleground in the struggle between the Protestants and Rome. An Ireland which was being drawn into the orbit of Counter-Reformation Catholicism, and which was turning to foreign States for help against the English, was a deeply disturbing prospect for Elizabeth and her ministers. But equal, or greater, dangers faced them still nearer home. An increasing number of young priests trained at William Allen's college of Douai were slipping into England in the later 1570s and the first Jesuits, Edmund Campion and Robert Parsons, arrived in 1580. Even where the desire existed, conversion and conspiracy were not easily kept apart. Mary Queen of Scots was languishing in prison, a poignant figure on whom were focused the sympathies and hopes of Catholic Europe. Sooner or later English Catholic priests and laity were bound to find themselves caught in the twisting threads of conspiracy which led, through a European labyrinth, to the captive queen. Everyone was caught up in them in time: Don John of Austria and Gregory XIII; Philip II and the duke of Guise; Esmé Stuart, earl of Lennox, who from 1579 was the dominant figure at the court of the young James VI, and was determined to bring back Scotland into the Guise and Catholic camp; Bernardino de Mendoza, Philip II's ambassador in London; and the English and Scottish Catholic exiles, who hovered hopefully on the fringes of the Catholic courts of Europe, or returned home at the risk of their lives to plot insurrection and invasion, and the murder of Elizabeth.

In 1583 Sir Francis Walsingham, the queen's principal secretary and a supreme unraveller of plots, uncovered clues which led to the arrest of an English Catholic, Francis Throckmorton. The prisoner's confessions under torture revealed the full extent of the conspiracy, and irrevocably implicated the Spanish ambassador, Mendoza, who had used Throckmorton as his go-between for communication with Mary Queen of Scots. The ambassador was called before the council in January 1584 and ordered to leave the country. The plot had been foiled, but Anglo-Spanish relations had suffered a further setback, and the country had become more than ever aware of the dangers that threatened it from the international Catholic conspiracy. It was clear, however, that the dangers in England were of a different kind from those posed by Catholicism in Ireland. Where, in Ireland, Rome and Spain might one day be able to call on widespread popular support, the English Catholics by the 1580s were a small and uncertain minority, and the country as a whole was becoming increasingly Protestant in temper. The threat in England was likely to come, not from the uprising of a repressed Catholic laity, but from the solitary act of a lone assassin, who, by killing Elizabeth, would plunge the country into an acute succession crisis. The life and safety of the queen therefore became more than ever the pre-eminent concern of ministers and nation. The queen herself, a desperately vulnerable figure in a world of treachery, represented the sole guarantee of continuing tranquillity and order. Only her life stood between the country and the perils of civil strife and Spanish and Catholic domination. Loyalty to the queen therefore became charged with new emotional overtones, at a time when English nationalism was being powerfully intensified by the swift growth of Protestant hatred of Rome and patriotic hatred of the Spaniards.

The new wave of Protestant patriotism in England eased the queen's task in domestic affairs by enhancing national solidarity, but at the same time made her conduct of foreign affairs more difficult by thrusting constant demands upon her for a more aggressive policy. These demands for a 'Protestant' foreign policy were all the more difficult to resist because they were vigorously pressed by influential spokesmen in the council and at court – notably the earl of Leicester and Sir Francis Walsingham. For years this faction had been pressing the queen and Burghley to intervene more decisively on the continent, in support of the Dutch rebels and the Huguenots in France. It was this faction, too, which, in alliance with London merchants and west-country gentry, had done so much to promote the movement of oceanic enterprise that was so important an element in the rise of English nationalism and in the decline of Anglo-Spanish relations. Elizabeth had connived at, or supported, acts of piracy when they suited her purpose, but she and Burghley had done their best to avoid any irrevocable action, which would drive the Spaniards to retaliate.

The hesitations of the queen's foreign policy appeared both unworthy and futile to the Walsingham-Leicester faction. In a struggle for the salvation of Protestantism itself, England had no right to remain on the sidelines. Nor could neutrality serve any useful purpose. Spain and Rome were embarked on a grand design to exterminate Protestantism on the continent, and an attack on England itself was no more than, a matter of time. Self-interest, therefore, as well as the innate rightness of the cause, demanded English intervention in Europe to save the Protestants. The Throckmorton conspiracy and the assassination of William of Orange had shown the true colour of Spain's intentions. Failure to support the Dutch revolt at this critical moment could lead only to disaster.

How far did Walsingham's thesis rest on a correct assessment of Philip II's intentions? There were strong, and growing, pressures on the king of Spain for a confrontation with England. In 1583 the marquis of Santa Cruz, fresh from his triumph in the Azores, advised the king to launch an invasion of England in the following year. But Philip set the plan on one side, for, like Elizabeth, he too shrank from open confrontation. It was one of the ironies of the early 1580s that the two principals, Philip and Elizabeth, were reluctant adversaries. But each was constantly being driven a little closer to the brink of war. Where Walsingham and his friends strove to influence the queen with their spectre of an international Catholic conspiracy, so cardinal Granvelle and his fellow-activists in Spain conjured up with equal plausibility the spectre of an international Protestant plot. There was evidence enough to support the claim: covert English help for the Huguenots and the Dutch; the activities of John Casimir of the Palatinate and the German *reiter* in France and the Netherlands; the privateering of the English in the Atlantic and Caribbean; the Anglo-French support for the prior of Crato and his schemes for the reconquest of Portugal and the Azores. Were not the times now favourable, as Granvelle suggested, for a pre-emptive strike, perhaps in Ireland, which would force the English to limit their help to the Dutch and keep their ships heavily occupied in home waters?

The year 1584 was critical both for Philip and Elizabeth. The deaths within a few weeks of each other of Alençon and William of Orange changed overnight the complexion of international affairs. While Elizabeth found herself being inexorably sucked into the vortex of affairs in the Netherlands, so Philip found himself being sucked no less inexorably into the vortex of French domestic strife. With Alençon's death, the Protestant Henry of Navarre became heir presumptive to a childless Henry III. This itself was serious enough, but Philip's most immediate anxieties centred on the Netherlands. Ever since the outbreak of the revolt the prime aim of his foreign policy in northern Europe had been to prevent the French from meddling in Netherlands affairs. Now that Alençon and Orange were both dead, the Dutch in despair were offering the sovereignty of the Low Countries to the king of France. At all costs Henry III must be deterred from accepting the offer and from intervening on the side of the rebels. This could best be achieved by keeping him fully occupied at home, and Philip was even ready to offer Henry of Navarre a handsome payment and regular monthly subsidies if he would take up arms against the king and resume the civil wars in France.

There were, however, more promising and more likely allies in France than the heretic of Navarre. For the duke of Guise and the Catholics the death of Alençon was a disaster, in that it brought them face to face with the prospect of a Bourbon and Protestant succession. But it also offered opportunities from which Guise was not the man to shrink. The house of Lorraine claimed descent from Charlemagne, and therefore insisted that it had a prior right to the throne over both Valois and Bourbons, who were merely descendants of the usurper Hugh Capet. Did not the death of Alençon, then, make Henry of Guise – not Henry of Navarre – the heir apparent to the crown?

The king of Navarre enjoyed the advantage of being recognized as the legal heir by Catherine and the king; and he was already skilfully moving to identify his own cause with the survival of the State. But Guise was a challenger with an exceptionally powerful following. He possessed the full support of the great territorial magnates of the Guise-Lorraine connection: his brother the duke of Mayenne, and the dukes of Nevers, Mercoeur, Aumale and Elboeuf. The Savoyard ambassador singled out the provinces of Normandy, Picardy and Champagne as being especially devoted to Guise, and he considered the nobility in general to be 'well affected to the house of Guise, and many of them discontented with the present state of things.'[2] The duke had, too, the city of Paris on his side, together with the clients of the Guise connection, and an army of office-holders whose prime loyalty was to himself rather than to the king. He could also count on the fervent support of a large section of the clergy and the populace. The prospect of a Protestant succession had re-awakened all the old Catholic fears, and the Sainte-Union or League, which had been defunct since 1577, was revived in 1584 on the death of Alençon. To the League, the duke of Guise was the man destined to save France from the horrors of Huguenot domination.

If Philip II was concerned to prevent Henry III from embarking on a new adventure in the Netherlands, he clearly had ample material to hand in the French domestic crisis. The populace was growing restless under the weight of heavy taxes and mounting economic distress; the extreme Catholics were again taking to arms; and the Guises themselves were turning with contempt against a king who showered gifts and offices on his favourites, the dukes of Joyeuse and Epernon. This was plainly a moment in which a modest outlay of silver might reap handsome dividends. The duke of Guise had in fact been receiving money from Spanish agents at least since 1582, but the events of 1584 made it mutually advantageous to establish a closer and more formal relationship. On 31 December 1584 the Guises concluded the secret treaty of Joinville (their ancestral home) with Philip's envoy, Juan Batista de Tassis. In return for a monthly subvention of 50,000 *escudos* the Guises pledged themselves and the League to work for the extermination of heresy in France, and for the succession of the elderly cardinal of Bourbon, in place of his heretical nephew, Henry of Navarre. There was still no question of Spanish military intervention, but Philip had taken a major step towards involvement in the domestic affairs of France.

Bernardino de Mendoza, now Spanish ambassador in Paris, brought heavy pressure to bear on Henry III during the winter of 1584–1585 to prevent him from accepting the sovereignty of the Netherlands. Mendoza's diplomatic weapons were forcefully seconded by a growing display of Guise power. The League was receiving massive support from the urban population of the Catholic north, which hated the Huguenots and was oppressed by the heavy burden of taxes caused by the collapse of government finance. At the same time, Guise was able to build up his support among the nobility by exploiting the unpopularity of the royal favourite Epernon and his Gascon following. There was, as the Savoyard ambassador explained, no lack of pretexts on which Guise could draw to justify a recourse to arms. He could claim to be resisting a 'tyrant' in the duke of Epernon, and to be struggling to relieve the people 'oppressed by subsidies and *tailles.*'

Faced with a classic example of aristocratic faction exploiting popular and religious discontent, the distracted Henry III could only prevaricate and retreat. At the end of February 1585 he finally declined the Dutch offer of sovereignty. In March the League issued, in the name of the cardinal of Bourbon, the declaration of Péronne, which protested against maladministration and the Protestant tendencies of the crown, and called all true Catholics to arms. This was an obvious Guise bid for control of the government, and Henry lacked the stamina and the resources to resist. In July, in spite of the pleas of Elizabeth, he signed the treaty of Nemours, by which he surrendered to Guise demands that all past edicts of pacification should be revoked and heresy proscribed. The duke of Guise had played with the king as the king and his nobles played with yo-yos in Paris this year.[3] It was a humiliation which Henry would never forgive him.

The king's surrender to the League was totally unacceptable to Henry of Navarre, since it meant a return to the worst days of Catholic repression. But Navarre was now called upon to fight not only for his faith but also for his rights. The treaty of Nemours was followed by an edict debarring him from succession to the throne, and in September 1585 the new pope, Sixtus V, rashly excommunicated him. The eighth and last of the French civil wars which now broke out – the 'War of the Three Henries' (the king, Guise, and Navarre) – was in reality a war for the succession. Like its predecessors it was shot through with religious antipathies, but where it was to Guise's advantage to exacerbate them, it was to Navarre's to play them down. Guise badly needed the religious issue, both to rally popular Catholicism to his side, and to justify, on the grounds of his opponent's heresy, his own tampering with the order of succession. Navarre, on the other hand, needed to detach moderate Catholic opinion from the duke of Guise. Unless he were immediately converted – and this would forfeit him the support of the Huguenots without ensuring him that of devout Catholics – he could only achieve this by presenting himself as the upholder of legitimacy and the defender of the State. His policy was therefore to damp down religious passion wherever possible, and present himself as the symbol of French national aspirations against an alien house of Lorraine enjoying Spanish support, and against a papacy which had unwisely revived the old Gallican suspicions by interfering with the succession laws of France.

It was one of the ironies of the moment, however, that in order to sustain his struggle against the Guises, Navarre was compelled to combine his patriotic stance with appeals for external aid. Only the queen of England could supply him with the cash to pay for German mercenaries. Elizabeth therefore found herself faced simultaneously in 1585 with urgent requests for help from the Protestants of both the Netherlands and France. There was nothing new about this, and she had acquired through long experience an uncanny skill in deflecting appeals for men and money. But the position on the continent was by now so grave that a more positive response was clearly needed. Antwerp was close to surrender, and the case for sending English troops to the help of the Dutch was becoming overwhelming. The news of the Guise alliance with Philip II and Henry III's capitulation to the League could only reinforce it. If a Spanish-controlled puppet régime were once established in France, Spain would be close to securing hegemony over the continent, and Farnese's army, victorious in the Netherlands, would be freed for the invasion of England.

Elizabeth and Burghley therefore found themselves driven to accept the policies long advocated by the Leicester-Walsingham faction for a more active commitment to the continental Protestants. Over the last ten years this faction had built up a close personal relationship with the circle round William of Orange – men such as Joachim Ortell and Paulus Buys, who had come to think of England as the source of Dutch salvation. With the ground thus well prepared, an embassy was despatched to Elizabeth in June 1585 to offer her the sovereignty of the Low Countries. Acceptance of the offer would have committed the queen to unlimited support for the Dutch, whom she continued to regard as rebels with no right to barter away a title that belonged to the king of Spain. But she declared herself graciously willing to take the Dutch under her protection, and it was on this basis that a settlement was at length negotiated. On 20 August 1585, three days after the fall of Antwerp, the treaty of Nonsuch was signed. The queen agreed to provide an army of 5,000 foot and 1,000 horse, under English command, for the duration of the war. As security for the repayment of expenses, the ports of Flushing and Brill would be garrisoned by English troops.

The earl of Leicester, who was appointed commander of the expeditionary force to the Netherlands, landed at Flushing in December 1585. He arrived at a moment when the fortunes of the rebels had reached their lowest ebb. Antwerp had fallen; only the four provinces of Holland, Zealand, Utrecht and Friesland still held out, together with part of Gelderland; and these provinces themselves were disunited and demoralized. The Catholics remained strong and were potential sources of treachery: the loss in 1580 of the north-eastern province of Groningen to the royalists through the defection of its Catholic stadholder the count of Rennenberg had inflicted deep psychological wounds which were still far from healing. The Catholic danger, too, had strengthened the hand of the more extreme Calvinists. The town regents were at loggerheads with the powerful Calvinist preachers, and the poorer provinces were at loggerheads with Holland, which carried the main financial burden of the war and claimed a corresponding pre-eminence in the formulation of policy. It was into this morass that the earl of Leicester stepped.

It soon became painfully clear that the man who was at first acclaimed as the saviour of the Netherlands lacked the tact and finesse for what, in any event, was an almost impossibly delicate mission. He infuriated Elizabeth by accepting without her permission the title of governor-general, and he antagonized the regent class of Holland and Zealand by striking up an alliance with the extreme Calvinist popular party of Utrecht. In particular he clashed sharply with the Estates of Holland and their Advocate, Jan van Oldenbarneveldt, over an attempt to prohibit all Dutch trade with Spain – a policy which was enthusiastically supported by the preachers of Utrecht, but which spelt ruin to the merchants of Holland. Nor could he command the military success which might have restored his reputation. Sir Philip Sidney's death at Zutphen in 1586 conferred a tinge of chivalry on a useful but mismanaged campaign which dug deeply into the limited resources of Elizabeth's exchequer. Intervention could be an expensive business, as Philip also was finding in France.

2 The Brink of War

Regardless of its success or failure, the mere fact of the Leicester expedition might suggest that Elizabeth now accepted the inevitability of war with Spain. A similar impression might also be given by the dramatic intensification of English maritime enterprise in 1585. Although war remained obstinately undeclared, this was the year in which England and Spain effectively began their struggle for the domination of the seas. In April Sir Richard Grenville sailed for Roanoke Island to found the first English colony in the Americas. In May, Philip seized all the English ships in Iberian ports, as part of a general embargo designed to destroy the trade of the Dutch rebels with the Iberian peninsula. The seizure provoked a violent response among the English merchants engaged in the Iberian trade, and they demanded and received from the government the right to retaliate. From the summer, merchants and sea-faring gentry were combining in a campaign of plunder and privateering off the Iberian coast. In September, the queen authorized a new voyage by Sir Francis Drake. The nominal purpose of his expedition was to release the embargoed merchantmen; but its real object was to intercept the silver fleet and raid the Spanish Main.

Yet even while Drake was attacking Vigo, and sailing the Atlantic to pillage Santo Domingo and Cartagena, Elizabeth herself was still obstinately pursuing any initiative which offered the faintest hope of avoiding open war. She was acting less out of duplicity than out of a prudent sense of the realities of power. It was one thing to allow Drake to undertake an expedition which could be regarded as no more than a legitimate reprisal. It was another to invite and seek out a full-scale confrontation with the most powerful State in the world. In any such confrontation, England stood at a clear disadvantage. Her financial resources were small compared with those of Spain, although Burghley had succeeded in building up a reserve of £300,000 by 1585. The Leicester expedition and the subsidies to Henry of Navarre had strained the exchequer; and Drake and Hawkins in turn failed to bring home the Spanish silver that might make good the loss. In spite of the rich prizes brought by privateering, war meant a loss of prosperity and consequent distress. Nor could there be any great confidence in England's capacity as a fighting power. Admittedly, English seamanship was probably equal to that of the Spaniards, although no one could know if the country possessed the capacity for sustained naval war. But on land an inexperienced militia, drawn from a population less than half the size of Spain's, did not look much of a match for the *tercios* of Flanders.

The decisive move for war was therefore more likely to come from Spain than England, in spite of the growing popular clamour in England for vigorous anti-Spanish policies. Cardinal Granvelle had long been pressing Philip for more energetic action, both against Henry III and Elizabeth. With his habitual grasp of strategic realities, he had appreciated that the distraction of the Ottoman Empire by developments along its frontier with Persia provided Philip with a unique opportunity to turn his attention to the Atlantic and the North – an opportunity that could most effectively be exploited from the vantage-point of Lisbon. But Philip was growing weary of his importunate minister. In the spring of 1583 he left Lisbon for Madrid, where he consulted the cardinal less and less. When the king fell seriously ill in 1585, and created a special new body known as the *Junta de Noche* to advise him, Granvelle found himself excluded. The men of power in Madrid were now Cristóbal de Moura, who had engineered the Portuguese succession; Mateo Vázquez, the king's secretary; and Juan de Idiáquez, Granvelle's confidant and colleague, who was increasingly to bear the burden of government as the king grew old and infirm. Granvelle himself watched disillusioned from the sidelines, and died – four years after the other strong man of the reign, the duke of Alba – in September 1586.

Yet Philip, true to character, was slowly and hesitantly appropriating the cardinal's policies even as he rejected the man himself. The arguments for restraint in his dealings with England had been sensibly weakened by the events of 1584–1585. Not only was English intervention in the Netherlands threatening to prevent the successful conclusion of Farnese's campaign of reconquest, but English privateers were increasingly jeopardizing the safety of the Indies and Spain's transatlantic lifelines. Among the Spanish mercantile community the growth of the English maritime offensive was now leading to a belief that the best way to protect the Iberian Atlantic economy was to launch a direct attack on England. Certainly the international situation was more favourable to such an enterprise than at any previous moment in the reign. Fear of the French reaction had always tended to inhibit Philip in his attitude to England; but now, with Henry III neutralized by the pro-Spanish Guises, the danger of French intervention in support of Elizabeth appeared finally to have passed.

From the late summer of 1585, then, Philip was toying with Santa Cruz's proposals for the 'enterprise of England'. But he still needed a clear legal and moral pretext for an act of war. This was provided in the spring of 1586 by Mary Queen of Scots. Earlier in the year, Walsingham, in the hope of securing irrefutable proof of her complicity in the plots against Elizabeth, had conveniently devised a means for her to communicate with France. In a letter of 20 May to Mendoza in Paris, she declared herself ready to transfer in her will

the succession rights to the English throne from her heretical son
James to Philip of Spain. In return, Philip would take her under his
personal protection, and avenge the wrongs of an injured queen.

Philip's favourable response to Mary's letter committed him to her
support; but it seemed that both her own and Philip's interests might
be better served by the assassination of Elizabeth than by a costly and
difficult invasion of England. In July Mendoza was privately informed
of a conspiracy being devised by Anthony Babington, and was asked if
Spanish help would be forthcoming in the event of Catholic risings in
England and Scotland. But Walsingham as well as Mendoza was privy
to the plot, and Babington and his accomplices were seized and
executed. There remained the agonizing problem of Mary herself.
Those who wished to see an end to her troublesome life had been
greatly helped by the overthrow in Scotland in the autumn of 1585 of
the French party built up by Esmé Stuart, duke of Lennox, who had
died in 1583. The signing with James VI of the treaty of Berwick in
July 1586 afforded them further encouragement. By this treaty England and Scotland promised each other every assistance in the event of
a foreign invasion, and James was offered a subsidy of £4,000 a year.
The delicate subject of the English succession remained, as ever,
taboo, but James had good reason to believe that, if he conducted
himself circumspectly in the eyes of Elizabeth, the prize would come
his way in the end. If one day he had to choose between the English
crown and the life of his mother, there was now little doubt where his
choice would lie.

In October 1586 a commission was set up for the trial of Mary
Queen of Scots, and duly found her guilty. Elizabeth could not bring
herself to kill a sister queen, and James's pleas for clemency fortified
her resistance to the demands of her council and her people for Mary's
execution. But when James hinted in private correspondence that he
would not annul the treaty of Berwick in order to save his mother,
Elizabeth was left alone to defend a hopeless cause. For weeks she
suffered agonies of indecision, but at last the death warrant was
extracted from her, and Mary went to the scaffold at Fotheringay on
18 February 1587.

While Mary's fate still hung in the balance, Juan de Idiáquez drafted
a memorandum for Philip outlining the arguments for and against an
invasion of England. The costs of the enterprise, he conceded, might
well exceed the profits, in terms of the revenues of a conquered
England. 'But if one goes deeper into the question, the enterprise
appears unavoidable, simply as a defensive measure devoid of aggressive or ambitious intent. Possessions as widely dispersed as those of
Your Majesty cannot be protected or preserved without rigorous
punishment of anyone who is so bold as to attack them.' If England
were successfully conquered and the Queen of Scots was by this time

dead, Philip would then be free to dispose of the country as he wished, 'for it is in this way that monarchs have increased their power and monarchies have grown – not by appropriating everything for themselves, but by distributing much of it among their creatures and dependents. If Your Majesty should place a dependent on the throne of England, which is at present stirring up the Netherlands, troubling the Indies and infesting the ocean, there will be no one in Christendom left to provoke you, especially as France (which alone has the capacity) will find its opportunities gone.' The case for invasion, then, was overwhelming. Moreover, the cause was just, and the king could undoubtedly expect his due reward from God.

Idiáquez's memorandum vividly reveals the considerations governing policy-making in Madrid in those crucial months before a firm decision was reached on the enterprise of England: the deep sense of frustration at the inability of Spanish power to crush the Dutch revolt and ensure the safety of Spain's maritime economy; the conception of a form of hegemony, whereby faithful clients of the king of Spain ruled the States of Europe, and his traditional enemy, France, was firmly held in check; and the belief in a coincidence of God's will and the interests of Spain. The news of Mary's execution merely reinforced a case that already seemed sufficiently strong. In some ways, however, it eased Philip's task. As long as Mary lived, she remained the rightful heir to the English throne, and a conquest of England which made her queen would be less advantageous to Spain than to France and her Guise relations. Now she was safely, if tragically, dead, and her appointed heir was Philip. The king could therefore present himself to the world as the avenger of a martyred queen, the champion of legitimacy, and the paladin of the Catholic cause against two heretical rulers – Elizabeth of England and James VI of Scotland.

In fighting for the Catholic cause, Philip required not only the pope's spiritual blessing but also his financial support. During the long pontificate of Gregory XIII, there had been the usual friction between Philip and the papacy; but the pope, while impatient and erratic, had been reluctantly forced to accept that, in the end, the king of Spain called the tune. If he protested, as he often did, against Philip's prevarications and delays, he was likely to find himself put firmly in his place by the equally irascible count of Olivares, who had come to Rome as Spanish ambassador in 1582.[4] But on 10 April 1585 Gregory died at the age of eighty-three, and Olivares found himself faced, in Sixtus V, with a pope of very different mettle.

Like others before him, Olivares had tended to underestimate Sixtus, partly, no doubt, because he talked too much. But it was the extraordinary fluency of his sermons that first started Felice Peretti, the son of a peasant-gardener of Slav ancestry, on his spectacular ecclesiastical career. Entering the Franciscan order he acquired fame through his preaching, and was raised to the purple as cardinal Montalto by Pius V. Domestic Italian feuds were carried over into the conclave following Gregory's death, which was characterized by a bitter struggle between cardinals Farnese and Medici. The king of Spain's announcement of his neutrality suggested that the luckless cardinal Farnese might achieve the tiara at last; and it was to prevent this unfortunate outcome that the cardinal of Medici surreptitiously – and with eventual success – marshalled support for cardinal Montalto.

In elevating the sixty-four year-old Montalto to the papal throne, the cardinals appreciated that they had chosen a relatively young and vigorous successor to Gregory, but nobody was prepared for the whirlwind energy of the five-year pontificate of Sixtus V. Here was a man who not only talked but acted; who threw himself with tumultuous energy into every kind of enterprise, from the reform of the papal finances to the revision of the Vulgate, from the administrative reconstruction of the papacy's temporal states to the physical reconstruction of the Eternal City. If any one action symbolized the character of the new pontificate, it was the erection of the great obelisk in St Peter's Square in 1586. Everyone told him that the feat was impossible. But at the imperious command of Sixtus, a project of which popes had dreamed for a hundred and thirty years was carried through in as many days by the papal architect, Domenico Fontana. There could have been no more striking confirmation of Sixtus's firm conviction that the human will, under the divine impulsion, could surmount every obstacle. If the final assessment of his pontificate does not entirely confirm the truth of his conviction – if at times there seems to have been more sound and fury than solid achievement – this was because, even for a Sixtus, there are certain things which are, alas, impossible.

It was, for instance, unfortunate for Sixtus that both Henry of Navarre and Elizabeth of England happened to be heretics. They were rulers after his own heart, and he longed to see them both embraced within the welcoming arms of the church. This was not only because of their great personal qualities, but also because he saw in them what he most required – effective counterweights to the overwhelming power of Spain. Like his predecessors he found this intolerably oppressive, and the situation was exacerbated by the marriage, in the opening year of his pontificate, of Philip's younger daughter Catherine to the young Charles Emmanuel, who had succeeded his father, Emmanuel Philibert, as duke of Savoy in 1580. The marriage, which threatened to extend Spanish influence throughout northern Italy, filled him with foreboding and drew him closer to Tuscany and Venice, which feared Spanish domination as much as himself.

Yet there was no escaping the dilemma which had dogged his predecessors. Against the instinctive papal dislike and distrust of

Spain must be set the promotion and extension of the faith, unhappily dependent on the force of Spanish arms. In France, Sixtus's zeal for the faith led him at the start of his reign into policies which he later bitterly regretted. He realized too late that his support for the League and his excommunication of Henry of Navarre had merely strength-ened Philip's influence, driven Navarre even closer to Elizabeth, and stirred up the dangerous forces of Gallicanism. And yet, as long as the League fought almost alone for the faith, and Navarre rejected the idea of conversion, what else could Sixtus do? Similarly with England, where his overtures to Elizabeth were – not surprisingly – ignored. To whom could he turn for help but to Philip against that Jezebel?

It was the execution of Mary Queen of Scots which finally brought Sixtus to concur in Spanish plans. He raged in the consistory against the English queen, and, as a gesture of defiance, made William Allen a cardinal. Already at the end of 1585 he had renewed the Spanish *cruzada* for a further seven years. Now, in July 1587, he reached an agreement with Olivares to provide a subsidy of one million ducats, on condition that an expedition set sail to England before the end of the year, and that Philip placed on the English throne a prince who would restore the Roman faith. From this moment, then, the enter-prise of England looked assured of papal support. As the ships for the great expedition were made ready in the dockyards of Spain, it seemed as though the lines of secular and religious division had finally con-verged. Ranged against the Protestants of England, France and Hol-land were the forces of Spain and the 'Counter-Reformation'. Yet this conveys the impression of an incomparably more monolithic combin-ation than in reality existed. If the principal forces of the 'Counter-Reformation' were Spain, the pope and the Jesuits, then even at this moment of crisis the alliance was scarcely very firm. Here was a pope who disliked the Jesuits and hated the Spaniards; who was desperately anxious for the restoration of Catholicism in England, but who saw with anguish that this would entail the establishment of a client of Philip II on the English throne; and who suspected, and perhaps in his heart almost dared to hope, that the enterprise to which he had given his blessing would end in failure and defeat. The triumph of the faith was the highest ideal of king and pope alike. But if for once, in 1587–1588, diplomacy and dogmatism walked hand in hand, it was pain-fully difficult not to hanker for a parting of the ways.

3   The Armada and the League

The fitting out of the Spanish Armada was a laborious affair. The marquis of Santa Cruz had originally envisaged a fleet of some 500 ships, carrying 60,000 soldiers and costing a grand total of nearly four million ducats. Ships had to be constructed in the dockyards of Spain and Italy; contracts had to be prepared for ordnance, timber and supplies, much of which could only be acquired at great expense from Northern Europe and the Baltic. Then in April 1587 Sir Francis Drake, freshly returned from his pillaging expedition in the Caribbean, made his famous raid on Cadiz. Here he destroyed twenty-four ships and a quantity of stores, before making for Cape St Vincent, where he harried Spanish shipping and captured large quantities of barrel-staves which were required for the casks that were to hold the provisions of the fleet.

The effect of Drake's Cadiz expedition was to delay until 1588 an invasion which had been intended for 1587. Not only had Drake's activities seriously interfered with the Armada's preparation, but they had forced Santa Cruz to sail for the Azores in June to protect the silver fleet. Although the fleet in due course reached Seville in safety, Santa Cruz and his men were in no condition on their return to Lisbon to embark at once on the English expedition. The sailing of the fleet was therefore postponed, and it was still not ready in February 1588 when Santa Cruz died in Lisbon. His reluctant successor was the duke of Medina Sidonia, whose long experience of fitting out fleets in Andalusia made him an obvious choice for the final organization of the Armada, while his high social status would help to ensure obedience to his orders among the serving officers under his command. Once arrived in Lisbon he pressed ahead with the last arrangements, under the distant but watchful surveillance of a king who was becoming uncharacteristically impatient; and by 30 May his Armada of 130 ships was standing out to sea.

The strategy governing the Armada expedition had been worked out by the king after lengthy consultation with Santa Cruz and Alexander Farnese, in the course of which it was subjected to constant changes of plan. As finally decided, it envisaged a junction between the Armada and Farnese's army, which would be embarked in barges and escorted by the Armada across the English channel. This demanded a degree of coordination highly improbable in sixteenth-century conditions, and the scheme was endangered from the outset by the lack of a deep-water port in the Netherlands for the galleons. Farnese, with his sharp eye for essentials, was painfully aware of the strategic and logistic problems involved. He had always felt deep anxiety about a hazardous and uncertain enterprise, which would entail the relegation of his own plans for the reduction of the Netherlands to a secondary place. The invasion of England, too, would deprive him of the reinforcements and money of which he already considered himself unjustifiably starved. He therefore insisted in his correspondence with the king on certain preconditions before the invasion fleet put to sea: there must be absolute secrecy concerning its objectives; the southern Netherlands must be well defended to deter any attempts at invasion from France; and France itself must be immobilized by its domestic troubles, so that Henry III would be unable to give any form of assistance to Elizabeth.

The delay in the despatch of the Armada had already jeopardized the secrecy on which Farnese had insisted. On the other hand, his stipulation about the passivity of France had been largely met as a result of the events of 1587. For a time, the situation had looked unpromising. Elizabeth's subsidies had enabled Henry of Navarre to hire a large force of Swiss and German mercenaries, which crossed the borders of Lorraine in August 1587 under the command of baron von Dohna. In order to prevent a junction of Navarre's forces and Dohna's relieving army, Henry III established himself on the Loire with the main body of the royal troops. From here he sent Guise to fight the Germans, anticipating his defeat, and his favourite Joyeuse to fight Navarre, whom he did not expect to be brought to battle. Unfortunately for the king, he had once again miscalculated. Navarre defeated and killed Joyeuse at Coutras on 20 October, and on 24 November, at Auneau, Guise routed Dohna and his German *reiter*, whom Navarre had failed to join. As a result, the victorious duke of Guise was greeted with wild acclaim as the hero of Catholic France, while the League was everywhere agitating against Henry III and his favourite, the duke of Epernon.

Guise's victory at Auneau seemed of more immediate consequence than Navarre's at Coutras, and Spain's ambassador in Paris, Mendoza, had reason to feel well pleased. There was every chance now that the League would be in a position to hold Henry III in check, as it would certainly wish to do for motives both of self-interest and conviction. The League may have been little more than an ill-assorted coalition of the House of Lorraine, disaffected gentry, extremist clergy and disgruntled citizens, but it represented a vigorous movement of protest which Spain might justifiably hope to turn to its own account.

The duke of Guise was reliable enough as long as Spanish silver could be used to bait the trap. He would always welcome foreign assistance if it improved his own chances of securing the succession; and Spain's interest in exploiting the weakness of the monarchy nicely coincided with his own. He could confidently expect the support of his large following which would remain loyal to him wherever he led, and also of the cities of northern and eastern France, where discontent was running deep. Almost thirty years of unrest and war had depressed trade and industry, and some regions had suffered devastation from marauding bands. On top of this, royal insolvency had given rise to endless tax demands – the *taille* alone rose from seven million *livres* in 1576 to eighteen million in 1588. The increased taxes fell most heavily on the towns; and this meant in practice the towns of northern France, since the South had effectively broken away to form a Huguenot-*politique* State on its own. Called upon to shoulder a burden made all the heavier by the defection of the South, the northern cities lavished their hatred on the Huguenots who paid no taxes, and on the profligate king in whose name they were raised.

Within the towns, certain sections of the population had good reasons of their own to exploit the general discontent. Until the 1570s the sale by the crown of increasing numbers of judicial and administrative offices had made possible a considerable degree of social mobility; but under Charles IX and Henry III the growing tendency of the monarchy to sanction hereditary succession in office had begun to turn the office-holders into a closed and self-perpetuating caste. The opportunities for office were therefore diminishing at exactly the moment when difficult economic circumstances made governmental or judicial office a highly desirable alternative to industry or trade. This meant that every important town by the 1580s had its aspiring and disgruntled citizens. In particular the lawyers and notaries looked enviously at the positions of influence achieved by the office-holding families.

Debarred from office in the *parlements* and the royal administration, many of these lawyers had none the less succeeded in forcing their way into municipal posts and urban corporations. By 1578 this class of ambitious *avocats* dominated many a town government. They enjoyed their power, but it was insufficient to satisfy their ambitions. Increasingly they began to think of themselves as the champions of virtually autonomous communes, defending the interests of municipality and people against their enemies and oppressors – the gentry, the office-holders, and the agents of a crumbling royal authority. In seeking to rally the populace to their cause, they found allies in the *curés* and the mendicants – Franciscans, Dominicans and Carmelites who denounced the wealth of the church establishment, and preached the need for a return to absolute purity of faith and morals with a passion and eloquence equalling that of their Calvinist rivals in the Netherlands. It was the preachers, too, who – as in the Netherlands – acted as the agitators and the organizers of revolt. Between them they forged the links in a conspiratorial chain which, by the end of 1587, united in a single subversive movement the Paris League and its counterparts in the provinces.

Inevitably, preachers and agitators moved farther and faster than municipal corporations. Even where these were dominated by League sympathizers, the instinctive fear of popular unrest characteristic of all town councils prompted them throughout 1587 to hold the League in check. But where the government of the provincial towns at least showed themselves sympathetic to League ideas, the government of the capital, although disillusioned with the king, remained hostile to the League. The hostility of the city government forced the Paris League into extremist courses from the start. Lawyers, notaries, clerics and doctors of the ultra-Catholic Sorbonne were the natural leaders of revolt, while artisans and shopkeepers were forged into a militant organization which in due course could be unleashed against the king and the municipal authorities alike. The city was divided into sections, eventually sixteen in number; a secret council, which came to be known as the Council of Sixteen, was set up; and agents were sent out to make contact with the provincial cities, and to propagate League ideals among the Paris population.

Throughout 1587 the inhabitants of the capital were restless and excited. Food prices were high; the city was hungry; and the priests and friars whipped up religious enthusiasm by such devices as recounting in gory detail the sufferings of Mary Queen of Scots and the English Catholic martyrs. Henry III was well aware of the dangers to himself of a hostile capital, and imprisoned three of the most notorious preachers on 2 September 1587. But at the sound of the tocsin the League turned out in force to defy the royal authority, and Henry III shied away from further energetic measures which might have re-established his mastery over the capital. The Paris League was now aware of its strength, and the duke of Guise's victory at Auneau increased its confidence. There could no longer be any doubt about its value both to Guise and to Mendoza. Successfully manipulated it was capable of bringing decisive pressure to bear on Henry III at a crucial moment in the affairs both of France and Europe. For Guise, it could be used to destroy the king's intolerable favourite, Epernon. For Mendoza, it could help to pin down the king while the Armada was sailing against England, and so prevent him from coming to Elizabeth's defence.

In the early months of 1588 Guise and Mendoza were working in close collaboration. Guise was happy enough to support the design for an invasion of England. It would avenge the death of his cousin, Mary Queen of Scots; and anyhow he would be well rewarded by the Spaniards for his pains. Guise's lieutenants were therefore instructed to secure the Channel ports as havens for the Armada in case of emergency. Mendoza and Guise were also in close contact with the Council of Sixteen. Long ago the Sixteen had prepared plans for the seizure of power in Paris, and Mendoza was anxious that any such move should be synchronized with the sailing of the Armada.

But the Spanish ambassador and the duke of Guise were not the only men with ambitious designs in the spring of 1588. Henry III found it intolerable that his authority should be challenged by the citizens of Paris, and he watched with growing anxiety the consolidation of Guise power and the Spanish preparations for the conquest of England. The time had come for decisive counter-measures to save both himself and the English. This time, instead of making a few arrests, he would use his troops on Paris. Meanwhile, the duke of Nevers, his newly appointed governor in Picardy, would force the Guisard duke of Aumale to relinquish his recent conquests; and the duke of Epernon, as governor of Normandy, would clear the Channel ports and go to the assistance of the English, either directly, or indirectly by means of an attack on Flanders.

Towards the end of April 1588 Henry moved four thousand Swiss troops into the Faubourg Saint-Denis. The leaders of the League were well enough prepared to be able to unleash a popular revolt at any moment. It is possible that they held back at the request of Mendoza, who wished for no decisive action until the Armada put to sea; but the degree of collusion between Mendoza and the Paris League is not easily determined. The Sixteen may simply have been concerned to avoid the risks entailed in a popular insurrection. If Guise could be induced to come to Paris, his presence alone might be sufficient to overawe the king. In response to the Sixteen's urgent appeals that he should move to the city's help, the duke set out from Soissons for Paris, which he entered on 9 May to the accompaniment of wildly enthusiastic crowds who cheered him on his way. His first act was to pay his respects to a startled Catherine de Medici, and then, with typical bravado, he rode on for an audience with his king, who had strictly forbidden him to set foot in the capital. Henry might, if he had wished, have killed Guise at this moment; but there were frenzied crowds outside the Louvre, and he shrank from an act of violence.

Instead, the king planned a military *coup* which would deliver into his hands the leaders of the Paris League and the duke himself. The city militia was to occupy the strategic points in preparation for the entry of the Swiss troops and the French guards who were stationed in the suburbs. The militia was in fact by this stage no longer to be trusted; but the king's troops marched into a silent city without opposition in the early morning of 12 May. The king, it seemed, had taken his capital without a shot being fired.

The only quarter which showed any signs of being ready to defend itself was the Latin Quarter, whose inhabitants began building barricades across the streets. Meanwhile the Swiss stood at their action stations, waiting for orders that never came. Seeing that nothing was happening, the populace grew bolder. Everywhere, barricades sprang up; and beneath the hot afternoon sun, tempers began to flare. Then, as the tocsins sounded, the crowds turned on the troops, who found their retreat barred by the barricades. Under the hail of missiles many of the soldiers laid down their arms. The king, for his part, was completely taken aback by the turn of events, and desperately appealed to Guise to rescue the Swiss and placate a mob which only he was strong enough to control. As the duke rode out unarmed into the streets, rebellion merged into a triumphant victory celebration. The barricades came down; the defeated royal regiments were permitted to leave the city; and the bonfires blazed through the night. But while Paris was celebrating, the king slipped quietly through the unguarded Porte Neuve, and away from a capital which, for a few short hours, he had believed was his.

In spite of the king's escape, the outcome of the Day of the Barricades was so satisfactory for the Spaniards that it might have been engineered by the Spanish ambassador. Perhaps it was. But more probably it was the consequence, half accidental and half planned, of a series of events originally set in train by the king's own decision in April to order his troops to the outskirts of Paris. Once this had happened, and the leaders of the League had summoned the duke of Guise to their help, a popular explosion could scarcely be avoided in a city where emotions had for months been tuned to fever-pitch. But in any event Mendoza was fully justified in looking back with satisfaction on this momentous day. It meant, as he wrote to Philip II, that 'the French king will be unable to assist the English in any way.'[5] This assessment proved correct. Henry's flight had left him powerless, and Epernon abandoned his Normandy government and retired to Angoulême. When the Armada at last began to move majestically up the English Channel, in the last week of July and the first week of August, Farnese had nothing to fear from the Flanders frontier, nor Medina Sidonia from the coast of France.

The fate of England now depended on its seamen and its ships. The queen's navy had been well nursed by its treasurer, John Hawkins, but the English commanders had no experience of a full-scale naval battle, and there could be no certainty about either their response or the outcome. As the ships of Howard and Drake dogged the crescent-shaped Spanish formation up the Channel, two rival systems of naval warfare found themselves on trial. The two fleets were well matched in numbers and tonnage. The Armada totalled 130 ships, of which the hard core was formed by the twenty galleons of the Castilian and Portuguese squadrons and four great ships from New Spain. There were also 41 merchantmen and numerous smaller vessels and supply ships; and the fleet carried 2,431 pieces of artillery and 22,000 seamen and soldiers. The hard core of the English fleet – about one sixth of its total – consisted of the thirty-four ships of the royal navy, of very varied tonnage and fighting power. Alongside these were some thirty merchantmen whose power was comparable or scarcely inferior to that of the queen's ships in their class.

Although the combatants looked roughly equal in numbers and size, they differed considerably in their sailing and fighting capabilities. Philip II had wisely abandoned Santa Cruz's plan for using Mediterranean galleys in rough northern waters. Galleys, with their freedom of movement, may have won Lepanto, but they were ill-equipped to face the Atlantic breakers, and were no match for the large, heavily-gunned English sailing-ships, whose advent would eventually lead to the triumph of sail over oar. Philip had therefore opted for galleons, which were ideally equipped for grappling and boarding. These galleons were mounted for the occasion with heavy-shotted but short-ranged artillery, intended to impair the sailing capacity of the English ships, so that they would stand to be boarded. The English ships, on the other hand, carried long-range guns in order to be able to ward off the galleons and prevent them from grappling. In the event, the English vessels proved far superior in mobility and sailing quality, but their long-range guns turned out to be too light to pierce the galleons.

Medina Sidonia's great ships maintained a superb discipline as they moved up the Channel, but the original defect in Philip's plan became glaringly apparent as they approached Calais. With an English squadron and Dutch flyboats patrolling the shallows off Dunkirk and Nieuwport, it was impossible for Farnese's invasion barges to move out to sea unprotected. But it was equally impossible for the galleons to move close enough in to the shore to give them the escort without which they could not move. As a result, the rendezvous was never effected, and the Armada waited helplessly off Calais for the barges that Farnese dared not send. It was now that the English sent their fireships against the galleons. As the fireships approached, the Armada broke its superb formation, and its ships were scattered in their attempt to escape. Although Medina Sidonia succeeded in rallying them again off Gravelines on 8 August, they presented sitting targets for the English fleet – close enough to bring its artillery into range, but too far away to allow the Spaniards to grapple. Even now, however, the weight of shot from the English guns was not sufficient to enable them to destroy the Spanish fleet. Although the Armada was damaged, at least it had survived; but it no longer had any chance of effecting the junction with Farnese, and it was hopelessly exposed to the perils of wind and weather. Caught by the south-west wind the battered fleet was driven into the North Sea, from where it made its way as best it could round the British Isles, limping home to Spanish ports. Superb seamanship prevented a total disaster, and perhaps two thirds of its fighting strength was saved, but wrecks littered the coasts of Scotland and Ireland, and the loss of life was heavy.

In terms of fighting power, then, the defeat of the Armada represented a serious, but not an overwhelming, blow to Spain. Only four galleons had been lost, and within two years Philip had reconstructed his Indies fleets. Spanish naval power in the 1590s – as Drake and Hawkins discovered to their cost – was if anything more formidable than it had been before the Armada ever set sail. The blow to the

Spanish merchant marine, however, was much heavier with the loss of eighteen of the forty-one merchantmen and large numbers of skilled seamen. But although the victory allowed the English to recover the initiative in the Atlantic, Spain's monopoly of the American trade was still unbroken, and its Indies routes intact.

The political and psychological consequences of the English victory, on the other hand, were of incalculable importance. Philip II received the news of the disaster with his customary impassivity, but it hit Castilian national morale with shattering effect. How was it that a chosen people could have been abandoned by their God? The defeat of the Armada was a subject of universal discussion, and the king himself was widely criticized, both for choosing a mistaken strategy and for pursuing expensive policies that imposed an intolerable burden on his peoples. Some were even bold enough to lay the blame squarely on Philip's personal sins, which had brought down divine retribution in their wake. Later sixteenth-century Castile was a society in which the highly charged religious atmosphere was productive both of saints and charlatans. By the time of her death in 1582 Teresa of Avila, who had been involved in many a brush with authority as she set about the reform of the Carmelite order and underwent a series of mystical experiences of such transcendence as to arouse the deepest suspicions, had established a reputation for sanctity which would be officially confirmed by her canonization in 1622. But other visionaries of more dubious character could equally well find a ready following. One of these was a certain Lucrecia de León, a young woman on the fringes of the court, who claimed to have experienced a long succession of vivid dreams, many of them with a strong political content. Her dreams enabled her to prophesy the failure of the Enterprise of England, and her reputation soared as her prophecy came true. Eventually she was arrested by the Inquisition, but not before her accusations against the king for oppressing the poor and leading Spain to ruin had brought her at least a transient fame.

While Spaniards mourned the loss of their fleet, and agonized over the causes of the disaster, there was exultation among the English, the Huguenots and the Dutch. England's victory was seen as the salvation of Protestant Europe. 'I had always cherished the hope,' wrote the Huguenot leader La Noue in great excitement to Sir Francis Walsingham, 'that you would have the advantage over your enemies on the sea ... The prince of Parma has been frustrated in his design, and has seen beneath his very nose the chariots of Egypt submerged beneath the waves.... The Spaniard wanted to take Flanders by way of England, but it is now for you to take Spain by way of the Indies ... In saving yourselves you will save all the rest...'[6]

The new confidence evinced by the leaders of Protestant Europe was felt also in another, and more unexpected, quarter. Since the humiliation of the Day of the Barricades, Henry III had been a cowed and abject man, whose last vestiges of authority had been brutally stripped away. 'From that day', wrote the contemporary French historian, De Thou, 'the majesty of the throne remained, so to say, buried in deep oblivion until the reign of Henry IV.'[7] But if the majesty was gone, the man himself remained, morally and politically defeated, but harbouring, deep down in that twisted mind, secret dreams of revenge against the duke of Guise, that swashbuckling adventurer who now behaved as if he were the uncrowned king of Catholic France. In the months that followed the Day of the Barricades, Henry had been subjected to a whole series of humiliations. In signing the Edict of Union of July 1588 he had been forced to consent to all the League's demands. He had been compelled to appoint Guise lieutenant general of the realm and to name the cardinal of Bourbon as first prince of the blood and next in succession to the throne. But with the news of the defeat of the Armada, his spirits and courage began to revive. Perhaps he could after all throw off the tyranny of the Guises, the arrogant puppets of a defeated king of Spain.

The financial straits of the crown had made it necessary to call a new meeting of the Estates-General at Blois in September. At the beginning of the month, the king suddenly dismissed his ministers – his chancellor, Cheverny, his *surintendant des finances*, Bellièvre, and his three secretaries of state, Brulart, Pinart, and the indispensable Villeroy. This unexpected action has never been fully explained, but it seems plausible to see it as the culmination of a gradual process of disillusionment with his advisers, and especially with Villeroy, which dated back at least to 1584. France's involvement in the Netherlands in support of Alençon had been a disaster, and for a time Henry was convinced that it would push his country into open war with Spain. If in the end he succeeded in extricating himself from his predicament, it was only at a heavy expense in prestige. Since then he had suffered nothing but humiliations, culminating in the Edict of Union and his effective surrender to the Guises. It was easy to blame himself for the long series of humiliating failures, but easier still to blame his advisers. So it was that Henry dismissed his ministers, hoping by this apparently decisive action to wipe the slate clean and prove to the world that he was now in command.[8]

The Estates-General of Blois were packed with the adherents of the League and especially with those ambitious *avocats* who dominated the French municipalities and constituted no less than half the members of the third Estate. Of the 505 deputies present, 380 were Leaguers. No Huguenots attended. An assembly like this provided an obvious forum for the apotheosis of the duke of Guise, who shrugged off Mendoza's warnings about the dangers of making a personal appearance. Temperamentally a shallow and glittering adventurer, Guise was a man incapable of grasping that even the luckiest man could push his luck too far. The assembly opened, however, under the shadow of a national humiliation whose consequences might have alerted a wiser man to the dangers of the exposed position in which his policies had placed him. Philip II's son-in-law, Charles Emmanuel of Savoy – yet another inveterate gambler in that reckless age – marched his troops into the marquisate of Saluzzo, a French enclave within the borders of Piedmont. He was occupying it, he explained, to save it from the Huguenots of the Dauphiné. This implausible explanation convinced nobody. The occupation of Saluzzo, which closed the gateway of Italy to France, was of obvious advantage to Philip II; and the duke of Guise, as Philip's ally, naturally fell under suspicion of complicity and treacherous intent.

The loss of Saluzzo temporarily brought king and Estates-General together in a mutual sense of shock, but it was not long before all the old hatreds revived. Henry had been brave enough to criticize the League in his opening speech, but pressure from Guise and the Estates forced him to swear to the Edict of Union once again. In spite of his compliance, the deputies proved as obdurate as ever in voting subsidies, and insisted on the reduction of the *taille* to its level of 1576. The obstructive behaviour of the Estates was attributed by the king to the Guises, and increased his determination to rid himself of this brood of vipers in the bosom of the realm.

As Henry reflected during those winter days at Blois on the indignities to which he was subjected, long periods of brooding melancholy were interrupted by sudden outbursts of rage against the tyrant duke. Guise knew all this, but he refused to be disturbed. The king was a coward; and there was anyhow no drawing back for a man whose life consisted of a series of calculated risks. 'He who gives up the game has lost it', he is alleged to have remarked.[9] But there were various possible ways of losing this particular game. On the morning of 23 December the duke was summoned from the council chamber for an audience with the king, and walked straight into the trap that had been carefully prepared. In the royal antechamber, almost at the door of the king's cabinet, he was surrounded and cut down by assassins. His brother, the cardinal of Guise, was taken into custody along with the cardinal of Bourbon, and was murdered by his guards on Christmas Eve.

Henry III felt a great sense of release with his enemies dead. Now at last he was king – or so he hastened to assure his mother. Catherine knew better, and warned him at all costs to make sure of the towns. Her perception of the realities of power was as acute as ever, but she was old and mortally ill, and there was nothing more she could do for the monarchy and the dynasty she had fought so tenaciously to preserve. Broken by the recent terrible sequence of events, she died on 5

January 1589. No one, according to De Thou, felt either very pleased or very sad when they heard the news of her death.

Henry's elation at the murder of the Guises soon proved to be as misplaced as Mendoza's deep despair. Guise might be dead, but the League survived – stunned at first by the murder of its leader, but soon thirsting for revenge against the 'murderous tyrant'. In Paris the populace rose in a spontaneous outburst of fury; and this time, unlike the Day of the Barricades, the example of the capital was followed in the provinces. Town after town rose in support of the League under its new leader, Guise's brother, the duke of Mayenne. All payment of taxes to royal officials was forbidden by the League. The Council of Sixteen in Paris began a formal trial of the king in his absence; and the Theology Faculty of the Sorbonne declared French citizens released from their oath of allegiance and free to take up arms against a tyrant. It was one of the supreme ironies of this moment that the doctrines of resistance, formerly devised and elaborated by the Huguenots, were now appropriated for use by the Catholics. From 1589 the Catholic presses poured out their pamphlets insisting that power lay with the people, and that a king who broke his contract could be resisted, deposed and slain.

The flames of League violence in the spring of 1589 were fanned from Rome, where Sixtus V, with typical impetuosity, responded to the murders in the manner of a medieval pontiff – by ordering Henry III to appear in Rome in person or by proxy within sixty days to answer for the death of the cardinal of Guise, a prince of the church. The threat of excommunication, however, was only one, and perhaps not the greatest, of the troubles that beset the wretched king. Half the country was in revolt against him; he was without money; and his enemies were crying out for his life.

Even before the arrival of Sixtus's brief, there was only one course open to him – alliance with Henry of Navarre. In April 1589, after difficult negotiations, the two kings reached agreement. Navarre declared himself willing to bring his troops to Henry's help, and by July the royal army, reinforced by Swiss and German mercenaries, was laying siege to Paris. In the besieged capital itself the hatred of the king had reached new heights of hysteria. There were fanatics enough to be found in the streets of Paris, and on 1 August – the day before Navarre planned his final assault on the city – one of them, a young Jacobin friar, Jacques Clément, gained access to Henry III at Saint-Cloud and stabbed him. Henry, the last of the Valois, died the following morning.

Before he died, Henry recognized the king of Navarre as his successor. Instinctively the last of Catherine's sons had learnt the lesson she had tried to teach him: at all costs the legitimate succession, the very foundation of monarchical authority, must be preserved. The League might proceed to proclaim the cardinal of Bourbon their king as 'Charles X', but Navarre possessed in his legitimate rights to the crown a weapon of incalculable advantage. The years to come would show that he was shrewd enough to know how to use it.

At the moment of his accession, however, Navarre was still a Protestant. Because of his religion, many nobles and towns gave him only provisional and conditional allegiance; and a large part of the country, which placed religion before legitimacy, refused entirely to accept him. Philip II, for his part, had always refrained from a final break with Henry III, who was, after all, the lawful and consecrated king. But Henry of Navarre, in his eyes, had no such claim to the crown. Ever since the death of Guise, Philip had been preparing for direct intervention in France. Now that Henry III, too, was dead, there was no further reason for delay. Farnese in the Netherlands was instructed to prepare his troops for action. Once again, as in 1588, the suppression of the Dutch revolt was to be subordinated to a grand, and possibly chimerical, design with endless ramifications. But if Farnese had ever cared to ask whether the purpose of that design was to keep France Catholic, or to keep it weak and divided, perhaps not even Philip himself could have given him the answer.

The Discomfiture of Spain

1 France and Spain

'The affairs of France', wrote Philip II to Farnese in the autumn of 1589, 'are at this moment the principal thing.'[1] In spite of obtaining the support of Juan de Idiáquez, Farnese's objections to the employment of his army in France were overruled by Madrid. The king's other principal adviser, Cristóbal de Moura, seems to have argued successfully that the struggle for the Netherlands would be decided in France. Flanders would be in immediate danger if Henry of Navarre became king of France, because the heretic king would undoubtedly come to the help of his fellow-heretics, the Dutch. If, on the other hand, the League were victorious, the complete reconquest of the Netherlands should not be difficult.

Against Moura, Idiáquez seems to have maintained that Spain's resources were insufficient to enable it to fight simultaneously on two fronts; and he agreed with Farnese that they would be better employed in recovering the Netherlands. Nor was it for the king of Spain to incur universal odium by acting as the defender of Catholicism throughout the continent. This task properly belonged to the papacy. The rival French factions were best left to fight their battle out between themselves, and their consequent exhaustion would leave the field free to Spain.

Philip's dilemma, which was resolved in favour of intervention, was as nothing compared with that of Sixtus V. For the Holy See, the loss of France would be a disaster of unparalleled magnitude, and would make the victory of Protestantism in northern and central Europe irreversible. The immediate consequence of Henry III's assassination was therefore a *rapprochement* between Sixtus and the Spaniards, both equally appalled at the prospect of a Protestant king. Cardinal Cajetan was sent as papal legate to France to work for the 'conservation of the Holy Catholic faith throughout the realm', and to detach

Catholic support from Henry and unite it with the League. Yet hardly had Cajetan set out on his mission when Sixtus began to experience misgivings. A victory for the League was a victory for Spain, as the Venetians hastened to point out when Sixtus berated them for receiving an ambassador from Henry. Already Philip was aspiring to be recognized as the official 'protector' of the realm; and when 'Charles X', the cardinal of Bourbon, died in May 1590, Philip put forward the claims of his elder daughter, Isabella Clara Eugenia, (the grand-daughter of Henry II and Catherine de Medici), in bland defiance of the Salic law which governed the French succession. Philip's behaviour confirmed Sixtus's worst fears about Spanish designs. There were violent scenes as Sixtus raged away at the count of Olivares, and refused to endorse Philip's policy in France.

A Protestant victory in France could mean the end of European Catholicism. A Spanish victory in France could mean the end of papal independence. It was therefore essential for Rome that France should be kept both Catholic and strong. It was clear that wholehearted support for a Spanish-dominated League, such as Cajetan recommended, could not achieve the second of these ends. Only one way of escape from the dilemma suggested itself: the conversion of Henry of Navarre. During the last turbulent months of his life, Sixtus's conviction grew that Henry must, and could, be brought back to the church. When he died on 27 August 1590 – appropriately enough in the middle of a thunderstorm – he had already moved sufficiently far from his first position of unqualified support for the League to make it possible for his successors to reverse his policy.

It was to be some time, however, before any successor appeared with both the desire and the capacity to enter the promised land which Sixtus had pointed out from afar. The one-and-a-half years following the death of Sixtus were years of a quite remarkable papal mortality. Sixtus was followed to the grave in quick succession by Urban VII (pope for twelve days), Gregory XIV (ten months), and Innocent IX (two months). It was only with the election of cardinal Aldobrandini as Clement VIII in January 1592 that the spell was broken, and a pontificate opened which was to last for thirteen years. But sudden death was not the only unhappy characteristic of this strange interlude. In the earlier conclaves of his reign, Philip II had done little more than make his likes and dislikes strongly known. But the conclaves of 1590–1592 were distinguished by the direct intervention of Spain. Philip could not afford another Sixtus V, and his ambassadors were instructed to work actively for the election of candidates whose reliability was assured. The conclaves grew increasingly resentful of Spanish interference, but it was only in the close-fought election of January 1592 that the Spanish nominee was finally defeated, and a pope was chosen who had no leading-strings to Spain.

Clement VIII was an able and intelligent man, as prudent as Sixtus had been reckless and unpredictable. It was his achievement to disengage the papacy from the commitments to Spain incurred by his immediate predecessors and to steer it back to the policy advocated by Sixtus in the closing months of his life. But he had to move with infinite care and diplomacy, knowing that the success of his policy would ultimately be determined not by himself but by the personal decision of Henry of Navarre. Would Henry become a genuine Catholic, and, if so, when and how?

Although he was no doubt well aware that the logic of events would some day compel him to renounce his Protestant faith, Henry was shrewd enough to appreciate that it was essential to bide his time. The pressures upon him to announce his conversion were considerable, but a precipitate abjuration would almost certainly lose him the support of his loyal Huguenot followers, while bringing him little compensation in the form of new Catholic adherents. His personal religious record was, after all, very dubious. Baptized a Catholic and given an ambiguous religious education at court, he had been instructed in Calvinist doctrines during the first years of his adolescence by his remarkable mother, Jeanne d'Albret. At the time of the massacre of St Bartholomew he had been compelled to return to Rome, but had abjured again four years later to become the leader of the Huguenots. In Catholic eyes, therefore, he was already a double apostate, and a sudden new conversion would be regarded as characteristically insincere.

Henry had already shown himself a man of resourcefulness and political acumen, and he now proceeded to play a difficult hand with exceptional skill. In his proclamation of 4 August 1589 on the death of Henry III, he promised to maintain and preserve the Roman Catholic faith in France, and to follow the spiritual guidance of a 'free and lawful general, or national, council'. In reviving the old Gallican idea of a national religious council, Henry was making a shrewd bid for moderate Catholic support at a highly propitious time. Sixtus's bull excommunicating him in 1585 had sparked off violent controversy in France about the character and extent of papal power. A generation acquainted with Bodin's conclusion that freedom from external interference was an essential attribute of sovereignty was unlikely to show much enthusiasm for Sixtus's adherence to the principles enunciated in 1302 by Boniface VIII, whereby the papacy claimed supreme power in the temporal sphere as well as the spiritual, and assumed to itself the right to make and unmake kings. The Jesuit Robert Bellarmine published in 1586 a more moderate statement of the papal position, claiming for the papacy no more than an indirect temporal jurisdiction, although this still included the power of deposition over princes who infringed the spiritual rights of their subjects.

But Sixtus V denounced such faint-hearted doctrines and ordered the first volume of Bellarmine's *Controversies* to be placed on the Index.

Even Bellarmine's theory of indirect papal power was scarcely calculated to allay suspicion about the intentions of Rome. It seemed obvious to the more moderate French clergy and laity that papal power was on the increase, in clear defiance of the decrees of the Councils of Constance and Basle, to which the Gallican church had always been firmly attached. The repression of heresy was beginning to look like a self-defeating policy, and one which threatened the traditional independence of the French national church. Moreover, in spite of Sixtus's feuds with the Spanish ambassador, Rome was too closely identified with the political ambitions of Spain. It was also too closely identified with doctrines which sought to justify the subversion of authority and popular revolt. Could not the horrific act of regicide of 1589 be attributed to the monstrous teachings of the Jesuits about rights of resistance and popular sovereignty? Disenchantment reached its climax when the papacy proceeded to disregard the fundamental laws of the French monarchy which laid down the direct order of succession to the throne. This contempt for the fundamental law gravely affronted the legalistically minded *parlementaires*, who regarded themselves as the guardians of France's constitutional tradition. When Henry IV made his appeal to Gallican sentiments, therefore, it awoke strong answering echoes among those who were alarmed by the increasing intrusions of Rome into French national life, and who feared that a victory of the League would bring with it foreign domination and a forcible imposition on France of the Tridentine decrees.

Although a number of moderate Catholics may have been encouraged by Henry's manifesto to see him as the long-awaited saviour of France, his position was exceptionally difficult during the opening years of his reign. Certainly he possessed magnetic qualities of leadership, such as no king had displayed in France for half a century or more. But he lacked the revenues from taxation which had sustained some semblance of royal authority until the last tragic months of the reign of Henry III, and he was faced with the open revolt of Paris and half the population. In March 1590 he won a great victory over Mayenne and the League forces at Ivry, but the sequel to his victory proved sadly disappointing. His army marched on Paris, and hopes ran high that the civil wars would end with the rapid subjection of the capital. But this was to reckon without the fanatical attachment of the Parisians to the League, and the ability of Farnese to bring them assistance from Flanders.

Under the energetic but increasingly repressive government of the Council of Sixteen, the capital prepared itself for the siege. The Jesuits and the friars urged the citizens to stand firm against the forces of impiety and heresy. The Spanish ambassador, Mendoza, was tireless in distributing food supplies and in organizing public relief. The city's sufferings were horrible, almost beyond belief. 'They chase dogs and eat grass that grows in the streets', reported Pierre de L'Estoile, that sharply critical observer of Parisian life and of the follies of the League. 'The only thing that is cheap in Paris is the sermons, where the preachers fill the poor people up with...lies and stupidities.'[2] By August, with 13,000 inhabitants dead of starvation, Paris was on the point of surrender. But at the moment when Henry seemed to have the capital within his grasp, Farnese crossed the border, and forced Henry, in a brilliant campaign, to raise the siege and retire to Normandy.

Farnese's intervention radically changed the character of the conflict. Until this moment the war in France had been primarily a civil war, to the advantage of local magnates and one or two covetous neighbours. Gradually the country was being dismembered into fragments. The duke of Mercoeur ruled Brittany, and the duke of Mayenne Burgundy; Champagne was coveted by the duke of Lorraine, and Provence was invaded by the irrepressible Charles-Emmanuel of Savoy in the summer of 1590. But now, for the first time, Spanish troops had intervened. Although assistance for the League remained the nominal pretext for intervention, Philip's general policy and his attempt to secure the throne for the Infanta Isabella suggested that his real intention was to ensure Spanish domination over France as a whole. In October 1590, 3,500 Spaniards landed in Brittany, of which the Infanta claimed the title of duchess. The possession of Brittany would provide Spain with a staging-post on the Lisbon-Antwerp sea-route, and a valuable base for the prosecution of its war with England. But Spanish military intervention was not confined to Brittany. In the spring of 1591 Spanish troops invaded Languedoc, and a Spanish garrison was introduced into Paris. In August, Alexander Farnese was ordered back into France for a fresh campaign, which compelled Henry to raise the siege of Rouen in April 1592.

Spain appeared to have embarked on a career of open aggression, with the enthusiastic approval of a client papacy. In the circumstances, Henry could present himself as the defender not merely of France but of all Europe against the grandiose ambitions of Philip II and the Holy See. Once again, therefore, a local conflict was internationalized. Elizabeth would have preferred to confine her wars against the Spaniards to the high seas, especially after the failure of the English expedition which had been sent to Portugal in 1589. The purpose of the expedition, led by Drake and Norris, had been to capture Lisbon and provoke a popular insurrection which would restore the prior of Crato to the throne. But the campaign had been disastrously mismanaged, and the Portuguese had failed to rise. Even worse, the expedition had missed a supreme opportunity for following up the defeat of the Armada, by striking decisively at the crippled Spanish fleet while it was being refitted at Santander.

As a result of the English failure in 1589, Spanish naval power in the 1590s was too formidable to be directly challenged, and Philip was sufficiently confident of his naval and financial strength to be able to risk large-scale intervention in France. The presence of Spanish armies in Normandy and Brittany posed a threat to English interests which Elizabeth could not afford to ignore. If the Channel ports fell under Spanish control, the British Isles and the Netherlands would at once be endangered, and Philip would again be close to universal domination. Reluctantly, therefore, Elizabeth found herself driven back to expensive land-warfare on the continent. An expeditionary force under Norris was sent to Brittany in 1590, and another, under the earl of Essex, to Normandy in 1591.

Spanish power never looked more formidable than in 1591 and 1592. There were, however, increasing signs that it was seriously over-extended. At home the strain of war was beginning to tell. Philip was now spending over twelve million ducats a year. About a quarter of this was provided by the silver of the Indies, and the rest had to be raised by taxation, mostly in Castile. In 1590 the Cortes of Castile were persuaded to vote a new tax, the *millones*, levied on articles of consumption and designed to yield eight million ducats over a period of six years – a novel tax in that it applied, at least nominally, to all classes of society. These new fiscal demands provoked agonized debate in the Cortes over the purpose as well as over the expense of the war. Castile's messianic nationalism still had its fervent exponents, like the deputy for Murcia who dismissed the argument of economic exhaustion with a wave of the hand: 'If we are defending God's cause, as we are, there is no reason to abandon it on grounds of impossibility, for He will find us new Indies and a new Potosí.' But other deputies preferred economics to metaphysics, and made their feelings clear. If the rest of Europe wished to destroy itself, then let it go ahead. There was no justification for letting Castile bleed to death to save the Netherlands and France.

While Philip's policies were being subjected to surprisingly out-spoken criticism in the Cortes of Castile, he also found himself faced with troubles in Aragon. Whereas royal government was firmly estab-lished in Castile, and a relatively high standard of justice had been maintained by the king, the liberties of the Crown of Aragon had always subjected the viceroys to sharp constitutional and administrative restraints. In the kingdom of Aragon itself, the *fueros* or liberties gave ample scope to the local nobility and gentry to abuse their wide powers of jurisdiction with little fear of viceregal intervention. When Philip tried to grasp the nettle in 1590 by sending a non-Aragonese noble to govern the kingdom, there were fierce protests from the Aragonese ruling class about this unwarranted attempt to deprive it of its liberties. As ill luck would have it, it was at this moment that Antonio Pérez escaped from his gaol in Madrid and fled across the frontier into Aragon, out of reach of royal justice. Philip's desperate efforts to recover both his secretary and the documents in his possession provoked a riot in Zaragoza in May 1591. Pérez was set free by the mob as he was being taken to the prison of the Inquisition, and the marquis of Almenara, the king's special representative, lost his life as a result of mob violence when his palace was stormed.

Philip could not afford to take any chances as long as Antonio Pérez was present to direct the revolt. Pérez was clever enough to think of turning Aragon into an independent republic under the protection of France, and if this happened Spain would find herself with a second Flanders, in the peninsula itself. A royal army of 12,000 men was assembled on the frontier, and crossed into Aragon in October 1591. It met with almost no resistance, and the ring-leaders of the revolt were captured and executed. But the elusive Pérez once again escaped, this time over the mountains into Béarn. It was to be the beginning of a long and disillusioned life of exile, in which the king's former secretary moved pathetically to and fro between the courts of France and England, hoping to blackmail his way back into his master's favour by threatening to sell to Spain's enemies the precious secrets of the Escorial.

Having repressed the revolt with severity, Philip settled the affairs of Aragon with moderation. Instead of destroying the liberties of Aragon, he preferred to stand by his promise to preserve its laws and privileges, and he made only minor institutional changes. In retrospect, the troubles of Aragon seem a relatively small and localized affair. But in many respects Philip had been fortunate. Events in France and the Netherlands had shown the dangerous possibilities of the aristocratic constitutionalism professed by the Aragonese. Fortunately for Philip there proved to be little popular enthusiasm for the aristocratic protest: there was neither a sufficiently strong spirit of Aragonese nationalism, nor a movement of religious dissent, to unite different social classes in a generalized rebellion. Nor was Henry of Navarre in a position to provide the external assistance which sixteenth-century risings appeared to need for success. But the revolt in Aragon did reveal that even Spain was vulnerable – that a Philip II who encouraged armed risings against his fellow monarchs could not reasonably expect that he alone should remain immune.

The need to attend to Aragonese affairs necessarily interfered to some extent with Philip's schemes for intervention in France. But his principal difficulty lay not in rebellion at home, but in the impossibly heavy nature of his commitments abroad. Throughout 1591 Farnese was short of money, and ceaselessly warned Philip of the serious consequences of his policy of intervention in France. Farnese's forebodings proved to be fully justified. In the Netherlands, Maurice of Nassau, the young son of William the Silent, had been appointed captain-general in 1588, and had begun to reform the armies of the United Provinces under the guidance of his cousin, William-Louis of Nassau. On his cousin's advice he had steeped himself in Roman and Byzantine military treatises, as well as in the study of mathematics and geometry. Inspired by classical military ideals he proceeded to instil some discipline into the ragged mercenary bands, dividing them into battalions of 550 men, which were more manoeuvrable and more economical of manpower than the great Spanish *tercios*. Along with his organizational and administrative reforms, he also provided specialized training for the pioneer corps and for military engineers. Farnese's intervention in France made it possible for this reformed and reorganized army to assume the offensive. In the spring of 1590 the Dutch captured Breda, and in 1591 Maurice launched a spectacular offensive which won him Zutphen, Deventer and Nijmegen, thus restoring communications between the north-eastern Netherlands and the main body of the United Provinces.

The circumstances in which Maurice achieved his successes were remarkably similar to those of nearly twenty years before. In 1572 the rebels had gained their first foothold when Alba had been forced to turn south in order to meet the threat of invasion from France. Now, in 1590–1591, the rebels decisively consolidated their position and made Dutch independence assured, because Farnese was forced to turn southwards like Alba, to intervene in France. The interdependence of Dutch and French affairs – that recurrent theme of later sixteenth-century European history – had once again been revealed, and Farnese's assessment of the situation had been proved strikingly correct. But he earned no gratitude for his foresight or his pains. Philip II was growing increasingly suspicious of his commander, and by February 1592 he had decided to recall him. But Providence, as so often happened, moved faster than the king of Spain. In the spring of 1592, just after relieving Rouen, Farnese was badly wounded in the arm. His health had already been undermined by his exertions, and by the autumn it was clear that he was dying. In the event there was no need for his successor, the count of Fuentes, to present the letter of recall; for Farnese died at Arras on 3 December, while on the way to his third expeditionary campaign in France.

The death of Farnese at the age of forty-seven deprived Philip of a great captain and a shrewd and realistic adviser. With his passing, the chances of Spanish success in France were still further reduced. But in the long run the fate of Philip's French policy would not be determined by the skill of his commanders, but by the ability or the failure of Henry IV to win the allegiance of a majority of his subjects. Military victory might help Henry in this, but it would not by itself be enough. Somehow the mass of the nation would have to be persuaded that its own best interests lay with the cause of lawful and consecrated kingship.

2 The Rallying to the King

A mass movement in support of Henry was likely to be triggered off as much by the mistakes and failures of the League as by any positive action on Henry's part. A great debate was agitating Catholic France in the early 1590s, and it was on the outcome of this debate that Henry's fortunes depended. The arguments of both sides were nowhere better put than in a brilliant fictional dialogue, the *Dialogue d'entre le Maheustre et le Manant*. The original version was written in 1593 by a member of the radical wing of the League against its aristocratic wing led by the duke of Mayenne, but it subsequently reappeared in 1594, after being doctored by a royalist editor, who skilfully strengthened the *Maheustre*'s arguments to win support for the cause of Henry IV. The *Manant*, the Parisian *petit bourgeois* with radical League sympathies, explained that he and his friends were fighting for the 'conservation of the Catholic, Apostolic and Roman religion', the extirpation of heresy and the reform of injustice, impiety and vice. In reply, the swashbuckling gentleman, the *Maheustre*, gave his reasons for supporting Henry of Navarre – reasons which go a long way towards revealing why Henry's appeal proved in the long run stronger than that of his opponents.

In the adapted version the *Maheustre* was able to argue in the first place that he was supporting the 'legitimate and natural king of France'. He put his finger here on a fatal weakness of the League: its disregard for the principle of hereditary succession through the male line. It was true that vestigial traces of the idea of elective monarchy still survived, and acquired fresh currency in pamphlets of the League. But the sense of mystical kingship had been carefully fostered by the Valois and Catherine de Medici. The majority of Frenchmen in the later sixteenth century were therefore likely to look askance at the idea of electing their king in the manner of the Poles. 'We wanted a natural – not an artificial – king and leader', remarks the representative of the third estate in another famous pamphlet of 1593, the *Satyre Ménippée*.[3] Against this national predilection for hereditary succession it was not easy to persuade the country that Henry had forfeited his claims on the grounds of heresy. It was made still harder by the absence of any credible alternative. The extent of the League's embarrassment was painfully revealed by the meeting of the Estates-General summoned by Mayenne at Paris in January 1593. When Philip II's representatives put forward the idea that the Salic law should be abrogated and the Infanta be accepted as queen, there was an angry response from the delegates, who wanted neither a foreigner nor a female on the throne.

Moreover, the League's disregard for legitimate right affronted vested interests as well as national instincts. Alongside the old aristocracy and gentry there was now a powerful *haute bourgeoisie*, consisting of families which had come into wealth through trade, finance or office. The presidents, judges and *conseillers* of the *parlements*, who represented the dominant element in this class, were professionally and personally interested in the survival of a strong and legally-based monarchy. As the guardians of customary tradition, such men as Pierre de L'Estoile and Jacques-Auguste de Thou regarded the law as sacrosanct; as the holders of offices which could now be transmitted by hereditary succession they regarded a hereditary monarchy as the natural champion of their rights. Legalist in temperament, Gallican and moderate Catholic in religion, traditionalist in their outlook on politics and society, they were profoundly out of sympathy with the apparent determination of the League to flout the fundamental principles of order and legality.

Nothing, indeed, could have been more calculated to alarm the more prosperous section of the community and to alienate aristocratic sympathies than the League's challenge to the established social order. The *Maheustre* significantly gave as his second reason for supporting Henry of Navarre his abhorrence of popular violence. 'This wishes to establish itself at the expense of aristocratic privilege, which is to be abolished and replaced by a democracy.' The growing fear of democracy 'in the manner of the Swiss' arose partly from the communal tendencies of the provincial towns, which had shown themselves bitterly hostile to the local nobility, and partly from the activities of the radical popular wing of the Paris League. Already in 1588 the Council of Sixteen had overthrown the city charter of Paris and arrogated to itself the functions of municipal government. Its members were drawn from the ranks of those discontented lawyers and small tradesmen who resented the dominance of the nobility and *gens de robe* in national and local life. Sworn to uphold the word of God, as revealed in the inspired utterances of the Faculty of Theology of the Sorbonne, these men and the friars and *curés* were the heart and soul of Paris's resistance during the terrible siege of 1590.

During the siege and its aftermath, the Sixteen tightened their hold over the capital. The Paris depicted by Pierre de L'Estoile is a city in the grip of terror, ruled by a close-knit band of fanatical upstarts who planned to strike down all those whom they suspected of wishing to compromise with Henry of Navarre. The duke of Mayenne, the nominal leader of the League, had none of his late brother's dynamic qualities, and found it impossible to hold the radical and aristocratic wings of the movement together. The only check on the radicals was the *parlement* of Paris – an institution which was for them the very symbol of oligarchical exclusiveness. During the autumn of 1591 it became clear that a showdown between the extreme and the *politique* members of the League could not be long delayed. The Sixteen laid their plans accordingly. A ten-man committee of public safety was formed, and the League preachers were instructed to whip up public opinion against the traitors in the city's midst. On 15 November the moderate president of the *parlement* of Paris, Barnabé Brisson, was arrested and executed along with two other magistrates.

This time the Sixteen had gone too far, even for some of their own fervent supporters. The continuing domination of the city by a group of demagogues and fanatics was more than Mayenne was prepared to tolerate. He moved his troops into the capital, seized and hanged four of the ring-leaders, and declared the Sixteen disbanded. Jean Bussy-Leclerc, one of the most fanatical of the leaders, was spared, and the duke of Mayenne dared not touch the preachers; but the reign of terror was over. For the nobility and *haute bourgeoisie* it had been a gruelling experience, and its lesson was not lost on them. 'Democracy threatens you...the beggars (*les gueux*) are in command', an anti-League pamphlet of 1590 had warned the aristocracy. 'They have conspired against our lives and have aspired to free themselves from the subjection to which God has ordained them.'[4] Here was the unforgiveable crime. In France, as in the Netherlands, the collapse of authority had aggravated social tensions and had stimulated dangerous egalitarian doctrines. When the *Manant* could argue that virtue, not birth, should be the criterion for titles of nobility, the moment had come to call a halt. If the League was going to challenge the principle of hierarchy – the very foundation of the social order – it was time to turn to the natural defender of that order, the king, even if the king himself were still a heretic.

The *Maheustre* had one further reason for turning to Henry of Navarre: 'to chase out the Spaniard who has been called into France'. The reaction of the States General of the League in the spring of 1593 to the proposal for a Spanish queen showed that many of the League's supporters could not stomach the prospect of consigning their country into the hands of its greatest enemy. Henry of Navarre was well informed of these doubts and dissensions in the League, and his impeccable sense of timing suggested that the moment had now come to make the inevitable concession. On 25 July 1593 he abjured his faith at Saint-Denis.

Henry's renunciation of Protestantism removed the last rational grounds for refusing to recognize his kingship. But Clement VIII was too doubtful of the sincerity of his conversion, and too frightened of the Spaniards, to feel able to pronounce immediate absolution. The pope's hesitation provided a specious justification for those Leaguers who still chose to continue the fight. But the unhappy paradox of their position was vividly suggested by the *Manant*'s profession of faith: 'I would rather be a Spanish Catholic to live in my religion and win my salvation, than a French heretic destined to lose my soul.'

With every passing month, the defections from the League increased. Following its Gallican principles the national church defied Rome and the Jesuits, and consented to Henry's coronation at Chartres in February 1594. The next month, Henry felt strong enough to take possession of a capital which was worth a mass, and the Spanish garrison marched out of Paris without a shot being fired. Even the Sorbonne now recognized Henry as the lawful king of France. Where formerly it had demanded resistance and regicide, it now insisted on absolute obedience; and when a young student called Jean Chastel, who had been educated at the Jesuit college at Clermont, made an attempt on Henry's life in December, the Sorbonne joined in the mass movement of revulsion against those considered responsible for the heinous crime of laying hands on the Lord's anointed. The Jesuits in fact had no knowledge of Chastel's intentions, and their teachings on tyrannicide were no different from those of the general run of scholastic theologians. But they had refused to pray for the king until he was granted papal absolution. In the circumstances, Chastel's crime was sufficient pretext for the expulsion from France of an Order whose Ultramontane tendencies aroused the deepest Gallican suspicions.

The dramatic change of mood in the capital in 1593–1594 was reflected throughout the country. The rural population of France was weary of ceaseless war. Starvation and plague were threatening, and in a devastated Brittany great packs of wolves were on the prowl. To the peasantry there was 'one enemy: the captain; one protector: the king'. It was to the idealized figure of a patriarchal king, the upholder of justice, the champion of order, that they now instinctively turned. In province after province the peasants banded together against the League and the nobles, and compelled the municipal authorities to come to terms with Henry IV. It was an extraordinary spontaneous movement, compounded of a hatred of anarchy and social oppression, and a mass rallying of the people of France to their anointed king. In south-western France at the end of 1593 vast masses of peasants – dubbed *croquants* by their enemies – banded together and agreed to sink their differences in a struggle against an oppressive nobility and in defence of the king 'our lord'. It was as if the country were purging itself of the religious hatreds of half a century. 'We all promise and swear before God to love and cherish each other.' There would be 'no more war among them, nor reproach for diversity of religion, and each would be free to live as he desired.'[5]

As the country rallied to Henry, the League's resistance crumbled away. On 17 September 1595 Clement VIII at last gave him absolution on certain conditions, some of them for the time being unenforceable, like the implementation of the decrees of the Council of Trent. The papal absolution revealed the futility of further resistance, and Henry knew all the arts of turning enemies into friends. In so far as the Wars of Religion in France had been largely an urban conflict, it was essential for him to recover the support of the towns. Many members of the ruling elites in the cities adhering to the Catholic League had become disillusioned by the League's failure to restore order and unity, and looked instinctively to the king for the answer to their problems. Henry for his part showed himself to be a supremely adept politician, with a shrewd understanding of the internal workings of municipal politics. He placed his own men in important magisterial posts throughout the country, made a lavish display of his magnanimity by offering to reissue the charters of rebellious League towns, and exploited existing clientage systems to build up a network of loyal supporters in city governments. While he was perfectly prepared to resort to force when it served his purposes, essentially it was a combination of patient negotiation and the skilful manipulation of clientage systems in ways that had eluded his Valois predecessors that gave legitimacy to his government and restored stability to France.

Inevitably, Henry's loyal Huguenot supporters – men like Philippe Du Plessis-Mornay – were bitterly disillusioned with the recent turn of events. But Henry was a man who forgot as easily as he forgave, and forgiveness at this moment mattered more than forgetfulness. Lavish bribes won over one League leader after another, until Mayenne himself surrendered in January 1596. Papal help would still be needed to induce the remaining fanatics to lay down their arms, especially in Brittany, where the duke of Mercoeur continued to resist. But to all intents and purposes the civil wars were at an end. Henry had been accepted by his nation. Now it remained for him to expel the Spaniards, and to restore religious peace.

3 Nantes and Vervins

Henry formally declared war on Spain on 17 January 1595. Since the collapse of the League had deprived Philip II of most of the allies on whom he depended for carrying the war into the centre of France, hostilities during the next two or three years would be confined to the border provinces: Brittany, Burgundy, the north-east frontier region, and Provence. Even where there was strong local resistance to Henry IV, as in Brittany, there was little or no effective cooperation between the Spaniards and the rebels, and warfare soon degenerated into banditry and pillage. But the danger from Spain could not be disregarded. As long as Spanish troops were stationed on French soil or could cross into France with relative impunity, the embers of civil war would be kept alive, and the security of all north-west Europe would continue to be imperilled.

Philip II, with the years closing in upon him, was now mobilizing all his financial, military and naval resources for a massive strike against his northern enemies. England and France, as always, held the key to the Netherlands; and Philip's determination to maintain Catholicism and Spanish primacy in Northern Europe had become inextricably confused. In spite of Castile's exhaustion, he could still draw on large sums of money in the early 1590s, and it was this that tempted him to gamble on a dramatic final throw. Never had the American mines been more productive, nor the European bankers more amenable. Paradoxically, the sudden supply of riches derived as much from poverty as from affluence. In Castile and Antwerp the story was the same: war conditions had drastically reduced the attractiveness of domestic investment. Since its recapture by Farnese in 1585, Antwerp had ceased to be a centre of international maritime trade. Its industry had been destroyed; its population had shrunk as a result of emigration and of the famine of 1585–1586, from 80,000 to a mere 42,000 in 1589. With their commercial prospects ruined, the Antwerp merchants lacked the usual outlets for their capital. Like the Genoese and the Castilian bankers they found that loans to the Spanish Crown now offered the best return.

The flow of American silver and the easiness of the bankers enabled Philip in the early 1590s to pour money into the bottomless pit of Flanders. There was, of course, never enough to satisfy the commanders of the army, not even enough, it was said, for count Mansfield, the temporary governor, to buy himself a dinner.[6] Yet the quantities disbursed were enormous. They reached their peak in July 1595 with the conclusion of an *asiento* with a group of bankers for the vast total of 4 million *escudos*, to be made available in Flanders at the rate of 280,000 a month. This prodigious effort was timed to coincide with the arrival in Flanders of a new governor-general. After Farnese's death Philip had selected as his successor the hapless archduke Ernest, the Emperor Rudolph's younger brother. The choice reflected Philip's anxiety to hold together the Austrian and Spanish branches of the Habsburgs; and it was planned in due course to marry Ernest to the Infanta Isabella. But Ernest, who arrived in the Netherlands in 1594, died early in 1595, leaving little to show for his abortive life except a pile of debts which Philip and the Emperor each declined to pay. Philip now replaced him with the youngest and most hispanicized of the Austrian archdukes, Albert, whom he had previously employed as governor of Portugal. On Albert's arrival in the Netherlands at the beginning of 1596, the count of Fuentes, who had been acting as interim governor, was recalled to Spain. In Fuentes, the army had lost a good commander; but at least there was an adequate supply of money for a spring campaign. Under a French refugee general appointed by Albert, the army suddenly advanced on Calais, which was totally unprepared, and captured it without great difficulty in April 1596.

With Calais in Spanish hands the threat to Northern Europe seemed as serious at this moment as at any time in recent years. It was not surprising that the 'alarm of Calais' kept the aged Lord Burghley awake all night, and stirred up in him 'many cogitations'.[7] There were other troubles, too, to keep Burghley from his sleep. Revolt had broken out in Ulster in 1593, and it was joined in 1595 by the most powerful of the Irish nobles, Hugh O'Neill, earl of Tyrone. The rebels had promptly appealed to Philip II for help, and persistent intelligence reports suggested that a new Armada was being prepared in Spain for the assistance of the Irish or a new 'enterprise of England'. It was for this reason that Drake and Hawkins were authorized to spend no more than six months on their proposed new expedition to the isthmus of Panama at the end of 1595 – they would be needed at home in the spring to defend British shores against a probable invasion. But the Indies raid proved a disastrous failure, for the Spaniards had advance warning and had strengthened their defences. The English attacks were successfully beaten off, and Drake himself died at sea in February 1596. It was a defeated and demoralized expedition which returned home to England a week or two after Calais had fallen to the Spaniards.

Although Elizabeth was scandalized by Henry IV's 'great apostasy', the common danger in the spring of 1596 was sufficient to bring England and France together once again. By a treaty signed on 24 May, Henry promised not to conclude a separate peace with Spain, in return for a force of 2,000 men and an ungenerous loan. The Dutch, too, were permitted to join in the treaty as equal partners. With great reluctance, Elizabeth had swallowed her habitual dislike of rebels, and the United Provinces for the first time took their place among the sovereign states of Europe.

In 1596, therefore, William of Orange's dream of a *politique* coalition against Spanish power was posthumously achieved, although regrettably without the adherence of the German princes. English participation in the coalition would be more than a formality: the new favourite at Elizabeth's court, the earl of Essex, would make sure of that. As the leader of the bellicose anti-Spanish faction, Essex was determined to seize the initiative before the Armada sailed. His attack on Cadiz at the end of June 1596 was a brilliant success. The Spaniards, taken completely by surprise, suffered the novel experience of having their own territory pillaged and devastated for two weeks by a foreign army. Stung to reply, Philip despatched his new Armada to the assistance of the Irish rebels in October, but a gale drove it back to the Spanish coast with heavy losses. Another great fleet was similarly thwarted in the autumn of 1597, when a storm dispersed the ships as they neared the English Channel. It seemed that God did not favour the enterprise of England.

The cost of preparing these large naval expeditions and of sustaining the campaigns in France and Flanders was becoming increasingly hard to meet. On 29 November 1596 Philip suddenly suspended payments to the bankers – once again, as in 1575, the Crown had defaulted on its debts. This time it took one year, instead of two, to reach a compromise agreement with the royal bankers, but the delicate machinery of credit had been severely damaged in the process. The great Castilian fairs of Medina del Campo never really recovered from this fresh catastrophe. Matters were made worse by the coincidence of financial collapse with a series of natural disasters. Cold wet weather had produced a run of bad harvests, and prices in Castile and Andalusia were rising steeply from 1596. How much longer could an exhausted country support the crippling burden of war in Northern Europe?

Sufficient money was still found for a new campaign in France, and Spanish forces captured Amiens in March 1597. But every new Spanish military effort in France involved a diversion of forces from the Netherlands. The archduke Albert, like Farnese before him, saw that he was being called upon to achieve the impossible, and urged Madrid to cease dissipating its shrinking resources. This time the pleas from Brussels met with a more sympathetic response. Philip was tired, ill, and cruelly disillusioned. Time, on which he had drawn so heavily in the past, was no longer a friend but an enemy. He knew that he had not much longer to live, and that his young son was painfully ill-equipped by temperament and intellect to bear the heavy burden of governing the Monarchy. Spain's vast commitments must be reduced before it was too late.

The place to begin was France, where it was becoming increasingly difficult to maintain a Spanish presence among a hostile population. Although Henry succeeded in recapturing Amiens in September 1597, he too had his reasons for wishing to end the war. The six-months' siege of Amiens, even if it ended in success, had brought home the alarming vulnerability of his own position. Large parts of the country had been devastated; money was short; and it was proving difficult or impossible to obtain financial and military help from abroad. Still more serious was the threat of renewed civil war, instigated this time by his former Huguenot supporters.

Henry had promised the Huguenots in his Edict of Mantes of 1591 that he would revoke the anti-Protestant decrees of Henry III's later years, and revert to the relatively favourable situation created by the Edict of Poitiers of 1577. As a temporary solution this might have satisfied the Huguenots, if it had not been followed in 1593 by Henry's abjuration. The king's betrayal of their cause aroused deep fears for their rights. In 1595 their general assembly met without royal permission at Sainte-Foy to consider the best means of securing adequate guarantees from the king, and to provide their movement with a firm political organization. They wanted a new edict from the king, and they were quick to appreciate that the war with Spain favoured their chances of extracting concessions. When the king hesitated they made approaches to the English and the Dutch, and withdrew their contingents from the royal army in mid-campaign. With their refusal to send troops to help Henry during the siege of Amiens it began to look as though civil war was once more very close.

In the autumn and winter of 1597 the national situation and the international acted and reacted on each other. Henry needed peace with the Huguenots to fight his war with Spain, and he needed peace with Spain in order to meet the Huguenot challenge. In the circumstances, the case for negotiations, both at home and abroad, was becoming very strong, Clement VIII had expressed with increasing urgency his fear that the conflict of France and Spain would in the end redound only to the advantage of Protestant Northern Europe, and Henry as well as Philip was now prepared to listen. As a tough round of bargaining opened with the Huguenots, sympathetic responses were made to the first overtures from Philip. On 30 April 1598, while Spanish and French delegates were still in conference at Vervins, Henry signed the Edict of Nantes for the 'union, concord and tranquillity' of his subjects, both Huguenot and Catholic.

The Edict of Nantes was a civil measure, an act of state imposed on a country in which two competing religions had reached momentary deadlock. If the king had been stronger, it would not have been necessary; if he had been weaker, it would not have survived. The Edict, intended as a provisional measure, acquired a degree of permanence by default. Like the peace of Augsburg of 1555 it was essentially a religious truce between warring creeds, neither of which was ready to abandon its claims to universality; but it differed from the Augsburg settlement in that a territorial division, while logical in Germany, was unthinkable in France. Protestantism in France remained a minority religion – perhaps one in ten Frenchmen were

Huguenots at the most, and their numbers had shrunk as the wars continued. This minority, too, was widely dispersed, although there were sizeable concentrations of Huguenots in Normandy, Dauphiné, Languedoc and Aquitaine. They were not sizeable enough, however, to justify territorial division along religious lines, even if this had been a politically viable solution. Nor was the total number of Huguenots in France sufficient to justify the grant of absolute equality to the two faiths, for only in a very few towns were Protestants in an actual majority. As a result, Henry, like his predecessors, was forced to seek a solution which recognized the failure of Protestantism to become more than a minority religion, while at the same time conceding its title to existence.

In the event, the Huguenots secured as much as they deserved, but a good deal less than that for which they hoped. Much of the Edict of Nantes was little more than a repetition of the Edict of Poitiers, although the right of public worship was marginally extended. One or two places in every *bailliage* or *sénéchaussée* were added to the towns designated in 1577. The Huguenots were also allowed to retain their *places fortes*. They were guaranteed admission into public office and into colleges and universities. They were to enjoy full civil rights, which were to be protected by special chambers in the *parlements*. And they could hold religious assemblies with royal permission. In many respects these were liberal terms, although there would be innumerable problems concerning the exact interpretation of an often ambiguous text. Yet the Edict can also be interpreted as a drastic setback for the Huguenots, or at least for their future hopes. While giving them rights and guarantees, it imposed such strict limitations on their cult as to make later expansion impossible, whereas Roman Catholic worship was to be everywhere allowed. Since French Catholicism was already showing signs of a new vitality, there was a strong probability that the Huguenots would in time become no more than a barely tolerated minority, their religion condemned to permanent stagnation.

At the time of the Edict itself, however, there was as much dissatisfaction in the Catholic as in the Protestant ranks. From the standpoint of Rome the Edict was highly unpalatable, in that it formally sanctioned the existence of two religions in one state. This, after all, was not Transylvania or Poland but France, the very heart of Catholic Europe. Clement VIII was appalled: 'the worst edict that can possibly be imagined...An edict that permits liberty of conscience, the worst thing in the world.' Nantes, in effect, represented a direct challenge to Rome's claim to be an exclusive and universal church, just as it also represented a direct challenge to the traditional political axiom of sixteenth-century monarchies – *un roi, une foi, une loi*. It represented, too, the defeat of Philip's hopes for France. He had wanted a France that was Catholic but weak. But now it had a king who legally sanctioned heresy and who was actively reviving the power of the State.

The signing of the Edict, however, had no effect on the peace negotiations between the two powers. Two days later, on 2 May 1598, a treaty was concluded at Vervins. This effectively re-established the treaty of Cateau-Cambrésis of nearly forty years before. The Spaniards agreed to abandon Brittany and Calais, together with their conquests along the Netherlands frontier. France, therefore, had recovered her territorial integrity, and the period of Spanish intervention had been brought to a close.

Philip II was now free to concentrate on his war with the Protestant states – England and the United Provinces – neither of which had been willing to join France in the peace settlement. Four days after Vervins Philip made over the Netherlands to the archduke Albert and his future wife, the Infanta Isabella. They were to rule the Netherlands as 'sovereign princes', but there was a certain deliberate ambiguity about the meaning of these words. They were not intended to imply any renunciation by Spain of its rights to the Netherlands, and the government in Brussels was always to be gently but firmly tied to the government in Madrid. Philip was no doubt hoping by this means to ensure an easier inheritance for his son. Or perhaps he saw in the government of the 'archdukes' a viable means of preserving Spain's presence in the southern Netherlands, while at the same time continuing the war against the rebels in the north. But the transfer of sovereignty in the Low Countries, when taken with the peace of Vervins, marked the beginnings of Spain's slow retreat from Northern Europe – a retreat which would be intensified by peace with England in 1604 and by the truce signed with the Dutch in 1609.

It was a disappointing conclusion to the prodigious Castilian efforts of Philip II's later years. Admittedly, France had not been lost to the heretics, and this might be considered a vindication of Philip's policies. But Spain had not defeated the England of Elizabeth, and it had failed in the prime purpose of its northern policy – the restoration of the Dutch rebels to obedience to their king. In pursuit of this aim, Philip had spent all – and more than – he had, and had reduced to misery his kingdom of Castile. It was time to call a halt. In June the king was struck by sickness, and insisted on being removed from Madrid to the Escorial where he wished to meet his end. He prepared for death as he had prepared for every event of his life, with an infinitely meticulous attention to detail. After an agonizing illness, borne without complaint, he died on 13 September 1598, at the age of seventy-one. Sometimes it must have seemed to a Europe which had lived beneath his shadow for so long, that he would never die. But even the king of Spain proved mortal in the end.

12

The Divided Continent

1 The Mediterranean World

'It is certain,' wrote the French historian Jacques-Auguste de Thou in 1604, 'that empires, like men, have their beginning, their growth, their decadence and their end; and that Providence has fixed certain bounds which neither force nor prudence can cross.'[1] By the end of the sixteenth century there were many who believed that Spain and its empire had passed their peak and had started downwards on their inexorable decline. Neither force nor prudence had availed Philip II in the end. The defeat of the Armada; the failure in the Netherlands; the peace of Vervins; the anticipated exhaustion of the American mines – did not all these suggest that the sun was slowly setting on the splendour of Spain?

In Spain itself – the Spain of the young king Philip III – the voices of alarm were beginning to be raised. The country was tired and psychologically defeated. The close of the century was a terrible period, when bankruptcy and harvest failure were accompanied by the northwards march of famine and the southwards march of plague. Already the *arbitristas* – projectors, economists and pamphleteers – were hard at work diagnosing the sickness and prescribing the remedies for an ailing body politic. It was easy enough to see that things had gone wrong; and it was only natural that a Castile which had been buoyed up for so long by a profound faith in its providential mission should abandon itself to an orgy of national introspection when it found itself defrauded.

An extravagantly ambitious foreign policy, which took no account of the country's capacity to bear the cost, had undoubtedly taken its toll of Castile. The burden of taxation, especially in the last years of Philip II, had been crippling; and the whole character of royal finance had helped to distort the Castilian economy and to stunt the opportunities for increasing the national wealth. The high returns on *juros* or credit bonds to service the royal debt had lured private capital away from more hazardous but potentially more useful investment in agricultural and industrial enterprise. The Crown's resort to foreign bankers had placed many of the sources of wealth in foreign hands and had correspondingly sapped the strength and the morale of the native entrepreneurial class. Yet in spite of the drastic consequences of Habsburg foreign policy for Castilian economic life, it is easy to overestimate – as Castilians themselves tended to overestimate – the extent and the uniqueness of Castile's difficulties at the end of the century.

If Castile's imperial adventures placed her in a class by herself, many of her problems were common to the Mediterranean world as a whole. The population of this world had by now drastically outstripped the capacity of the region to provide it with food and work. It had perhaps doubled over the course of a hundred years – from some thirty million in 1500 to sixty million in 1600.[2] Although this increase was part of a wider, European, phenomenon, it created problems which were felt with particular intensity in the Mediterranean lands. The Mediterranean sun was hot, and much of the land was mountainous and arid. Transport, irrigation and land-exploitation all presented challenges to ingenuity and determination which tended to be harsher than comparable challenges in the more temperate climes of Northern Europe. Whether these challenges could ever have been met from the limited resources of sixteenth-century technology is open to doubt. But conservatism, self-interest and a fatalistic outlook may often have prevented the inauguration or completion of projects which were not themselves hopelessly beyond the range of contemporary technical expertise. A project for making the river Tagus navigable from Toledo to Lisbon was begun by an Italian engineer with some success in the 1580s, but was abandoned before the end of the century, largely because of the opposition of local interests. It seems as if a mental revolution was needed before the resources of nature could begin to be systematically harnessed by men. A few enlightened spirits, like Olivier de Serres, the Huguenot agriculturalist, accepted the possibility that men could improve their own environment, and made proposals to that end. But Serres himself was scathing in his denunciations of the bovine Languedoc peasants among whom he lived. Against the dead weight of tradition in a still largely illiterate society, and the self-interest created by exaggerated notions of property, there was very little possibility of introducing change.

Unable to tackle the causes of poverty and hunger, the Mediterranean States dealt with their consequences as best they could. Hungry men, as governments knew to their cost, all too easily became vagabonds and bandits – bandits especially in a part of the world where vendettas stretched back into time immemorial, where the hand of government scarcely extended beyond the city walls, and where impoverished nobles and gentry lorded it over the countryside with their bands of retainers. In the later decades of the century the scourge of banditry seems to have grown more acute throughout the Mediterranean lands. Only Castile remained relatively free, perhaps because the hungry and unemployed could find escape from their troubles in the *tercios* of Flanders or the great open spaces of the Indies, and because justice was sure, if not swift, as long as Philip II sat on the Spanish throne. But Castile still had its professional rogues, its *pícaros*; and beyond Castile, in Catalonia or Languedoc or Italy, the *pícaro* was transformed through desperation or bravado into the bandit – the outlaw who lived with his fellows by a private code of law which regulated the conduct of their state within the state.

Banditry was nowhere more virulent at this time than in the lands of the papacy, which displayed as in microcosm all the problems of social and political order of the Mediterranean world. On balance, the Papal States had been exporters of grain until around 1575, but in the last quarter of the century the situation changed. Italy, like much of Mediterranean Europe, seems to have suffered climatic changes in this period. Some years saw heavy rains and disastrous floods, and there were frequent harvest failures, as in 1589 and 1590, when banditry reached new heights. But climatic conditions were not alone responsible for the failure of the grain supply. As in Castile, the heavy burden of taxation depopulated the countryside and reduced the supply of cheap rural labour. Moreover, the growth of Rome as a great capital city – from 30,000 inhabitants in 1500 to 100,000 by the end of the century – created a valuable market for meat as well as for grain. This led to sharp competition for land between the corn and the cattle interest, for which only a small labour force was required. While much agricultural land was given over to pasture, other good land was driven out of use by the spread of malaria; and although Sixtus V made heroic efforts to drain the Pontine marshes, drainage schemes were expensive and technically difficult, and were slow to yield results. The *Campagna*, therefore, like the Castilian countryside, was unable to rise to the challenge of increased demand.

The *Campagna* was dominated by feudal barons who resented the prosperity of the capital and feared the slow but steady extension of papal control over their lands. The temporal domain of the papacy was administered by the cardinal chamberlain through governors in the major towns and through a growing army of officials and tax-collectors. Like their secular colleagues, sixteenth-century popes had made strenuous attempts to improve the effectiveness of their government and to increase their revenues from taxation in their own domain, at a time when the Protestant secession had drastically diminished their traditional sources of income from other parts of Europe. By the end of the century they had made considerable progress on both fronts. Taxation in the Papal States increased ten-fold over the course of the century (far more than the rise in prices); and the increasing tendency of popes to appoint ecclesiastics to the higher administrative offices was leading to loud complaints about the tyranny of a government of priests.

In the course of the papal search for new sources of revenue, Gregory XIII began in 1578 a systematic investigation of the title deeds by which the barons held their fiefs. Numerous castles were claimed by the Apostolic Chamber from their indignant but illegal occupiers, who responded to attempts at dispossession by resort to armed resistance. The conjunction of harvest failure and famine with this revolt of the rural aristocracy produced a violent outbreak of banditry, which represented at once a rebellion of the countryside against the capital, and a rebellion of the untamed forces of localism against the claims of the central power. This was typical Mediterranean-style banditry – a movement of rural unrest abetted and exploited by a discontented and backward aristocracy for its own particular ends. But it is also recognizable as a bastard brother of the movements which had produced the rising in Aragon and the civil wars in France. It needed only a greater degree of sophistication for aristocratic banditry to be transformed into a rising in defence of 'liberties', and a dash of patriotism and religion to turn brigands into *Gueux*. Throughout the sixteenth century the dividing-line between anarchy and aristocratic constitutionalism was a narrow one, which was crossed and recrossed haphazardly by the brigand, the malcontent and the patriot alike.

From 1578 to 1595 the Papal States were submerged beneath the tidal wave of banditry which at times lapped against the walls of Rome itself, and cut the road to Naples. For a moment it seemed that Sixtus V had got the better of the bandits, after launching a massive campaign and meting out savage sentences against those who were caught. But the dearth and starvation of the closing years of his pontificate brought them out again; and even the notorious bandit-noble Alfonso Piccolomini, who had been pardoned by Gregory XIII, reappeared in July 1590, a month before Sixtus's death. It was only around 1595, during the pontificate of Clement VIII, that the intense bandit movement which had started in 1578 began to die away. Vigorous and persistent police action gradually achieved the desired results. One bandit leader after another met his death on the gallows, and the nobles who sheltered and abetted the bandits were hunted down and defeated. Many of their clients and retainers were drafted into the papal army, or amnestied on condition that they left for Hungary to join the war against the Turks.

While military action subdued the countryside, Rome itself was taking captive the nobility whose connivance and support had done so much to keep rural banditry alive. As the popes set the fashion in the embellishment of their capital, nobles vied with each other in building expensive urban places. The high standards of comfort and luxury set by the new aristocracy of the papal families challenged the habits of the old Roman nobility, and involved them in heavy expenditure which loaded them with debts. It was debt which forced famous families like the Orsinis to sell their rural castles and turn to papal patronage for survival. By degrees, therefore, the old nobility was subdued and civilized, and tied by silken threads to the court of the popes.

In taming and civilizing the old military aristocracy, the popes were doing no more than their secular colleagues, who were everywhere attempting by a judicious combination of *douceur* and violence to curb the more dangerous manifestations of aristocratic unrest. The very return to peace at the close of the century would itself speed the process by diverting expenditure from armies to courts. Tempted by patronage and seduced by luxury, the nobility of Europe would gradually be persuaded to shed old habits which were less suited to the life of the court than the camp. But beneath the nobility were the people, crowded together in the rapidly growing cities, and prone to riot and rebellion if taxes became unbearable and bread became too dear. Here the problems were so great as to defy solution within the context of the Mediterranean world alone. Salvation, when it came, would come from outside the region, brought by the grain-ships of Northern Europe.

From the beginning of the 1570s, more and more northern vessels were to be seen in Mediterranean ports. The English, in their search for new markets for their cloth and tin, were growing increasingly active from around 1573. Their peculiar blend of trade and piracy, which had already created such havoc in the Spanish Atlantic, was causing deep anxiety to Venice by the later 1570s; and the concession of trading facilities by the sultan proved sufficient to justify the founding of a Levant Company in 1581. The Dutch, for their part, had vigorously persisted in their trade with the Iberian peninsula, undeterred by the fact that they were at war with Spain. When the earl of Leicester attempted to prohibit their Iberian trade[3] he found all the merchants and shipowners of Holland ranged against him, angrily defending their lucrative occupation as purveyors of northern foodstuffs and naval stores to their Spanish enemies. They had their eyes, too, on the legendary trade of Seville. The increasing preoccupation of the Genoese with the Spanish Crown's finances had left a partial vacuum in the Seville trade, which the Dutch were determined to fill. Through their clandestine agents and factors, especially the

Portuguese-Jewish *marranos*, Dutch merchants successfully penetrated the Indies trade with the tacit assent of a Spanish government which was painfully aware of its dependence on the rebels as buyers of colonial produce and suppliers of northern goods.

With the English showing a marked interest in Mediterranean markets, and with the Dutch secretly established in Lisbon and Seville, a full-scale entry of northern merchants into the Mediterranean was only a question of time. It was the grain crisis in the Mediterranean basin which precipitated the invasion. In the Ottoman Empire, grain was in short supply in the mid-1560s, and then again from 1572–81, and from 1585–1590. In Naples there were six famine years between 1560 and the end of the century. Even Sicily, the granary of the Mediterranean, went through a phase of bad harvests between 1575 and 1580, although it remained a major exporter of grain well into the seventeenth century. Unable to feed themselves, the Mediterranean countries turned to Northern and Eastern Europe for help. In response, English, Dutch and Hanseatic ships swarmed through the straits of Gibraltar, carrying the Baltic corn which could mean the difference between starvation and survival.

The penetration of northern shipping into the Mediteranean in the closing years of the century inevitably changed the commercial and economic balance of southern Europe. Tuscany, under the skilful government of the former cardinal of Medici, now the grand duke Ferdinand (1587–1609), seized its opportunity and declared Leghorn a free port in 1593. It became in consequence the favoured Italian port of northern merchants, and a major distribution centre for northern grain. On the profits of this new commercial activity, the grand duke became perhaps the richest prince in Europe.

Where Tuscany gained, Venice lost. It had already suffered severely from the loss of Cyprus to the Turks in 1571 and from the depredations of pirates – not only the Barbary corsairs but also Spanish, Florentine and Maltese privateers, and those water-bandits of the Adriatic, the Uskoks, operating from their impregnable base of Segna, near Fiume. Now, towards the end of the century, northern pirates – the unassimilated surplus, like the Italian bandits, of over-populated societies – joined their southern brethren in the game. More and more Venetian merchantmen found themselves under attack from English or Dutch-owned *bertoni*: tall and broad three-masted ships of medium tonnage, which rode the seas well and carried twenty cannons or more. Venice proved singularly incapable of meeting this pirate challenge. The traditional galley-fleet was technically ill-equipped to tackle the *bertoni*, which were too high for easy boarding from the low hulls of the galleys. Venice was finding it difficult, too, to recruit galley crews. While the industrial development of the mainland was beginning to attract the interest of Venetian businessmen more than their traditional maritime trade, naval service was losing its prestige and the morale of seamen was declining. Above all, Venice herself had become too easy-going and too rich. Her closed, self-perpetuating oligarchy apparently lacked the desire and the ability to devise new methods for new circumstances. Venice, like Castile in the later sixteenth century, was showing all the symptoms of a hardening of the arteries.

Although the response varied from port to port and from state to state, there was no escaping the crucial fact of south European life in the late sixteenth century – the transformation of the Mediterranean into an Anglo-Dutch lake. This was the context within which late sixteenth-century Spain faced its difficulties. All the Mediterranean States were victims, in a greater or lesser degree, of a situation in which there seemed to be no escape from dependence on the North. There were, of course, desperate attempts to fight back. In 1585 Philip placed his first embargo on northern shipping in Iberian ports. In 1595, and again in 1598, he seized some five hundred Dutch ships at anchor in Spanish and Portuguese harbours. But the embargoes proved to be hopelessly self-defeating. It was impossible for the Iberian peninsula to live for long without northern grain and supplies, and the Spaniards lacked the merchant marine to fetch these vital commodities for themselves. They were driven back, therefore, to reliance on their enemies. Moreover, the cure could well prove more drastic than the disease. When the Dutch were deprived in 1598 of access to Portuguese salt at Setubal, they simply responded by making direct for the Caribbean and the salt-pans of Araya off the coast of Venezuela. It seemed that, whatever Spain did, it was fated to lose. Having failed to defeat the English and crush the Dutch revolt, it was now condemned to watch impotently the spectacular advance of its northern enemies at the expense of its own overseas possessions and its economic life.

The defeat of Spain, then, was part of a wider defeat of Southern Europe by the North. The Mediterranean countries, which for so long had called the tune in Europe, seemed now to be entering on a new phase of life marked by economic subservience to the North European states. But at the close of the century this transformation still tended to be masked by the prestige of Spanish military power and of Mediterranean civilization. The Spanish Monarchy was still regarded by contemporaries as the greatest power in the world, and Spanish cultural influence was never greater than in the opening years of the new century, at a time when Spain's real military and political strength had already passed its peak. Above all, the civilization of the Italian Mediterranean continued to exercise a deep fascination over a continent which was accustomed to look southwards for its art and its ideas. The North was impressed, as it was meant to be impressed, by the rising baroque splendours of the city of Sixtus V and Clement VIII. It was excited, as Italy was excited, by the new anti-Mannerist styles of Annibale Caracci and Caravaggio. And a continent in spiritual turmoil still felt the lure of Rome.

2 Rome and the North

The great rebuilding of Rome, which drained the *Campagna* of its wealth, was a triumphant assertion of the church's faith in its own future, at a time when it was on the point of rediscovering the joys of independence. For over a generation Rome had lived beneath the shadow of the power of Habsburg Spain. But during the 1590s the shadow began to lift, and all Italy glimpsed the sunshine which had been absent for so long. Earlier attempts to break free of Spanish influence had led only to frustration and disappointment: Sixtus V had raged in vain against the count of Olivares, and little had come of the struggle of 1582–1583 within the Venetian oligarchy between the old men, the *vecchi*, who clung to their policy of placating Philip II, and the *giovani* who wanted the Republic to show a greater firmness in its dealings with Spain. Although the leaders of the *giovani*, Leonardo Donà and Nicolò Contarini, met with some success in their attempts to introduce governmental reforms, they found – as their elders had found before them – that there was little chance of pursuing a genuinely independent foreign policy as long as France was too weak to counter-balance Spanish power. But with the emergence of Henry IV as the strong king of a re-united France, the international situation was dramatically changed. Henry's adherents and publicists were quick to seize their opportunity, and to present their king to the world as a Gallic Hercules, who would break the Spanish shackles which held Christendom enslaved.

Venice, Tuscany and Rome all saw Henry IV as their potential saviour from Spanish domination, but it was the Holy See which stood to gain most from the recovery of France. Once Henry IV and Clement VIII had made their peace, the papacy was in a position to return to the balance of power politics which had served it so well before Spain became supreme. The possibilities of the new situation were strikingly revealed in 1597, when Alfonso II d'Este, the duke of Ferrara, died without heirs. Ferrara was a papal fief, and Clement VIII was determined to recover it, although Spain indicated its sympathy for the claims of Cesare d'Este. The precedents of the past decades pointed to success for the Spanish candidate, but Clement appealed to Henry IV for support. The Gallic Hercules, anxious to prove himself a faithful son of the church, declared himself ready to lead an army across the Alps in defence of the papal cause. Against the threat of

Henry IV, Philip II was not prepared to press his case, and the duchy of Ferrara duly reverted to the Holy See.

The papal success at Ferrara suggested something of the new opportunities created for Rome by the revival of France under a strong, and Catholic, king. But whether it could exploit these opportunities to recover the allegiance of central and northern Europe without recourse to the embarrassing assistance of Spain would depend on the goodwill of its non-Spanish secular supporters, and on the effectiveness of its own agencies of conversion. Here, over the last few decades, considerable progress had been made. In Rome itself the reforms of Sixtus V had set the seal on a long process of re-organization which had concentrated supreme authority in the hands of the pope, and had divided the work of the ecclesiastical bureaucracy into specialized departments, each with a separate function to perform. There was now an effective papal diplomatic corps, and the secretary of state was entrusted with the conduct of foreign affairs. The cardinals, whose number was fixed at seventy by Sixtus V, were divided into fifteen 'congregations', which were in effect permanent committees with specialized duties relating to the spiritual and administrative life of the church.

With special congregations for the Inquisition, the Index, the bishops and religious orders, Rome was better equipped to pursue systematic policies which were capable of the requisite adaptation to suit local needs. At the same time, the Holy See was careful to strengthen its ties with bishops and clergy in distant parts of Europe, and it made increasing use of papal nuncios to represent its interests at the courts of secular princes and to coordinate the various local agencies for conversion and reform. The religious orders, and particularly the Jesuits, had a vital part to play in this local field. By the end of the century the Jesuit order had a total membership of 13,112, and was divided into thirty-two provinces. Through its numerous colleges, of which there were 372 by 1600, it had begun to win back the new generation to Rome. It was notable, for instance, how Catholicism acquired a new impetus in the duke of Mayenne's Burgundy after the coming of the Jesuits and their installation at the Collège des Godrans in 1581. Admittedly, the Jesuits suffered a temporary setback with Henry IV's decree expelling them from the country in 1594.[4] But in several parts of France the decree seems never to have been carried out, and the order made a significant contribution to the education of a generation which was to promote the French Catholic revival of the early seventeenth century.

The story was similar in the German and Austrian lands. Wherever the religious orders could secure an entry, the work of re-Catholicization was energetically advanced. But the opposition remained strong, and the difficulties formidable. Among the aristocracy of the Habsburg lands, Protestantism was deeply entrenched: as late as 1609 the Estates of the archduchy of Austria had three hundred Protestant members against only eighty Roman Catholics. Nor did resistance come only from the Protestants. This, at least, was the experience of Melchior Khlesl, the converted son of a Viennese baker, who was placed in charge of the Catholic reform movement in Upper and Lower Austria in 1590 and became bishop of Vienna in 1598. There were interminable bickerings and feuds between the various orders; and the parish clergy, which had for so long been neglected by Rome, proved tiresomely recalcitrant in the face of attempts to raise its standards of morals and learning to the level expected of the post-Tridentine church.

In circumstances such as these, the attitude of the secular prince could make all the difference between failure and success. But, as the papacy was uneasily aware, it was at this point that a question mark hung over the lands of central Europe. The record of the Austrian Habsburgs was by no means reassuring. The Catholicism of the new generation of Habsburgs, unlike that of their father Maximilian II, was fortunately not in doubt: in particular, the archduke Albert was a devoted son of the church, and the governor of the Tyrol, the archduke Maximilian, was an enthusiastic patron of the Capuchins, and noted for his piety. But the Emperor Rudolph II himself, while generally sympathetic to the work of Catholic reform, was so melancholic and volatile in temperament as to be alarmingly unreliable. Quite apart from any personal idiosyncrasies, Rudolph was also closely identified as Emperor with a tradition of mediation which aroused the gravest suspicions in Rome. The continuing pursuit of a higher religious synthesis which would reconcile the warring creeds within the Empire, and the equivocal approach of the Austrian Habsburgs to the problem of heresy in the Netherlands – these suggested a lack of dogmatic commitment deeply disturbing to the papacy.

It was particularly unfortunate for a papacy whose Catholicism was not that of Madrid, that it also found itself out of sympathy with the Catholicism of Vienna and Prague. Each branch of the Habsburgs, the Spanish and the Austrian, regarded itself as divinely entrusted with the Holy Grail of the true Catholic tradition, and in neither instance could the papacy bring itself to support the claim. Rome's hopes of escaping from the constricting grasp of Spanish advocacy were therefore frustrated in central Europe by the absence of a viable alternative. While the Austrian Habsburgs were profuse in their expressions of support for the work of Catholic reformation, there was a lack of urgency, and even a passivity, about their attitude which alarmed both Rome and Madrid. Almost by default, therefore, the task of stiffening the Catholic response in the Habsburg lands devolved upon the

Spaniards; and the papacy found itself in a position where it had little choice but to acquiesce.

It had always been the task of the Spanish ambassador at the Imperial court to urge the Emperor towards firmer and more militant policies. The task was delicate and unrewarding, because of the mutual jealousies of the Spanish and Austrian Habsburgs and the inevitable divergencies of their respective interests. Philip II was permanently alarmed about the character and extent of Imperial intervention in the Netherlands. He was concerned, too, that the influence of the Emperor would be insufficient to prevent the German princes from entering into alliances with France and the Dutch; and he was deeply worried about the personal eccentricities and potential religious unreliability of his nephew Rudolph II. The Spanish ambassador in Prague in the 1580s and 1590s, a vigorous diplomat of Catalan origin, Guillén de San Clemente, therefore occupied a position of exceptional importance. Like his colleague Mendoza in Paris, his responsibility was to champion Spanish interests and Spanish Catholicism at a court where the Catholicism of the monarch left much to be desired.

During the last ambitious years of the reign of Philip II, Spanish policy in central and eastern Europe, as conducted by San Clemente, was as dynamic and interventionist in character as it was in western Europe. Madrid intervened in the Polish election which followed the death of Stephen Báthory in 1586, and threw its weight – although without success – behind the candidature of the archduke Maximilian. On the outbreak of hostilities between the Empire and the Turks in 1593, Madrid did what it could to stiffen the Emperor's resolution, and sent him a subsidy to help with the campaign. In the last months of his life, Philip II was actually contemplating the despatch of an expedition from Italy to the Balkans to relieve the Ottoman pressure on the borders of the Empire. But it was not only the revival of Turkish ambitions which alarmed the king of Spain. He was deeply perturbed by San Clemente's reports of the weakness of Rudolph's response to the Protestant menace in the Habsburg lands and Bohemia. If Rudolph would do nothing, then the duty fell on Spain. San Clemente therefore built up in Prague during the 1590s a strongly pro-Spanish party among the Bohemian Catholic nobility, which began campaigning for more vigorous anti-Protestant policies.

At a time, then, when the papacy was at last beginning to emancipate itself from Spain in western Europe, it still found itself heavily dependent on Spanish initiative in the Imperial lands. This unhappy state of affairs would continue as long as Rudolph reigned. But future prospects fortunately appeared a little brighter. None of Maximilian II's five sons had any children, and the future of the dynasty lay with their cousin, the archduke Ferdinand, who would eventually succeed Matthias as Emperor in 1619. In Ferdinand of Styria the church at last found an Austrian Habsburg such as it desired. Educated by the Jesuits at Ingolstadt, Ferdinand was the prototype of the new-style Catholic prince – narrow, pious, rigid, and utterly reliable. After assuming the government of the lands of Central Austria in 1596, Ferdinand made a pilgrimage to Loreto and Rome. At Ferrara he knelt at the feet of Clement VIII and vowed to devote his life to the restoration of Catholicism in his hereditary lands; and on returning home to Austria, he proved as good as his word. Defying the aristocracy, and ignoring the warnings of Rudolph II, he expelled the Protestant pastors and teachers from his principality and from his capital of Graz. It was the beginning of a career which would end with Counter-Reformation Catholicism triumphant throughout the Habsburg lands.

Beyond Austria and Bohemia lay Poland and the North. Here again, sympathetic rulers were essential for any systematic reconversion of lands and people lost to Rome. The short reign of Stephen Báthory in Poland had shown what could be achieved by a well-intentioned monarch, even when hampered by drastic constitutional restrictions. Báthory's patronage of the Jesuits was already beginning to show results: by the end of his reign there were 360 members of the order in Poland, and twelve Jesuit colleges. It was therefore a matter of deep concern to Rome that Báthory should have a successor who would follow in his steps. The papacy, like Madrid, supported the archduke Maximilian. Many of the Polish nobles, however, including Báthory's former supporters, backed the claims of the young prince Sigismund Vasa, the son of John III of Sweden and his Jagiello wife. There was still a sentimental loyalty in Poland to the old Jagiello dynasty; and the Báthory party hoped that the election of a Vasa would involve Sweden in their plans for the conquest of Muscovy.

In the election diet of 1587, Sigismund obtained the majority vote. But a minority proceeded to proclaim the archduke Maximilian king, with the enthusiastic support of San Clemente. Aided by a large Spanish subsidy, Maximilian decided to fight for the throne; but he was defeated and taken prisoner in the Armada year, 1588, and Rome and Madrid both found it prudent to abandon their opposition to a Vasa ruler, now Sigismund III. In originally supporting Maximilian, Sixtus V had once again characteristically taken a precipitate decision, for Sigismund was in some ways a more promising figure than Maximilian from the standpoint of Rome. Like Ferdinand of Styria he had been educated by Jesuits, and was exceptionally devout. Moreover, as heir to the throne of Sweden, he might prove the chosen instrument for the recovery of Scandinavia. The Swedish aristocracy were well aware that the election of Sigismund to the throne of Catholic Poland threatened to bring back their own country into the Roman orbit. But the political advantages to Sweden of John III's dynastic policies might well outweigh the religious risks. John III, like Eric XIV, had pursued a foreign policy aimed at Sweden's expansion towards the east; and a close association between Sweden and Poland would strengthen both countries against their common enemy, Russia. The Swedish nobles also glimpsed the possibility of private advantage in the long periods of royal absenteeism to be expected once the new king of Poland was also king of Sweden. But they were careful to leave nothing to chance. Before leaving for Poland in the autumn of 1587, Sigismund was made to sign the Statutes of Kalmar, which were designed to ensure that the union of the crowns should neither endanger the country's independence nor prejudice its faith. The rights of the Swedish church were guaranteed; no Roman Catholic propaganda was to be permitted; and Sweden was to be governed by an aristocratic regency council of seven during the periods of Sigismund's absence in Poland.

In spite of the obdurate Lutheranism of the Swedish aristocracy, the papacy was sanguine about the prospects of reconversion. In 1592 Clement VIII appointed to Poland a papal nuncio, Germanico Malaspina, whose specific task was to prepare the way for the recovery of Sweden. John III's death in November of this year led to Sigismund's accession, and the new king was attended by the nuncio and a Catholic retinue on his visit to Stockholm in 1593. But he found on his arrival that he was confronted by that same combination of religious and aristocratic opposition which had bedevilled the lives of his fellow-princes in other parts of Europe. The Swedish aristocracy's fear of arbitrary power had been increased by John III's use of base-born secretaries for the conduct of his government. This was a common enough aristocratic complaint; but the Swedish nobles of the 1590s were a more sophisticated generation than their fathers who had deposed Eric XIV in 1568. They had travelled more and read more, and they were well acquainted with the results of antiquarian researches into Sweden's past, and with the more recent political literature of western Europe, including the works of Du Plessis-Mornay, Hotman and Buchanan. Under the leadership of Eric Sparre, they had begun to think of themselves as the historic guardians of Sweden's laws and liberties, and they staked their claim for a major share in government before the death of John III.

At the time of Sigismund's coronation in 1594 a decisive meeting of the Estates or *Riksdag* was held at Uppsala. During Sigismund's absence the country had effectively been governed by his uncle, the last of the sons of Gustavus Vasa, duke Charles of Södermanland. This formidable character, a Lutheran with neo-Calvinist tendencies, turned up for the meeting of the Estates with a large armed following. The Estates themselves, firmly Lutheran, were determined to place a curb on Sigismund's Catholicism, while the aristocracy was equally determined to impose new restrictions on the powers of the crown. Sigismund's defeat at the hands of the Estates represented a victory both for Protestantism and for the idea of contractual government based on the rule of law. The king returned disappointed to Poland, leaving Sweden in the hands of an uneasy coalition of duke Charles and the råd, or council, dominated by the higher aristocracy.

The following years in Sweden saw a confused tripartite struggle between duke Charles, the aristocracy, and Sigismund, who returned from Poland with an army in 1598. In the end, it was duke Charles who emerged victorious. Sigismund, after gaining some initial advantages, suddenly threw in his hand and left again for Poland. He was formally deposed by the Estates in 1599 – the second king of Sweden to be deposed in under half a century. Duke Charles, as the surviving representative of the dynasty and the crown, then rounded on the aristocratic opponents of the royal power. Eric Sparre and three of his colleagues were executed in 1600 for 'treasonable' activities, and the duke accepted the crown four years later as Charles IX of Sweden.

The victory of duke Charles over aristocratic constitutionalism proved in the end to be no more than a transient success, for the nobility had won sufficient concessions from the crown over the course of the years to make it difficult for future rulers to challenge a constitutional system based on representative Estates and a contractual relationship between the ruler and the ruled. But the victory over Sigismund was permanent and decisive. The abortive union of the Swedish and Polish crowns was irrevocably dissolved, and Rome's hopes for the recovery of Scandinavia were correspondingly shattered. Charles saw himself, and was seen by his subjects, as the saviour of Protestantism in Sweden, just as his son, Gustavus Adolphus, would one day be seen as the saviour of Protestantism in Europe. Whether Catholicism would really have been restored in Sweden if Sigismund had remained on the throne, may, however, be questioned. Lutheranism had shown itself a tougher plant in Swedish soil than in other parts of Europe, and it is doubtful whether king and nuncio would have succeeded in uprooting it. But the triumph of duke Charles marked cleanly and decisively the line of division between the Protestants and Rome. While Poland under Sigismund III returned by degrees to its Catholic allegiance, Scandinavia was henceforth firmly planted in the Protestant camp.

By the end of the century, this camp contained – besides Scandinavia – England, Scotland, the United Provinces, seven Swiss cantons and considerable parts of Germany. The Protestants were also very strong in Bohemia and Transylvania; and less strong, but still influential, in Poland, France, and the Habsburg hereditary lands. But the Roman church could look back on a series of solid successes since the conclusion of the Council of Trent in 1563. The Mediterranean lands, Celtic Ireland, and much of France had remained loyal to the faith. Lost ground had been won back in Bavaria, the southern Netherlands, Germany and Austria; and the kingdoms of France and Poland had been plucked like brands from the burning when it seemed that all was lost. The church itself was better equipped, and its morale infinitely higher, than half a century before. The phase of survival was over: recovery was well under way. But it would be folly for Rome to rest on its laurels, for Christendom, more than ever, was divided against itself.

3   Division and Unity

The extent to which Europeans were divided by the end of the century is suggested by their inability even to agree on the date. The Council of Trent was the latest in a succession of church councils to take note of the disparity between the Julian and the solar calendars – a disparity which meant that Easter and other holy days no longer conformed to the provisions laid down by the Council of Nicaea in the year 325. The Julian calendar made the year too long by 11 minutes and 14 seconds, and the cumulative effects of this had created a divergence of ten days over the course of the centuries. At the request of the Council of Trent, Gregory XIII referred the question to distinguished mathematicians and astronomers. Their labours culminated in the new 'Gregorian' calendar, which was sanctioned by a papal bull of February 1582, and which involved the suppression of ten days between 5 and 15 October of that year. Unfortunately, the technical superiority of the Gregorian to the Julian calendar failed to outweigh for Protestants the grievous original sin of its popish provenance. Consequently, while the Catholic states, including France, adopted it within the year, neither the Orthodox East nor the Protestant North was prepared to follow suit. Not until 1700 did Protestant Germany and Switzerland, Denmark and the United Provinces[5] decide to fall into line; and England and Sweden maintained a heroic rearguard resistance until 1752 and 1753.

Chronological schism was no doubt among the least of Europe's many ills. But it was symptomatic of the wider division brought about by the conflict of creeds. Mutual comprehension had become more difficult and mutual antipathies had been exacerbated as the results of nearly half a century of war. Yet there still remained, transcending all the disagreements, a European civility. For all the disruptions of the past few years Europe's community of merchants and its community of scholars survived more or less intact. Universities may have become more national and more parochial, but scholars of European repute continued to be courted by patrons, and even by universities, regardless of their faith. The Netherlands-born moralist and philosopher, Justus Lipsius (1547–1606), a protégé of cardinal Granvelle, accepted a post at the German Protestant university of Jena at the request of the Lutheran duke of Saxe-Weimar. Later, at the height of the Dutch revolt, he moved from Catholic Louvain to Calvinist Leyden, where he wrote a treatise on politics which even advocated the extermination of heretics. From Leyden he moved in 1591 to the presumably more compatible company of the Jesuits of Mainz, before accepting from among a host of offers the chair of history and literature at his old university of Louvain.

The European community, partially disrupted by war, quickly re-established itself on the return of peace. But ideas and attitudes had nevertheless been profoundly affected by the national and international dissensions of the preceding years. Indeed, it could hardly be otherwise, given the extreme bitterness and violence of the times. This was a society in which over-population, with a consequent shortage of food and employment, had created tensions which the social and political framework proved unable to contain. The possessing classes reacted by emphasizing with renewed determination the exclusive nature of their rights and their privileges, while the dispossessed responded by resorting to violence in any one of its multifarious forms – piracy and banditry, riot and rebellion, looting and pillage and frenzied iconoclasm. Violence was no doubt a normal way of life in Early Modern Europe, and war was seen as an accepted institution rather than as an unfortunate aberration from a long cycle of peace. But the very insolubility of the social and economic problems created by over-population, together with the collapse of Europe's religious consensus, and the fortuitous weakness of many monarchies, had created a situation in which the State was no longer able to fulfil its expected function of confining violence within accepted limits. The consequence of this was a descent from (modified) order into total disorder, on the horrors of which Shakespeare was characteristically eloquent:

> *Civil dissension is a viperous worm,*
> *That gnaws the bowels of the commonwealth.*[6]

The common response to this frightening situation was predictable enough: extreme political and social conservatism. The radical voice of the early sixteenth-century humanists, protesting against privilege and property, was silent in the later years of the century. An era of social experiment had given way to an era remarkable for its siege mentality. It was no accident that the three most creative minds of the second half of the century – Montaigne, Bodin and Shakespeare

– should all have been deeply conservative in their attitude to government and society. Intelligent men dwelt on the need for good government – synonymous with strong kingship – as the answer to public disorder. In a world like this, where order was at a premium, innovation stood at a discount.

Along with the extreme conservatism of later sixteenth-century societies went another phenomenon highly characteristic of the age – an enhanced sense of nationalism. A society where divisions ran deep – where Montaigne's own family were part Protestant and part Catholic – may subconsciously have sought compensation for its divisions in the common bonds of nationality. While nationalism could bring a new cohesion to a community threatened with dissolution through religious dissension, so also it might itself draw new vitality from the religious enthusiasm of a community which felt its beliefs imperilled by foreign and domestic enemies. Catholic Spain and Protestant England both displayed an intensified form of providential nationalism under Philip II and Elizabeth. Both considered themselves specially chosen of God to bear aloft His banner. No doubt this conviction led to terrible inhumanities by the nationals of both countries, and to tragic absurdities, as when the Spanish historian Juan de Mariana carefully censored his own writing to avoid giving comfort to Spain's enemies. But providential nationalism played its part in creating a climate in which a Cervantes or a Shakespeare could attain instinctive insights into the community to which they belonged, and were moved to dig deep into popular and vernacular traditions for fresh sources of inspiration.

Europe's intellectual order, like its social and political order, was hard hit by the grim struggles of the later sixteenth century. The demands of religious controversy inevitably bred narrow, dogmatic minds. As a result, the fruitful humanist speculation of the earlier part of the century often withered in its later years beneath a stifling orthodoxy. Each faith – Lutheran, Calvinist, Catholic – claimed a monopoly of truth, and each created its own private scholasticism which placed fidelity to the letter before originality of the mind. This was an age, anyhow, which tended to rate method above content; an age which was inclined to prefer the classification of old facts to the discovery of new. Its tone was set by Petrus Ramus – Pierre de la Ramée (1515–1572) – the French Protestant dialectician, whose famous Method, with its curious mnemonic devices, was concerned to sort ideas into convenient groupings and so to provide European youth with an educational system in which logic was the key to all the arts. No doubt Ramism was an autonomous product of the continuing scholastic tradition, but its popularity derived at least in part from the deep concern with order felt by a generation condemned to live its life in a disordered world.

The perennial search for an order within the universe appears indeed to have been intensified by the desire to escape from the disorders of a religiously divided Europe. It was natural enough that the scholars and philosophers who hoped through occultism and magic to decipher the riddles of the universe should also have been closely associated with attempts at religious reunion, for a higher religious synthesis would properly emerge from an understanding of the cosmic harmony. This at least was the hope of Guillaume Postel (1510–1581), the French orientalist and scholar-mystic, who dedicated his life to achieving the *concordia mundi*. It was the hope, too, of that even more remarkable figure, Giordano Bruno (1548–1600). Both men belonged to that strange third world between dogmatic Catholicism and dogmatic Protestantism, the citizens of which were to be found in the Valois and Habsburg courts, in the London of Sir Philip Sidney and the Antwerp of the printer Christophe Plantin and the Spanish theologian Benito Arias Montano. It was a world whose secrets were locked away in the mysteries of neo-Platonism and 'Egyptian' magic; a world of affinities and harmonies, which was controlled by the movements of the celestial bodies. Its esoteric quest for a cosmic harmony contributed incidentally – through its mathematical and magical pre-occupations – to the development of European science; and Bruno himself made a great imaginative leap from the Copernican theory to the conception of an infinite universe. But neither mystery nor magic could find an answer to the problem of Europe's religious division.

Men of letters were as much at hazard as anyone else from the consequences of this division, and perhaps even ran an extra occupational risk of their own. Ramus lost his life in the massacre of St Bartholomew; the Spanish poet and theologian Luis de León was shut away in the cells of the Inquisition; and Giordano Bruno was burnt at the stake for heresy. It was not surprising that Justus Lipsius, who had seen his native Netherlands devastated by war, should have devoted much thought to the attitude to be adopted by the scholar in the midst of war and conflict. He gave his answer to the world in his *De Constantia* of 1583. With Seneca, he counselled resignation: 'We are obliged to endure novelties, and to refrain from troubling ourselves about what we cannot prevent.' Lipsius's Christianized neo-Stoicism proved to be a philosophy well suited to the times. It offered his contemporaries a rational faith with a highly respectable classical ancestry and it provided a self-contained moral code based on a fatalistic resignation, but with a sufficient veneer of Christianity to disarm the scruples of the pious.

Not everyone, however, was able to find lasting satisfaction in Stoic humanism. The great Michel de Montaigne (1533–1592) was attracted to it for a time, but his enthusiasm had already waned when he came to publish his *Essays* in 1580. Its veneration for the powers of human reason seemed to him arrogant and presumptuous. For a man with Montaigne's sceptical cast of mind there was more to be said for the Pyrrhonist doctrine that it was impossible for man to attain to certainty of knowledge. It was as a Pyrrhonist that he asked himself the memorable question: 'Que sçais-je?' But the beginning of wisdom was to be found, not in the study of Pyrrho or Cicero, but in the study of oneself. Self-study, concluded Montaigne, was alone capable of teaching a man the complicated art of living. It would hardly seem a coincidence that an age in which the collapse of social cohesion left the individual defenceless and alone, should have seen the first tentative explorations of individual psychology. Montaigne's *Essays* – the word as used in this context was his own invention and was characteristic of the man – probed with subtlety the recesses of character to find the springs of human action. With Montaigne, sixteenth-century man, having discovered the world, embarked on the still more hazardous voyage which would lead to the discovery of himself.

Montaigne's view of mankind – sceptical, detached, and keenly alive to the follies of men and to their infinite diversity – inevitably led him to dislike and distrust extremes. While himself remaining a loyal Catholic, he had no use for the passionate fanaticism of the League. On the other hand, he disapproved of the edicts of toleration, for innovation in religion would lead to the dissolution of society. Yet his own humane outlook and the high value which he placed on the individual conscience made him a natural moderate in a society torn by the violence of its religious disputes. In this, as in so much else, he resembled his compatriot, Jean Bodin, whose massive mind at first sight contrasts so sharply with Montaigne's incisive and graceful wit. But Montaigne and Bodin were united in their horror of civil disorder and in their desire to see an effective government. They shared the view that religion was the natural cement of society, but both of them had achieved a relativism in their approach to their own society which made them shrink from dogma in considering the form which that religion should take. Bodin's astonishing *Heptaplomeres* widens the religious discussion to include the sceptic, the Jew and the Moham-medan, as well as representatives of the warring Christian creeds. In the quicksands of comparative history and comparative religion, there remained little firm foundation for dogmatic faith.

Yet, by a typical irony of this complex age, the Bodin who had achieved such remarkable religious detachment was also the Bodin who demanded death for the witches. There remained dark chasms of the human mind which it would need more than a Montaigne to explore. Tolerance and moderation are elusive qualities, difficult of acquisition and precarious when attained. But, at a time when it seemed that everything conspired to extinguish them, there were deep forces at work to keep them alive. The discovery of extra-European societies made it possible for European man to approach his own society with fresh perspectives and a new sense of detachment. Simultaneously, a growing awareness of the futility and inconclusiveness of religious conflict led to an increasing acceptance of the necessity for toleration on pragmatic grounds. 'Experience teaches us', wrote De Thou in 1604, 'that the sword and flames, exile and proscription, are more likely to exacerbate than to cure an ill.'[7] Such a realization might suffice to make liberty of conscience a fact long before it ever became an article of faith.

But could so fragile a plant as freedom of conscience ever survive in a dogma-ridden world? Neither Catholic nor dogmatic Calvinist societies would appear conducive to its growth. The best hope lay with those societies where *politique* principles were sufficiently established to keep the bigots at bay; and these societies, around 1600, were to be found in the Protestant North rather than (with the partial exception of Venice) in the Catholic South. Neither in the England of Elizabeth, the Scotland of James VI, nor in the United Provinces of William of Orange and Oldenbarnevelt did the Calvinist preachers succeed in securing the supreme power in the State; and Lutheran Sweden successfully resisted the Calvinizing tendencies of Charles IX. In all these countries lay control was preserved, and the Protestant Reformation was partially secularized.

A Protestant lay society might be expected in practice, if not in theory, to adopt a reasonably tolerant and moderate outlook on life. There was less room for superstition and bigotry in an educated society, and the very insistence of Protestantism on the study of the Scriptures encouraged the promotion of education and the spread of literacy. It is not surprising that Catherine de Medici, confronted with a galaxy of Huguenot talent, should have admitted that three quarters of the best educated of her subjects were Huguenots.[8] But something more than educational attainment appears to have been involved. Later sixteenth-century Protestantism seems to have created across Europe a new and recognizable breed of leaders of society – Coligny, Walsingham, Oldenbarnevelt, Du Plessis-Mornay, La Noue – distinguished by a high seriousness of purpose and integrity of mind. They were men who were prepared to dedicate their lives to a cause, but who did so on the basis of a high assessment of the moral worth and individual judgment of their associates. Indeed, the very structure of Protestant church life itself encouraged individual participation and the reaching of collective decisions through discussion – processes which were likely to be carried over into secular affairs. Self-discipline demanded a respect for the opinions of others in a community, whether religious or secular, which was founded on a faith in the primacy of law and in the importance of individual consent.

Although the second half of the sixteenth century was in many parts of Europe a period distinguished by the revival of constitutionalist ideas, it would hardly seem a coincidence, therefore, that these appeared more firmly established by the end of the century in those States where Protestantism had become the national faith. The conception of power as deriving from God through the people, and the idea of a contractual relationship between the ruler and the ruled – these were the principles that had been confirmed and vindicated in the great upheavals in France and the Netherlands. Political liberty, as guaranteed by Estates and parliamentary institutions, was a necessary pre-condition for acceptance of liberty of the mind. Constitutionalism in its sixteenth-century form may have been socially conservative and even repressive, but at least it allowed a little more scope for the varieties of individual opinion than an absolute monarchical power.

Change was slow and hesitant, but perhaps the sails of northern ships in Mediterranean waters were a sign of things to come. For the turmoil of the later sixteenth century had not left Europe as it found it: already a shift of emphasis could be observed, away from Mediterranean Europe to the Atlantic North. In these northern societies a new dynamism was to be detected, as they began to acquire certain recognizable characteristics of their own – a degree of political representation and political liberty, an insistence on the high priority to be given to commercial activity and business enterprise, a concern for precision and exact observation, and a modified acceptance of intellectual and religious dissent. Already by 1600 there were hints of a growing divergence of character between these societies and those of southern Europe. But a divided Christendom remained an essentially united continent. There was still a European civility; and all Europe continued to feel itself threatened by the presence of the Turks at its gates. Certainly its civil wars had been divisive and horribly barbarous. But they had nevertheless bequeathed to a basically unified society that most vitalizing of legacies – a diversity of cultures and a diversity of faiths.

Notes

Chapter 1   The International Scene

1   Quoted by John Lynch, *Spain 1516–1598* (Oxford, 1991), p. 255.
2   Below, p. 33.
3   Below, p. 115.
4   Quoted by J. E. Neale, *Elizabeth I and her Parliaments, 1559–1581* (London, 1953), p. 57.
5   'El Memorial de Luis de Ortiz', ed. M. Fernández Alvarez, *Anales de Economía* XVII (1957), p. 134.
6   This and the information that follows is drawn from Emmanuel Le Roy Ladurie, *Les Paysans de Languedoc*, vol. 1 (Paris, 1966), pp. 333–56.
7   See *Beloved Son Felix* (translated Sean Jennett, London, 1961), for a vivid contemporary description of sixteenth-century student life.

Chapter 2   The European Economy

1   Below, pp. 181.
2   Figures converted into Spanish ducats from the table given on p. 34 of Earl J. Hamilton, *American Treasure and the Price Revolution in Spain* (Cambridge, Mass. 1934).
3   See Marjorie Grice-Hutchinson, *The School of Salamanca. Readings in Spanish Monetary Theory, 1544–1605* (Oxford, 1952), pp. 91–6.
4   C. M. Cipolla, 'La prétendue révolution des prix', *Annales* X (1955), pp. 513–16. Eng. trans. in *Economy and Society in Early Modern Europe*, ed. Peter Burke (London, 1972), ch. 3.
5   *Discours politiques et militaires du seigneur de la Noue* (Basle, 1587, new ed. Geneva, 1967), c. VIII.

Chapter 3   The Problem of the State

1   Armagil Waad, quoted by Patrick Collinson, *The Elizabethan Puritan Movement* (London, 1967), p. 30.

2 Quoted by Lawrence Stone, *The Crisis of the Aristocracy* (Oxford, 1965), p. 257.

3 Quoted by H. Pirenne, *Histoire de Belgique* vol. III (Brussels, 1923), p. 400n.1.

4 The Netherlands were ruled by a governor, whose duties were comparable to those of a viceroy.

5 Below, pp. 182 ff.

6 Quoted from an anonymous paper of c. 1626 by G. N. Clark, 'The Birth of the Dutch Republic', *Proceedings of the British Academy* vol. XXXII (1946), p. 9. See also pp. 27–31 for an interesting discussion of the word 'State'.

7 Quoted by W. F. Church, *Constitutional Thought in Sixteenth Century France* (Cambridge, Mass., 1941), pp. 160–1n. 94.

8 For this trend among French jurists, see Julian H. Franklin, *Jean Bodin and the Sixteenth-Century Revolution in the Methodology of Law and History* (New York, 1963), part I, and Donald R. Kelley, *Foundations of Modern Historical Scholarship. Language, Law and History in the Renaissance* (New York and London, 1970).

9 Pedro Cornejo, *Compendio y breve relación de la Liga* (Brussels, 1591), f. 6.

10 A subject of intense study since H. R. Trevor-Roper's pioneering essay, 'The European Witch-craze of the Sixteenth and Seventeenth Centuries', first published in his *Religion, the Reformation and Social Change* (London, 1967), pp. 90–192. For recent bibliography see the section on Further Reading at the end of this book.

11 Robert M. Kingdon, *Geneva and the Coming of the Wars of Religion in France, 1555–1563 (Geneva, 1956), p. 6.*

12 Quoted by Lucien Romier, *Le Royaume de Cathérine de Médicis* vol. II (3rd ed. Paris, 1925), p. 261.

13 Below, ch. 4.

Chapter 4   Protestantism and Revolt

1 For the Granada revolt, see below, chap. 6. In the first edition of this book (1968) I provocatively suggested that this clustering of revolts (including the Corsican uprising of 1564 thrown in for good measure) might justify historians in postulating a 'general crisis of the 1560s', comparable to the 'general crisis of the 1640s', at that time the subject of vigorous historical debate. That same year, an Inaugural Lecture at King's College, London, on 'Revolution and Continuity in Early Modern Europe' (reprinted as chapter 5 of J. H. Elliott, *Spain and its World, 1500–1700*, New Haven and London, 1989), gave me an opportunity to speculate on possible reasons why the 1640s rather than the 1560s should have been singled out for special treatment. The challenge was not seriously taken up, and the publication of *The European Crisis of the 1590s*, ed. Peter Clark (London, 1985) introduced yet another decade of alleged 'crisis', which may suggest (as I pointed out in that volume) that

the notion of 'crisis' was in danger of being overworked. But this does not rule out the desirability of European-wide analysis when a number of states are simultaneously struck by movements of revolt, as they were in the 1560s.

2 Quoted by Vittorio de Caprariis, *Propaganda e pensiero politico in Francia durante le guerre di religione*, vol. I (Naples, 1959), p. 106.

3 Quoted by A. W. Whitehead, *Gaspard de Coligny* (London, 1904), p. 33.

4 Caprariis, *ibid.*, p. 102.

5 Quoted by P. F. Geisendorf, *Théodore de Bèze* (Geneva, 1949), p. 116.

6 Quoted by H. Pirenne, *Histoire de Belgique* vol. III (3rd ed., Brussels, 1923), p. 428n.1.

7 Huguenot military and naval organization has been studied by Jean de Pablo in two articles entitled 'Contribution à l'étude de l'histoire des institutions militaires Huguenots', *Archiv für Reformationsgeschichte* vols. 47–8 (1956–1957). For the royal army, see James B. Wood, *The King's Army: Warfare, Soldiers and Society during the Wars of Religion in France, 1562–1576* (Cambridge, 1996).

8 On being (wrongly) informed that Dreux was a Huguenot victory, Catherine reacted entirely in character. 'Eh bien!' she is said to have remarked. 'Désormais nous prierons Dieu en français.'

9 Cf. his opponents' cry: 'God save us from the toothpick of the Admiral!'

10 As a prince of the Empire, Louis of Nassau could be Lutheran with impunity. The course of William's own religious evolution is not entirely clear. He was still going to mass in 1566, but was a Lutheran by the end of 1567, and became a Calvinist in 1573. How far these conversions were tactical, and how far they corresponded to a genuine evolution of his religious beliefs, it is not possible to say.

11 For interesting details about certain members of this community, see Paul J. Hauben, 'Marcus Pérez and Marrano Calvinism in the Dutch Revolt and the Reformation', *Bibliothèque d'Humanisme et Renaissance. Travaux et Documents*, vol. XXIX (1967), pp. 121–32.

12 Above, p. 14.

13 Information on Antwerp wage-earners is taken from the admirably meticulous study by E. Scholliers, *De Levensstandaard in de XVe en XVIe Eeuw te Antwerpen* (Antwerp, 1960), which contains a long French summary of the author's findings.

14 M. Delmotte, 'Het Calvinisme in de verschillende bevolkingslagen te Gent (1566–1567)', *Tijdschrift voor Geschiedenis* vol. 76 (1963), pp. 145–76.

Chapter 5 Catholicism and Repression

1 Quoted by M. Van Durme, *El Cardenal Granvela* (Barcelona, 1957), pp. 403–4.

2 Above, p. 79.

3 Quoted by J. M. March, *Don Luis de Requesens* (2nd ed., Madrid, 1946), p. 247.

4   Below, ch. 6.
5   Quoted by Bernard de Meester, *Le Saint-Siège et les Troubles des Pays-Bas* (Louvain, 1934), p. 47.
6   Above p. 79.
7   J. Craeybeckz, 'Alva's Tiende Penning Een Mythe?', *Bijdragen En Mededelingen van het Historisch Genootschap* vol. 76 (1962), pp. 10–42.

Chapter 6   The War with Islam

1   Above, p. 13.
2   *The Turkish Letters of Ogier Ghiselin De Busbecq*, ed. E. S. Forster (Oxford, 1927), pp. 60–1.
3   Elizabeth of Valois bore Philip two daughters, Isabella Clara Eugenia (the future ruler of Flanders) and Catherine. He married in 1570 as his fourth wife Anne of Austria, the daughter of his cousin, the Emperor Maximilian II. The future Philip III was born of this marriage in 1578.
4   William of Orange to John of Nassau, 20 Feb. 1570 (G. Groen Van Prinsterer, *Archives ou Correspondance Inédite de la Maison d'Orange-Nassau*, vol. III, Leyden, 1836, Letter CCCXXXVIII).
5   Below, p. 186.

Chapter 7   Crisis in the North: 1572

1   Above, pp. 87
2   Above, p. 79.
3   Above, p. 79.
4   Below, pp. 157 ff.

Chapter 8   A Middle Way?

1   Below, pp. 186 ff.
2   Madame Du Mornay, quoted in Raoul Patry, *Philippe Du Plessis-Mornay* (Paris, 1933), p. 29.
3   See Frances A. Yates, *The Valois Tapestries* (London, 1959) for a brilliant piece of detective work on the political symbolism concealed in the designs for these tapestries, including the tapestry of the Polish ambassadors.
4   Below, p. 259.
5   Fausto Sozzini (1539–1604) was a native of Siena who settled in Poland in 1579. Here he exercised a great influence on the anti-Trinitarian Anabaptists, and after his death the Polish Brethren – pacifist and anti-Trinitarian – became known as 'Socinians'.
6   His concern for these regions is well illustrated by his decision to create a special congregation of eight cardinals (including cardinal Hosius and his

secretary of state Ptolemy Gallio, cardinal of Como) for the reconversion of the Teutonic nations.

7 Above, p. 164.

8 For cardinal Borromeo, see above, p. 104. Borromeo's influence on Henry III is examined by Frances Yates, *The French Academies of the Sixteenth Century* (London, 1947), cs. VIII and X, and I have followed her illuminating assessment of Henry's character and policies.

9 So called after 'Monsieur' – the king's brother, Alençon, who was rewarded for his treachery with the rich appanage of Berry, Touraine and Anjou. He thus succeeded to Henry's title of duke of Anjou; but, in order to avoid confusion, it seems best to continue referring to him by the title under which he was known during the reign of Charles IX.

10 Henry, whose father had been assassinated in 1563, was nicknamed 'le balafré' – scarface – after a wound received in battle in 1575.

11 Quoted by N. M. Sutherland, *The French Secretaries of State in the Age of Catherine de Medici* (London, 1962), p. 223.

12 Above, p. 165.

13 For Requesens, see above, p. 107. Requesens, a Catalan name, is pronounced Rica-sens.

14 Quoted by Meester, *Le Saint-Siège et les Troubles des Pays-Bas*, p. 95.

15 Orange to the counts of Nassau, 5 February 1573 (Groen van Prinsterer, *Correspondance*, vol. IV p. 50).

16 Above, p. 160.

17 Above, p. 8.

18 Below, p. 180.

Chapter 9   The Growth of Spanish Power

1 Above, p. 129.

2 Above, p. 36.

3 Below, pp. 186 ff.

4 Although Sebastian's body was later recovered from the Moors and buried with due pomp at Belem, there was great popular reluctance to believe that the body was really that of the king. Hence the strange phenomenon of *Sebastianismo* – the belief, which lingered on for generations, that Sebastian was still alive and would one day return to reclaim his kingdom.

5 The combined Spanish and Portuguese fleets now totalled 250,000–300,000 tons. This may be compared with the Netherlands – 232,000 tons; Germany – 110,000; France – 80,000; England – 42,000 (cf. A. P. Usher, 'Spanish ships and shipping in the 16th and 17th centuries', *Facts and Factors in Economic History. Essays presented to Edwin Francis Gay* (Cambridge, Mass., 1932), pp. 189–213).

6 Above, pp. 46–7.

7 The first Netherlands editions of Las Casas' *Brief Account of the Destruction of the Indies* – an essential source-book for the black legend – had appeared in 1578.

8   Above, p. 150.

Chapter 10   The International Conflict

1   Quoted by Whitehead, *Gaspard de Coligny*, p. 243.
2   René de Lucinge, *Lettres sur les débuts de la Ligue*, ed. A. Dufour (Geneva, 1964), p. 26 (Letter of 25 March 1585).
3   Nancy L. Roelker, *The Paris of Henry of Navarre as seen by Pierre de l'Estoile* (Cambridge, Mass., 1958), p. 113. This passage was kindly brought to my attention by Professor Franklin Ford of Harvard University.
4   Ambassador from 1582–1591, Enrique de Guzmán, count of Olivares, was the father of Philip IV's great minister and favourite, Gaspar de Guzmán, the count-duke of Olivares, who was born in Rome in 1587.
5   Quoted by De Lamar Jensen, 'Franco-Spanish Diplomacy and the Armada', *From the Renaissance to the Counter-Reformation*, ed. C. H. Carter (London, 1966), p. 219.
6   Letter of 17 August 1588, printed as an appendix to Henri Hauser, *François de La Noue, 1531–1591* (Paris, 1892), pp. 315–19.
7   J. A. De Thou, *Histoire Universelle* (ed. London, 1734), vol. X, p. 261.
8   The evidence for this interpretation is provided by Edmund H. Dickerman and Anita M. Walker, 'The Language of Blame: Henri III and the Dismissal of his Ministers', *French History*, 13 (1999), pp. 77–98.
9   Quoted in De Lamar Jensen, *Diplomacy and Dogmatism* (Cambridge, Mass., 1964), p. 168.

Chapter 11   The Discomfiture of Spain

1   L. Van Der Essen, *Alexandre Farnèse*, vol. V (Brussels, 1937), p. 280.
2   *The Paris of Henry of Navarre* (ed. N. L. Roelker), p. 190.
3   Quoted by Robert Mandrou, *Introduction à la France Moderne* (Paris, 1961), p. 169.
4   Quoted by Corrado Vivanti, *Lotta politica e pace religiosa in Francia fra Cinque e Seicento* (Turin, 1963), p. 46.
5   Vivanti, pp. 42 and 45. The etymology of the name *Croquant* remains uncertain. It may denote a peasant wielding a *croc* or cudgel. It may also derive from the village of Crocq in Limousin (see Yves-Marie Bercé, *History of Peasant Revolts*, Oxford, 1990, pp. 279–84).
6   H. Lapeyre, *Simon Ruiz et les Asientos de Philippe II* (Paris, 1953), p. 87.
7   Conyers Read, *Lord Burghley and Queen Elizabeth* (London, 1960), p. 516.

Chapter 12   The Divided Continent

1   *Histoire Universelle* (London, 1734), vol. 1, book 1, p. 17.

2 See F. Braudel, *The Mediterranean and the Mediterranean World in the Age of Philip II* (2 vols., London, 1972–1973), vol. 1, pp. 402 ff. for this and other population figures for the Mediterranean region. The author rightly stresses the great element of uncertainty in his figures.

3 Above, p. 210.

4 Above, p. 240.

5 Except Holland and Zealand, which adopted the new calendar in 1582.

6 *Henry VI*, part I, Act III, Sc. I, ls. 72–3.

7 *Histoire Universelle* vol. I, p. 313.

8 Trevor-Roper, *Religion, the Reformation and Social Change*, p. 209.

Further Reading

1 General Works

The history of sixteenth-century Europe is covered by a number of general works, including most recently Richard Bonney, *The European Dynastic States, 1494–1660* (Oxford, 1991) and Richard MacKenney, *Sixteenth Century Europe. Expansion and Conflict* (London, 1993). H. G. Koenigsberger, George L. Mosse and G. Q. Bowler, *Europe in the Sixteenth Century* (2nd ed., London 1989) adopts a thematic approach, while H. G. Koenigsberger, *Early Modern Europe, 1500–1700* (London, 1987) provides an admirable short survey. Social developments are explored in Henry Kamen, *European Society, 1500–1700* (London, 1984; originally published in 1971 under the title of *The Iron Century*), while the first section of *Early Modern Europe. An Oxford History*, ed. Euan Cameron (Oxford, 1999) surveys in short compass 'The conditions of life for the masses', 'Renaissance and Reformation', and 'War, Religion and the State'. Perry Anderson, *Lineages of the Absolutist State* (London, 1974) is a comparative survey of Early Modern Europe from a Marxist perspective.

For reasons that became increasingly clear to me as I wrote this book, syntheses confined to the history of the second half of the century are in short supply. *The New Cambridge History*, vol. III (ed. R. Wernham, 1968) covers roughly the same period, but as a collective work it inevitably lacks unity, although it contains some excellent chapters, in particular the long chapter by H. G. Koenigsberger on 'Western Europe and the Power of Spain', which has not been displaced by more recent work, and is reprinted in his *The Habsburgs and Europe, 1516–1660* (Ithaca and London, 1971). Indeed there is still much to be gained from consulting older surveys, like Henri Hauser, *La Prépondérance Espagnole, 1559–1660* (3rd ed., Paris, 1948), which was of particular help to me in composing this book.

2   Kingship and the State

Much work has been done in recent years on different aspects of the history of states and state formation in the Early Modern period. In particular, it has now become fashionable to see sixteenth-century European states as 'composite monarchies', and to pay special attention to some of the ways in which these composite monarchies were articulated and held together – notably through the court and court culture, the deployment of imagery to project the majesty of kingship, and the exploitation of patronage to create and sustain clientage systems and networks of loyalty and dependence.

J. H. Elliott, 'A Europe of Composite Monarchies', *Past and Present*, 137 (1992), pp. 48–71, provides a brief introduction to the theme, while the essays by different authors in *Conquest and Coalescence*, ed. Mark Greengrass (London, 1991) discuss the various ways in which a number of six-teenth- and seventeenth-century rulers addressed the question of how to handle territories that were nominally subject to them but retained strongly independent identities. Elements of the new approach to what used to be called 'state-building' can also be found in two volumes of essays by various hands published under the auspices of The European Science Foundation: *Economic Systems and State Finance*, ed. Richard Bonney (Oxford, 1995), and *Power Elites and State Building*, ed. Wolfgang Reinhard (Oxford, 1996). Peter Clark (ed.), *The European Crisis of the 1590s: Essays in Comparative History* (London, 1985) is another collective volume containing valuable contributions on the problems facing the rulers of European states following the wars and upheavals of the later sixteenth century. For detailed studies of the history of individual states in this period, see the section on 'National Histories', below.

The book that has done most to promote the study of the court over the last few decades is Norbert Elias, *The Court Society* (Oxford, 1983), translated by Edmund Jephcott from the German edition of 1969, itself a revised version of a thesis completed in 1933, but not published at the time for political reasons. While in many respects very suggestive, it is much too reductive in its approach to court history, taking the court of Louis XIV as its model. For a critical appraisal see Jeroen Duindam, *Myths of Power* (Amsterdam, 1995). A. G. Dickens (ed.) *The Courts of Europe: Politics, Patronage and Royalty, 1400–1800* (London, 1977) is a well-illustrated survey of several Early Mod-ern courts by different authors, and contains much interesting material. Another collective volume, Ronald G. Asch and Adolf M. Birke (eds), *Princes, Patronage and the Nobility: The Court at the Beginning of the Modern Age, c. 1450–1650* (Oxford, 1991) is more reflective of trends in modern scholarship. So too are *The Princely Courts of Europe, 1500–1700*, ed. John Adamson (London, 1999), and *The World of the Favourite*, ed. J. H. Elliott and L. W. B. Brockliss (New Haven and London, 1999), a collection of essays on the favourite, who emerges in the sixteenth century as a European figure who was to play a critical part in linking king, court and country, not least through the use of patronage and the organization of clientage.

The rituals and symbols of kingship, and its projection through the written word, visual imagery and ceremonial appearances, have received much attention in recent years. A pioneering figure in this field is Frances Yates, whose *The Valois Tapestries* (London, 1959), and *Astraea: The Imperial Theme in the Sixteenth Century* (London, 1975) throw a brilliant shaft of light on different aspects of sixteenth-century politics and religion. Roy Strong pursues the theme of art and power in *Splendour at Court: Renaissance Spectacle and Illusion* (London, 1973) and subsequent works. Some of the ceremonies surrounding French kingship are examined by Ralph E. Giesey, *The Royal Funerary Ceremony in Renaissance France* (Geneva, 1960), and Sarah Hanley, *The Lit de Justice of the Kings of France* (Princeton, 1983), while Edward Muir explores the rituals of a city state in his *Civic Ritual in Renaissance Venice* (Princeton, 1981), and is the author of a more wide-ranging survey, *Ritual in Early Modern Europe* (Cambridge, 1997).

The best current introduction to theories of the state in the Early Modern period is Quentin Skinner, *The Foundations of Modern Political Thought* (2 vols, Cambridge, 1978), which can be supplemented by *The Cambridge History of Political Thought, 1450–1700*, ed. J. H. Burns (Cambridge, 1991), and Richard Tuck, *Philosophy and Government, 1572–1651* (Cambridge, 1993). But there is still gold to be mined in J. N. Figgis's essays, *From Gerson to Grotius*, first published in 1907. Donald R. Kelley, *Foundations of Modern Historical Scholarship. Language, Law and History in the Renaissance* (New York and London, 1970) is an important study of the contribution made by French jurists to the development of constitutionalist thinking, while Julian H. Franklin, *Jean Bodin and the Rise of Absolutist Theory* (Cambridge, 1973) explores the contribution of Bodin to the reassertion of royal power towards the end of the sixteenth century. There is an abridged version by M. J. Tooley of Jean Bodin, *Six Books of the Commonwealth* (Oxford, n.d.). Two classics of Huguenot constitutionalist and resistance theory have now received worthy editions in English translation: François Hotman, *Francogallia*, ed. Ralph E. Giesey and J. H. M. Salmon (Cambridge, 1973), and the *Vindiciae Contra Tyrannos*, ed. George Garnett (Cambridge, 1994). For resistance theory in the Dutch revolt, see section 7, below (*The Netherlands*). Gerhard Oestreich, *Neostoicism and the Early Modern State* (Cambridge, 1982) provides valuable assessments of the impact of the neo-Stoic writings of Justus Lipsius, and of the development of ideas about the state.

Constitutionalist theories found their natural home in representative institutions and Estates, which have also been the subject of renewed attention in recent years. A brief survey of their fluctuating history may be found in A. R. Myers, *European Parliaments before 1789* (London, 1975), while C. Griffiths, *Representative Government in Western Europe in the Sixteenth Century* (Oxford, 1968) is a useful source-book. J. Russell Major explores *Representative Government in Early Modern France* (New Haven and London, 1980) on a massive scale, while F. L. Carsten provides a comprehensive study of *Princes and Parliaments in Germany* (Oxford, 1959). Important essays on aspects of constitutional theory and practice are to be found in two volumes of selected essays by H. G. Koenigsberger, *Estates and Revolutions* (Ithaca and London, 1971) and *Politicians and Virtuosi* (London and Ronceverte, 1986).

A wide-ranging interpretative survey of revolts and revolutions in this period is provided by P. Zagorin, *Rebels and Rulers, 1500–1660* (2 vols. Cambridge, 1982), while Yves-Marie Bercé, *Revolt and Revolution in Early Modern Europe: An Essay on the History of Political Violence* (Manchester, 1987) provides an intelligent thematic analysis of the origins and mechanism of political violence in specific historical contexts. See also, as an introduction the subject, J. H. Elliott, 'Revolution and Continuity in Early Modern Europe', *Past and Present*, 42 (1969), pp. 35–56 (reprinted in J. H. Elliott, *Spain and its World, 1500–1700*, (New Haven and London, 1989). A valuable comparative study by H. G. Koenigsberger, 'The Organization of Revolutionary Parties in France and the Netherlands', first published in 1955, is reprinted in his *Estates and Revolutions*, mentioned above.

3 Social and Economic History

Some of the greatest achievements of twentieth-century historiography have been in the realm of social and economic history, particularly in relation to the Early Modern period. French historians, and in particular those associated with the journal known since 1946 as *Annales: économies, sociétés, civilisations*, have here made a major contribution, and a good sample of essays from the *Annales*, in translation, is to be found in Peter Burke (ed.) *Economy and Society in Early Modern Europe. Essays from Annales* (London, 1972).

One of the founders of *Annales* was Lucien Febvre, whose *Philippe II et la Franche-Comté* (Paris, 1912), is a superb pioneer work, now somewhat neglected, in the realm of 'total history' to which the *Annalistes* aspired. But the most famous of all the works associated with the *Annales* school, and one that has had a profound impact on historical writing, is Fernand Braudel, *La Méditerranée et le Monde Méditerranéan*, first published in 1949 and reissued in two volumes, after extensive revision, in 1966. There is a fine English translation by Siân Reynolds of this revised edition, *The Mediterranean and the Mediterranean World in the Age of Philip II* (2 vols, London 1972–3). With the passage of time some of the weaknesses of Braudel's book have become increasingly apparent. Many would regard it as excessively determinist in its explanation of historical developments, and the third of the three sections into which the book is divided, 'Events, Politics and People' is poorly related to the preceding two sections on 'The Role of the Environment' and 'Collective Destinies', which more clearly engaged Braudel's enthusiasm. But even if many of Braudel's interpretations are open to challenge, and his attempt to produce a work of 'total history' is ultimately accounted a failure, *The Mediterranean* will continue to be read, if only for the fertility of the historical imagination it displays, and for its brilliant vignettes of people and places.

Two other major works of French historical scholarship also deserve special mention. Emmanuel Le Roy Ladurie, *Les Paysans de Languedoc* (2 vols, Paris, 1966) casts a searching light on rural society in southern France in the sixteenth century, and he has followed this up with further suggestive and original studies on sixteenth-century life and society, notably *Carnival: A People's Uprising at Romans, 1579–1580* (Harmondsworth, 1981). A third classic work of twentieth-century French historiography, although in a very different mould, is Pierre Chaunu, *Séville et l'Atlantique* (8 vols, Paris, 1955–9). This is no *Mediterranean*, but rather a vast compendium of information, much of it heavily quantitative in character, on trade between Seville and Spain's expanding American empire. Chaunu's monumental work has placed the 'Spanish Atlantic' and the workings of its trading system firmly on the map of sixteenth-century history. Readers who blench at the thought of embarking on this flotilla of volumes will find their contents very efficiently summarized on pp. 88–99 of the same author's *L'Amérique et les Amériques* (Paris, 1964). Since Chaunu, much work has been done on the economic character and consequences of Europe's transatlantic expansion in the sixteenth century, particularly by Anglo-American historians. Ralph Davis, *The Rise of the Atlantic Economies* (Ithaca, 1973) is a useful survey which can be supplemented by the essays in two volumes edited by James D. Tracy, *The Rise of Merchant Empires* (Cambridge, 1990) and *The Political Economy of Merchant Empires* (Cambridge, 1991). Immanuel Wallerstein, *The Modern World-System: Capitalist Agriculture and the Origins of the European World-Economy in the Sixteenth Century* (New York and London, 1974) is a highly ambitious, and controversial, attempt to chart the creation by Europe of a capitalist world economy.

Volumes 4 and 5 of *The Cambridge Economic History of Europe* (Cambridge 1967 and 1977) remain standard works of reference on the economic life of Early Modern Europe, which is treated in shorter compass in the volume edited by Carlo M. Cipolla, *The Sixteenth and Seventeenth Centuries* in *The Fontana Economic History of Europe* (London, 1974). See also H. A. Miskimin, *The Economy of Later Renaissance Europe, 1460–1600* (Cambridge, 1977), and, for central and eastern Europe, the essays assembled in *East-Central Europe in Transition*, ed. Antoni Mączak, Henryk Samsonowicz and Peter Burke (Cambridge, 1985). For towns and urbanization, Jan de Vries, *European Urbanisation, 1500–1800* (London, 1984) and C. J. Friedrichs, *The Early Modern City, 1450–1750* (London, 1995). Brian Pullan, *Rich and Poor in Renaissance Venice* (Oxford, 1971) is a fascinating study of the administration of poor relief, and of the way in which it was used to preserve political and social stability in Venice.

Gender and family history have received much attention in recent years. See in particular Olwen Hufton, *The Prospect Before Her. A History of Women in Western Europe, 1500–1800* (vol. 1, London, 1995), Natalie Zemon Davis and Arlette Farge (eds), *A History of Women in the West* (vol. 3, *Renaissance and Enlightenment Paradoxes*, Cambridge, Mass., 1993) and Roger Chartier (ed.), *A History of Private Life* (vol. 3, *Passions of the Renaissance*, Cambridge, Mass., 1989). Natalie Zemon Davis has brought fame to an obscure one-legged soldier, and, in the process, illuminated hidden aspects of village life in sixteenth-century France, in her celebrated *The Return of Martin Guerre* (Cambridge, Mass., 1983).

4 Religion and Culture

Euan Cameron, *The European Reformation* (Oxford, 1991) is an accessible and up-to-date synthesis of the development of Protestantism, although with the emphasis on the earlier stages of the Reformation. Much discussion in recent years has centred on the Reformation's 'success' or 'failure', the subject of a wide-ranging survey article by Geoffrey Parker, 'Success and Failure during the First Century of the Reformation', *Past and Present*, 136 (1992), pp. 43–82. For more detailed studies see Gerald Strauss, *Luther's House of Learning: Indoctrination of the Young in the German Reformation* (Baltimore, 1978) and R. Po-Chia Hsia, *Social Discipline in the Reformation: Central Europe, 1550–1750* (London, 1989).

On Geneva and the consolidation and spread of Calvinism, R. M. Kingdon, *Geneva and the Coming of the Wars of Religion in France, 1555–1563* (Geneva, 1956) and *Geneva and the Consolidation of the French Protestant Movement, 1564–1572* (Geneva, 1967) remain standard works. To these should now be added W. G. Naphy, *Calvin and the Consolidation of the Genevan Reformation* (Manchester, 1994). *International Calvinism, 1541–1715*, ed. Menna Prestwich (Oxford, 1985) contains some excellent essays on the diffusion of Calvinism through Europe.

The Counter-Reformation is much better served now than it was when the first edition of this book appeared in 1968, although that year saw the publication of an outstanding short work of synthesis, A. G. Dickens, *The Counter Reformation* (London, 1968), which still retains its freshness. It can usefully be supplemented by N. S. Davidson's Historical Association booklet, *The Counter-Reformation* (Oxford, 1987), and by R. Po-Chia Hsia, *The World of Catholic Renewal, 1540–1770* (Cambridge, 1998), which takes into account the large body of work produced since the close of Vatican II, and contains an extensive bibliographical essay. John Bossy, 'The Counter-Reformation and the People of Catholic Europe', *Past and Present*, 47 (1970), pp. 51–70, is a suggestive essay linking religious and social change, while his *Christianity in the West, 1400–1700* (Oxford 1985) explores the breakdown of medieval Christianity and the ways in which it was superseded (on both sides of the religious divide) during the sixteenth century. Louis Châtellier, *The Europe of the Devout: The Catholic Reformation and the Formation of a New Society* (Cambridge, 1987), is another exploration of the relationship between religion and society, this time by way of the Marian congregations founded by the Jesuits at the end of the sixteenth century. H. O. Evennett, *The Spirit of the Counter-Reformation* (Cambridge, 1968) is a subtle and sensitive introduction to aspects of Counter-Reformation spirituality. The early stages of the Jesuit Order are the subject of John W. O'Malley, *The First Jesuits* (Cambridge, Mass. and London, 1993). For the life and work of St Charles Borromeo, see the essays in *San Carlo Borromeo*, ed. J. M. Headley and J. B. Tomaro (Washington, 1998). The best local study of the impact of the Counter-Reformation in Spain is Sara T. Nalle, *God in La Mancha: Religious Reform and the People of Cuenca, 1500–1650* (Baltimore, 1992), while Henry Kamen adduces much new information in *The*

Phoenix and the Flame: Catalonia and the Counter Reformation (New Haven and London, 1993).

For the papacy, Leopold von Ranke's *The History of the Popes* (Eng. trans., 3 vols. London, 1907) still makes superb reading, and L. von Pastor's monumental *History of the Popes*, vols. 15–24 (Eng. trans., London, 1928–1933) is an inexhaustible quarry. There is a useful essay by Peter Partner on 'The Papal State, 1417–1600' in Mark Greengrass, ed., *Conquest and Coalescence*. Urban life and problems in the Rome of the Counter-Reformation popes are studied at length by Jean Delumeau, *Vie Economique et Sociale de Rome dans la seconde moitié du XVIe siècle* (2 vols, Paris, 1957–1959).

The impact of the Counter-Reformation on the arts remains a much-debated subject. John Shearman, *Mannerism* (London, 1967) is an admirably level-headed introduction to a complex style. My information on Andrea Gilio's recommendation for a 'judicious mixture' of the old and new is drawn from Federico Zeri, *Pittura e Controriforma* (Turin, 1957). While the importance of Gilio's treatise has since been contested, the eclectic character of later sixteenth-century art is obvious. Much depended, as with the artists patronized by Cardinal Farnese, on questions of patronage, which have received considerable attention in recent art-historical studies. R. G. Mann, for instance, has studied *El Greco and his Patrons* (Cambridge, 1996), while Thomas DaCosta Kaufmann, *Court, Cloister and City* (London, 1995) provides what has long been missing, a comprehensive survey of art in central Europe. Among the major patrons was the Emperor Rudolph II, whose patronage and aesthetic interests are the subject of a brilliant study by R. J. W. Evans, *Rudolf II and his World* (Oxford, 1973). Attention should also be drawn to John Hale, *The Civilization of Europe in the Renaissance* (London, 1993), a magnificent survey of the arts, letters and learning over the course of 'the long sixteenth century'.

The more repressive aspects of Counter-Reformation Catholicism have also been the subject of much recent research, with Inquisition studies as a major growth area, in part because they provide such rich archival information on individual case histories. *The Inquisition in Early Modern Europe: Studies in Sources and Methods*, ed. G. Henningsen and J. Tedeschi (De Kalb, Ill., 1986) provides the best introduction. The Spanish Inquisition has been subject to revisionist interpretations by Henry Kamen, of which the most recent is *The Spanish Inquisition: an Historical Revision* (London, 1997), while the differing concerns and modes of operation of the different tribunals provide the theme for William Monter, *Frontiers of Heresy* (Cambridge, 1990) whose account embraces Sicily as well as Spain itself. For Italy, see P. F. Grendler, *The Roman Inquisition and the Venetian Press, 1540–1605* (Princeton, 1977) and Brian Pullan, *The Jews of Europe and the Inquisition of Venice, 1550–1670* (Oxford, 1983). Jonathan I. Israel, *European Jewry in the Age of Mercantilism, 1550–1750* (2nd ed., Oxford, 1989) is a valuable survey of the fortunes and misfortunes of the Jewish communities of Early Modern Europe. Carlo Ginzburg, *The Cheese and the Worms: The Cosmos of a Sixteenth-Century Miller* (Eng. trans., Baltimore, 1980), based on the inquiry of the Inquisition into the highly personal cosmology of a miller of Friuli, has become a historical (or micro-historical) classic.

There has also been considerable interest in exploring the religious border-land between dogmatic Catholicism and dogmatic Protestantism, with Frances Yates again as a pioneer. Especially valuable for an understanding of the religious climate among those who continued to think in terms of toleration and ecumenicism are her *The French Academies of the Sixteenth Century* (London, 1947), *The Valois Tapestries* (cited under section 2, above) and *Giordano Bruno and the Hermetic Tradition* (London, 1964). William J. Bouwsma, *Concordia Mundi* (Cambridge, Mass., 1957) explores the ideas of another figure in the same tradition, Guillaume Postel. For an abortive attempt at religious reconciliation see Donald Nugent, *Ecumenism in the Age of the Reformation: the Colloquy of Poissy* (Cambridge, Mass., 1974). Thierry Wanegffelen, *Ni Rome ni Genève: Des fidèles entre deux chaires en France au XVIe siècle* (Paris, 1997) analyses literary and political texts that fell between the two confessions in France, while Howard Louthan, *The Quest for Compromise. Peacemakers in Counter-Reformation Vienna* (Cambridge, 1997) explores ecumenical tendencies at the Imperial court in Vienna, a subject to which R. J. W. Evans has made an important contribution in his *Rudolf II and his World* (cited above) and his *The Making of the Habsburg Monarchy, 1550–1700* (Oxford, 1979). For recent work on toleration, see the essays collected in Ole Peter Grell and Bob Scribner, (eds), *Tolerance and Intolerance in the European Reformation* (Cambridge, 1996). Olivier Christin, *Les paix de religion: L'autonomisation de la raison politique au XVIe siècle* (Paris, 1997) provides an illuminating comparison of religious peace settlements in Germany and France.

H. R. Trevor-Roper, *Religion, the Reformation and Social Change* (London, 1967), is a collection of essays which provide a consistently luminous vision of the complex interplay between ideas, politics and society in Early Modern Europe. There is a difficult but rewarding study of Ramus by Walter J. Ong, *Ramus: Method and the Decay of Dialogue* (Cambridge, Mass., 1958), and the influence of Ramism is fascinatingly explored by Frances A. Yates in *The Art of Memory* (London, 1966). For the sixteenth-century revival of Stoicism see in particular Gerhard Oestreich, *Neostoicism and the Early Modern State*, cited above under section 2. On the consequences of the coming of print culture, see Elizabeth Eisenstein, *The Printing Press as an Agent of Change* (Cambridge, 1979), Lucien Febvre and Henri-Jean Martin, *The Coming of the Book: the Impact of Printing, 1450–1800* (London, 1976) and Roger Chartier, *The Cultural Uses of Print in Early Modern France* (Princeton, 1987). The impact of the discovery and settlement of the New World of America on sixteenth-century European civilization is discussed by J. H. Elliott in *The Old World and the New* (Cambridge, 1970, repr. 1992), and in the collection of essays in *America in European Consciousness, 1493–1750*, ed. Karen Ordahl Kupperman (Chapel Hill and London, 1995), while Anthony Pagden, *The Fall of Natural Man* (revised ed., Cambridge, 1986) examines the debate about the nature of the American Indian and explores the origins of comparative ethnology.

For an introduction to the currently very fashionable genre of 'popular culture', see Peter Burke, *Popular Culture in Early Modern Europe* (London, 1978; 2nd ed. 1994), and for the contribution of an outstandingly successful practitioner of the genre, Natalie Zemon Davis, *Society and Culture in Early*

Modern France. Eight Essays (Stanford, 1975). Witchcraft in Early Modern Europe has also been the subject of intensive recent study. Good introductions to current thinking on the subject are provided by the essays edited by Jonathan Barry, Marianne Hester and Gareth Roberts, *Witchcraft in Early Modern Europe* (Cambridge, 1996), and by Lyndal Roper, *Oedipus and the Devil: Witchcraft, Sexuality and Religion in Early Modern Europe* (London, 1994), which extends beyond witchcraft to probe into many other aspects of sixteenth-century life and behaviour. Stuart Clark, *Thinking with Demons: the Idea of Witchcraft in Early Modern Europe* (Oxford, 1997) is a massive and powerful study of the witchcraft beliefs held by European intellectuals. Other important studies are R. Briggs, *Witches and Neighbours: the Social and Cultural Context of European Witchcraft* (London, 1997) and Wolfgang Behringer, *Witchcraft Persecutions in Bavaria* (Cambridge, 1997).

5 International Relations and Warfare

The best study of diplomatic sixteenth-century procedure remains Garrett Mattingly, *Renaissance Diplomacy* (London, 1955), while Gaston Zeller, in the second volume of *Histoire des Relations Internationales* (ed. Pierre Renouvin, Paris, 1953) provides a good survey of international relations in this period. R. B. Wernham has studied the evolution of Elizabethan foreign policy in his *Before the Armada* (London, 1966) and provides an overall view of the subject in *The Making of Elizabethan Foreign Policy, 1558–1603* (Berkeley, 1980). He carries his story to a conclusion in *The Return of the Armadas. The Last Years of the Elizabethan War against Spain, 1595–1603* (Oxford, 1994). I found particularly helpful, in spite of its obvious bias, Kervyn de Lettenhove, *Les Huguenots et les Gueux* (6 vols, Bruges, 1883–1888). Bernard de Meester, *Le Saint-Siège et les Troubles des Pays* (Louvain, 1934) is informative on papal policy towards the Netherlands, while Charles Wilson, *Queen Elizabeth and the Revolt of the Netherlands* (London, 1970) traces the grudging evolution of Elizabeth's policies towards the Dutch rebels. De Lamar Jensen, *Diplomacy and Dogmatism: Bernardino de Mendoza and the French Catholic League* (Cambridge, Mass., 1964) shows a famous Spanish ambassador at work. John Bossy, *Giordano Bruno and the Embassay Affair* (New Haven and London, 1991) is an exciting piece of detective work into the murky world of sixteenth-century espionage.

In recent years, warfare, both on land and sea, has interested sixteenth-century historians more than diplomacy. A vivid introduction to the subject is provided by J. R. Hale, *War and Society in Renaissance Europe, 1450–1620* (London, 1985). The so-called 'military revolution' of 1560–1660 has been the subject of intense historical debate since the idea was first launched in 1956 by Michael Roberts in an inaugural lecture, subsequently reprinted with some amendments in his *Essays in Swedish History* (London, 1967). Leading contributions to the debate are reprinted in Clifford J. Rogers (ed.), *The Military Revolution Debate* (Boulder, 1995), while Geoffrey Parker, as a principal participant, provides a sweeping survey of military innovation and the rise of the West between 1500 and 1800 in his *The Military Revolution* (Cambridge, 1988).

Geoffrey Parker's *The Army of Flanders and the Spanish Road, 1567–1659* (Cambridge, 1972) is a path-breaking account of the logistical problems facing the Spaniards in their war against the rebels in the Netherlands, and he explores further aspects of the problem in his collection of essays, *Spain and the Netherlands, 1559–1659* (London, 1979). His *The Grand Strategy of Philip II* (New Haven and London, 1998) advances the hypothesis that Philip possessed a 'grand strategy', and then proceeds to analyse its conceptualization and execution on the basis of a wealth of archival information and the findings of modern strategic and management studies. I. A. A. Thompson, *War and Government in Habsburg Spain, 1560–1620* (London, 1976) is an impressive account of the way in which Spain tried to organize and run its military machine. James B. Wood sheds much light on the military difficulties confronting the French monarchy in his *The King's Army: Warfare, Soldiers and Society during the Wars of Religion, 1562–1576* (Cambridge, 1996).

Understanding of the character and problems of naval warfare in the Mediterranean, on which Braudel has much to say, has been greatly enhanced by John F. Guilmartin, *Gunpowder and Galleys: Changing Technology and Mediterranean Warfare at Sea in the Sixteenth Century* (Cambridge, 1974). Andrew Hess sets the battle of Lepanto into context in 'The Battle of Lepanto and its Place in Mediterranean History', *Past and Present*, 57 (1972), pp. 71–87. The fourth centenary in 1988 of the failure of Philip II's 'Enterprise of England' generated a wealth of studies in a field hitherto dominated by Garrett Mattingly, *The Defeat of the Spanish Armada* (London, 1959), which remains unrivalled for its readability and for its skill in pulling together the diplomatic and political threads in the months preceding the sailing of the fleet. Attention is drawn in particular to Colin Martin and Geoffrey Parker, *The Spanish Armada* (London, 1988), which makes use of the results of underwater archaeology, and to the collection of essays by British and Spanish historians in M. J. Rodríguez-Salgado and Simon Adams (eds), *England, Spain and the Gran Armada, 1585–1604* (Edinburgh, 1991). Peter Pierson, *Commander of the Armada: The Seventh Duke of Medina Sidonia* (New Haven and London, 1989) uses new archival information to explore the background and career of a reluctant commander.

For piracy and its impact in the Atlantic and Mediterranean respectively, see K. R. Andrews, *Elizabethan Privateering* (Cambridge, 1964), and Alberto Tenenti, *Piracy and the Decline of Venice, 1580–1615* (London, 1967).

6   Biographies

One of the best approaches to later sixteenth-century Europe is through biographies of leading figures. Serious historical biography went into relative eclipse in the decades following the Second World War, but this seems now to be drawing to an end. Philip II, for example, has recently received considerable biographical attention, some of it stimulated by the fourth centenary, in 1998, of his death. Braudel's *Mediterranean* still gives an incomparable picture of the king, but recent work has added much new detail. Peter Pierson, *Philip II of Spain* (London, 1975) provides a good starting-point for the study of the king and his reign. Geoffrey Parker, *Philip II* (Boston-Toronto, 1978, and London 1979) is particularly fresh on the more personal aspects of Philip's life, while he devotes close attention to his decision-making processes in his *The Grand Strategy of Philip II* (see section 5, above). The most recent biography in English, Henry Kamen, *Philip II of Spain* (New Haven and London, 1997) is enriched by numerous quotations from Philip's papers, but goes too far in its attempts to redress what it regards as an excessively negative image of the king. Philip's first favourite, Ruy Gómez de Silva, prince of Eboli, is the subject of a recent short biography by James M. Boyden, *The Courtier and the King* (Berkeley and London, 1995), while William S. Maltby has written a life of his rival, the Duke of Alba, in *Alba: A Biography of Fernando Alvarez de Toledo, Third Duke of Alba, 1507–1582* (Berkeley, Los Angeles, London, 1983). A. W. Lovett looks at Philip at work through a study of one of his secretaries, in *Philip II and Mateo Vázquez de Leca: the Government of Spain, 1572–1592* (Geneva, 1977). Gregorio Marañón, *Antonio Pérez* (London, 1954) is an abridged English translation of a fascinating study which tells us almost as much about the king as about its nominal subject, the most notorious of Philip's secretaries. The 'great' biography of Philip II, however, remains unwritten, and may well be unwriteable.

While Philip II and his Spain dominate the history of Europe in the second half of the sixteenth century, there are many noteworthy biographical studies of other significant figures of the period, several of them written in the earlier part of this century. The list that follows is inevitably very arbitrary: James Brodrick, *Robert Bellarmine* (London, 1961); David Buisseret, *Henry IV* (London, 1984); Gaetano Cozzi, *Il Doge Nicolò Contarini* (Venice, 1959); Ivan Cloulas, *Cathérine de Médicis* (Paris, 1979), but Catherine still awaits a really satisfactory biography; Léon Van Der Essen, *Alexandre Farnèse* (5 vols, Brussels, 1933–7) – a superb study of Farnese as a commander; R. J. W. Evans, *Rudolf II and his World* (Oxford, 1973); H. O. Evennett, *The Cardinal of Lorraine and the Council of Trent* (Cambridge, 1930); Paul F. Geisendorf, *Théodore de Bèze* (Geneva, 1949; 2nd ed., 1967); Gordon Griffiths, *William of Hornes, Lord of Hèze and the Revolt of the Netherlands, 1576–1580* (Berkeley, 1954) – useful for the 'Malcontent' movement; Henri Hauser, *François De La Noue, 1531–1591* (Paris, 1892) – an admirable study of a Huguenot leader; Mack P. Holt, *The Duke of Anjou and the Politique Struggle during the Wars of Religion* (Cambridge, 1986); A. De Hubner, *Sixte-Quint* (2 vols, Paris, 1870) – not worthy of its tempestuous subject; Raoul Patry, *Philippe Du Plessis Mornay* (Paris, 1933); Nancy L. Roelker, *Queen of Navarre: Jeanne d'Albret, 1528–1572* (Cambridge, Mass., 1968); Jonathan Spence, *The Memory Palace of Matteo Ricci* (New York, 1984) – an ingenious study of a famous Jesuit's encounter with China; P. O. De Törne, *Don Juan d'Autriche et les Projects de Conquête de l'Angleterre* (Helsinki, 1915); M. Van Durme, *El Cardenal Granvela* (Spanish translation from the Flemish, Barcelona, 1957); C. V. Wedgwood, *William the Silent* (London, 1944; repr. 1989).

7   Histories of States and Regions

The following is a list (confined to continental Europe) of a number of particularly useful studies of states and regions in the second half of the sixteenth century.

France

Mack Holt, *The French Wars of Religion, 1562–1629* (Cambridge, 1995) is a balanced summary of recent research, with many suggestions for further reading in English, while Mark Greengrass, *The French Reformation* (Oxford, 1987) is an excellent introductory essay on French religious developments. Two classic French works, Lucien Romier, *Le Royaume de Cathérine de Médicis* (2 vols, Paris, 1922) and H. Drouot, *Mayenne et la Bourgogne, 1587–1596* (2 vols, Paris, 1937) remain fundamental to a study of the period, and to these should be added another monumental monograph, Denis Crouzet, *Les guerriers de Dieu* (2 vols, Paris, 1990), which counterbalances the political and social interpretation of Drouot by interpreting violence as a religious phenomenon.

For a comprehensive survey of developments in France during the religious wars, see J. H. M. Salmon, *Society in Crisis: France in the Sixteenth Century* (London, 1975), to which should be added his volume of essays, *Renaissance and Revolt. Essays in the Intellectual and Social History of Early Modern France* (Cambridge, 1987), which includes a social analysis of the Paris Sixteen. The essays in Natalie Zemon Davis, *Society and Culture in Early Modern France*, cited above in section 4 under the discussion of popular culture, provide many insights into the religious and social climate of France in this period. Donald R. Kelley, *The Beginning of Ideology: Consciousness and Society in the French Reformation* (Cambridge, 1981) uses contemporary pamphlets to trace the development of a revolutionary Protestant 'ideology'.

N. M. Sutherland, *Catherine de Medici and the Ancien Regime* (Historical Association pamphlet, London, 1966) remains a useful brief introduction to a period she has studied in detail, notably in *The Massacre of St Bartholomew and the European Conflict, 1559–1572* (London, 1973), a close political and diplomatic narrative in which she seeks to absolve Catherine from blame for the initial attack on Coligny. Her *French Secretaries of State in the Age of Catherine de Medici* (London, 1962) studies an important aspect of royal administration. For the military aspects of the conflict see in particular James B. Wood, *The King's Army*, cited in section 5, on warfare. Stuart Carroll looks at the Guise faction and its activities in Normandy in his *Noble Power during the French Wars of Religion* (Cambridge, 1998), and Philip Benedict, *Rouen during the Wars of Religion* (Cambridge, 1981) is an illuminating account of the impact of civil strife on a major city, with constant reference to developments in other parts of the country.

For an admirable account of Henry IV and the restoration of order, see Mark Greengrass, *France in the Age of Henry IV* (2nd ed., London, 1995). Henry's abjuration of Calvinism is the subject of Michael Wolfe's monograph, *The Conversion of Henry IV: Politics, Power and Religious Belief in*

Early Modern France (Cambridge, Mass., 1993), and his strategies for recovering the obedience and loyalty of the cities are analysed by S. Annette Finley-Crosthwaite, *Henry IV and the Towns* (Cambridge, 1999). C. Vivanti, *Lotta politica e pace religiosa in Francia fra Cinque e Seicento* (Turin, 1963) gives important insights into the final phase of the civil wars and the reign of Henry IV, for which also see the classic study by R. Mousnier, *L'Assassinat d'Henri IV* (Paris, 1964), translated as *The Assassination of Henry IV: The Tyrannicide Problem and the Consolidation of Absolute Monarchy in the Early Seventeenth Century* (London, 1973).

Germany and the Empire

Hajo Holborn, *A History of Modern Germany. The Reformation* (London, 1965) remains a good general survey, and can be complemented by Bob Scribner, *Germany. A New Social and Economic History, 1450–1630* (London, 1996). F. L. Carsten, *Princes and Parliaments in Germany* (Oxford, 1959) is essential for constitutional developments. Claus-Peter Clasen, *The Palatinate in European History, 1559–1660* (Oxford, 1969) is a valuable booklet on one of Europe's trouble-spots. For the Empire, R. J. W. Evans, *The Making of the Habsburg Monarchy* (Oxford, 1979) is fundamental. See also R. J. W. Evans and T. V. Thomas (eds), *Crown, Church and Estates. Central European Politics in the Sixteenth and Seventeenth Centuries* (London, 1991). For the reigns of Maximilian II and Rudolph II, Bohdan Chudoba, *Spain and the Empire, 1519–1643* (Chicago, 1952) is still worth consulting.

Italy

A general survey can be found in in vol. 2 of *Storia d'Italia*, ed. Nino Valeri (Turin, 1959). Eric Cochrane's *Italy, 1530–1630* (London, 1988) was left unfinished at the time of his death, and lacks the coherence of his *Florence in the Forgotten Centuries, 1527–1800* (Chicago and London, 1973). William J. Bouwsma, *Venice and the Defense of Republican Liberty* (Berkeley and Los Angeles, 1968) is a fine study, and can be read in conjunction with Brian Pullan's *Rich and Poor in Renaissance Venice* (section 3, above) to gain an understanding of the elements that contributed to the survival of a republic in a strongly monarchical age. M. E. Mallett and J. R. Hale's impressive *The Military Organization of a Renaissance State: Venice, c. 1400–1617* (Cambridge, 1984) throws new light on the relationship of Venetian myth and reality from a military angle.

Italian historians are now re-evaluating the period of Spanish dominion of the peninsula, a field in which H. G. Koenigsberger was a pioneer with his *The Government of Sicily under Philip II of Spain* (London, 1951; amended ed. *The Practice of Empire*, Ithaca, 1969). The revisionist work currently being undertaken in Italy still has to find its way into English-language literature, but two recent studies provide valuable insights into the character and consequences of Spanish rule in Naples: Thomas Astarita, *The Continuity of Feudal Power. The Caracciolo di Brienza in Spanish Naples* (Cambridge, 1992) and Antonio Calabria, *The Cost of Empire. The Finances of the Kingdom of Naples in the time of Spanish Rule* (Cambridge, 1991).

The Netherlands

The volume in the *Oxford History of Early Modern Europe* by Jonathan Israel, *The Dutch Republic: Its Rise, Greatness and Fall, 1477–1806* (Oxford, 1995) is an impressive achievement. Offering firm answers to many vexed questions, it provides an essential point of reference. For a long time P. Geyl, *The Revolt of the Netherlands* (London, 1932) held the field as the standard account of the revolt in English, and it still makes good reading, but the years have taken their toll. Unlike Geyl, Geoffrey Parker, *The Dutch Revolt* (London, 1977) gives proper weight to the Spanish side of the story, which also provides the theme of his essays, *Spain and the Netherlands*, and his *The Army of Flanders and the Spanish Road*, both cited in section 5 on warfare. See also the biographical studies of Alexander Farnese and William the Silent, cited in section 6. For the religious background and character of the revolt, see the sensitive essays by Alastair Duke collected in his *Reformation and Revolt in the Low Countries* (London, 1990), and Phyllis Mack Crew, *Calvinist Preaching and Iconoclasm in the Netherlands, 1544–1569* (Cambridge, 1978). Robert S. DuPlessis, *Lille and the Dutch Revolt* (Cambridge, 1991) studies the case of a city in which public order was preseved. The theoretical justifications of the revolt are discussed by Martin Van Gelderen, *The Political Thought of the Dutch Revolt, 1559–1590* (Cambridge, 1992) and can be studied in two collections of texts that have been made available in translation: E. H. Kossmann and A. F. Mellink, *Texts Concerning the Revolt of the Netherlands* (Cambridge, 1974), and Martin Van Gelderen, *The Dutch Revolt* (Cambridge, 1993). For a modern reprint, edited by H. Wansink, of the 1581 English translation of William of Orange's *Apology*, see *The Apologie of Prince William of Orange Against the Proclamation of the King of Spaine* (Leiden, 1969). Simon Schama, *The Embarrassment of Riches* (New York, 1987) is a bravura account of the evolution of Dutch Golden Age culture.

The Ottoman Empire

Halil Inalcik, *The Ottoman Empire. The Classical Age, 1300–1600* (London, 1973) provides a general survey, and further information is available in Metin Kunt and Christine Woodhead (eds.), *Süleyman the Magnificent and his Age. The Ottoman Empire in the Early Modern World* (London, 1995). Braudel's *Mediterranean* offers many insights into the confrontation between the Ottoman and Spanish Empires, which long ago inspired the parallel surveys of Leopold Von Ranke, *The Ottoman and the Spanish Empires* (Eng. trans, London, 1843). Much still needs to be done on sixteenth-century Ottoman history if the parallels and contrasts are to be developed. Andrew Hess, however, in *The Forgotten Frontier. A History of the Sixteenth-Century Ibero-African Frontier* (Chicago and London, 1978) gives an illuminating account of the expansion of the Ottoman Empire into North Africa, and of the confontation of the two civilizations on the borderlands of empire. Chapter 9 of H. Inalcik's volume of essays, *The Ottoman Empire: Conquest, Organization, Economy* (Variorum reprints, London, 1978) is a brief account of the Lepanto campaign written from Ottoman sources. Dorothy M. Vaughan, *Europe and the Turk* (Liverpool, 1954; 2nd ed., 1967) is a careful survey of Turkish relations with the West, and W. E. D. Allen's booklet, *Problems of Turkish Power in the Sixteenth Century* (London, Central Asian Research Centre, 1963) is illuminating about events on the Ottoman Empire's Asian borders.

Poland and Eastern Europe

For an introduction, see Norman Davies, *God's Playground* (vol. 1, *The Origins to 1795*, Oxford, 1981), and *The Cambridge History of Poland* (2 vols, Cambridge, 1941). Karin Maag (ed.) *The Reformation in Eastern and Central Europe* (Aldershot, 1997) is a collection of essays on religious change in different East European states. On the Polish election I have used especially H. De Noailles, *Henri de Valois et la Pologne en 1572* (3 vols Paris, 1867) and P. Champion, *Henri III, roi de Pologne* (Paris, 1943). Various aspects of the life of Báthory are studied in *Etienne Báthory, Roi de Pologne, Prince de Transylvanie* (Cracow, 1935). William H. McNeill, *Europe's Steppe Frontier* (Chicago, 1964) is a lively survey of problems and developments in eastern Europe, and to this should be added *East Central Europe in Transition* (cited in section 3, above). Jerome Blum, *Lord and Peasant in Russia* (Princeton, 1961) surveys economic and social developments in Muscovy.

Scandinavia

The Baltic region is comprehensively surveyed in David Kirby, *Northern Europe in the Early Modern Period: The Baltic World, 1492–1772* (London, 1990). For the Reformation and attempts at Counter-Reformation, see O. P. Grell (ed.), *The Scandinavian Reformation: From Evangelical Movement to Institutionalized Reform* (Cambridge, 1995), and O. Garstein, *Rome and the Counter-Reformation in Scandinavia*, vol. 1 (Oslo, 1963). For Swedish history, Michael Roberts, *The Early Vasas: A History of Sweden, 1523–1611* (Cambridge, 1968), and *The Swedish Imperial Experience, 1560–1718* (Cambridge, 1979), are indispensable.

Spain

For general background to the period, see John Lynch, *Spain, 1516–1598: From Nation State to Empire* (Oxford, 1991); J. H. Elliott, *Imperial Spain, 1469–1716* (London, 1963 and subsequent reprints); Henry Kamen, *Spain, 1469–1714: A Society of Conflict* (London, 1983). James Casey, *Early Modern Spain. A Social History* (London and New York, 1999) is a perceptive and up-to-date survey of Early Modern Spanish society, with much new illustrative detail. Discussion of several significant topics, including the question of Spain's 'decline', can be found in the following volumes of essays: J. H. Elliott, *Spain and its World, 1500–1700* (New Haven and London, 1989); Richard L. Kagan and Geoffrey Parker, *Spain, Europe and the Atlantic World* (Cambridge, 1995); I. A. A. Thompson, *War and Society in Habsburg Spain* (Aldershot, 1991) and *Crown and Cortes* (Aldershot, 1993);

and Henry Kamen, *Crisis and Change in Early Modern Spain* (Aldershot, 1993).

The transition from the Empire of Charles V to the *monarquía española* of Philip II is richly documented by M. J. Rodríguez-Salgado, *The Changing Face of Empire; Charles V, Philip II and Habsburg Authority, 1551–1559* (Cambridge, 1988). For biographical studies of Philip II and some of his closest advisers, see the relevant paragraph in section 6, above (Biographies), and for Spanish military organization and the Armada campaign, section 7 on warfare. Richard Kagan, *Lucrecia's Dreams: Politics and Prophecy in Sixteenth-Century Spain* (Berkeley and Los Angeles, 1990) uses the dreams of a visionary to explore the opposition to Philip's policies. There is no monograph in English on Philip's acquisition of Portugal, but see E. W. Bovill's readable account of Portugal's disaster in Africa which made it possible, *The Battle of Alcazar* (London, 1952) and J. H. Elliott, 'The Spanish Monarchy and the Kingdom of Portugal' in *Conquest and Coalescence*, ed. Mark Greengrass.

There is now a large literature on sixteenth-century Spanish America. J. H. Parry, *The Spanish Seaborne Empire* (London, 1966) remains a useful introduction. See also vols 1 and 2 of *The Cambridge History of Latin America*, ed. Leslie Bethell (Cambridge, 1984), and the lucid survey in the relevant chapters of Peter Bakewell, *A History of Latin America* (Oxford, 1997).

Index

Abjuration, Edict of (1581) 197
administrative systems 47–51, 119, 120
Aerschot, duke of 84, 177, 191
Africa 130
agriculture 25–8, 40–1, 252–4
Alba, Fernando Alvarez de Toledo, duke of
    Cateau-Cambrésis 5
    disgrace of 182
    Eboli, prince of 46
    England 113, 139
    French aid for Protestants 144–5, 146,
        152–3
    meeting with French court at Bayonne
        (1565) 80
    Netherlands 92–3, 108–12, 140–4,
        152–3, 172–3, 174
    Portuguese campaign 187–8
Albert, archduke 243, 244, 247, 257
Albert of Brandenburg 14
Albert V, duke of Bavaria 56, 95, 105,
    167, 168
Alcázarquivir, battle of (1578) 130, 186,
    187, 204
Alençon, Francis, duke of 171
    attempts to supplant Henry III 169
    Azores 189–90
    Coligny 146
    death 206
    Elizabeth of England 160
    Huguenot-*politique* alliance 151, 170
    Netherlands 192–3, 195–9
    Poland 155
Alfonso d'Este, duke of Ferrara 255
Algiers 126
Ali Pasha 127
Allen, William 216
Almenara, marquis of 235
Amboise, conspiracy of (1560) 9, 62, 72
Amboise, Edict of (1563) 79, 87
Amboise, Pacification of (1563) 79

Amiens 244, 245
Amsterdam 28, 91, 111, 142
Anabaptism 82, 90, 155
Andelot, François d' 4, 59
Anjou, François, duke of see Alençon,
    duke of
Anjou, Henry, duke of see Henry III
Anne of Saxony 84
anti-Trinitarians 155, 163
Antoine de Bourbon, king of Navarre 44,
    60, 63, 72, 73, 79
Antonio, Dom, prior of Crato 186,
    187–90, 206, 233
Antwerp
    Alençon 198
    Eastern European trade 28–9
    fall to Spanish (1585) 200, 209, 210
    famine (1565–66) 89–90
    loans to Spanish Crown 242
    revolt (1566) 91, 92
    sack of (1576) 176, 180, 183
    Sea Beggars 141
Aragon 53, 234–5
architecture 101, 103
Arias Montano, Benito 265
Arras, treaty of (1579) 193
Arras, Union of (1579) 192
art 100–3
Atlantic trade 29–35
    English privateers 206, 211, 212, 217
    Huguenot fleet 78–9
    Spanish naval power 223–4
Augsburg, banking 28
Augsburg, peace of (1555) 10, 16, 21, 88,
    166, 167–8
Augustus I, elector of Saxony 167
Aumale, duke of 207, 221
Auneau, battle of (1587) 218, 220
Austria
    Estates 54

Ottoman Empire 117, 130
religion 167, 256–9
Azores 189–90, 206, 217
Azpilcueta Navarro, Martín de 37

Babington, Anthony 213
Baltic 14–15, 24–9, 89
banditry 249–52
banking 3, 24, 35, 179–81
Barcelona, silver route 181
Baroque 102–3
Bavaria 56
Bayonne 79–80, 109, 144
Beaulieu, edict of (1576) 170, 171
Beggars 88
Bellarmine, Robert 98, 231–2
Berlaymont, baron of 83, 88
Berwick, treaty of (1586) 213
Besançon 180–1
Beza, Theodore
aid to Huguenots 75
Catherine de Medici 73
Coligny 81
colloquy of Poissy 63–4
and Condé 72
Geneva Academy 16
hymns 78
nobility 60
right of resistance 72, 74, 149–50
Blois, Estates of 170–1
Blois, treaty of (1572) 139
Bodin, Jean 37, 39, 57, 151, 231, 263–4, 266
Bohemia 54, 166
Bohemian Brethren 155, 166
Bolivia 31
Boniface VIII 231
Borromeo, Charles, cardinal 98–9, 101, 104, 107, 169
Bourbon, house of
clientage network 46
power over monarchy 44
Protestantism 59, 60, 76–7
rivalry with Guises 73
see also Antoine de Bourbon; Condé; Henry IV
Brabant
Alba 111, 152
Calvinism 82, 177, 192
deposition of Philip II 197
ecclesiastical reorganization 85
Farnese 200
Braganza, duchess of 186
Brandenburg 54
Brederode, Henry, count of 88, 92, 93
Brès, Guy de 17, 82, 92
Brill 135–6, 139–40, 210
Brisson, Barnabé 239
Brittany 233, 234, 241, 242, 247
Bruno, Giordano 265

Brussels 191, 200
Buchanan, George 260
Burghley, William Cecil, lord
administrative machinery 49
aid to Dutch Protestants 138, 144, 209
aid to Huguenots 209
financial reserve 211
rising of the northern earls 113
Scotland 8, 9
Spain 205, 243
Burgundy 256
Bussy-Leclerc, Jean 239
Buys, Paulus 209

Cadiz 217, 244
Cajetan, cardinal 229–30
Calais 4, 5–6, 243, 247
calendars 262
Calvin, John 16, 60, 71–2
Calvinism 16–23, 267
'democratic element' 70–1
England 175–6, 267
France see Huguenots
Geneva 16–17, 20
Germany 166–8
literacy 18–19
literature 17–18
and Lutheranism 163–4
Netherlands 17, 18, 82–3, 87–93, 110, 141, 174–7, 191–2
nobility 59–61, 71, 72, 76
Poland 155
response to persecution 71–3, 75, 149–50
St Bartholomew, massacre of 149–50
scholasticism 264
Scotland 17, 267
Sweden 164, 267
United Provinces 267
see also Huguenots
Campagna 250–1
Campion, Edmund 204
Canisius, Peter 167
Caribbean 30, 33, 78–9, 113, 206
Carlos, Don 44, 108, 121–2
Carranza, Bartolomé de, archbishop of Toledo 106
Cassander, George 164–5, 166
Casimir, John, Count Palatine 80, 192, 206
Castile
bankruptcy 248–9
Cortes 52–3, 116, 234
financial problems 178–80
Moriscos 124–5
New World 29–30
pícaros 250
revenues 12
Sea Beggars 172
taxation 179–80, 234

Catalonia   53
Cateau-Cambrésis, peace of (1559)   3–7,
    8, 9, 13, 16–17, 30
Catherine de Medici, queen of France
    attempts at religious reconciliation   73
    clientage network   46
    and Coligny   145–7, 148
    Coligny's plans to aid Dutch
        Protestants   143–4, 144–7
    court ceremonial   43
    death   226–7
    death of Henry II   7
    Estates-General   52
    Habsburg-Valois struggle   9–10
    Henry of Guise   221
    Henry III   169–70
    Huguenot-*politique* alliance   151
    marriages of children   136–7
    Mary Queen of Scots   138–9
    Mary Stuart   9
    Netherlands   109, 143–7, 160, 196
    Poissy, colloquy of   63–4
    Poland   157, 159–60, 161
    Portuguese throne   186–7, 189–90
    regent to Charles IX   63
    religious reconciliation   62–3, 73–4, 87,
        136
    restricted power   164
    royal progress (1564–5)   79–80
    St Bartholomew, massacre of   144,
        145–9, 151–3
    third war of religion   80
    vulnerability of   44, 45
    war of religion   79, 80
Catherine, infanta of Spain   215
Catholic Reformation   94–104
Cecil, William see   Burghley, lord
censorship
    Calvinist literature   18
    see also   Index
Cervantes, Miguel de   128, 264
Charles, cardinal of Bourbon
    (Charles X)   208, 225, 226, 227–8,
        230
Charles Emmanuel, duke of Savoy   44,
    215, 226, 233
Charles IX, king of France
    aid for Dutch Protestants   137–8,
        143–4, 145, 146–7
    clergy   52
    Coligny   147
    death   160–1
    Guises   62–3
    Holy Roman Empire   159–60
    marriage   136, 137
    officials   219
    royal progress (1564–5)   79–80
    St Bartholomew, massacre of   147–9
    vulnerability of   44
    wars of religion   74

Charles IX, king of Sweden (duke of
    Södermanland)   165, 260–1
Charles V, Emperor   10, 11
    administrative system   48
    Cortes   53
    England   4
    finance for war   33
    Netherlands   54, 85, 90
    Ottoman Empire   13
    religion   16, 18
Charles X see   Charles, cardinal of
    Bourbon
Chastel, Jean   240
Châtillon, house of   59, 60
Châtillon, Odet de   59
Christopher, duke Palatine   160
cities, growth of   26
Clément, Jacques   227
Clement VIII   230–1, 245
    Edict of Nantes   246
    Ferdinand II   259
    Henry IV   240, 241, 255–6
    Papal States   251
    Sweden   260
clientage system   45–7, 76
Coligny, Gaspard de, admiral   69
    aid for Dutch Protestants   140, 143–7
    anti-Spanish plans   137–9, 203
    attempted murder of   145
    and Catherine de Medici   73
    character of   80–1
    murder of duke of Guise   79
    Protestantism   4, 59, 77, 267
    reconciliation policies   136–9
    St Bartholomew, massacre of   144–5,
        147–8
Coligny, Louise de   199
Cologne   168
Commendone, cardinal   155, 156
composite monarchy   42
Compromise (of 1566)   88–9, 91, 110
Condé, Louis I de Bourbon, prince of
    army   78
    Catherine de Medici   73–4
    death   80
    Francis II   62
    international assistance   75–6
    meeting with Beza at Nérac   72
    Protestantism   59, 60
    religious wars   79, 80
    support of Calvinist churches   76–8
Contarini, Nicolò   255
Convocation Diet (1573)   157–8
Corfu   125
corruption   50–1
corsairs   116, 118–19, 123, 126, 131, 137,
        189
Corsica   7
Corso, Sampiero   7
Counter-Reformation   56, 99–114, 123

Coutras, battle of (1587) 218
Crete 125
Cromwell, Thomas 49
currency, debasement of 39
Cyprus 125-9

Danzig 28, 162
Dathenus, Peter 177, 191
Dauphiné 170, 246
Day of the Barricades 221-2, 225
Denmark 14-15, 262
Desmond, earl of 204
Dialogue d'entre le Maheustre et le
    Manant 237-40
Djerba 115-16
Dohna, baron von 218
Donà, Leonardo 255
Dordrecht 142
Doria, Andrea 35
Douai, university of 85
Drake, Sir Francis 114, 189, 211
    Cadiz 217
    death 243
    Portuguese expedition (1589) 233
    Spanish Armada 222, 223
Dreux, battle of 79
Du Plessis-Mornay, Philippe 145, 177
    conversion to Protestantism 59
    Henry IV's renunciation of
        Protestantism 241
    on Lepanto 138
    Protestantism 267
    Vindiciae contra Tyrannos 150

Eastern Europe 25-8
Eboli, princess of 185
Eboli, Ruy Gómez de Silva, prince of 152
    and Alba 46, 112
    Carlos, Don 122
    Cateau-Cambrésis 5
    conciliation policy 108
    death 172, 182
    England 113
economy 24-41
Edinburgh, treaty of (1560) 9
education 22-3, 262-3
Egmont, Lamoral, count of
    arrest and execution 110
    conflict with Granvelle 85
    Council of State 86
    Gueux 88
    Netherlands Council of State 83, 84
    religious toleration 87
    revolt (1566) 92
El Greco 106
El-Mansur 189
Elboeuf, duke of 207
Elizabeth of Austria 136, 137
Elizabeth, queen of England
    and Alençon 160, 196

anti-Spanish alliance with France 138-9
Calvinism 175-6
Cateau-Cambrésis 4-6
Catholic plots against 204-6
clientage networks 46
court ceremonial 43
German Protestantism 167
Henry of Anjou 136
Huguenots 75, 209
Ireland 204
Mary Queen of Scots 213
nationalism 264
Netherlands 137, 144, 195, 196, 200,
    206, 209-11
parliament 54, 56
Portuguese throne 189
religion 17, 58, 61
Scotland 8-9
Sea Beggars 139
Sixtus V 215, 216
Spain 112-14, 205-6, 211, 218, 233-4,
    243-4
'State' 49
vulnerability of 44, 45
Elizabeth of Valois 7, 79, 122, 195
Emden 28
Emmanuel Philibert, duke of Savoy
    Calvinism 20
    Cateau-Cambrésis 6
    marriage 7
    Piedmont 54-5
    Portuguese throne 186
    and Spain 11
    vulnerability of 45
England
    administrative machinery 49
    American colonies 211
    Cateau-Cambrésis 4-7
    cloth trade 28
    composite monarchy 42
    court ceremonial 43
    Don John of Austria's invasion
        plans 183-4
    France 72, 75-6, 112, 209
    Ireland 203-4, 243-4
    Jesuits 204
    Julian calendar 262
    Mary Queen of Scots 112-13
    Mediterranean trade 252-3, 253-4
    nationalism 264
    Netherlands 108, 111-12, 137, 144,
        195, 196, 200, 206, 209-11, 212
    parliament 54, 55-6
    Philip II 112-14
    Portugal 189, 233-4
    privateers 206, 211, 212, 253-4
    Protestantism 17, 61, 175-6, 267
    Ridolfi plot (1571) 113
    rising of the northern earls 69, 113
    Roman Catholicism 113, 203-6

England (*Cont.*)
  St Bartholomew, massacre of 152
  Scotland 8–9, 213
  Sea Beggars 139
  Sixtus V 216
  Spain 211–14, 216–18, 222–4, 243–4
  vulnerability of monarchy 44, 45
Epernon, duke of 207, 208, 218, 220,
  221, 222
Eric XIV, king of Sweden 14–15, 44, 45,
  50, 164
Ernest, archduke of Austria 155, 156,
  242–3
Escobedo, Juan de 183–4
Espinosa, cardinal 123
Essex, Robert Devereux, earl of 234, 244
Estates 51–7, 116, 170–1, 234
Este, Cesare d' 255
Estienne, Henri 17
Estonia 14–15
Euldj Ali, king of Algiers 126, 128, 129,
  178

famine 250, 253–4
Farnese, Alexander, prince of Parma
  death 236
  France 228, 229, 233, 236
  marriage 88
  Netherlands 184, 186, 190–6, 200, 212
  Piacenza 47
  Spanish Armada 217–18, 222, 223, 224
Farnese, cardinal 102, 135, 215
Farnese, house of 46–7
  see also Margaret of Parma
Farnese, Ottavio 47
Farnese, Ranuccio 186
Ferdinand I, Emperor 10, 13, 21, 95, 96
Ferdinand II, Emperor 259
Ferrara 255–6
Fez 186, 189
Fitzgerald, James Fitzmaurice 204
Flanders 242–3
  Alba 111, 152
  Calvinism 17, 82, 91, 177, 192
  deposition of Philip II 197
  Farnese 193, 200
  revolt 1566 90, 91
  tercios 84, 86, 93
Florence 6, 116
flota 32
Flushing 140, 210
Fontana, Domenico 215
food
  inflation 37–40
  see also grain
Formula of Concord (1580) 167
France 207–8, 209, 228, 229–30
  administrative machinery 48–9, 51, 219
  Azores 189–90
  bankruptcy of monarchy 3, 33

Calvinism see Huguenots
Caribbean 30, 33
Cateau-Cambrésis 3–7
Charles Emmanuel of Savoy 226
clientage networks 46
composite monarchy 42
Corsica 7
Council of Trent 21, 94–5, 97
court ceremonial 42–3
croquants 240–1
Day of the Barricades 221–2, 225
Edict of Amboise 79
Edict of Mantes (1591) 245
Edict of Nantes (1598) 245–7
Edict of Poitiers (1577) 245, 246
Edict of Union (1588) 225, 226
England 8–9, 138–9
Estates-General 51–2, 170–1
Gallicanism 62, 97, 216, 231–2
Henry IV 229–41
inflation 37, 39, 41
Italian territories 6–7, 9
January Edict (1592) 64, 73
Jesuits 232–3, 240, 256
League (1576) 170–1
Netherlands 111, 137–9, 143–7, 192,
  195–9, 206–8
papal power 231–2
parlements 52
Polish throne 157, 159
politiques 87–8
religious toleration 62–5, 169–71
Roman Law 56–7
St Bartholomew, massacre of 135–6,
  144–53
Scotland 8–9
Spain 137–9, 218, 229–34, 241–7
taxation 52, 218–19
trade 24–5
vulnerability of monarchy 44, 45
wars of religion 69, 71–81, 112, 136,
  149, 169–71, 209, 218–22
William of Orange 160
Franche-Comté 10, 22, 84–5, 86
Francis II, king of France 7–8, 9, 44, 52,
  56, 62
Frederick II, king of Denmark 15
Frederick III, Elector Palatine 17, 75, 80,
  109, 166
French Reformed Church 76–8
  see also Huguenots
Fuentes, count of 236, 243
Fugger family 24, 35, 180

galeones 32
Gallicanism 62, 97, 216, 231–2
Gallio, Ptolemy 105
Gembloux, battle of (1578) 184, 191
Geneva 16–17, 20
  Alba's campaign 109

Huguenots 75, 76–7
  nobility and Calvinism 59
  response to persecution 71–2
  right of resistance 149–50
  St Bartholomew, massacre of 149–50
Geneva Academy 16–17, 22, 59
Genlis, seigneur de 143
Genoa
  bankers to Philip II 35, 179–81, 182, 252
  Corsica 7
  New World trade 32, 35
  Ottoman Empire 116, 127
George, John, elector of Brandenburg 167
Gérard, Balthasar 199
Germany
  Calvinism 166–8
  Council of Trent 94–5, 97
  Diets 55–6
  French religious wars 72, 75
  Julian calendar 262
  Netherlands 108, 160
  religious conflicts 16, 164, 165–8
  St Bartholomew, massacre of 152
  trade 28
Ghent 90–1, 192, 200
Ghent, Pacification of (1576) 176–7, 191, 193
Gilio da Fabriano, Andrea 100–2
gold 30–1, 36
Gonzaga, cardinal 96
Gouda 141
government administration 47–51, 119, 120
grain trade 252–4
Granada 122–5
Granvelle, Antoine Perrenot, cardinal 10
  as adviser to Philip II 185–6
  Cateau-Cambrésis 3–4, 5
  Catholic Reformation 94
  as civil servant 47
  Compromise 89
  death 212
  ecclesiastical reorganization 85–6
  England 206, 212
  Franche-Comté 84–5
  Netherlands 83–4, 86, 92, 108, 112, 190, 191, 194
  Portuguese throne 187–8
  Spanish financial problems 178
Gregorian calendar 262
Gregory XIII
  calendar 262
  election 135
  England 204
  Holy League 128–9
  music 101
  papal nuncios 105
  Papal States 251
  and Philip II 214

re-conversion of Protestant Europe 163
  St Bartholomew, massacre of 148
Gregory XIV 230
Grenville, Sir Richard 211
Groningen 82, 210
Guerrero, Pedro, archbishop of Granada 94–5
Gueux 88; see also Sea Beggars
Guise, house of
  anti-Calvinism 62
  Charles IX 62–3
  clientage network 46
  Coligny 145, 147
  Edict of Beaulieu 170
  Henry of Guise as heir apparent 207–9
  Huguenot-politique alliance 151
  Mary Queen of Scots 8–9
  power over monarchy 44
  rivalry with Bourbons 73
  St Bartholomew, massacre of 144, 145, 148–9
  third religious war (1568–70) 80–1
  see also Lorraine, cardinal of
Guise, Francis, duke of
  accession of Francis II 7–8
  anti-Calvinism 63–5
  death 79, 96
  First War of Religion (1562–63) 79
  murder 144, 145
  Scotland 4
  taking of Paris (1562) 74
Guise, Henry, duke of
  death of 226
  England 204
  as heir apparent 207–9
  League 170
  Nemours treaty 208–9
  Paris League 220–2, 225–7
  and Spanish alliance 218
  Spanish Armada 220–1
  stalemate with Henry of Navarre 171
  wars of religion 209, 218–22
Guise, Louis, cardinal of 226
Gustavus Vasa, king of Sweden 54

Haarlem 152–3
Habsburgs
  Cateau-Cambrésis 3–7
  Estates 54
  Poland 156
  re-Catholicization of northern Europe 256–9
  see also Charles V; Ferdinand I; Matthias; Maximilian II; Philip II; Rudolph II; Spanish Monarchy
Hainault 53, 82, 152, 193
Hamilton, Earl J. 37
Hampton Court, treaty of (1562) 75–6
Hanseatic League 253

Hawkins, John 113, 114, 211, 222, 223, 243
Hembyze, Jan van 191, 200
Henry, cardinal, king of Portugal 186, 187–8
Henry II, king of France 3–7, 9–10, 42–3, 47, 48–9
Henry III, king of France (duke of Anjou)
  Alençon's sovereignty in Netherlands 196, 198
  Coligny 146, 147
  Day of the Barricades 222, 225
  death 227, 229
  death of Henry of Guise 226–7
  Elizabeth of England 136
  Netherlands 196, 198, 200, 206–8
  officials 219
  Paris League 220–2, 225–7
  Poland 153, 155, 157–61
  religious toleration 169–71
  Spanish Armada 218, 220–1, 222
  treaty of Nemours (1585) 208–9
  wars of religion 80, 209, 218–22
Henry IV, king of France (Henry of Navarre) 237–41
  confrontation with Huguenots 245–7
  conversion to Roman Catholicism 230–1, 239–40
  Edict of Nantes (1598) 245–7
  Gallicanism 232
  as heir apparent 206–9
  Henry of Guise 171
  Henry III 227–8
  Huguenots-politiques alliance 170
  Jesuits 256
  marriage 136, 144, 147
  papacy 215, 216, 255–6
  Paris 232–3
  Spain 229–37, 241–7
  Spanish Armada 218
  succession 227–8
  treaty of Nemours 24, 208–9
  wars of religion 209, 218
Henry VIII, king of England 54
Hesse, landgrave of 93
Hèze, William of Hornes, lord of 191–2, 193
Holland
  Anabaptism 82
  Calvinism 174–5
  deposition of Philip II 197
  Leicester, earl of 210
  Pacification of Ghent 176–7
  Sea Beggars 140, 141–3, 152
Holy League 120, 123, 126–9, 135, 181
Holy Roman Empire
  Council of Trent 21, 97
  Estates 54
  Philip II 258
  power of emperor 11

religion 154, 165–8, 256–9
Turkish threat 117–18
see also Austria; Germany
Horn, count of 84, 88, 110
Hosius, cardinal Stanislas 105, 155, 156
Hotman, François 57, 72, 150, 260
Howard of Effingham, Charles Howard, 2nd baron 222
Howard of Effingham, William Howard, 1st baron 5
Huguenots 17–19, 169–71
  Alba's campaign 109
  army 78
  autonomy in southern France 170–1, 219
  Azores 189–90
  conspiracy of Amboise 9
  Dutch Protestants 108, 137–9, 196
  Edict of Amboise 79
  Edict of Nantes (1598) 245–7
  fleet 78–9
  Henry of Anjou as king of Poland 159, 161
  and Henry IV 241, 245–7
  international aid 75–6
  January Edict (1562) 64
  Montpellier 18–19
  New World 114
  nobility 59, 60
  politique alliance 151, 170, 219
  religious wars 72–81, 80–1, 136, 209
  St Bartholomew, massacre of 135–6, 144–53
humanism 102, 103, 264, 265–6
Hungary 54, 117–18, 163, 166

iconoclasm 70, 91–2, 100, 142, 192
Idiáquez, Don Juan de 185, 212, 213–15, 229
Illyricus, Flacius 98, 164, 167
Index 97–8, 99, 256
Indies see New World
inflation 37–41
Innocent IX 230
Inquisition 58, 99, 256, 265
  congregation 256
  Counter-Reformation 99
  Netherlands 85, 87, 88
  Spain 106, 123
Ireland 203–4, 205, 206, 243–4
Isabella Clara Eugenia, infanta of Spain 230, 233, 238, 242, 247
Isabella, Empress 186
Islam 115–31
Italy
  banditry 250–2
  Cateau-Cambrésis 6–7
  conflict between papacy and Philip II 107
  Council of Trent 94–5

inflation 37
  Ottoman Empire 120
  Spain 11–12, 178–9, 181, 215, 255
  Turks 115–16
Ivan IV, tsar of Muscovy 14–15, 27, 157, 159, 162
Ivry, battle of (1590) 232

Jagiello, house of 155, 259
Jagiello, Anne 161
James VI, King of Scotland 204, 213
January Edict (1562) 64, 73
Jarnac, battle of (1569) 80, 157
Jeanne d'Albret, queen of Navarre 60, 81, 137, 140, 231
Jesuits
  Burgundy 256
  and Calvinism 20
  Catholic Reformation 94, 98
  England 204
  France 232–3, 240, 256
  Germany 167
  hostility of Paul IV 102
  membership 256
  Netherlands 85
  Poland 155, 163, 259
  Portugal 187
  Sixtus V 216
  Sweden 165
John of Austria, Don
  England 204
  Morisco revolt 124
  Netherlands 176–7, 182–5, 190, 191–2
  Ottoman Empire 126–7, 128–9
  Poland 155
John III, king of Sweden 162–3, 164–5, 259–60
Joinville, treaty of (1584) 208
Joyeuse, duke of 207, 218
Judaism, Netherlands 88
Julian calendar 262

Kalmar, Statues of (1587) 260
Kazan, Khanate of 14
Khevenhüller, Hans 128
Khlesl, Melchior 257
Knox, John 8, 17, 71, 150

La Marck, William de 139–40
La Noue, François de 140
  clientage networks 45–6
  defeat of the Spanish Armada 224
  inflation 41
  politique alliance 151
  Protestantism 267
  third religious war 81
La Renaudie, Jean de Barry, seigneur de 62, 72
La Rochelle 76, 78–9, 81, 139, 149, 153, 159

La Valette, John de 116
landowners, price rises 40–1
Languedoc 170
Languet, Hubert 150, 195
Laubespine, Claude de 48, 49
Laynez, Diego 64
Le Havre 75–6, 79
League (1576–7) 170–1
League (1584–96) 171, 207–9, 216, 218–22, 232–3
League, Netherlands see Compromise
Leicester, earl of 205–6, 209, 210–11, 252
Lennox, Esmé Stuart, earl of 204, 213
Leo X 18
León, Lucrecia de 224
León, Luis de 265
Lepanto, battle of (1571) 120, 127–8, 138
L'Estoile, Pierre de 233, 238
Levant Company 252
Leyden, siege of (1574) 174
L'Hôpital, Michel de 52, 55, 60–1, 80, 87
Lines of Demarcation 30
Lipsius, Justus 263, 265
literacy, Calvinism and 18–19
literature 100
Lithuania 14
Livonia 14–15, 162
Longjumeau, peace of (1568) 80
'Lords of the Congregation' 8
Lorraine, Charles of Guise, cardinal of 145
  accession of Francis II 7–8
  Cateau-Cambrésis 3–4, 5
  Council of Trent 21, 94, 96
  death 170
  dismissal of L'Hôpital 80
  national council 62
  Poissy, colloquy of 63–4
  St Bartholomew, massacre of 144, 148
  wars of religion 69
Lorraine, duke of 233
Los Vélez, Pedro Fajardo, marquis of 124, 182, 184
Louis, Elector Palatine 167
Louis I de Bourbon, Prince of Condé
  see Condé
Louis of Nassau 93
  alliance with France and Poland at Blamont (1573) 160
  capture of Brill by Sea Beggars 140
  Compromise 88
  death 160
  defeat by Alba (1568) 110
  French aid 137–8
  invasion of Groningen (1568) 139
  invasion of Netherlands (1572) 140–1, 143, 152
  Mook, battle of (1574) 173
  Protestantism 87
  Sea Beggars 139, 140

Lublin, Union of (1569) 14
Luther, Martin 16
Lutheranism
    Bavaria 56
    death of Luther 16
    French wars of religion 73
    Germany 165–8
    influence in Estates 56
    literature 18
    Netherlands 82, 91–2
    Philippists 164
    Poland 155
    scholasticism 264
    Sweden 164–5, 260–1, 267
Lyons 32, 39, 75, 77, 148

Maastricht 193
malaria 250
Malaspina, Germanico 260
Malcontents 192–4
Malta 116–17
Mannerism 100–3
Mansfeld, count 92, 242
Mantes, Edict of (1591) 245
Manuzio, Paolo 98
Margaret of Parma 86
    Franche-Comté 85
    Netherlands 81–2, 83–4, 88–9, 90,
        91–3, 108, 109–10, 190–1
    Piacenza 47
Marguerite of Valois 6, 7, 136, 147
Maria of Portugal 88
Mariana, Juan de 264
Marillac, Charles de, archbishop of
    Vienne 52
Marnix de Sainte Aldegonde, Jean de 59,
    88, 92
Marnix de Sainte Aldegonde, Philippe
    de 59, 88, 141
Marranos 88
Mary of Hungary 84
Mary I, queen of England 4, 44
Mary of Lorraine, queen regent of
    Scotland 4, 8
Mary Queen of Scots
    accession of Francis II 7–8
    alienation of nobility 45
    deposition 69, 71
    English throne 8–9, 112–13, 204–5
    France 4, 7–8, 138–9
    John of Austria 183
    parliament 56
    Philip II 212–14
    trial and execution 213, 214, 216
    vulnerability of 44
Matthias, archduke 184, 191–2, 196–7
Maurice, Elector of Saxony 84
Maurice of Nassau 236
Maximilian, archduke 257, 258, 259
Maximilian II, Emperor

    acceptance as king of the Romans 96
    Netherlands 112, 174
    Ottoman Empire 117–18
    Poland 156–7, 161–2
    religion 106, 136, 164, 165–6
Mayenne, Charles, duke of 207, 227, 232,
    233, 237–8, 239, 241, 256
Medici, Cosimo de, grand duke of
    Tuscany 6, 11
Medici, Ferdinand de, grand duke of
    Tuscany 253
Medici, Francis de, grand duke of
    Tuscany 180
Medina Celi, duke of 112, 152
Medina del Campo 32, 244
Medina Sidonia, duke of 45, 217, 222,
    223
Mediterranean 34–5, 115–17, 118–31,
    248–55
Melancthon, Philip 164
Mendoza, Bernardino de 204, 205
    death of Henry of Guise 227
    France 208, 218, 220, 221, 222, 225,
        233
    Mary Queen of Scots 212–13
Mercoeur, duke of 207, 233, 241
Method 264
Metz 6
Mexico 30–1, 32
Middelburg 172, 173
mignons 169, 170
migration 39
Milan 12, 99, 107
Modrzewski, Andrew 156
monarchy 42–51
    administrative systems 47–51
    clientage networks 46–7
    Estates 51–7
    financial crises 51
    religious conflict 59, 61–5
    tyranny 150–1
    vulnerability 43–5
Mondéjar, marquis of 123–4
Monsieur, peace of (1576) 170
Montaigne, Michel de 263–4, 265–6
Montcontour, battle of 80, 159
Montigny, baron de 84, 86, 122, 191–2
Montluc, bishop of Valence 157
Montmorency, Anne de, Constable 3–4, 5,
    7, 63–4, 79, 80
Montmorency, François de 136
Montmorency, house of 44, 46, 69
Montmorency-Damville, Henry, duke
    of 151, 170
Montpellier 18–19
Mook, battle of (1574) 160, 173
Moriscos 69, 118, 122–5
Morocco 186
Morone, cardinal 96
Moura, Cristóbal de 187, 212, 229

Mulai Mohammed 186
Muscovy 14–15, 26–7, 121, 130, 157,
  162–3
music 100, 101

Naarden 152
Nantes, Edict of (1598) 245–7
Naples 107, 164–5, 178, 253
Narva 14
Nasi, Joseph, duke of Naxos 119
nationalism 205, 264
Nemours, treaty of (1585) 208
neo-Platonism 103, 265
neo-Stoicism 265
Nérac 72
Netherlands 172–7, 182–5
  Accord (1566) 91–2
  Alba 108–12
  archduke Albert and Isabella 247
  Baltic trade 27–9
  Calvinism 17, 18, 87–93, 141, 174–7,
    191–2
  Cateau-Cambrésis 5
  Compromise 88–9
  Council of State 83–4, 85, 86, 87
  Council of Troubles 110–11, 172
  ecclesiastical reorganization 85–6
  English aid 206, 209–11, 212
  Estates 53–4
  financial problems of Spanish
    Monarchy 180–2
  Henry III 206–8
  Henry IV 229
  Huguenot fleet 79
  Inquisition 85, 87, 88
  invasion by Orange (1572) 140–4, 152–3
  Malcontents 192–4
  Mediterranean trade 253–4
  mutiny of Spanish Army 173–4, 176–7
  Pacification of Ghent (1576) 176–7,
    191, 193
  Perpetual Edict (1577) 177, 183, 193
  Philip II's return to Spain 10
  Protestantism 82–3, 87–93, 108–12
  religious toleration 168, 172–7
  revolt (1566) 69, 71, 81–93, 108
  Roman Catholicism 90–2
  Sea Beggars 135–6, 139–43, 152, 172
  Spain 190–200
  Spanish Armada 217–18, 224
  split of northern and southern
    provinces 192–4
  States General 111
  taxation 111
  tercios 84, 86, 93, 173–4, 176–7, 181,
    183, 193–4
  trade with Baltic 27–8
  trade with Spain 252–3
  Union of Arras (1579) 192
  Union of Utrecht (1579) 192, 197

  see also United Provinces
Nevers, duke of 207, 221
New World 10, 29–37, 114, 181, 188,
  189–90, 211
Nîmes 170
nobility
  banditry 251–2
  Calvinism 71, 72, 76
  Eastern Europe 26–7
  Estates 56–7
  power over monarchy 44–6
  relationship with royal officials 50, 51
  religious disunity 59–61
  unrest 251–2
Nonsuch, treaty of (1585) 210
Norris, Sir John 233, 234
North Africa, Spain 118–19, 124, 128
Northern Seven Years War (1563–70)
  14–15, 89
Norvegus, Laurentius 164, 165
Norway 105
Nostradamus 70

officials, France 219
Oldenbarneveldt, Jan van 210, 267
Olivares, Enrique de Guzmán, count
  of 214, 216, 230, 255
Ortell, Joachim 209
Ortiz, Luis de 17
Ottoman Empire 115–31
  armed forces 119–20
  Austria 117–18
  English trade 252
  famine 253
  Lepanto 127–8
  Malta 116–17
  Morisco revolt (1568–70) 123–5
  Muscovy 121
  officials 119
  Poland 157
  Spain 13–14, 106, 107, 178, 181, 258
  threat to Italy 12
Overijssel, Anabaptism in 82

paganism, art 100, 101
Palestrina, Giovanni Periluigi da 101
Panama 32, 243
papacy
  Council of Trent 94–6, 97
  Henry IV 255–6
  Ireland 204
  Papal States 250–2
  power over monarchies 231–2
  re-Catholicization of northern
    Europe 256–62
  Spanish domination 106–8, 255, 257–8
Papal States, banditry 250–2
Paris 74, 147–8, 207, 221–2, 232, 238–40
Paris League 219–22, 225–8, 230, 237–41
Parma 47

Parsons, Robert 204
patronage networks 45–7
Paul III 47, 94
Paul IV 18, 20, 97, 102, 104
peasants
  price rises 40–1
  serfdom 25–7
Peñón de Vélez 116
Peretti, Felice see Sixtus V
Pérez, Antonio 48, 172, 182–5, 235
Pérez, Gonzalo 48
Pérez, Marcus 92
Péronne, declaration of (1585) 208
Perpetual Edict (1577) 177, 183, 193
Perrenot, Antoine see Granvelle
Persia, Ottoman Empire 121, 129, 130
Peru, trade 30
Philip II, king of Spain 10–13
  administrative system 48
  Antwerp 200
  Aragon rebellion (1591) 234–5
  Armada 217, 222–4
  Calvinism 22
  Cateau-Cambrésis 3–7, 10
  character 121
  Charles Emmanuel of Savoy 226
  clientage networks 46–7
  composite monarchy 42
  Cortes 52–3, 234
  Council of Trent 21, 96, 97
  Counter-Reformation 106–9
  court ceremonial 42–3
  death 247
  Don Carlos 121–2
  Empire 258
  England 4, 8–9, 112–14, 211–14
  Ferrara 255–6
  financial problems 3, 10–11, 35,
    178–82, 242–3, 244, 248–9
  France 79–80, 206–8, 228, 229–30,
    233–4, 235–7, 238, 241–7
  Henry of Guise 207–8, 209
  Irish revolt 243–4
  Italian possessions 11–12
  John III of Sweden 164, 165
  marriage to Elizabeth of Valois 7
  Mary Queen of Scots 204–6, 212–14
  Mary Tudor 4
  Milan 107
  Morisco revolt (1568–70) 122–5
  murder of Juan de Escobedo 184
  Naples 107
  nationalism 264
  Netherlands 10–11, 61, 83–8, 92–3,
    108–12, 121, 153, 172–3, 176–7,
    182–5, 193–7, 242–3
  New World territories 30–1
  northern shipping in the
    Mediterranean 254
  Orange's Apology 194–5

Ottoman Empire 13, 107, 115–17,
    118–31, 181, 258
papacy 135, 215–16, 230–1
Pérez, Antonio 182–5
Portugal 156, 182, 185, 186–90
Protestantism 61, 87–8
  return to Spain 10–11
  revenues 12–13
  St Bartholomew, massacre of 152
  Sicily 107
  United Provinces 197
  vulnerability 44–5
Philip III, king of Spain 125, 248
Philippists 164, 167
Piacenza 47, 181, 190, 200
Piali Pasha 115, 117
pícaros 250
Piccolomini, Alfonso 251
Piedmont 6, 54–5, 226
piracy, Mediterranean trade 252
Pius IV
  character 104
  Council of Trent 20–1, 96
  death 98
  music 101
  Ottoman Empire 117
  reform 105
Pius V 104–5
  Cosimo de Medici 11
  death 135
  England 112, 113
  Geneva 109
  Netherlands 108, 112
  Ottoman Empire 120–1, 126, 128
  Spain 107–8, 178, 179
Placards, Netherlands 85, 88
Plantin, Christophe 265
Platter, Felix 22
Poissy, colloquy of (1561) 63–4
Poitiers, edict of (1577) 171, 245, 246
Poland 154–63
  Anjou 153
  Council of Trent 97
  election of Sigismund III 259–60
  Henry, duke of Alençon 146
  Ivan IV of Muscovy 14
  Jesuits 259
  John III of Sweden 164
  Livonia 162
  religion 61–2, 105, 155–8, 161–3
  St Bartholomew, massacre of 152
  Spanish intervention 258
  trade with West 27–8
  Union of Lublin 14
  union with Sweden 261
politiques 87–8, 136, 150–1, 159, 161,
    170, 267
population growth 25, 38–9, 249
Portugal
  Council of Trent 97

England 206, 233–4
    Jesuits 187
    New World 29, 30
    Ottoman Empire 130
    Philip II 156, 182, 185, 186–90
Possevino, Antonio 165
Postel, Guillaume 265
prices, rise in 37–41
privateers, Mediterranean 253–4
prophecy 70
Protestant Reformation,
    secularization 267
Protestantism 16–23
    Alba's campaign in Netherlands 109
    attempts to re-Catholicize northern
        Europe 256–62
    Austria 167, 257
    Counter-Reformation 99–114
    England 17, 203–6
    fanaticism 58–9
    French religious wars 69–93
    Germany 165–8
    internal feuds 163–4
    literature 17–18
    Netherlands 82–3, 87–93, 108–12
    nobility 59–61
    Poland 155–8, 159–63
    Renaissance 103–4
    revolution 71–3
    St Bartholomew, massacre of 135–6,
        144–53
    Scotland 8–9
    spread of 17–18
    Sweden 164–5
    see also Anabaptism; Calvinism;
        Huguenots; Lutheranism
Provence 170, 233, 242
Prussia 27
publishing 17–18, 98
Pyrrhonism 266

Quiroga, Gaspar de, archbishop of
    Toledo 106, 182

Ragazzoni, Jerome 96–7
Ramism 264
Ramus, Petrus 264
Reconquista 118
reiter 80, 206, 218
religion 15–23, 58–65
    confessional reunion 95, 154, 166
    monarchy and Estates 56
    Protestant revolts 69–93
    see also Protestantism; Roman
        Catholicism
Renaissance 103–4
Renard, Simon 84–5, 86
Rennenberg, count of 210
Requesens, Don Luis de 107, 108–9,
    172–7, 178, 182

resistance, theory of 71–2, 74–5, 149–51,
    197, 227
revolution, Protestantism 71–3
Rhine Palatinate 17, 109
Ridolfi plot (1571) 113
Roanoke Island 211
Roman Catholicism
    art 100–3
    Austria 256–9
    Baroque style 102–3
    Catholic Reformation 94–104
    confessional-box 99
    Counter-Reformation 99–114, 256–62
    England 113, 203–6
    episcopal residence 95, 96, 97
    fanaticism 58–9
    French religious wars 70
    growing power 203–4
    Holy Roman Empire 165–8
    Index 18, 97–8, 99, 256
    Ireland 203–4, 205
    music 101
    Netherlands revolt (1566) 90–2
    Poland 62, 105, 155–8, 160–3
    Protestantism 16–23
    publishing 98
    reform of 20
    Spanish domination 257–8
    special congregations 105
    Sweden 164–5, 260–1
    Vulgate 98
Roman Law, France 56–7
Rome 98, 255–62
Rouen 148, 233
royal officials 47–51
Roye, Eléonore de 59
Rudolph II, Emperor 166–8, 257, 258,
    259
Ruiz, Simón 180
Russia 14–15, 26–7, 162
    see also Muscovy

St Bartholomew, massacre of 135–6,
    144–53, 157
St Germain, peace of 136
St John of Malta, Knights of 13,
    116–17
St Quentin, battle of (1557) 4, 5, 6
Saint-André, Maréchal de 5, 63
Saint-Germain, peace of (1570) 81, 112
Saluzzo 226
San Clemente, Guillén 258, 259
Sandomir, Consensus of (1570) 155, 163
Santa Cruz, marquis of 127–8, 190, 206,
    212, 216–17, 222–3
Sardinia 11
Savoy 6–7, 116, 215
    see also Charles Emmanuel; Emmanuel
        Philibert
Saxony 54, 167

Scotland
  deposition of Mary Queen of Scots 69,
    71
  English invasion (1560) 8–9
  Francis II of France 7–8
  parliament 56
  religion 8–9, 17, 71, 204, 267
  treaty of Berwick with England 213
  vulnerability of monarchy 45
Sea Beggars 135–6, 139–43, 152, 172
Sebastian, king of Portugal 44, 186
secretaries of State 48–50, 225
Selim II, Ottoman Sultan 117–18, 119,
  125, 129
serfdom 25–7
Seripando, cardinal 95, 96, 98
Serres, Olivier de 249
Seville 31–4, 181, 252–3
Sforza, Bona 164
Shakespeare, William 263–4
Sicily 11, 53, 107, 178, 253
Sidney, Sir Philip 167, 210, 265
Siena 6
Sigismund II Augustus, king of Poland
  61–2, 155–7
Sigismund III Vasa, king of Poland 259,
  260–1
Sigismund Zapolyai, prince of
  Transylvania 13, 161
silver
  Genoese bankers 180–1
  inflation 37, 39–40
  New World 11, 30–3, 35–7
  Spanish trade 189
Simonetta, cardinal 94
Sixteen, Council of 220–1, 238–9
Sixtus V 214–16
  Henry III 227
  Henry IV 209, 229–30, 231
  papal power over monarchies 231–2
  Papal States 250, 251
  Polish throne 259
  re-organization of Rome 256
  Spain 215–16, 255
Socinus 163
Sökölli, Mehmed 117, 120, 121, 130
Sorbonne 64, 227, 238, 240
Sores, Jacques de 79
Spain and Spanish monarchy 178–200
  administrative system 47–8, 51
  alliance with papacy against
    Protestantism 107–8
  armed forces of 12
  Cateau-Cambrésis 3–7
  Clement VIII 230–1
  clientage networks 46
  Coligny 137–9
  composite monarchy 42
  Cortes 52–3
  Council of Trent 21, 94–5, 106

  court ceremonial 42–3
  death of Mary Tudor 4
  England 8–9, 204–6, 211–14, 216–18,
    222–4
  English and Dutch trade in
    Mediterranean 254
  financial problems 3, 33, 178–82,
    248–9
  France 79–80, 137–9, 209, 218, 228,
    229–34, 241–7
  growth of power 203
  Henry of Guise 209
  Holy Roman Empire 258
  inflation 37, 39
  Inquisition 18, 106, 123
  Ireland 204
  Italian possessions 6–7, 11–12
  lines of communication 189–90
  Moriscos 69, 118, 122–5
  nationalism 264
  Netherlands 108–12, 172–7, 190–200
  New World trade 11, 29–35, 181
  nobility 45
  North Africa 118–19
  Ottoman Empire 115–17, 118–31, 181,
    258
  power 11–13
  Protestant literature 17, 18
  return of Philip II 10–11
  revenues 12–13
  St Bartholomew, massacre of 148
  Sixtus V 215–16
  taxation 53, 179–80
  trade 24–5, 252–3
  Tunis 126, 129, 130
  vulnerability of monarchy 44–5
Spanish Armada 216–18, 220–1, 222–4
Spanish Netherlands, split from northern
  provinces 192–4
Sparre, Eric 260, 261
Spes, Don Guerau de 113
Speyer, treaty of (1544) 28
State-building 49
Stephen Báthory, king of Poland and prince
  of Transylvania 161–3, 258, 259
Stettin, peace of (1570) 14–15
Strozzi, Filippo 190
Stukely, Sir Thomas 204
Sulaiman the Magnificent, Ottoman
  Sultan 13, 117–18, 119
Sweden
  election of Sigismund as king of
    Poland 259–60
  Ivan IV of Muscovy 14
  Julian calendar 262
  Northern Seven Years War (1563–70)
    14–15
  Poland 157, 162–3
  religion 164–5, 260–1, 267
  Riksdag 54

vulnerability of monarchy 45
Switzerland
  Council of Trent 97
  French Wars of Religion 72
  Julian calendar 262

Tassis, Juan Batista de 208
taxation
  Castile 234
  Estates 52, 53, 54–5
  France 52, 218–19
  Netherlands 111
  Papal States 251
  Spain 53, 179–80
tercios 84, 86, 93, 109, 111, 173–4,
  176–7, 181, 183, 193–4
Teresa of Avila, St 224
Terranova, duke of 178
Teutonic Order, Knights of 14
Thou, Jacques-Auguste de 225, 227, 238,
  248, 267
Throckmorton, Francis 204–5, 206
Toledo, Don Fadrique de 152
Toledo, Don García de 116–17
Tordesillas, treaty of (1494) 30
Torres, Don Luis de 126
Toul 6
Tournai 17
trade
  Atlantic 29–35, 78–9, 206, 211, 212,
    217, 223–4
  Baltic 27–9
  Eastern Europe 25–8
  grain 252–4
  Mediterranean 252–4
  New World 11, 29–35, 181
Transylvania 117, 158
Trent, Council of 20–1, 87, 94–104, 105,
  262
Tripoli 13, 115
Truchsess, Gebhard 168
Tunis 126, 129, 130, 178
Tuscany 11, 215, 253
Tyrone, Hugh O'Neill, earl of 243
Tyrone, Shane O'Neill, earl of 204

unemployment 39, 40
Union, Edict of (1588) 225, 226
United Provinces
  Calvinism 267
  constitution 197–8
  Edict of Abjuration (1581) 197
  Julian calendar 262
  Maurice of Nassau 236
  treaty with England and France
    (1596) 243–4
  see also Netherlands
universities 22–3, 262–3
Urban VII 230
Uskoks 253

Utrecht, Union of (1579) 192, 197

Valencia, Cortes 53
Valenciennes 17, 78, 92, 140
Valois, house of 3–7, 42
  see also Alençon; Charles IX; Francis II;
    Henry II; Henry III
Vassy 73
Vázquez, Mateo 185, 212
Venice
  aristocratic control 57
  Council of Trent 97
  Ottoman Empire 120, 125–9
  piracy 253–4
  Spanish domination 11, 215, 255
  trade 34–5, 252, 253–4
Verdun 6
Vervins 245, 247
Viglius, Ulrich 5, 83
Villeroy, Nicolas de Neufville, seigneur
  de 49, 171–2, 225
Vindiciae contra Tyrannos 150, 197
Viret, Pierre 69
Vulgate Bible 98

wages, price rises 39, 40, 89–90
Walsingham, Sir Francis
  aid to Dutch Protestants 209
  Babington plot 213
  Catholic plots 204–6
  Mary Queen of Scots 212
  Protestantism 267
  Spanish Armada 224
War of the Three Henries 209, 218–22
Warsaw, Confederation of (1573) 158,
  162
Western Europe, trade with Eastern
  Europe 25–8
William of Nassau, prince of Orange
  Alençon 195–9
  Apology 194–5, 196
  Calvinism 175–6, 177, 191, 195
  Cateau-Cambrésis 5
  Catholic opposition to 191–2
  Council of State 83, 86
  count of Holland and Zealand 197
  death 199, 206
  France 137, 160
  Franche-Comté 84–5
  Granvelle 85–6
  growth of Spanish power 203
  Gueux 88
  invasion of Netherlands (1568) 110
  invasion of Netherlands (1572) 140–4,
    152–3
  Malcontents 192
  marriages 84, 199
  Morisco revolt 124
  proclaimed an outlaw 194, 196
  religious toleration 87–8, 173, 177

William of Nassau, prince of Orange (*cont.*)
   revolt (1566) 90, 91–3
   St Bartholomew, massacre of 152
   Sea Beggars 139, 140
   siege of Leyden (1574) 174
   split of northern and southern
     provinces 192
William-Louis of Nassau 236
witch-hunts 58
women, Calvinism and 19
Wootton, Nicholas 5
Württemberg 54

Zamoyski, John 162
Zborowskis 159, 160
Zealand
   Anabaptism 82
   Calvinism 174–5
   deposition of Philip II 197
   Leicester, earl of 210
   Pacification of Ghent 176–7
   Sea Beggars 140, 141
Zutphen 152